GETTING STARTED with GRE
A Strategic Approach

We know you're serious about acing the GRE. That's why REA developed a brand-new book with online diagnostics to ensure that you succeed on the world's leading graduate-admissions test. Our content is completely new and 100% aligned with the GRE.

Flexibly structured to help test candidates learn, practice, and refine an efficient approach to the test, the book is designed to meet you wherever you are in your GRE prep.

At REA, we bring you a class-in-a-book, prepared by a nationally recognized one-on-one tutor, with all the print and digital resources you need from one convenient source. We focus strictly on helping you do your best.

With that in mind, REA's *GRE: A Strategic Approach* offers:

1 Focused tutorials
Cover everything you need to conquer each of the three sections of the GRE revised General Test: Verbal, Quantitative, and Analytical Writing.

2 Flexible study plan
Create your own study schedule based on how many weeks you have before the test and how much material you need to learn.

3 **Online diagnostics**
REA's exclusive diagnostic feedback pinpoints your strengths and weaknesses in each section of the test, saving you time and focusing your efforts.

4 **Three full-length practice tests**
The book includes two full-length GRE practice tests with fully explained answers. One additional diagnostic practice test is available online.

5 **Proven GRE test-item strategies**
Drawing from his years of experience as a GRE tutor and test-prep expert, our author gives you the winning tips and strategies that will turn the test to your advantage.

6 **Resources galore**
You'll find many extras, including handy references for the math and verbal portions of the GRE, warm-up drills, and graduate school admissions advice.

Good Luck on the GRE!

COMPLETELY ALIGNED WITH THE GRE REVISED GENERAL TEST

GRE® A STRATEGIC APPROACH

Doug Tarnopol, M.A.

with
Norman Levy, Ph.D.
Elizabeth Rollins, M.A.
Gerri Budd, Ph.D.

Research & Education Association
Visit our website at www.rea.com/gre

Planet Friendly Publishing
✓ Made in the United States
✓ Printed on Recycled Paper
   Text: 10%   Cover: 10%
Learn more: www.greenedition.org

At REA we're committed to producing books in an Earth-friendly manner and to helping our customers make greener choices.

Manufacturing books in the United States ensures compliance with strict environmental laws and eliminates the need for international freight shipping, a major contributor to global air pollution.

And printing on recycled paper helps minimize our consumption of trees, water and fossil fuels. This book was printed on paper made with **10% post-consumer waste**. According to the Environmental Paper Network's Paper Calculator, by using this innovative paper instead of conventional papers, we achieved the following environmental benefits:

Trees Saved: 8 • Air Emissions Eliminated: 1,618 pounds
Water Saved: 1,379 gallons • Solid Waste Eliminated: 475 pounds

Courier Corporation, the manufacturer of this book, owns the Green Edition Trademark.
For more information on our environmental practices, please visit us online at www.rea.com/green

Research & Education Association
61 Ethel Road West
Piscataway, New Jersey 08854
E-mail: info@rea.com

 **GRE®: A Strategic Approach**

Published 2013
Copyright © 2012 by Research & Education Association, Inc.
Prior editions copyright © 2010 under the title *GRE General Test* and copyright © 2003, 2002, 1999, 1998 under the title *The Best Test Preparation for the GRE General Test* by Research & Education Association, Inc. All rights reserved. No part of this book may be reproduced in any form without permission of the publisher.

Printed in the United States of America

Library of Congress Control Number 2011931153

ISBN-13: 978-0-7386-0895-2
ISBN-10: 0-7386-0895-5

GRE® is a registered trademark of Educational Testing Service (ETS). All other trademarks cited in this publication are the property of their respective owners.

LIMIT OF LIABILITY/DISCLAIMER OF WARRANTY: Publication of this work is for the purpose of test preparation and related use and subjects as set forth herein. While every effort has been made to achieve a work of high quality, neither Research & Education Association, Inc., nor the authors and other contributors of this work guarantee the accuracy or completeness of or assume any liability in connection with the information and opinions contained herein and in REA's companion software and online materials. REA and the authors and other contributors shall in no event be liable for any personal injury, property or other damages of any nature whatsoever, whether special, indirect, consequential or compensatory, directly or indirectly resulting from the publication, use or reliance upon this work.

Cover image © iStockphoto.com/GrenouilleFilms

REA® is a registered trademark of
Research & Education Association, Inc.

CONTENTS

Letter to the Student vii
About the Authors ix
About Research & Education Association xii
REA Acknowledgments xiii
Going Online to Take the Diagnostic Test xiv
Your Diagnostic Test Score xv
    Understanding Your Score xv
    Elements of the Score Report xvi
    Scores in the Application Process xviii
    Planning Your Preparation xviii

CHAPTER 1: ABOUT THE GRE   1

Content 2
Structure and Timing 2
Scoring 5
Registering for the GRE 6
About the GRE Subject Tests 8
Taking the GRE Revised General Test for Business School 10

CHAPTER 2: GLOBAL STRATEGIES   11

Stand the Test of Time 12
Test Anxiety 12

CHAPTER 3: THE VERBAL SECTION   15

Form and Function 16
Sentence Equivalence Items (SEs) and Text Completions (TCs) 22
    Content Review 22
Sentence Equivalence (SE) Strategies 25
Text Completion (TC) Strategies 38
Reading Comprehension (RC) 52
    Content Review 53
Reading Comprehension (RC) Strategies 55

CHAPTER 4: THE MATH SECTION — 67

Form and Function 68
Math Content Review 70
Quantitative Comparison (QC) Strategies 120
Problem Solving (PS) Strategies 128
Data Analysis (DA) Strategies 138

CHAPTER 5: THE ANALYTICAL WRITING SECTION — 147

Introduction to the Essays 148

SUMMING UP — 169

PAPER-AND-PENCIL TEST 1 — 173

Answers 220
Explanations 226

PAPER-AND-PENCIL TEST 2 — 261

Answers 306
Explanations 312

APPENDICES — 347

Appendix A: Score Conversion Table 347
Appendix B: Math Reference 351
Appendix C: GRE Vocabulary Enhancer 373
Appendix D: Drills and Practice Questions 407
Appendix E: A Quick Reference Guide to Graduate School 465

INDEX — 499

LETTER TO THE STUDENT

Welcome to the wonderful world of GRE test preparation! Well, OK, it's not so wonderful. I took the GRE back in the day while in the process of applying to graduate school in the history of science. No, I didn't quite see the relevance either.

But whatever your (or my) opinion of the GRE, or of standardized testing in general, the reality is that you'll have to take this test. Doing as well as you can will not only increase your chances for acceptance to graduate programs but can also play a significant role in getting internal or external funding both before and during your dissertation.

Fortunately, there is nothing on this test that you haven't already learned. Unfortunately, much of it you learned a decade or more ago and haven't really used since, especially the material found in the math section. The formula for the volume of a right cylinder doesn't often come up at cocktail parties. Furthermore, the content, regardless of how familiar it may or may not be, comes packaged in mostly unfamiliar question types (we'll call them "item types" for reasons that will be made clear)—and, what's worse, you don't have all day to answer each item. This is a speed test at least as much as it is a content test.

Your task, then, is to master not only the content, but also the specific ways in which the content is tested in various item types—and then you must apply that mastery as fast as you possibly can without being careless or taking too many risks.

So, what is to be done? First of all, we must break up the tasks in order not to become overwhelmed. Then we'll diagnose your strengths and weaknesses by taking you through a full-length, computer-based diagnostic test. Next, we'll take you through the structure, timing, and scoring of the test. All of the strategies in this book have been reverse-engineered from the structure, timing, and scoring of the test.

Then we'll dive into a concise review of the content tested on each section. These sections will be followed by out-of-format items designed to reinforce your content knowledge. It's important to get the content down cold before confronting how that content is tested in the sometimes weird-looking item types.

Each item type will be presented and analyzed—the anatomy and physiology of the item type, so to speak. Next, a variety of strategies, each of which has been reverse-engineered from the item types, will be presented. Part of your job will be to figure out through practice which particular strategies work best for you. We're very empirical! And we'll provide a large "test bank" of in-format items to practice with.

Finally, we'll bring in the all-important aspect of timing, both at the item and section level. To this end, we'll have two more full-length, paper-based practice tests you can use for practice.

As you no doubt know, if learning were simply a matter of information exchange, life would be much simpler. But it isn't. Emotions and attitudes play a large, often decisive role in learning. Attention must be paid to such affective issues, and, to the extent that a book can do so, this one will. Based on my years of tutoring, I have a good sense of how anxiety and other entirely understandable emotional responses can interfere with learning, and I'll give suggestions of how to overcome these normal, nearly ubiquitous reactions.

I hope you find this book helpful! I welcome your reactions; feel free to e-mail me at dtarnopol@rea.com.

—*Doug*

ABOUT THE AUTHORS

The book's lead author (core review and strategies), Doug Tarnopol, M.A., brings a unique mix of talents and experience to test-prep teaching, tutoring, and instructional design. Doug has fifteen years of varied experience in test preparation. He has taught and tutored students of all backgrounds and advised both students and parents; he has also developed instructional print materials, designed online tests and courses, and run online academic support. Doug combines over a decade of test-preparation experience in teaching, instructional design, and front-line customer and academic support with an academically rigorous education.

Doug graduated magna cum laude from Cornell University in 1992, earning an A.B. (Cornellese for "B.A.") in History and writing a senior honors thesis on twentieth-century evolutionary theory. He continued his work in the history and sociology of science at the University of Pennsylvania, receiving an M.A. in 1996.

While in graduate school in the 1990s, Doug began teaching SAT classes for Kaplan Test Prep. After completing his graduate work, Doug moved to New York City and continued teaching for Kaplan, adding PSAT, SCI HI, SAT II: Writing, SAT II: Math, GMAT, GRE, and other courses to his repertoire. In 1999, after serving as Pre-College Student Advisor at Kaplan's flagship Manhattan center, Doug became a curriculum developer in what was then called the Kaplan Learning Services division, designing instructional material for state proficiency exams. He was soon promoted to Assistant Editor.

In 2000, after serving briefly as Manager of Pre-College Curriculum for Kaplan Test Prep, Doug joined the brand-new Kaplan Test Prep Online division, becoming Manager of Academic Services. Later promoted to Associate Director, Doug helped to create, coordinate, and maintain website, product, technical, and academic support activities, including management of admission and GMAT/GRE essay review services and the design of online course homepages and assets.

In November of 2002, Doug joined Peterson's new Test Prep division as Associate Program Manager, designing and gathering content for online tests for SAT, ACT, GMAT, GRE, and several CLEPs, as well as doing market research on various SAT online courses. He also worked on Peterson's adaptive online course for the SAT, which won Brandon Hall's Gold Excellence in E-Learning Award for 2003. Promoted to Program Manager in early 2003, Doug designed and edited Peterson's adaptive PSAT online course.

In October of 2003, Doug launched Tarnopol Learning Services, LLC, a tutoring and instructional design company. In addition to private tutoring, Doug authored six titles in SparkNotes' 2005 *SAT Power Tactics* series— *Test-taking Strategies, Critical Reading: Sentence Completions, Critical Reading: Reading Passages, Writing: Multiple-Choice Questions, The Essay, and Vocabulary Builder*, all of which are available, complete with pre- and post-tests authored by Doug, online.

Doug has also edited scholarly books and articles in the history of science; designed Flash simulations and diagnostic skills assessments for corporate training courses; expert-reviewed test-prep books, such as Peterson's current ARCO AP Biology book; written and edited learning objects for adaptive online courses for the Texas high-stakes exit exam; and developed instructor-led training materials for both California's high-stakes exit exam and a thirteen-lesson basic writing skills course.

Since moving to Rhode Island in 2005, Doug has been tutoring students for the SAT and ACT, as well as admissions-essay review, GRE, and GMAT. He has also tutored high school students in American history, English literature, biology, and writing, as well as college students in history, writing skills, and algebra.

Currently, when not tutoring students for the SAT, ACT or GRE, Doug is working on a book for the new AP Biology exam.

Doug also writes fiction and poetry. He is an avid drummer, beginning bassist, and voracious reader. He currently lives in Cranston, Rhode Island, with his wife, Donna. When not reading or watching classic films or *The Simpsons*, they can usually be found playing Scrabble or enjoying hide-and-seek with their recently acquired (and quite adorable) cat, Grendel. In fact, you can pretty much assume that most pages in this book were written with Grendel in his current position: on Doug's lap.

Elizabeth Rollins, M.A., has been a curriculum developer, editor, and content author for educational publishers for more than ten years. Formerly the Director of Research and Development for GRE Programs at the Princeton Review, Elizabeth directed a complete revision of the then existing GRE course. She has also written lessons and assessment material for high-stakes and national standardized tests.

Elizabeth wrote all of the verbal test items for the two paper-and-pencil and two computer-based practice tests.

Norman Levy, Ph.D., has been the Director of Mathematics and Testing for NJL College Preparation in Albertson N.Y., for the past twenty-five years. He coordinates all the instruction and materials for the math preparation required for AP Calculus, GRE, GMAT, LSAT, SAT I, ACT, SAT II, and PSAT. He also personally instructs individuals and groups in all levels of mathematics, ranging from middle school math through calculus. Previously, he was the Mathematics Coordinator for the Hebrew Academy of Nassau County (N.Y.). He supervised staff, participated in textbook selection, held teacher-training workshops, and implemented new programs as required to meet or exceed state standards.

Norm is a prolific author, having written more than 20 books in his career. Most recently he has written REA's *AP Calculus AB & BC*. He has also authored review books for PRAXIS II, ACT, Essential Math for the College Bound, Big 8 Mathematics, PSAT/NMSQT, Study Cards for the SAT I Math, CLEP Calculus, and SAT Subject Test: Math Levels I and II.

Norm wrote all of the quantitative test items for the two paper-and-pencil and two computer-based practice tests.

Gerri Budd, Ph.D., is a GRE rater for Educational Testing Service and a consultant for Sun Education Services. Previously, she worked as the Manager of Graduate Studies Support Services for Seton Hall University, where she created support services for grad students and managed graduate student admissions/recruitment.

Gerri shares her knowledge of the grad school application process in our appendix entitled "A Quick Reference Guide to Graduate School."

ABOUT RESEARCH & EDUCATION ASSOCIATION

Founded in 1959, Research & Education Association (REA) is dedicated to publishing the finest and most effective educational materials—including test preps and study guides—for students in elementary school, middle school, high school, college, graduate school, and beyond.

Today, REA's wide-ranging catalog is a leading resource for teachers, students, and professionals.

REA ACKNOWLEDGMENTS

In addition to our author team, REA would like to thank Wallie Walker-Hammond, former Assessment Specialist at Educational Testing Service, for her technical review of the verbal sections; Mel Friedman, REA's Lead Mathematics Editor, for his technical review of the math sections; Larry B. Kling, VP, Editorial, for supervising development; Pam Weston, Publisher, for setting the quality standards for production integrity and managing the publication to completion; Michael Reynolds, Managing Editor, for coordinating development of this edition; Stephanie Phelan and Maureen Mulligan for designing the book. John Paul Cording, Vice President, Technology, for coordinating the design, development, and testing of REA's software; Heena Patel, Software Project Manager, for her software testing efforts; Bob Pearson and PearSoft, Inc., for development of REA's online test delivery system, and Amy Jamison for ensuring the high quality of REA's online tests; S4Carlisle for typesetting; and Weymouth Design and Christine Saul for the cover design.

In addition, special appreciation is extended to John Kupetz, Instructor of Journalism and English at the College of Lake County, Grayslake, Illinois, and former Placement Director of the Medill School of Journalism at Northwestern University, for putting his eagle eye to REA's core GRE review and strategy materials.

STOP!

Before moving on, please go to
www.rea.com/gre
to take your full-length
diagnostic test.

YOUR DIAGNOSTIC TEST SCORE

Understanding Your Score

Now that you have completed the diagnostic test, we can review your score report and direct you to the most effective and efficient way to use this book.

Since August 1, 2011, the GRE score scale is 130 to 170, in increments of one point. The raw score, the actual number of correct items per section, is translated into the scaled score by a scoring rubric that ETS is still working on. REA has done its best to determine what that scoring rubric is, based on past raw to scaled score examples, but it is important to note that our scaled scores are just an approximation. As we learn more about ETS's scoring rubric, we will update ours online and in this book.

Your final score will be based on not only the raw to scaled scores of the four verbal and math sections, but also the two essays that make up the Analytical Writing section. For the immediate future, ETS will be using human readers to grade the essays.* Each one of your essays will be read by two readers and they will determine your score on a scale from zero to six, in half-point increments. This score will then be added to the rubric to determine your final scaled score. For our practice tests, you will score your essay yourself, and then REA will provide the scaled score.

You will be able to score your essays by using the examples of level 5 essays we provide. Based on your confidence in the essays you have written, you can enter the score you believe you would have gotten. Again, this is not infallible, but we believe it will give you an accurate assessment of your score, had you taken the actual GRE.

---

* The testing agency also employs a computerized essay reader known as eRater, which it uses to help grade other tests.

Elements of the Score Report

Here are the elements of the score report we will be using to diagnose your GRE test readiness:

- Raw score: this is simply the number of questions you got correct in each test section.

- Scaled score: using the best information currently available, REA attempts to translate the raw score into the score you will actually see on your test results. Know that we make no claims to exactitude, as ETS officials are still working on the metrics.

- Subscore by category: this is a very useful report. Here, each question is identified by type, and in the review section, we offer strategies for each type. Once you review your subscore by category, you can go to the book and study only what you need to.

- Correct items per section percentage: a quick way of seeing how well you did in a certain section. Again, pointing to where you need to dedicate your energies in studying.

- Elapsed time per section: how long it took you to complete a section. You may have done well, but if it took you a very long time, you may need to do some more prep.

Following is a screen grab of our score report, identifying all the information available about your test.

Practice GRE Score Report

Scoring Summary*

GRE revised General Test

82 Questions

Time Limit 03:45:00

User annsmith

Scaled Score

155 out of **170**

Section Score

See table at right

Analytical Writing
(2 Questions / Time Limit 01:00:00)
Scaled 5: 2 Correct / Elapsed Time 00:51:22

Verbal Reasoning
(40 Questions / Time Limit 01:00:00)
Scaled 156: 33 Correct / Elapsed Time 00:44:09

Quantitative Reasoning
(40 Questions / Time Limit 01:00:00)
Scaled 154: 32 Correct / Elapsed Time 00:53:29

Test Item Score

Verbal Reasoning
(40 Questions / Time Limit 01:00:00)
Scaled 156: 33 Correct / Elapsed Time 00:44:09

01: Text completion | [11/13] | 85%
02: Sentence equivalence | [11/14] | 79%
03: Reading comprehension | [11/13] | 85%

Quantitative Reasoning
(40 Questions / Time Limit 01:00:00)
Scaled 154: 32 Correct / Elapsed Time 00:53:29

01: Data analysis | [10/13] | 77%
02: Quantitative analysis | [11/13] | 85%
03: Problem solving | [11/14] | 79%

Individual Question Score
(Question number, Correct answer, Your response)

	Verbal Section 1		Verbal Section 2		Quantitative Section 1		Quantitative Section 2	
01	A	A	01	D	D	01	B	B	01	A	A
02	C	C	02	C	C	02	B	B	02	**B**	**E**
03	BD	BD	03	BD	BD	03	A	A	03	B	B
04	CD	CD	04	**ADCDH**	**ADCDH**	04	D	D	04	C	C
05	**CD**	**CE**	05	BD	BD	05	B	B	05	D	D
06	BFG	BFG	06	BDH	BDH	06	D	D	06	A	A
07	D	D	07	D	D	07	**A**	**B**	07	C	C
08	E	E	08	*See detailed explanations*		08	C	C	08	**B**	**C**
09	**E**	**C**	09	C	C	09	32	32	09	A	A
10	AB	AB	10	BC	BC	10	**B**	**C**	10	B	B
11	**C**	**B**	11	D	D	11	B	B	11	C	C
12	AC	AC	12	E	E	12	C	C	12	**2,997**	**985**
13	BE	BE	13	AC	AC	13	AC	AC	13	E	E
14	BF	BF	14	**BF**	**BE**	14	0,72	0,72	14	E	E
15	CD	CD	15	AD	AD	15	C	C	15	$\frac{11}{24}$	$\frac{11}{24}$
16	D	D	16	AE	AE	16	A	A	16	**B**	**A**
17	A	A	17	AC	AC	17	B	B	17	72	72
18	**A**	**C**	18	**E**	**C**	18	E	E	18	A	A
19	A	A	19	A	A	19	**AC**	**CD**	19	B	B
20	E	E	20	D	D	20	**E**	**A**	20	DE	DE

*Because REA is always refining our online testing system, there may be minor differences between this score report and the one you see when you complete your practice exam.

Scores in the Application Process

It is important to remember your score is the first part of the data a school will use in assessing your application. Of course, the admissions department wants to see exactly how well you did on the GRE, and the scaled score gives them that. But the second part is the percentile rank, the context in which that score exists. This tells how well you scored in relation to all the other people that took the GRE at that time. And maybe even more importantly, it reveals how well your score compared to all the other candidates applying to the same program you are.

It will take ETS some time to build the database required (from GRE General revised Tests already taken) to determine the percentile ranks, but it seems likely that previous test results will be used as a guide.

Planning Your Preparation

Now that you've interpreted and fleshed out your diagnostic score report, it's time to plan your preparation. I will give you some general principles; as I'll continue to emphasize throughout this book, it's up to you to apply these principles to your specific situation.

The main criteria are:

- *How much time you have to study before you take the official GRE.* That's not necessarily a matter of calendar-days. In fact, it's more a matter of total hours of study time—how many hours are you prepared (or able) to set aside between now and your test date?

- *What your target score is.* This is best defined by the average GRE score of the last-reported class of incoming first-years at the program or department into which you would most like to be admitted. However—and this is a big *however*—GRE scores often play a large role in graduate funding, especially, but not only, for dissertation support. If the latter is the case, especially if you're a Ph.D. candidate, the target score is not a limiting factor.

- *What your diagnostic score is.* This part you know already, as you've laid your score report on the table next to you as you read this chapter. (Right? ☺)

Let me give you an example. Let's say Doug Tarnopol, whose diagnostic score report you've just seen, has about 40 hours he can set aside to prepare. Given his scores—460 in Verbal and 620 in Quantitative—he's scoring in the middle range for both sections. (We will address his essay score later on.) In fact, he's at the 52nd percentile rank for each section, so he has a "balanced" score. Let's assume his target percentiles are 85th for each section—let's say he's applying to programs in quantitative history. According to the old scoring scale, he'll need a 600 in Verbal and a 760 in Quantitative.

Since he has a lot of time and balanced scores in the mid-range, Doug should really use this entire book. He could theoretically start with whichever section he likes—Verbal, Quantitative, Essays—after having read the introductory sections, but he might as well go in order. His scheduling task is pretty simple: split up the time evenly between Verbal and Quantitative, giving less attention to the Essays, which are scored separately from the other two sections, and on a six-point scale. They are also quite amenable to improvement, regardless of writing ability, as you'll see later on.

Let's take another example. Let's say a test-taker named Jane Doe has a Quantitative score of 700 and a Verbal score of 500. Assume Jane is going to be an engineer. She needs to get the highest Quantitative score possible, which is an 800 (soon to be a 170). As of the time of this writing a "perfect" score in Quantitative is actually "only" a 94th percentile rank, which tells you how many people cluster up in the "perfect" score range. No one at her engineering schools, let's assume for our current purposes, cares what she gets in Verbal as long as she's at or above 500, or, around a 60th–65th percentile rank, and they're not even going to look at her essay.

Jane's course is clear. Ignore everything in this book except the math section.

So, enough with the hypotheticals! Let's figure out what *you*, who are presumably non-hypothetical, need to do:

1. How many hours are you willing and able to put into this?

    Remember, as if you need reminding, that such notions as "diminishing returns" and "opportunity costs" are really real! Don't overdo your preparation, especially for relatively paltry potential benefits; remember you have other things, like grades or full-time work, perhaps, and definitely statements of purpose, to "resource."

Work out your estimate in the following space.

2. What is your target score?

   Verbal: _____

   Quantitative: _____

   Essay: _____

3. How'd you do on your diagnostic test?

   Verbal: _____

   Quantitative: _____

We must now deal with the essay score—if and only if you know it matters. If it doesn't matter to any program to which you're planning to apply, don't waste any time on this. If you can't rule out the essay matter, turn to the sample essay included with the online diagnostic test and do a quick-and-dirty self-score. Don't get too worked up about it; it'll be pretty clear whether you're in the lower range (i.e., 0–3) or the upper range (i.e., 4–6).

Put it all together now, and scope out your time to whatever degree of specificity you deem valuable. If you're mapping out your time down to the half-hour, of course, I'd say ease up a tad. If you're totally winging it, I'd say buckle down and sketch out some reasonable schedule.

Keep in mind that both your progress as you study and the general vagaries of life will probably end up altering your current plan a bit, but that's only to be expected. At least you'll exert some control over the future, and that reduction in anxiety alone is worth the effort!

CHAPTER 1
About the GRE

WHO TAKES THE GRE? Two different populations take the GRE: those individuals applying to graduate school and those applying to business school.

As with the SAT and ACT tests, the GRE requires you to master four main testing parameters: content, structure, timing, and scoring.

CONTENT

The GRE test has three main sections: Verbal, Quantitative, and Analytical Writing (a.k.a., essays).

The Verbal section tests your reading skills and indirectly your vocabulary. It also tests your grasp of sentence structure as well as logic as it applies to sentence structure. This is common-sense logic, not esoteric symbolic logic.

The Quantitative section tests your knowledge of junior-high-school math and a bit of basic data analysis. You once knew this material, which is not difficult compared with, say, calculus or even trigonometry. With that in mind, this section should not be a problem. However, if you're not a math person, it's possible you've avoided this topic since you took the SAT or ACT. If that's the case, don't worry. We'll help you review.

The Analytical Writing section includes two essays: an analysis of an issue and an analysis of an argument. These essays are more concerned with the structure and organization of an argument than the artfulness of written expression, as you'll see later in detail. The issue essay prompts you to build an effective argument and the argument essay prompts you to analyze someone else's less effective argument. They are mirror images of each other and will be covered later in more detail.

STRUCTURE AND TIMING

The computer-based GRE, which most readers will take, has the structure shown in the table on the next page.

Don't worry about which section(s), if any, is the unscored or research section; just treat each section the same. Also, don't freak out if you have a few more or a few less than 20 questions in a section. There may be some variability.

You get 3 hours and 45 minutes to take the test. It's a lengthy test. Several breaks should help: a 10-minute break after the third section, and 1-minute breaks between the other sections. You'll have plenty of opportunities to take

Format of the GRE revised General Test

Section	Number of Items	Timing (minutes)
Analytical Writing: Issue Essay Argument Essay	 1 1	 30 30
Verbal Reasoning: Section 1	About 20	30
Quantitative Reasoning: Section 1	About 20	35
Verbal Reasoning: Section 2	About 20	30
Quantitative Reasoning: Section 2	About 20	35
Possibly an **unscored section**, either Verbal or Quantitative, which may be inserted anywhere within the test	About 20	30 or 35
Possibly a **research section**, either Verbal or Quantitative, which will appear last	Varies	Varies

full-length practice tests: These will help you prepare for a major requirement of the GRE test: the ability to sit still and concentrate. The Germans call this ability sitzfleisch (ZITS-fl[eye]sh). You might call it "chair glue."

You will probably take this test on a computer, and we'll explore the interface, which you've already seen. Our hope is you're reading this after taking your diagnostic full-length test. Thus, you'll need to use scratch paper, which will be provided at the test center.

Besides the interface, the paper-based test differs from the computer-based test in a few ways. The paper-based testing time is 3 hours and 30 minutes, has approximately 25 questions in each Verbal and Quantitative reasoning sections, and allows 5 more minutes to complete each of those sections.

From this point, do not write anything in this book unless you're specifically told to do so! You need to get used to practicing on scratch paper from the start.

We'll also explore the anatomy of each item type in the relevant sections as we encounter them. For now, let's agree on some terms.

- "Item" is how we'll refer to what normal people call "questions." Not every "item" is framed like a question, and this term thus avoids confusion.

- We'll refer to "normal" multiple-choice items—in which you choose the one correct answer from several options as "multiple-choice items." These multiple-choice items are indicated by ovals on-screen, as you saw.

- We'll refer to the less-familiar multiple-choice items—in which you choose more than one (but not always more than one!) answer from several options—as "multiple-response items." Multiple-response items, by this definition, are indicated by boxes on-screen, as you saw.

- When you have to fill in an answer, we'll call that a…wait for it…"fill-in."

- The word-selection items in the Verbal section, which we will discuss later, will not be distinguished from multiple-choice items because it doesn't matter from your perspective whether you click on an oval or on the word itself.

- We'll refer to another type of item from the Verbal section, in which you highlight a sentence or other bit of text in a passage, as "highlighters." We'll refer to items that ask about a highlighted word or sentence as either multiple-choice or multiple-response items. That function is identical to line numbering in the SAT or ACT paper-based testing. Again, this doesn't change a thing from the test-taker's perspective.

- Any passage with associated items or a math figure or data set with multiple associated items will be called a "testlet." The term "testlet" is useful because it describes what these sets are: mini-tests within the big test. Besides, "testlet" is a term from psychometrics and you can use it to impress your friends and prospective employers.

We'll introduce a few section-specific terms of art later. Since psychologists state seven items is the maximum one can retain at once in short-term memory, that's enough for now.

This test includes both an online calculator and the ability to go back and forth within a section, using a review screen to reorient yourself. Go to our online practice-test center and ETS's PowerPrep online practice any time before your actual test to remove any unfamiliarity with how it works.

There's been much hoopla over the GRE's "section-level adaptivity." The bottom line for you, the test-taker, is it's not relevant. Based on extensive research and discussions with multiple psychometricians, we've determined that how you do on Section 1 of either the Verbal or Quantitative section determines your rough, or "fuzzy" score. That performance triggers the construction of Section 2, which tightens the focus on your score. Again, the upshot is that you should do what you'd normally do—the best you can with the time you're given. That's that.

SCORING

The GRE is scored as follows:

> Verbal and Quantitative raw scores (i.e., the number correct per section) are converted to a scaled score. The scale, which used to be 200–800 in 10-point increments, is now 130–170 in 1-point increments.

Keep two important points in mind. First, there is no penalty for answering incorrectly. Global strategy, No. 1, thus is to answer everything. Guessing can only help you. I'll provide some more global strategies in the next section.

Second, you may have noticed that we've been referring to the "old" 200- to 800-point scale. If you missed the alerts we've sprinkled around the book and online diagnostic test, you should be aware that the revised GRE is now based on a 130-170 score scale, in 1-point increments.

The actual scale isn't that crucial. It could be anything—1 to 300, or even A to Z, if you like. The real apples-to-apples comparison, the number that carries the most weight, is the percentile rank. For example, a score in the 80th percentile rank means your score, whatever the scale used, was better than 80 percent of test-takers, statistically speaking. Without the percentile rank, the scale means little. Think of the scaled score as the interface between your raw score and your percentile rank. That's all it is.

The analytical essays are scored "holistically" on a 6-point scale in half-point increments. Don't sweat that too much. We'll burn that bridge when we get to it.

If you take the computer-based test, you will see your unofficial scores for the Verbal Reasoning and Quantitative Reasoning measures at the test center. Because of the Analytical Writing essay scoring process, you will not be able to view your Analytical Writing score at the testing center. Your official scores will be mailed approximately 10-15 days after your test date.

If you take the paper-based test, your official scores will be sent within six weeks after your test date.

ETS reports all scores for tests taken within a five-year period. The scores your graduate program will use is up to them. They may use the most recent score, average the scores together, or use the best for each section regardless of which test it appears in. Ask each school and department how they do it. Ideally, your goal should be to take the GRE only once.

REGISTERING FOR THE GRE

A credit card allows you to register online to take the GRE. Go to *ets.org/gre/revised_general/register* and follow the directions to register through [My GRE Account]. You can also use your credit card to register by phone at 1-800-GRE-CALL. If you prefer to register by mail, the authorization voucher request form is in the GRE revised General Test Registration Bulletin. The GRE revised General Test is offered as a computer-based test throughout the year at most of the testing locations around the world. The paper-based test is offered up to three times yearly where computer-based testing is not easily available.

Registering online?

When you register online with a credit or debit card, you can print out your voucher once you complete the registration process.

Registering by phone?

If you're registering by phone, call the test center directly or you can call the Prometric Candidate Services Center at 1-443-751-4820 or 1-800-473-2255. You'll receive a confirmation number, the reporting time, and the address of the testing center when you call.

Registering by mail?

Download and complete the Authorization Voucher Request Form that's found in the GRE Bulletin. Then mail the voucher request form with the appropriate payment to the address printed on the voucher. You should allow up to three weeks for processing and delivery by mail. You'll have to make an appointment to take the test before the voucher expires.

Testing Outside the U.S.?

The computer-based test will not be given every day at every test center. You'll have to call your Regional Registration Center to verify the testing dates. The list of Regional Registration Center can be found at *http://www.ets.org/gre/revised_general/register/cbt*.

A Few Things to Remember When You Register

- Choose a testing date.

- Check the fees and make sure you read the reschedule and cancellation policies (probably best BEFORE you register!).

- Some of the test centers are not open on all of the dates.

- You cannot transfer your registration to another person (who would try to do that?).

- The name you register with must exactly match the name of the identification (ID) documents you'll present on test day. If the name doesn't *exactly* match, you may not be allowed to take the test or your test scores may be canceled after you take the test (ETS means business!). If you register by phone, make sure you are registered under your entire first and last names as they are found on your ID.

- When you register, you can request that your scores be sent to up to four graduate programs, business programs, or fellowship sponsors. You will be asked to choose your score recipients when you register for the test or at the test center the day you take the test.

You can take the GRE revised General Test only once every 60 days and you can take the test no more than five times within a 12-month period. (Remember, ideally, your goal should be to take the GRE only once.)

ABOUT THE GRE SUBJECT TESTS

The GRE Subject Tests are designed to show what you know about a particular subject—nothing earth-shattering about them. Subject tests may not be required by schools, but they can be a really great way to make you stand out from the crowd. You already know that a great score on the GRE revised General Test will help you get into that graduate program or business school you've dreamed of, and taking a GRE subject test in an area that you've studied extensively—that subject you majored in—can give you an edge! The Subject Tests enable the admissions officers to compare candidates from different colleges. You should check admissions requirements at the schools you're interested in to determine if the GRE Subject Tests are required (and if not, you still might want to consider taking one. It's up to you).

Scores and Test Dates

The Subject Tests are all multiple-choice, paper-and-pencil tests. They are designed to test subject areas that are learned in undergraduate school. You'll receive one point for each question answered correctly, but you'll be penalized for incorrect answers. Your score will be a "scaled" score that ranges from 200 to 900. Some of the Subject Tests contain subtests that contribute to subtest scores. The subtest scores range from 20 to 99. The Subject Tests are administered three times a year: October, November, and April. Go to *www.gre.org* for test dates and deadlines for registration.

Subjects

The eight Subject Tests, with a brief description for each, are:

- **Biochemistry, Cell and Molecular Biology**

    This test consists of about 175 multiple-choice questions based on laboratory situations, diagrams, or experiment results. The content is divided into biochemistry, cell biology, and molecular biology and genetics. There is an emphasis on questions that require problem solving, as well as content knowledge.

- **Biology**

    This test consists of about 200 multiple-choice questions based on descriptions of laboratory and field situations, diagrams, or experiment results. The content is divided into three major areas: cellular and molecular biology, organismal biology, and ecology and evolutions.

- **Chemistry**

    This test consists of about 130 multiple-choice questions. The content of the test covers analytical chemistry, inorganic chemistry, organic chemistry, and physical chemistry.

- **Computer Science**

    This test consists of about 70 multiple-choice questions that cover software systems and methodology, computer organization and architecture, theory and mathematical background, and other topics that include numerical analysis, artificial intelligence, computer graphics, cryptography, security, and social issues.

- **Literature in English**

    This test consists of about 230 questions on poetry, drama, biography, the essay, short story, novel criticism, literary theory, and the history of English. The questions are usually classified as factual and critical. The factual questions require the student to identify literary or critical movements, to determine in what literary period a work was written, to identify a writer, or to determine the author of a work based on the style and the content of the work.

- **Mathematics**

    This test consists of about 66 multiple-choice questions. About one-half of the questions assess knowledge of calculus and about one-quarter of the questions tests elementary algebra, linear algebra, abstract algebra, and number theory. The remaining questions test other areas of math that undergraduates study.

- **Physics**

    This test consists of about 100 multiple-choice questions, and most of the questions can be answered based on what was learned in the first three years of undergraduate physics. The major topics include classical mechanics, electromagnetism, optics and wave phenomena, thermodynamics and statistical mechanics, quantum mechanics, atomic physics, special relativity, and laboratory methods.

- **Psychology**

    This test consists of about 205 multiple-choice questions. The questions fall into three categories: experimental, social, and a "general" category. The experimental category includes questions in learning, language, memory, thinking, sensation and perception, and physiological neuroscience. The social category includes questions in clinical and abnormal psychology, lifespan development, personality, and social psychology. The other "general" category includes questions in the history of psychology, industrial-organizational, and educational psychology, as well as measurement and methodology.

There is a wealth of information on the GRE Subject Tests at *www.gre.org* that includes some free sample questions.

TAKING THE GRE REVISED GENERAL TEST FOR BUSINESS SCHOOL

There are hundreds of business schools across North America and overseas that now accept the GRE General Test for admission to MBA programs and there are good reasons for this.

1. If you're not sure what you want to do after you graduate, take the GRE. Whether you want to go to grad school or business school, the GRE revised General Test may be the only test you need.

2. GRE scores are accepted by more than 300 business schools, including those that are ranked high, like Harvard, MIT Sloan, NYU Stern, and Stanford University (you can find the full list at *http://www.ets.org/gre/general/about/mba/programs*).

3. According to ETS, the GRE revised General Test measures skills that are valued by business schools, such as verbal reasoning, quantitative reasoning, critical thinking, and analytical writing.

No matter the reason you are taking the GRE revised General Test, we are here to help you get that score you need!

CHAPTER 2
Global Strategies

STAND THE TEST OF TIME

The GRE tests speed as much as, if not more than, content. The goal is to get the maximum score within the allotted time. That may be obvious, but consider what follows from the obvious. First, you must fine-tune your sense of how much time to spend per item. This is a crucial and doable task. In fancy terms, you must develop what academicians call focused metacognition. In English, this means you must get used to doing the tasks while also watching yourself do them. This other "you" will keep a critical eye on an on-screen timer and a mental stopwatch, as if filming yourself. As you work through this book, you'll be learning how to do the tasks and building your timer and stopwatch. In poker terms, you have to know when to stick and when to fold. Your metacognitive ability to watch yourself will help you play your cards right when you take the GRE.

Second, you need to break yourself of the ingrained habit of starting at No. 1 and doing the items in order. ETS has put a lot of effort into making a quasi-adaptive test that lets test-takers skip around. This is a huge benefit for you. For example, GMAT sections are more traditionally adaptive tests in which performance on an item generates both your provisional score and the difficulty level of the subsequent item. You can't skip around, and thus you have no idea what's coming. In contrast, the GRE sections let you survey the field. You can thus deploy your knowledge efficiently over the entire section. You're free to grab the low-hanging fruit since each item is worth the same. This way, you maximize your score and leave the tough items for last.

You might be worried that, by using this approach, you'll lose your place in the heat of battle and miss answering some questions. You won't, though, because you're going to set this book down right now and go play with the review functionality in our diagnostic test at www.rea.com/gre and in ETS's free online PowerPrep (www.ets.org/gre/revised_general/prepare/powerprep2) until you're entirely confident you can skip around at will.

TEST ANXIETY

Test anxiety can affect you in two ways. First, it may cause you to procrastinate. That will only intensify your anxiety. Since you're reading this, you've taken the proverbial first step and have put your toe in the water. So go for it now. Dive in. Take that diagnostic if you haven't already. Nothing cures the fear of the unknown—How will I do? What's this test all about?—better than eliminating the unknown.

Did you ever see the movie *Jaws*? I'm guessing you have. Steven Spielberg gives you only tantalizing glimpses of the shark until the end. Ditto the monster in *Alien* and ditto nearly every horror flick of the past century. Why? We can imagine far scarier monsters than even the most depraved and talented special-effects person can conjure and put on a screen—and it's cheaper to have you do it. Nothing is as scary in the doing as in the anticipating. You know this. So, basically, I want you to start looking at the shark and sink your teeth into the GRE.

Second, test anxiety can also cause you to freeze during the test. The fear of freezing often causes procrastination and other avoidance behaviors. I have a simple solution. Practice. Practice, practice, practice. Practice till you become calm. Then keep practicing till you go beyond calm and become a bit bored with the GRE. Stop there—just short of complacency.

For those of you with hair aflame, furiously cramming for the GRE, here's the deal. First, are you absolutely certain that you have to take this so soon? If not, put it off, put more practice time in, and you'll be calmer. Second, if you have no choice but to take it now, embrace it. Let me introduce you to a useful phrase you've probably heard: "It is what it is." Don't freak. Transmute your fear into cold, steely-eyed determination to smack this test around. Turn the disadvantage of fear into something else: cold determination in pursuit of the perfect revenge—success.

I'll return to these emotional issues throughout the book. For those of you who don't need the advice or support, more power to you. Skip the sections or sentences that treat nervousness and fear. I'm writing one book for all students. Please don't take offense if you have nerves of steel.

And for the nervous among you, keep this in mind: Only one kind of organism experiences no anxiety: a dead one. Your anxiety means you're alive. Use it as any good organism does—to motivate you to succeed. Celebrate your life, and smack the GRE into submission.

OK. We've got a diagnostic under our belts, we have a study plan, and we're familiar with the test interface, structure, and timing. We've even touched on some test-taking strategies and dealt with some possible fears. It's time to dive in. We'll start with some content and item-specific strategies for the Verbal section.

CHAPTER 3
The Verbal Section

See *Appendix C: Verbal Enhancer* for added support.

FORM AND FUNCTION

The function of this section is to test reading skills. You already know how to read, so you're off and running.

The twist is you must first learn about the specific forms by which your reading skills are tested, then learn to recognize and deploy your ability to read, and practice doing that under time pressure.

Let's take a brief tour of this section, item-type by item-type, treating them as "ideal types," rather as people treat organisms in, say, a vertebrate anatomy class. Rather than go in the order in which items are presented on the test, we'll follow a different sequence—from the most discrete and localized kind of reading to the most complex and generalized kind of reading. "From molecules to man," in the sexist terminology of those halcyon days of biology-teaching.

First are **sentence equivalence** questions (hereafter, **SE**s). Here's one you've already seen in the full-length diagnostic:

> The interchangeability of not only the male but also the female leads in *The Importance of Being Earnest* wittily underscores their _____.
>
> A acuity
> B desperation
> C superficiality
> D hilarity
> E profundity
> F frivolity

You've got one sentence with one blank. Your task is to complete that sentence properly and plausibly by choosing two from among the six answer choices. The only relevant context is the logic and meaning of the sentence. That's what makes **SE**s "discrete." They are reading comprehension at the sentence level.

Variants of these items are considered to be Text Completions by ETS: items that provide five clickable words.

Here's one:

Choose the one best answer choice for the blank.

National epics often behave as _____ myths: since the origins of most, if not all, nation-states are bloody, national epics endeavor to sanctify the blood through the appeal to a higher, usually divinely inspired goal.

- Ⓐ confiscatory
- Ⓑ exculpatory
- Ⓒ revelatory
- Ⓓ foundational
- Ⓔ aspirational

Click on your selection.

Since these questions deal with one sentence and one blank, they should be categorized here. One sentence, one blank—this is a simpler, if not necessarily easier, task than the **SE**.

Next, you have **Text Completions** (hereafter, **TCs**). A familiar example:

According to Schwarzwald, only two cosmological possibilities exist. First, if the amount of matter in the universe is such that mutual gravitational attraction will not overcome the explosive force of the Big Bang, then we live in (i) _____, constantly expanding universe. Second, if the amount of matter in the universe is such that mutual attraction will eventually overcome the Big Bang, then we live in a presumably infinite, (ii) _____ universe, in which Big Bang is followed by Big Crunch and another Big Bang forever.

Blank (i)	Blank (ii)
Ⓐ a weak	Ⓓ oscillating
Ⓑ a finite	Ⓔ contracting
Ⓒ an ancillary	Ⓕ unpredictable

These go up a level in complexity: usually more than one sentence and usually more than one blank. You now have to deal with an argument that links the sentences and provides the main clues to the correct answers. But you only have one real task: For each blank pick a word that fits the logic and meaning of the paragraph.

The GRE then ratchets it up with **Reading Comprehension** sets (henceforth, **RC**s). Let's take two examples to show the progressive complexity. First, a paragraph-length **RC** set:

Questions 1–3 are based on the following passage:

The "central dogma of molecular biology," first promulgated in the late 1950s, is that the information contained in the genome can flow in only one direction: from nucleic acids to proteins. In the archetypal situation, information "originates" in an organism's DNA. DNA, a large macromolecule made up of nucleotides which contain nucleic acids, serves as a template for messenger RNA (mRNA), a kind of photonegative of its "parent" DNA. Like DNA, mRNA is composed of nucleic acids. This mRNA macromolecule itself forms the template for the protein-to-be, which is made up of a different kind of molecule, amino acids. But this isn't the whole story. In some special situations, RNA can transmit information to DNA. So there can be some "backflow," if you will, of information from RNA to DNA, but, as of yet, no one has shown that protein-based information can be transmitted back to the genetic material, whether DNA or RNA.

1. According to the passage, which of the following sequences would most closely conform to the central dogma of molecular biology?

    (A) Protein → DNA → RNA
    (B) RNA → DNA → Protein
    (C) DNA → RNA → Protein
    (D) DNA → Protein → RNA
    (E) Protein → RNA → DNA

2. In context, "archetypal" is closest in meaning to

    (A) ancient.
    (B) typical.
    (C) exceptional.
    (D) embryonic.
    (E) antediluvian.

3. The author of the passage mentions "backflow" chiefly in order to

- (A) suggest a fatal flaw in the central dogma of molecular biology.
- (B) argue that the central dogma of molecular biology needs to be radically reinterpreted.
- (C) demonstrate that in certain instances information can flow from protein to DNA.
- (D) indicate that in some cases information can flow from RNA to DNA.
- (E) cast doubt on the notion that DNA is made up of nucleotides.

You now have a full paragraph and multiple items that ask you to determine three things: first, a logical sequence from the text; second, the meaning of a particular word in the context of the paragraph; and third, the rhetorical purpose of a particular word choice.

I'm not including an example of another variant on the paragraph-length **RC**, but you'll recall that some paragraphs provide an argument you are expected to evaluate, strengthen or weaken. Sometimes you highlight a sentence in the paragraph to point out a feature of an argument. Sometimes you're asked about the function of a highlighted element. And sometimes an item may be multiple response instead of multiple choice. These variations are less important than you might think. What matters are the skills these items are designed to assess, as well as the degree of complexity each reading task presents.

Finally, the mother of all Verbal sets—a long passage set:

Questions 1–4 are based on the following passage:

Like other organisms, gypsy moths and humans share a liking for similar habitats. Aside from their pestilent nature, gypsy moths are still moths, and unlike fruit flies and other Diptera moths and butterflies (Lepidoptera) have long been collected and fancied. "Sugaring" tree trunks to attract specimens became popular in Britain during the 1840s; many other collecting methods and instruments of amateur entomology (such as "simbling"—catching a female moth in a box or cage and using her to attract males) are at least a hundred years older.

In his delightful autobiography, *Speak, Memory,* Vladimir Nabokov recounts the beginning of his obsession with lepidopterology.

Nabokov was born in 1899, and started chasing butterflies around 1905, but (if one can accept his self-described precociousness) he became seriously involved in reading the literature around 1908–1910—exactly when the German–Jewish biologist Richard B. Goldschmidt was beginning to use the gypsy moth in his groundbreaking studies on genetics and evolution. Thus, Nabokov gives us a picture of the knowledge, techniques, and social relations of central European lepidopterology at exactly the time Goldschmidt was becoming, as it were, scientifically involved with this organism. Most importantly, Nabokov emphasizes that "since the middle of the [nineteenth] century, Continental lepidopterology had been, on the whole, a simple and stable affair, smoothly run by the Germans...[who] did their best to ignore the new trends [in evolution and genetics] and continued to cherish the philately-like side of entomology."

But Goldschmidt differed from his stamp-collecting countrymen. He was an embryologist by training, part of the new generation of laboratory-based biologists that could be justly symbolized by the compound microscope. The gypsy moth—or perhaps we should now refer to it by its scientific name, *Lymantria dispar*—was meant to be experimented with, not collected and classified.

Nabokov captures the type of species-definition that Goldschmidt's new generation of biologists was promulgating. "The Victorian...kind of species," Nabokov writes, "hermetic and homogenous, with sundry (alpine, polar, insular, etc.) 'varieties' affixed to it from the outside, as it were, like incidental appendages, was replaced by a new, multiform and fluid kind of species, organically *consisting* of geographical races or subspecies." The genetic basis of geographic races was exactly what interested Goldschmidt in *Lymantria dispar,* and his investigations lasted a quarter of a century, through a world war, internment in an American prison camp, and other vicissitudes of life that people, like all other organisms, must inevitably negotiate. Ultimately, and for a variety of interesting reasons, Goldschmidt parted ways with *Lymantria dispar,* falling under the seductive spell of its Dipteran competitor, *Drosophila melanogaster* (the fruit fly), but his first love was to color Goldschmidt's genetic and evolutionary theories long after the romance had ended.

1. According to the passage, which of the following is true of fruit flies?

    A They are attracted to "sugared" tree trunks.
    B Unlike gypsy moths, they are pests to humans.
    C They belong to the classification category Diptera.
    D They share a liking for habitats humans also prefer.
    E They launched Nabokov's interests in lepidopterology.

2. In the third paragraph, the author is mainly interested in

   (A) using the proper scientific name for the gypsy moth.
   (B) criticizing Goldschmidt's rejection of nineteenth-century natural history.
   (C) comparing Nabokov's concern with the gypsy moth to Goldschmidt's.
   (D) highlighting a key difference between nineteenth-century natural history and twentieth-century biology.
   (E) establishing the compound microscope as a symbol for twentieth-century biologists.

3. According to the passage, the species definition that Goldschmidt and his generation of biologists were replacing most closely reflects which of the following?

   (A) A geographically grounded family of very similar populations of organisms
   (B) A stamp-collecting-like activity, rather than an experimental, scientific activity
   (C) A uniform population of organisms, accompanied by associated but relatively unimportant local varieties, that is entirely cut off from all other such populations
   (D) A more scientifically based definition as opposed to a more literary description
   (E) A definition lacking the insights of embryological investigations

4. It can be inferred from the passage that the author chose to begin referring to the gypsy moth by its scientific name because the author

   (A) is suggesting that Goldschmidt began to fall in love with his favored laboratory organism.
   (B) bemoans the disappearance of more emotionally resonant approaches to the natural world.
   (C) rejects Nabokov's more literary treatment of lepidopterology.
   (D) desires to highlight the analogy between a creature noted for its pestilent nature and Goldschmidt's internment in an American prison camp.
   (E) wanted to reflect and reinforce the shift from nineteenth-century natural history to twentieth-century biology.

Yikes. You now have multiple paragraphs, and the complexity increased by at least one order of magnitude. That's a lot to absorb. Furthermore, you have four or more items that assess your ability to glean relevant details, identify the purpose of a paragraph unit, follow an argument or definition, and make an inference about a rhetorical usage. Of course, there are other possible items, which we'll go over in detail in the relevant sections.

SENTENCE EQUIVALENCE ITEMS (SEs) AND TEXT COMPLETIONS (TCs)

Now that you've been introduced to them, you will be shown how to get along with **SE**s. Recall the background, though:

- **SE**s "lead in" to **TC**s. **TC**s are multi-blank versions of **SE**s, that is.

- The "Mad-Libs-like" nature of this item type. I may be dating myself here, but those fill-in-the-blanks games, in which the person who comes up with blanks is given no indication of the subject matter but must supply examples of the required part of speech, are similar to both **SE**s and **TC**s. They're both easier and far less funny. On the GRE, however, you're given the context, unlike a true Mad Lib.

- **SE**s and **TC**s engage both real-world reading comprehension and GRE Reading Comprehension (**RC**s). Instead of identifying key elements in finished text, as in **RC**s, test-takers must first identify what's missing and then provide that or those key elements. There are plenty of cross-item-type connections of this sort, and I'll point them out as they come up.

But before we jump into the step-methods and strategies, let's review some of the skills and content these items test.

Content Review

There won't be much review necessary for Sentence Equivalence Items and Text Completions. Instead, we'll focus on tactics and strategies that will give you the most mileage. As we'll discuss, while reviewing vocabulary lists can't hurt, list-mania is not the most efficient way to build your GRE vocabulary. For the GRE, you're better served by being able to scan sentences for clues—including roots, suffixes, and prefixes—that will point to the answers you need.

1. Sentence structure

Mastering sentence structure, rather than weighing yourself down with tons of new vocabulary words, is the royal road to success on Sentence Equivalence Items and Text Completions. In other words, the New GRE rewards you for being keen on context rather than just being able to spit out hundreds of impressive-sounding words that would light up the boardroom of *American Literary Review*. Realizing this will not only make your job easier on test day, but will also continue to redound to your benefit in graduate school and long afterward.

Let's not gloss over the fact, however, that vocabulary is always a strong indicator of success.

For now, a brief grammar review is in order.

First, remember that English is an "SVO" language—subject, verb, object. The GRE makes life tougher for you by sometimes inverting that order from the active (S-V-O) to the passive (O-V-S). It also peppers those SVO or OVS sentences with lots of clauses and phrases that split the "S" from the "V" and "V" from the "O." So keep your wits about you by remembering SVO is the key to untangling sentences no matter what phrases and clauses intervene.

Take this item for example—

The interchangeability of not only the male but also the female leads in *The Importance of Being Earnest* wittily underscores their _____.

It requires some untangling.

What's the subject? *Interchangeability*. That is modified by the direct article, *the,* and the prepositional unit *of not only…Earnest*, that *not-only-but-also* embeds. Then comes an adverb, *wittily*, modifying the verb, *underscores*. You must provide the object, which is modified by *their*. All that gobbledygook just masks the S-V-O pattern:

Interchangeability-*underscores*-**[missing object]**.
            S   V   O

Once you commit this pattern to memory you'll immediately orient yourself.

2. Logic and rhetoric

This sounds highfalutin, but it's simple. Check this example:

> The usual mode of human history is (i) _____ not tragic. In a tragedy, fates are inescapable and character is destiny; chance plays little or no role. But history is not the simple unfolding of (ii) _____ forces, whether divine or mundane; rather, it is more like the evolution of life: full of (iii) _____ and random events that combine in unpredictable ways. If there is any law to history, it is the law of unintended consequences.

"Say what?" you ask. Let's break it down into colloquial language, the kind you might use when talking to yourself:

"OK, it looks like the *mode* of human history is something other than tragic. What's a mode? If I know, I know; if I don't, I put it on the back burner and keep reading to see if I can infer its meaning.

Next I consider tragic modes, or tragedy, wherein fate and destiny are in charge. History, however, isn't like that—rather, it's like evolution. In what way? Well, the author defines that as full of something plus random events, and it's all rather unpredictable.

What have we said so far? Tragedy is inescapable and destined. History's not like that, but it is rather chancy.

Finally, I see the law of unintended consequences rules both evolution and, in this author's opinion, history, which isn't tragic. I don't need to know what *mode* means. I now know what's up here: some non-tragic and random "mode" governs history.

That's about all the deep knowledge of logic and rhetoric you'll need to predict answers to **TC** blanks. (You'll soon learn this strategy and make it entirely conscious.)

3. Vocabulary

Analogies and antonyms, which are no longer directly tested on the GRE, were never all that critical except for super-high-scorers to achieve super-high scores. Now they, and vocabulary generally, matter even less.

So do yourself a big favor and don't bother studying lists of hundreds of words supposedly likely to appear on the GRE. Study roots, suffixes, and prefixes. They are the units from which big, long Latinate words are built; learn what "circum-" means and you're more than halfway home to knowing the meanings of "circumnavigate," "circumvent," "circumscribe," "circumference," and so on. Learn what "ex-" means, and you've got another hint under your belt. And so on. we provide some good lists in Appendix C. Also, many are available online.

If you're familiar with a Romance or Germanic language, or with Latin or Greek, it also helps to activate your knowledge of foreign (i.e., non-English) languages. Given the mostly contingent wendings of peoples that make up much of history, other languages just haven't had much of an impact on English and are thus not helpful. But those listed contain many of the word parts that found their way into English; thus, you're already further ahead of the game than you may realize, even with the dangers of "false cognates."

That said, it does help to learn the meanings of words you encounter on official GRE tests—either on PowerPrep II or in the official book, free PDF(s), etc. You're already putting in the time. With marginal effort you can do a sweep every so often and make flashcards of unfamiliar words. By basing that effort on the official material, you have certain knowledge that those words could show up on the GRE.

SENTENCE EQUIVALENCE (SE) STRATEGIES

So, you have to pick **two** of the six answer choices in this multiple-response item, each of which completes the sentence. Often, you're just dealing with two synonyms; sometimes, however, there are non-synonymic ways of reasonably completing the same sentence. It'll be obvious when you run into the second, more challenging sub-type.

In this strategy section and in all subsequent sections of this type, we'll take a typical item you've already seen in the diagnostic test, and use it to show the strategies by walking you through a model explanation in "slow motion." We'll then provide a kind of "open hand" experience and take you through a version of the model with a different item that requires some responses from you. Finally we'll provide you with some untimed but testlike items for practice. We'll call the "open-hand" material "guided practice." When you're on your own, we'll call it "independent practice."[1]

There are two main types of strategies: what we'll call "the 'normal' way" and "reverse engineering." The "normal" way is simply the algorithm you should follow as a first resort. If that doesn't work, you can take advantage of the fact that this is a multiple-choice (or -response) test and work backwards. The "normal" way is the default tool. Reverse engineering is the backup tool. You'll need both in your toolbox, of course.

---

[1]Those destined for graduate work in education or related fields should stop laughing or wincing at our statement of the obvious. ☺

The "Normal" Way

Here's the algorithm you'll want to follow each time you see an **SE**.

Step 1: Cover the answer choices.

Step 2: Read the stem.

Step 3: Fill in the blanks with words or phrases of your own.

Step 4: Compare your words or phrases with those in the answer choices and eliminate those that fail to match.

Step 5: Plug whichever two choices remain into the blank and select the best fits or guess from among what's left.

The "Normal Way" in Slow Motion

As with virtually all of the strategies you're learning, the key element is to weaken the seductive power of the answer choices by providing plausible answers *before* you expose yourself to the wily answer choices. Four of them are known in the biz as "distractors"—and that's exactly what they're designed to do: distract you from recognizing the right answer. They act as camouflage.

Here's the item we'll use:

> The interchangeability of not only the male but also the female leads in *The Importance of Being Earnest* wittily underscores their _____.

Step 1: Cover the answer choices.

We've done that for you, but practice doing this on-screen with a piece of paper. It won't be that much of a challenge, but the point is you must make covering the answers a habit!

Step 2: Read the stem.

We've already parsed this as an example of how knowledge of sentence structure helps with **SE**s and **TC**s, but let's get a more colloquial sense of what the sentence says.

Rework the sentence in your head to get the meaning, or as your teachers always told you, put it into your own words. Example:

> "There are male and female leads in this play or story. Apparently, there are two each, because they are interchangeable. Usually, characters are distinct. Since they're not in this play or story, and since we know the play or story [it's a play] is witty, making the leads interchangeable would emphasize what?"

Step 3: Fill in the blanks with words or phrases of your own.

> "OK, that would emphasize that they're: not much different from each other; not particularly individualized, perhaps rather clone-like."

Step 4: Compare your words or phrases with those in the answer choices and eliminate those that fail to match.

Here they are:

"clone-like"

- Ⓐ acuity
- Ⓑ desperation
- Ⓒ superficiality
- Ⓓ hilarity
- Ⓔ profundity
- Ⓕ frivolity

Whoa. Our prediction of "clone-like" doesn't really match much, at first glance. Before we readjust, which will happen from time to time, let's see if any of the answer choices are just way out in left field. *Desperation* is so dissimilar to anything like "clone-like" or *interchangeability* that we can confidently eliminate that one.

Key point: When I say eliminate, I mean, when you practice on-line and during the real test, write on your blank sheet of paper six digits, like so:

1.

2.

(continued)

> ### The "Normal Way" in Slow Motion (Continued)
>
> **3.**
>
> **4.**
>
> **5.**
>
> **6.**
>
> Cross out whichever number corresponds to the choice you're consigning to the Outer Darkness, i.e., eliminating.
>
> I'm not sure I should do anything more than that. So let me rethink my prediction. If they're interchangeable, they're not particularly individualized. If they're not particularly individualized, what are they? Shallow? Let's try that, adjusting to the part of speech required:
>
> **"shallowness"**
> _____
>
> Ⓐ acuity
> Ⓑ desperation
> Ⓒ superficiality
> Ⓓ hilarity
> Ⓔ profundity
> Ⓕ frivolity
>
> Hmmm...*superficiality* and *frivolity* jump right out, and, moreover, are synonyms.
>
> **Step 5: Plug whichever *two* choices remain into the blank; select the best fits or guess among what's left.**
>
> We've nailed them.

OK, OK, I see you shifting uneasily in your chair. Yes, I assumed you knew what all the words meant. That won't always, or maybe even often, be so. We'll deal with that problem—partly now and partly later in the Reverse Engineering section.

All you need to know at this point, for the "normal" method, is never eliminate any answer choice whose meaning you're not pretty sure of. You could eliminate the right answer.

Sentence Equivalence (SE) Strategies

One last thing. Remember that we're categorizing those one-blank, select-a-word **TC**s as "**SE**s" for our own purposes. The "normal" way is the same, except you're only selecting one, instead of two, of the answers below the stem.

Now for some guided practice.

Guided Practice 1

Let's throw in one of those just-described **TC**s we're treating as an **SE**.

Step 1: Cover the answer choices

National epics often behave as _____ myths: since the origins of most, if not all, nation-states are bloody, national epics endeavor to sanctify the blood through the appeal to a higher, usually divinely inspired goal.

    confiscatory
    exculpatory
    revelatory
    foundational
    aspirational

Click on your selection.

You've covered the answer choices, right?

Step 2: Read the stem.

Put it into your own words in the space below.

CHAPTER 3
The Verbal Section

Compare that to this footnote.[2]

Step 3: Fill in the blanks with words or phrases of your own.

Write your prediction in the following space.

Now compare your prediction to this footnote.[3] If you feel you need to change your prediction, go ahead.

Step 4: Compare your words or phrases with those in the answer choices and eliminate all that do not match.

Here they are. Write your prediction in the space provided. Eliminate what you can:

- confiscatory
- exculpatory
- revelatory
- foundational
- aspirational

Step 5: Plug whichever choices remain into the blank; select the best fit or guess among what's left.

Do this as you see fit.

Turn to the end of the chapter for the answer.

---

[2] "OK, Self—this says that national epics are some kind of myth. What comes after the colon gives us the clue: It's the kind of myth that washes away the bloodiness of reality by dressing it up in some fashion. The old silk-hat-on-a-pig—in this author's opinion, which is all that matters!"

[3] I need something that expresses the silk-hat-on-a-pig, or, the washing away of the sin. How about "guilt-removing"? [Your prediction doesn't have to be "pretty" or even grammatical. It just has to work.]

Independent Practice

OK, you're on your own now! Don't worry about timing yourself. That's for the full-length tests. For now, just practice the method. Feel free to write the steps on a card or flip back and forth.

1. Largely due to the influence of trade-fueled population mixing, cities have always been centers of _____ the world's thoughts and traditions mix when the world's people mix.

    A provincialism
    B conflict
    C consumption
    D revelry
    E cosmopolitanism

2. Cafés have apparently often been associated with political _____ since coffee houses were, until modern times, one of the few places where people of all classes could mix and talk.

    A percolation
    B ferment
    C conformity
    D cuisine
    E bibulousness
    F radicalism

3. The second-century Roman writer Apuleius's book, *The Transformations of Lucius,* or, *The Golden Ass,* is not just one of the first novels but one of the most _____: writers from Cervantes and Boccaccio to Joyce and Borges have drawn from that gold mine.

    A protean
    B ancient
    C querulous
    D influential
    E quixotic
    F copious

Independent Practice Explanations

1. Largely due to the influence of trade-fueled population mixing, cities have always been centers of _____ the world's thoughts and traditions mix when the world's people's mix.

   A provincialism
   B conflict
   C consumption
   D revelry
   E cosmopolitanism

Trade fuels the mixing of populations in cities, and thus of different thoughts and traditions. A place that does that is a center of what? How about "worldly"? Leads right to *cosmopolitanism*. Note that "cosmo(s)" means "world" or "universe" and "poli(s)" means "city."

2. Cafés have apparently often been associated with political _____ since coffee houses were, until modern times, one of the few places where people of all classes could mix and talk.

   A percolation
   B ferment
   C conformity
   D cuisine
   E bibulousness
   F radicalism

All right: Cafés let people of all classes and kinds mingle and talk and exchange ideas. They're drinking coffee, and we all know how animated coffee makes us. So, we need a word that would capture the political developments associated with an unusual mix of enthusiastic people. How about "change" or "fervor" or something like that? Compare these to the answer choices: *ferment* and *radicalism* jump out. The others are distractors.

Sentence Equivalence (SE) Strategies | 33

3. The second-century Roman writer Apuleius's book, *The Transformations of Lucius,* or *The Golden Ass,* is not just one of the first novels but one of the most _____: writers from Cervantes and Boccaccio to Joyce and Borges have drawn from that gold mine.

   A protean
   B ancient
   C querulous
   D influential
   E quixotic
   F copious

This writer, "A," wrote a book that was one of the first novels. It's also something else, and we find it after the colon—a book that influenced many writers. It's a "gold mine" of a book. So it's a "rich" book—one of the richest. Note that the prediction doesn't have to be "pretty."

Protean is a nasty distractor—it means "taking many shapes or forms" and is a synonym for "transformations." *Ancient* doesn't match "rich"; gone. *Querulous* doesn't match "rich" (it means "liable to whine and complain"). *Influential* is good; so is *copious*. *Quixotic* is a nasty distractor. It is associated with Cervantes' *Don Quixote*, but means something other than "rich" (it means "impractically idealistic").

Reverse Engineering

One reverse-engineering strategy isn't really a reversal of the normal way but is a useful modification: If you cannot come up with a word for your prediction, decide whether you need a positive, negative, or neutral word.

Positive and negative mean more than morally positive or negative. An increase in magnitude is positive, for example. Not all blanks require something positive or negative. Sometimes it's just a descriptive word that is neutral. That gives you information, too.

For example, let's assume you couldn't come up with "clone-like" in the previous example. Perhaps you found your way to something negative. These word-charges are just unfocused versions of word-predictions. Especially under time constraint, they can come in very handy. Check it out:

> **"something negative"**
>
> - acuity
> - desperation
> - superficiality
> - hilarity
> - profundity
> - frivolity

Well, goodbye to *hilarity* and *profundity* and *acuity*—assuming you know the meanings of those words.

Which brings us to another reverse-engineering strategy: muddling through with less-than-perfect vocabulary knowledge. Besides applying your word-parts, knowledge of foreign languages, and so forth, you can do more. The good news is all you need to activate knowledge you already have!

Take, *acuity*. Maybe that word is unfamiliar. But what about a related word—"acute"? That can mean that little angle or it can mean a flare-up in a chronic disease—or it can mean perceptive. Take *profundity*. Shear off the suffix and what do you have? "Profound." That might be more familiar. The moral? Don't just balk at a word root that's been tarted up with lots of suffixes and prefixes. You may know enough about the word to guess at its meaning, or, failing that, at whether it's positive, negative, or neutral.

Keep in mind that the correct answers to most of these **SE**s are synonyms, or near-synonyms. This is a powerful fact: It means that even if you haven't got the slightest clue what the stem is talking about, you have a fairly good shot at getting the answers if you can identify two synonyms among the answer choices.

In our example, only *superficiality* and *frivolity* are near-synonyms. There's a good chance they would be right even if the stem had been sheer gibberish:

> **Inklebot hoopidink flurbaged the penguin, durbing the milltones to _____.**

That is, if the sentence had been entirely undecipherable to you!

These reverse-engineering strategies aren't foolproof. But you're in a kind of betting situation when you take the GRE. So you hedge your educated guesses to scrape out a few more raw points. A few more raw points will raise your scaled score and thus your percentile rank significantly.

You're now ready for some independent practice. Even if you see how to do these the normal way, you should still use reverse-engineering strategies.

Independent Practice

1. Determining human motivation is brutally difficult because the levels of causation are effectively _____: each of the innumerable genetic and environmental influences, some going back billions of years and all of which interact in some fashion, potentially plays a role in the motivation for one act.

    A infinite
    B inoperative
    C silenced
    D discrete
    E ignorable

2. The unit cost of computer memory continues to plummet: one can now spend twenty dollars on a ten-gigabyte, hand-held "jump drive"—that _____ cost a hundred times as much a few short years ago.

    A discrepancy
    B force
    C caliber
    D capacity
    E feature
    F information

3. Much of early twentieth-century classical music embraced a jarring, _____ aesthetic; like much of the visual art of that period, the need for art to be beautiful was being heavily challenged.

    A harmonious
    B dissonant
    C euphonious
    D discordant
    E symphonic
    F consensual

Independent Practice Explanations

1. Determining human motivation is brutally difficult because the levels of causation are effectively _____: each of the innumerable genetic and environmental influences, some going back billions of years and all of which interact in some fashion, potentially plays a role in the motivation for one act.

    A infinite
    B inoperative
    C silenced
    D discrete
    E ignorable

Let's use word charges for this one. We realize that there are lots and lots of levels of causation—genetic and environmental—which themselves interact. There's no way to calculate what the motivation was. Since we can't come up with a good word, we'll just say:

$$\text{``+''}$$

infinite
inoperative
silenced
discrete
ignorable

Well, what isn't positive? Actually, everything is negative except *infinite*, the biggest plus there is!

Do you see how this is a handy method?

2. The unit cost of computer memory continues to plummet: one can now spend twenty dollars on a ten-gigabyte, hand-held "jump drive"—that _____ cost a hundred times as much a few short years ago.

    A discrepancy
    B force
    C caliber
    D capacity
    E feature
    F information

Sentence Equivalence (SE) Strategies | 37

Let's try looking for near-synonyms in the answer choices. Only *capacity*, a quantifiable trait, and *feature*, a discrete trait, are more or less synonymous. None of the other words match. *Discrepancy* is about the difference between two quantities. *Force* is a measure of power, colloquially speaking. *Caliber* can refer to a specific quality in ammunition, or more generally to quality. *Information* is data.

3. Much of early twentieth-century classical music embraced a jarring, _____ aesthetic; like much of the visual art of that period, the need for art to be beautiful was being heavily challenged.

   A harmonious
   B dissonant
   C euphonious
   D discordant
   E symphonic
   F consensual

Let's look at word parts for this one, pretending that we don't know what some of these words mean. *Harmonious* hides the word "harmony," and that's not what we need here.

The prefix "dis-" means "not" or "the reverse of," as in "dissimilar." The "son" root has to do with sound—"sonic," "sonorous," and so on. So *dissonant* must mean something like "not sounding." Can it mean "silent" or "not sounding good"? A judgment call when you don't know the meaning, but we're hedging our bets here. ☺ Take *euphonious*. The prefix "eu-" means "good," as in "euphoria" (good feeling) or "eulogy" (speaking well of someone). The root "phon" has to do with sound—"phonics," "telephone," and so on. So it's "good sound." It must be wrong, as *jarring* doesn't meld with "good sound."

Check *discordant*. Another "dis-"; the form "discord" is probably more familiar. People in discord don't get along, as opposed to people in concord. So, *discordant* could mean "notes that don't get along"—that are *jarring*.

Symphonic, while a typical distractor—associated with music but not necessarily relevant here—has a prefix, "sym-," that means "together," as in "sympathy" (feeling connected to—"being together with"—other people's feelings). And there's that "phon" root.

Consensual has the "con-" prefix, which is the opposite of "dis-," and is also a form of "consensus." It's another "fitting well together" word and almost certainly wrong.

Only the near-synonyms of *discordant* and *dissonant* work.

TEXT COMPLETION (TC) STRATEGIES

Remember, there is no partial credit on **TCs**. You must fill all blanks correctly to score your point. You have two main strategies—again, the "normal" way and a variety of "reverse engineering" modes.

The "Normal" Way

Here's the algorithm you'll want to follow each time you see a text completion.

Step 1: Cover the answer choices.

Step 2: Read the stem.

Step 3: Fill in the blanks with words or phrases of your own.

Step 4: Compare your words or phrases with those in the answer choices and eliminate those that fail to match.

Step 5: Plug whichever choices remain into the relevant blank; select the best fit or guess from among what's left.

As with most strategies you're learning, always try to answer the item without reading those choices. The key is to weaken the seductive power of the answer choices by providing plausible answers *before* you expose yourself to the wily answer choices.

Let me take you through this method using a test-like item. As usual, we'll take it slow by playing "an open hand," as they say in cards.

The "Normal Way" in Slow Motion

Here's the item we'll use:

> The usual mode of human history is (i) _____ not tragic. In a tragedy, fates are inescapable and character is destiny; chance plays little or no role. But history is not the simple unfolding of (ii) _____ forces, whether divine or mundane; rather, it is more like the evolution of life: full of (iii) _____ and random events that combine in unpredictable ways. If there is any law to history, it is the law of unintended consequences.

Step 1: Cover the answer choices.

We've done that for you.

Step 2: Read the stem.

You cannot provide a prediction for the first blank until you've read the entire stem. This is not typical.

The second sentence provides a big clue: The author links the notion of tragedy—which human history is not, according to the author—to destiny, fate, and predetermination. After the semicolon in that sentence, the contrast to whatever mode the first blank stands for is hinted at: something having to do with chance.

Reading further, we see the author thinks history is more like biological evolution, which, according to the author, is full of random events and is thus unpredictable. Finally, he says the law of unintended consequences rules history. The third sentence carries through the contrast between fate and chance: History—to this author—is unlike destiny or fate.

Step 3: Fill in the blanks with words or phrases of your own.

Well, we know that the second blank must be filled by something like "non-chancy." Don't hesitate for a second over the grammar or silliness of your prediction. If it captures the idea, use it.

(continued)

The "Normal Way" in Slow Motion (Continued)

Check out the third blank. You have what I call a "blank-*and*" situation: whatever the blank is, it has to be at least more similar than not to whatever follows the *and*. A good prediction would be "chancy."

And, of course, the first blank has to refer to a mode that embraces "chanciness."

Perhaps you provided more specific predictions—if so, great! Perhaps you couldn't provide even these quick but useful predictions. If so, sit tight: other methods are coming.

Step 4: Compare your words or phrases with those in the answer choices and eliminate those that fail to match.

Time to look at the answer choices! Take them one at a time; start with whichever blank you feel the most confident about filling because the blanks are linked to each other. Nailing one may cause you to revise your other two choices. We'll keep it simple for now. Let's line up our predictions with the blank columns:

"a chancy mode"   "non-chancy"   "chancy"

Blank (i)	**Blank (ii)**	**Blank (iii)**
Ⓐ ironic	Ⓓ stochastic	Ⓖ unintelligible
Ⓑ heroic	Ⓔ deterministic	Ⓗ contingent
Ⓒ lyric	Ⓕ comprehensible	Ⓘ inevitable

Now, maximize your innate logic. Look at Blank (i). Ask yourself, "Which of these is definitely *not* a chancy mode? Let's pretend we're not quite sure what *ironic* means; it's a tough term, after all. If you don't know what a word in an answer choice means, don't eliminate. *Heroic* stories depend on effort of will or faith far more than on chance—gone. *Lyric* reminds one of song lyrics; "lyrical" conjures a picture of meadows and flute-toting shepherds and has nothing to do with chanciness. Gone. It looks like it's *ironic*. So choice (A) is it.

Check out Blank (ii). Tough words. But stick to your prediction—you need something like "non-chancy." Take *stochastic*. No idea what it means? Leave it. What about *deterministic*? As with any big word, break it up. Familiar with the word "determined"? Sure. If you're determined to do something, you're ready to impose your will toward some goal. That has nothing to do with chance! This one looks good, but check out the last one, *comprehensible*. We know what that means. It has nothing to do with chanciness or the lack of it. Gone. Choice (E) is looking good and gels with your choice in Blank (i).

Finally, Blank (iii) requires something like "chancy." Let's pretend we don't know what *unintelligible* means. Take off the prefix. Does "intelligible" ring a bell? Irrelevant here. Gone. No idea what *contingent* means? You're not alone—but don't eliminate it! Now *inevitable*. Has to do with time—something will definitely occur at a certain point if it's inevitable. Hmmm…. In the heat of the testing moment, it might seem OK, but note that it's not specifically about chanciness. If something has a low probability of occurring, like an asteroid impact, but there is enough time available, it's "inevitable." So, that one is gone too. You're left with *contingent*, choice (H).

Step 5: Plug whichever choices remain into the relevant blank. Select the best fit or guess from among what's left.

Choices (A), (E), and (H) work well. And they happen to be correct. But note that you didn't know what any of the right answers officially meant.

Let's try this with a different item.

Guided Practice 2

We'll use an item you've seen on the diagnostic test.

Step 1: Cover the answer choices.

Given that many multinational corporations have annual incomes greater than the gross domestic products of most nations, and that they are never democratically governed, we need to stop viewing private corporations as poor little individuals like ourselves, both equally (i) _____ by the all-powerful State. In fact, most economists and political scientists consider large multinational corporations, especially financial ones, to be a "virtual parliament" of immortal "individuals" whose investment choices (ii) _____ the actions of actual parliaments of mortal individuals.

Blank (i)	Blank (ii)
Ⓐ cowed	Ⓓ obliterate
Ⓑ supported	Ⓔ obviate
Ⓒ improved	Ⓕ substantiate

Step 2: Read the stem.

Put it into your own words in the space provided below.

OK, compare that to this footnote.[4]

---

[4]The author maintains that very rich multinationals are corporate institutions—not individuals—and are not governed democratically, and so they are not like actual, real, live people. Thus, they don't share some equal something-or-other with actual people. In fact, it looks like the virtual parliament of multinationals does something negative to the actions of actual parliaments that represent actual people.

Step 3: Fill in the blanks with words or phrases of your own.

Write your predictions in the following space.

Here are my predictions.[5]

Step 4: Compare your words or phrases with those in the answer choices and eliminate those that fail to match.

See what you can eliminate:

Blank (i)	Blank (ii)
Ⓐ cowed	Ⓓ obliterate
Ⓑ supported	Ⓔ obviate
Ⓒ improved	Ⓕ substantiate

Step 5: Plug whichever choices remain into the relevant blank. Select the best fit or guess from among what's left.

See the end of the chapter for the answer.

It's time for some independent practice.

---

[5]Blank (i): repressed and Blank (ii): override.

Independent Practice

1. Hockney has shown that most of the Old Masters were using optical aids to create their perfectly painted, photorealistic (i) _____ far earlier than was previously acknowledged. His research is a triumph of (ii) _____ of the value of simply looking at accumulated evidence without preconceptions, and letting the data tell their own story.

Blank (i)	Blank (ii)
(A) depictions	(D) cogitation
(B) perceptions	(E) deduction
(C) misrepresentations	(F) empiricism

2. What historians call the "Columbian Exchange" is only the most striking instance of a (i) _____ phenomenon. Ever since humanity spread out from Africa, (ii) _____ communities have harbored their own more-or-less unique disease organisms, crops, and even pack animals. The pre-human (iii) _____ distribution of such organisms determined much of subsequent human history, both before and after the rise of settled agriculture. There have been many smaller scale meetings of previously mostly isolated humans and their attendant species. The meeting of the old and new worlds, however, closed a loop that had begun millennia previously when a few intrepid people crossed the Bering Strait's land or ice bridge and populated North and South America.

Blank (i)	Blank (ii)	Blank (iii)
(A) perennial	(D) contiguous	(G) geographic
(B) unique	(E) disjunct	(H) efficient
(C) baroque	(F) competing	(I) ironic

3. We English-speakers should thank the Normans for invading England in 1066. That invasion brought the French into contact with the Germanic Anglo-Saxon language, complete with complex "declensions," that the influence of French almost entirely (i) _____, privileging instead a more Romance linguistic form. With surprising (ii) _____, within only three centuries of that invasion, Chaucer and others had invented a new language, English, which still benefits from the marriage of Romance and Germanic influences.

Blank (i)	Blank (ii)
(A) embraced	(D) enthusiasm
(B) effaced	(E) alacrity
(C) distorted	(F) deference

Independent Practice Explanations

1. Hockney has shown that most of the Old Masters were using optical aids to create their perfectly painted photorealistic (i) _____ far earlier than was previously acknowledged. His research is a triumph of (ii) _____ of the value of simply looking at accumulated evidence without preconceptions, and letting the data tell their own story.

Blank (i)	Blank (ii)
(A) depictions	(D) cogitation
(B) perceptions	(E) deduction
(C) misrepresentations	(F) empiricism

   You covered the answer choices, right? I won't mention this every time, but I will remind you from time to time!

   Hockney showed painters called "Old Masters" were using optical aids to make paintings that were as realistic as a photograph. We don't care what these optical aids were, of course, just that they were optical and that they aided the Old Masters, according to Hockney, and were in use long before art historians thought. The second blank has to be filled by a word that matches the definition after the dash.

   Prediction for (i)? How about "paintings"? Don't worry that you're repeating a word—usefulness, not beauty, governs your prediction. For (ii)? Probably tougher, but it's something that means just looking at the data. "Observation" would do.

   The only word that matches "paintings" is *depictions*. The only word that matches "observation" is *empiricism*. *Cogitation* means "thinking," and this is about a process that is more externally directed. *Deduction* happens inside the head.

2. What historians call the "Columbian Exchange" is only the most striking instance of a (i) _____ phenomenon. Ever since humanity spread out from Africa, (ii) _____ communities have harbored their own more-or-less unique disease organisms, crops, and even pack animals. The pre-human (iii) _____ distribution of such organisms determined much of subsequent human history, both before

and after the rise of settled agriculture. There have been many smaller scale meetings of previously mostly isolated humans and their attendant species. The meeting of the old and new worlds, however, closed a loop that had begun millennia previously when a few intrepid people crossed the Bering Strait's land or ice bridge and populated North and South America.

Blank (i)	Blank (ii)	Blank (iii)
Ⓐ perennial	Ⓓ contiguous	Ⓖ geographic
Ⓑ unique	Ⓔ disjunct	Ⓗ efficient
Ⓒ baroque	Ⓕ competing	Ⓘ ironic

What's going on? Well, we have something that historians call the "Columbian Exchange," which, we learn later—only by the end of the paragraph—must have been the exchange of those disease organisms, crops, and pack animals that were new to each side of the exchange. The second sentence provides an image of groups of humans spreading, making use of different organisms around them, getting immunity to different diseases, etc. They were making use of whatever they found wherever they went, as the third sentence implies.

Next we learn that such biological exchanges have been happening whenever relatively isolated human populations meet. Only during and after the Columbian Exchange did all of these different families of "hitchhiking" organisms meet, as people sailed back and forth between the last two isolated populations—those of the old and new worlds.

That wasn't easy. But now we can make some predictions. For (i), we need a word that means "happened continuously," and "happened continuously" will do just fine. For (ii), we need something that notes the isolation among human groups and their associated organisms—something like "separate." For (iii), we need something that modifies the noted distribution. From the logic of the sentence, it's clear that the modifier isn't needed—it's a matter of emphasis. What kind of distribution are we talking about? Across the world—or, "geographic."

Compare those predictions to the choices. You can get rid of *unique* and *baroque* and keep *perennial*, whether you know that word (note that well); you can kill *competing*. *Contiguous* means "geographically adjoining" and is the opposite of what you want. *Disjunct*, whether you've ever heard of it, must be right.

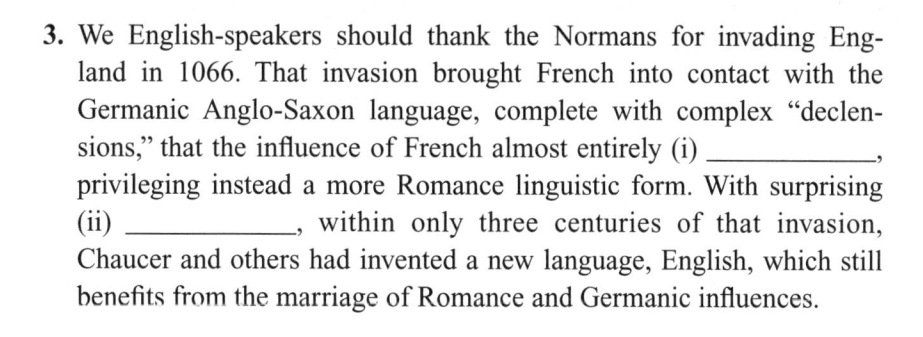

3. We English-speakers should thank the Normans for invading England in 1066. That invasion brought French into contact with the Germanic Anglo-Saxon language, complete with complex "declensions," that the influence of French almost entirely (i) _____, privileging instead a more Romance linguistic form. With surprising (ii) _____, within only three centuries of that invasion, Chaucer and others had invented a new language, English, which still benefits from the marriage of Romance and Germanic influences.

Blank (i)	Blank (ii)
Ⓐ embraced	Ⓓ enthusiasm
Ⓑ effaced	Ⓔ alacrity
Ⓒ distorted	Ⓕ deference

All right. The Norman invasion in 1066 brought French to a Germanic-speaking area. One result was that "complex 'declensions'"—whatever *those* are—were "de-privileged" or, say, "removed"? That's your prediction. Then, something surprising happened. Within "only" three centuries, a new language had been born. The prediction is this happened quickly, relatively speaking. Prediction? "Speed" would work.

Now compare. "Removed" doesn't match *embraced* or *distorted*. So *effaced*, whatever it means, is right by default. "Speed," likewise, doesn't match *enthusiasm* or *deference*. So *alacrity* wins by default.

Reverse Engineering

Pretty much all the strategies noted in the previous section on **SE**s apply here—word charges, focusing on other forms of the words listed, and so on. So please refer again to that section. I say "pretty much" because the synonym-I.D. strategy won't help here, of course.

Practice those strategies on the following items, even if you can do them the normal way.

Independent Practice

1. Martin Scorsese, at his best, gives voice and image to an entire (i) _____. Whether he's dealing with Italian-Americans in the 1970s, Lower-East-Side Manhattan, Jews in first-century Palestine, or Buddhists in twentieth-century Nepal, Scorsese brings an anthropologist's eye for telling cultural details and social rules to his dramas, which usually focus on an individual's struggle against the (ii) _____ of his specific culture.

Blank (i)	Blank (ii)
(A) subculture	(D) heritage
(B) syndicate	(E) mores
(C) elite	(F) absurdities

2. Conventional wisdom holds that technological developments (i) _____ scientific discoveries: science is in the driver's seat, technology is a passenger; science provides the rationale for technologies, technology puts science's rationale to material use. While this is often the case, especially since the late nineteenth century, it is far from the rule. Moreover, as an unacknowledged guide to pre-nineteenth-century science and technology, it's downright (ii) _____.

Blank (i)	Blank (ii)
(A) antecede	(D) confounding
(B) postdate	(E) enlightening
(C) impart	(F) predictive

3. As the saying goes, "You can't make an omelet without breaking a few eggs." True enough in general, and often, specifically, in personal relationships. As Esteves notes, the constant clarion cry for "civility" has its downside: the irrational fear of any form of conflict invariably consigns people to (i) _____, lonely, disconnected roles that disallow for growth and progress. Not all (ii) _____ communication is destructive.

Blank (i)	Blank (ii)
(A) contentious	(D) deleterious
(B) convivial	(E) dissentious
(C) hermitic	(F) disaffective

Independent Practice Explanations

1. Martin Scorsese, at his best, gives voice and image to an entire (i) _____. Whether he's dealing with Italian-Americans in the 1970s, Lower-East-Side Manhattan, Jews in first-century Palestine, or Buddhists in twentieth-century Nepal, Scorsese brings an anthropologist's eye for telling cultural details and social rules to his dramas, which usually focus on an individual's struggle against the (ii) _____ of his specific culture.

Blank (i)	Blank (ii)
(A) subculture	(D) heritage
(B) syndicate	(E) mores
(C) elite	(F) absurdities

Let's use charges for this one. First, you have an artist who gives voice and image to an entire [some kind of grouping of people]. In the next sentence, up to *Scorsese*, you get three examples of such groupings. Ask yourself—are any such groupings of people intended to be positive, negative, or neutral? Right—this is a neutral category, much like "grouping," actually. Compare your "neutral" prediction to the words provided: *subculture* is pretty neutral, whereas *syndicate* has a negative connotation and *elite* has either a negative or a positive connotation, depending on what you may think about elites. But it's not neutral. *Subculture* is it.

Moving on, we see that Scorsese's got an anthropologist's eye for details and social rules. His dramas, we're told, focus on an individual's struggle against something like "those rules"—but is a connotation implied? The tone of the entire passage is pretty neutral—Scorsese is compared to an anthropologist, who doesn't pass judgment, and not to a moralist, who does pass judgment. You thus need another neutral word. *Heritage* has a positive tone. *Absurdities* is clearly negative. *Mores*—a synonym for codes or rules—is just right.

2. Conventional wisdom holds that technological developments (i) _____ scientific discoveries: science is in the driver's seat, technology is a passenger; science provides the rationale for technologies, technology puts science's rationale to material use. While this is often the

case, especially since the late nineteenth century, it is far from the rule. Moreover, as an unacknowledged guide to pre-nineteenth-century science and technology, it's downright (ii) _____

Blank (i) **Blank (ii)**

(A) antecede   (D) confounding

(B) postdate   (E) enlightening

(C) impart   (F) predictive

We first must figure the logic of the sentence. Call conventional wisdom CW, science S, and technology T. It works like this:

$$CW = S \rightarrow T$$

I'm not using a mathematical/logical metaphor to vary the presentation. I want the math-heads to realize these skills can be transferred to language-comprehension. The relationship is a temporal one: science comes before technology.

Now comes the strategy. We need something like "come before" or "predate." But the words given as options are strange. We can get rid of *impart* because, assuming we don't know the meaning of the word, we can guess that since "im-" is a "negator"—"imperfect" = "not perfect"; "impervious" = "not pervious." Therefore, *impart* means "not parted" or "included within," so to speak. It's too vague to capture the diagrammed relationship. Gone. *Postdate* means "post" = "after," + date. That matches our "equation," but let's make sure by checking *antecede*. Well, "precede" means "to come before," so even if we're unfamiliar with *antecede* at first glance, we know that "ante-" means "before" ("antebellum," "antecedent"—the more familiar version of this word). So this must be a synonym for "precede." Gone.

As the author says, sometimes CW = S → T, especially recently. But for sci-tech that predates 1800, it's way off. Therefore, the pre-1800 rule is CW = T → S, or maybe there is no relationship at all between T and S pre-1800. Therefore, assuming CW = S → T for the pre-1800 era is wrong, will lead to opposite or entirely wrong conclusions. That would be a big negative.

Check the answer choices: Only *confounding* matches the prediction. *Enlightening* and *predictive* are positive and positive-neutral, respectively.

Text Completion (TC) Strategies | 51

3. As the saying goes, "You can't make an omelet without breaking a few eggs." True enough in general, and often, specifically, in personal relationships. As Esteves notes, the constant clarion cry for "civility" has its downside: the irrational fear of any form of conflict invariably consigns people to (i) _____, lonely, disconnected roles that disallow for growth and progress. Not all (ii) _____ communication is destructive.

Blank (i)	**Blank (ii)**
(A) contentious	(D) deleterious
(B) convivial	(E) dissentious
(C) hermitic	(F) disaffective

In this case, the logic isn't so tough, relatively speaking, as the vocab in the answer choices. We must put our vocab skills to good use.

The passage pretty much says that in personal relationships conflict is sometimes necessary and good. Blank (i) requires a word more or less like "lonely" and "disconnected." Blank (ii) requires a word something like "conflict-ish." Not pretty, but it works. If you chose "conflictual," more power to you.

Do what you can with those words. *Convivial*—break it down. The root "viv" means "life or lively," as in "vivacious," "vivisection," etc. The prefix "con-" means "together," so being lively together is probably close to *convivial*. That's not what you need. Gone.

I put in *contentious* to reinforce the point that these reverse-engineering strategies aren't foolproof. If you see "content" you can be forgiven, but the word is negative. It stems from "contention," not "content" as in "contentedness."

Anyway, "contention"—"conflict"—is suggested. It would be missing from those who take "civility" too far. So this word is the opposite of what you need.

You now know you need *hermitic*, whatever *that* is. But check it out: The word "hermit" is in there. In this case, you can trust the root. "Hermitic" means "hermit-like" just as "pathetic" means "pathos-like." That's what the suffix "–ic" usually means.

Now look at the next blank. Break these words apart: *Deleterious* hides the word "delete" so it's an adjectival form of "delete." Is that close enough to "conflict-ish"? Conflict, especially given the context of this passage, doesn't have to lead to deleting your "opponent," who in this case is by definition *not* your opponent.

Choices couched in extreme language are usually wrong for an interesting reason. If I make the extreme statement that all dogs are black, all you need to do to disprove me is one non-black dog. If "all dogs are black" were an answer choice, so to speak, it would be easy to eliminate. But if I say, "Some dogs are nice," how could you disprove it? What does "some" mean? How are you going to define a hopelessly subjective "nice"? That's the kind of answer-choice language that tends to be right. We'll talk more about this when we get into reading comprehension. Relax.

Dissentious hides "dissent"—a word that's pretty close to "conflict." Looks good! *Disaffective* breaks down like this:

- "dis-" is a negator.

- "affect" is the root of words like "affection," etc.

- "-ive" is a suffix that means "tending to" or "having the quality of."

In summary, you have a word that means something like "the quality of not being affectionate." But the point is that personal relationships, which are presumably and nearly by definition affectionate, need not reject all conflict. The author is not suggesting communication that lacks affection, so this is the wrong choice.

READING COMPREHENSION (RC)

Time to ratchet up yet further with the full-on reading comprehension stuff! You've already seen a variety of examples in the diagnostic test. The main **RC** set subtypes are:

- Short passage sets

- Long passage sets

- Argument passage sets (all short)

The questions (a.k.a., "items") you'll see in those passage sets will be discussed in this section.

There are two parts to an **RC** set: the passage and the associated items. I'll show you how to handle each. If short, the passages need to be read word-for-word. If long, you'll need to do a combination of reading and skimming. I'll teach you exactly how to skim, which is seldom taught. It's easy.

Besides skimming and the content we've reviewed, you'll need a quick brush-up on other skills. These include:

- Scanning

- Nonfiction structure and organization

- More on logic

- Notions like main idea, details, tone, and inference

- Rhetorical devices and tropes I'll raise as needed

I'll bring each of these up in their turn.

After the brief content review, we'll model the strategies, guide you through some practice, and then set you free to do some independent practice on a new passage set.

Content Review

The passages

Let's start with organization. Reach back to grade school—that same old essay structure is what you'll see on the GRE: introductory sentence/paragraph; supporting sentences/paragraph(s); concluding sentence/paragraph. Keep in mind that hierarchical, classic outline structure. It will help you navigate the passages.

Given that structure, you may or may not want to skim parts of the long passages. It depends on how fast you read. If you can't read the passage fast enough word-for-word, the general idea is to read the first paragraph, and the first and last sentence of the second and each of the subsequent paragraphs (if any). You then read the last paragraph word-for-word. To skim, move your finger or pencil along the lines on the screen (or when practicing, on the page) faster than you can possibly read, following the finger or pencil tip with your eyes. Let certain words pop out. They will, and enough will for you to have a sense of what's up.

Keep in mind that you want to know two main things when you finish with a long passage:

1. The main idea of the essay;

2. The main idea of each paragraph of the essay.

I'm going to use furniture for an analogy. You want to know that you're looking at a dresser as opposed to, say, a cabinet (i.e., you want to know what the main idea of the passage is). You then want to know that in drawer one you'll find socks, in drawer two you'll find sweaters, and so on (i.e., you want to know what the main idea of each paragraph is). You don't need to list all the socks and sweaters in each drawer. If you're asked about a particular sock (i.e., a particular detail), you'll open the relevant drawer and find it. Unless and until that happens, there's no need to worry too much about details, even if you're reading word-for-word.

When it happens, you can simply scan for the information. This isn't reading word-for-word. It's simply looking for the thing asked about. If you're asked about, say, Dizzy Gillespie in a jazz passage, scan for the shape of "Dizzy Gillespie" without allowing yourself to get bogged down reading. When you find the reference, read that portion, word-for-word.

For those argument passages I mentioned, you need to know a few basics of rhetoric. First, an argument is made up of an assertion, supporting evidence, and a conclusion. For example:

Assertion: Standing barefoot in the snow makes your feet cold.

Evidence: I measured the skin temperature of the feet of 12 people. Then I had them stand barefoot in the snow for two minutes. This took some doing. We went back inside and I measured their foot-skin temperature. It was lower. I asked them if their feet felt cold, to get a subjective line of evidence. They answered in the affirmative and threw some unprintable comments and several weighty items at me.

Conclusion: We see that standing in the snow not only makes your feet cold, but also increases the propensity to violence.

A bit silly but also to the point: You'll be asked some questions on more dubiously argued passages. You'll be required to expose hidden assumptions or flawed reasoning from evidence to conclusion or to strengthen the argument.

You'll also need these skills when you answer your Analyze-an-Argument essay prompt. We'll have more on that in the relevant section.

The items

Most items fall into a few content categories: main idea, details, tone, inference, and point of view.

The main idea is, well, the thesis of a given passage. What's it all about? This is often hard to put into words, but you must do it to make sure you understand the passage and then be ready for the main-idea item.

Detail items are like little research projects: go find fact x, and fact y.

Tone is just what you think it is—if the written material were spoken material, what would the tone be? You can say, "That movie was great, wasn't it?" Depending on your vocal tone, you could have loved or hated the movie. Writers also have a tone. It's their attitude toward their subject, and readers have to glean it from the word choices and other devices.

Inferences are what we do to move from one known fact to another known fact. How big the move is, is the nub, of course, but for GRE purposes an inference is pretty close to a known fact. For example:

Fact: When I went to sleep yesterday, there was still some snow in my yard.

Fact: This morning, there was no snow.

Warranted Inference: The snow melted.

The GRE isn't a test of formal logic—common sense and some attention to missing or hidden assumptions will do fine.

Point of view is simply from whose perspective a point is being made. It's not just a feature of fiction; in nonfiction, Professor A can have POV 1, whereas Professor B can have POV 2—and Passage Writer can have POV 3 when discussing Profs A and B.

In summary and to provide an orienting mantra for **RC** sets, keep uppermost in mind the 5 Ws plus H: who, what, where, when, why, and how.

READING COMPREHENSION (RC) STRATEGIES

We'll start with the mother-of-all-**RC**s—the long passage set. After working through how to handle the passage and items and giving you the usual guided and independent practice, we'll discuss the shorties and the argument passage sets. And that should do it.

The Passage: The Normal Way

Here are the steps you'll want to follow for the long passage.

Step 1: Read the first paragraph.

Step 2: Read the first and last sentences of each subsequent paragraph, skimming the rest.

Some provisos:

1. If you find you can read fast and accurately enough to read the whole passage word-for-word, feel free to do so. If you're not quite that fast, try reading the entire last paragraph and see how that helps.

2. For **short** and **argument** passages, read them in full.

3. It may well turn out that, whether it's a short, long, or argument passage, reading the stems of all the items first will help you read/skim of the passage. If so, that's your new Step 1. Remember, you can go back and forth within the section!

Our M.O. with RPs is to experiment. One size does not fit all. Here's the secret knowledge—whichever variation works is what you use. That's then your M.O. ☺

The "Normal Way" in Slow Motion

Remember the long passage you saw in the diagnostic test? We'll use that to run you through the steps:

Step 1: Read the first paragraph.

> Like other organisms, gypsy moths and humans share a liking for similar habitats. Aside from their pestilent nature, gypsy moths are still moths, and unlike fruit flies and other Diptera moths and butterflies (Lepidoptera) have long been collected and fancied. "Sugaring" tree trunks to attract specimens became popular in Britain during the 1840s; many other collecting methods and instruments of amateur entomology (such as "simbling"—catching a female moth in a box or cage and using her to attract males) are at least a hundred years older.

Step 2: Read the first and last sentences of each subsequent paragraph, skimming the rest.

We'll actually be even stricter and entirely omit the rest, just to prove a point about how much you can glean just from the first and last sentences.

They almost always contain the main idea of each paragraph and the transition to the next (or from the last) paragraph:

> In his delightful autobiography, *Speak, Memory*, Vladimir Nabokov recounts the beginning of his obsession with lepidopterology.
>
> ...
>
> Most importantly, Nabokov emphasizes that "since the middle of the [nineteenth] century, Continental lepidopterology had been, on the whole, a simple and stable affair, smoothly run by the Germans ... [who] did their best to ignore the new trends [in evolution and genetics] and continued to cherish the philately-like side of entomology."

The next one is short, so read the whole thing. Short paragraphs in the middle sometimes contain a big point or a key transition:

> But Goldschmidt differed from his stamp-collecting countrymen. He was an embryologist by training, part of the new generation of laboratory-based biologists that could be justly symbolized by the compound microscope. The gypsy moth—or perhaps we should now refer to it by its scientific name, *Lymantria dispar*—was meant to be experimented with, not collected and classified.

We'll assume we're not reading the whole last paragraph:

> Nabokov captures the type of species-definition that Goldschmidt's new generation of biologists was promulgating.
>
> ...
>
> Ultimately, and for a variety of interesting reasons, Goldschmidt parted ways with *Lymantria dispar*, falling under the seductive spell of its Dipteran competitor, *Drosophila melanogaster* (the fruit fly), but his first love was to color Goldschmidt's genetic and evolutionary theories long after the romance had ended.

Tell me what we know. Give doing this a shot on the next page:

(continued)

Main idea of passage	
Main idea of paragraph 1	
Main idea of paragraph 2	
Main idea of paragraph 3	
Main idea of paragraph 4	

Compare that to mine:

Main idea of passage	You don't have to read the whole passage to get a sense of its main idea. Sometimes the first paragraph provides the main idea.
	The main idea of this passage is how the study of life shifted from natural history/amateur/collecting to biology/professional/experimenting.
Main idea of paragraph 1	Butterflies and moths (Lepidoptera) were collected by fanciers back in the day.
Main idea of paragraph 2	Nabokov wrote about doing that in his memoir.
	Hmmm...tough quote. But the point is that whatever *philately* means, the lepidopterists were not into new trends in evolution and genetics.
Main idea of paragraph 3	*Philately* must mean "stamp-collecting." Goldschmidt was not a stamp-collecting kind of lepidopterist. He was a modern biologist.
Main idea of paragraph 4	Apparently, Goldschmidt's generation of biologists (who, according to the logic here, must have been into new trends in evolution and genetics) had a new definition of "species."
	Goldschmidt switched from gypsy moth to fruit fly, but the gypsy moth experience left its mark on his thought and science.

Unlike other items, there's no reverse engineering here. There is a range of options on how much of the passage to read, along with whether to read the item-stems first. You should try out on the practice materials. By the way, we'll provide some advice on practice materials in the concluding section of the book.

The Items: The Normal Way

There are only a few kinds of **RC** items: main idea, detail, vocab-in-context, and extended reasoning. The first three are self-explanatory. The last is probably unfamiliar. This is the bucket into which fall all questions of inference and other extensions beyond what's on the page, perhaps even including some questions of tone, like irony and metaphor. They usually tend to be tougher. So keep that in mind strategy-wise.

Luckily, you approach each item in the same way: The key idea is to have a prediction in mind before you look at the answer choices. Vocab-in-context items should be handled according to the step-method for **SE**s or **TC**s. Knock out the word whose definition is asked about to create a "blank." Predict an answer. Match to the choices.

Here's the recipe:

Step 1: Cover the answer choices.

Step 2: Read the stem carefully.

Step 3: Predict an answer, if possible.

Step 4: Match predicted answer to answer choices. Eliminate. Pick closest one.

The stem will tell you what to do: either to refer to your scribbled notes (or memory) of what the main idea of the passage (or a given paragraph) is; scan for a detail; make an inference; etc.

Let's try it with an item you saw on the diagnostic:

Like other organisms, gypsy moths and humans share a liking for similar habitats. Aside from their pestilent nature, gypsy moths are still moths, and, unlike fruit flies and other Diptera, moths and butterflies (Lepidoptera) have long been collected and fancied. "Sugaring" tree trunks to attract specimens became popular in Britain during the 1840s; many other collecting methods and instruments of amateur entomology (such as "simbling"—catching a

(continued)

> ## The Items: The Normal Way (Continued)
>
> female moth in a box or cage and using her to attract males) are at least as hundred years older.
>
> In his delightful autobiography, *Speak, Memory*, Vladimir Nabokov recounts the beginning of his obsession with lepidopterology. Nabokov was born in 1899, and started chasing butterflies around 1905, but (if one can accept his self-described precociousness) he became seriously involved in reading the literature around 1908–1910—exactly when the German-Jewish biologist Richard B. Goldschmidt was beginning to use the gypsy moth in his ground-breaking studies on genetics and evolution. Thus Nabokov gives us a picture of the knowledge, techniques, and social relations of central European lepidopterology at exactly the time Goldschmidt was becoming, as it were, scientifically involved with this organism. Most importantly, Nabokov emphasizes that "since the middle of the [nineteenth] century, Continental lepidopterology had been, on the whole, a simple and stable affair, smoothly run by the Germans … [who] did their best to ignore the new trends [in evolution and genetics] and continued to cherish the philately-like side of entomology."
>
> But Goldschmidt differed from his stamp-collecting countrymen. He was an embryologist by training, part of the new generation of laboratory-based biologists that could be justly symbolized by the compound microscope. The gypsy moth—or perhaps we should now refer to it by its scientific name, *Lymantria dispar*—was to be experimented with, not collected and classified.
>
> Nabokov captures the type of species-definition that Goldschmidt's new generation of biologists was promulgating. "The Victorian … kind of species," Nabokov writes, "hermetic and homogenous, with sundry (alpine, polar, insular, etc.) 'varieties' affixed to it from the outside, as it were, like incidental appendages, was replaced by a new, multiform and fluid kind of species, organically *consisting* of geographical races or subspecies." The genetic basis of geographic races was exactly what interested Goldschmidt in *Lymantria dispar*, and his investigations lasted a quarter of a century, through a world war, internment in an American prison camp, and other vicissitudes of life that people, like all other organisms, must inevitably negotiate. Ultimately, and for a variety of interesting reasons, Goldschmidt parted ways with *Lymantria dispar*, falling under the seductive spell of its Dipteran competitor, *Drosophila melanogaster* (the fruit fly), but his first love was to color Goldschmidt's genetic and evolutionary theories long after the romance had ended.
>
> **Step 1: Cover the answer choices.**
>
> According to the passage, which of the following is true of fruit flies?
>
> Done for you (turn the page and you'll find them).

Step 2: Read the stem carefully.

Check it out. The key is you'll probably have to research each reading question—three are false, one is true. This is then a high-investment item: You can't rely on a prediction, and you are at the mercy of the answer choices. Moreover, you may have to do four separate scans. Consider skipping this and doing an easier one in the set. Grab the low-hanging fruit fast!

However, for our purposes here, let's move to the research projects. No prediction is really possible so—

Step 3: Predict an answer, if possible.

— is out. Here are the answer choices:

- (A) They are attracted to "sugared" tree trunks.
- (B) Unlike gypsy moths, they are pests to humans.
- (C) They belong to the classification category Diptera.
- (D) They share a liking for habitats humans also prefer.
- (E) They launched Nabokov's interests in lepidopterology.

Treat each statement like a yes/no question:

- Are fruit flies attracted to "sugared" tree trunks?

No. The moths and butterflies are. Eliminate.

- Unlike gypsy moths, are fruit flies pests to humans?

No. Gypsy moths are big pests, too. Eliminate.

- Do fruit flies belong to the classification category Diptera?

Yes. But check the others.

- Do fruit flies share a liking for habitats humans also prefer?

Careful. You might think so, but the author doesn't mention it. Therefore, eliminate this option.

- Did fruit flies launch Nabokov's interests in lepidopterology?

No. They're not Lepidoptera and they didn't launch Nabokov's interest in that field.

Guided Practice

OK, now you try one. Feel free to refer back to the full passage.

> **Step 1: Cover the answer choices.**
>
> **In the third paragraph, the author is mainly interested in**
>
> - using the proper scientific name for the gypsy moth
> - criticizing Goldschmidt's rejection of nineteenth-century natural history
> - comparing Nabokov's concern with the gypsy moth to Goldschmidt's
> - highlighting a key difference between nineteenth-century natural history and twentieth-century biology
> - establishing the compound microscope as a symbol for twentieth-century biologists
>
> **Step 2: Read the stem carefully.**
>
> This is a very straightforward one: a little research project.
>
> **Step 3: Predict an answer, if possible.**
>
> You can make the prediction. Write your prediction here:
>
> Compare your answer to the footnote.[7]
>
> **Step 4: Match predicted answer to answer choices. Eliminate. Pick closest one.**
>
> - using the proper scientific name for the gypsy moth
> - criticizing Goldschmidt's rejection of nineteenth-century natural history
> - comparing Nabokov's concern with the gypsy moth to Goldschmidt's
> - highlighting a key difference between nineteenth-century natural history and twentieth-century biology
> - establishing the compound microscope as a symbol for twentieth-century biologists
>
> Only D matches the prediction.
>
> [7]The third paragraph was about how biology took over from stamp-collecting natural history.

It's time to do some independent practice: a couple of questions you've already seen relating to the long passage set we've been working through. There are plenty more practice sets in the practice tests.

Independent Practice

OK. You're on your own.

Take a second look at these two items from the diagnostic. Again, feel free to refer to your notes as well as the full passage.

1. According to the passage, the species definition that Goldschmidt and his generation of biologists were replacing most closely reflects which of the following?

    (A) A geographically grounded family of very similar populations of organisms
    (B) A stamp-collecting-like activity, rather than an experimental, scientific activity
    (C) A uniform population of organisms, accompanied by associated but relatively unimportant local varieties, that is entirely cut off from all other such populations
    (D) A more scientifically based definition as opposed to a more literary description
    (E) A definition lacking the insights of embryological investigations

2. It can be inferred from the passage that the author chose to begin referring to the gypsy moth by its scientific name because the author

    (A) is suggesting that Goldschmidt began to fall in love with his favored laboratory organism.
    (B) bemoans the disappearance of more emotionally resonant approaches to the natural world.
    (C) rejects Nabokov's more literary treatment of lepidopterology.
    (D) desires to highlight the analogy between a creature noted for its pestilent nature and Goldschmidt's internment in an American prison camp.
    (E) wanted to reflect and reinforce the shift from nineteenth-century natural history to twentieth-century biology.

Independent Practice: Explanations

1. According to the passage, the species definition that Goldschmidt and his generation of biologists were replacing most closely reflects which of the following?

    (A) A geographically grounded family of very similar populations of organisms
    (B) A stamp-collecting-like activity, rather than an experimental, scientific activity
    (C) A uniform population of organisms, accompanied by associated but relatively unimportant local varieties, that is entirely cut off from all other such populations
    (D) A more scientifically based definition as opposed to a more literary description
    (E) A definition lacking the insights of embryological investigations

Pay close attention to the stem. What should jump out?

- "species definition"

- that Goldschmidt's generation was **replacing**

We thus want the species definition that the older, nineteenth-century natural historians favored. You now have a search image; scan for it. Note that paragraph 4 begins with mentioning "species definition." OK. Look for the old one. The Nabokov quote supplies it, although in flowery and difficult language. But you can work it out. The Victorian species was:

- hermetic—as in the phrase "hermetically sealed," so not very open to the outside

- homogenous—as in all the same

- with varieties attached to the walled-off unit

Now you have a model to which you can compare the answer choices, and choice (C) matches. Note the tricky nature of (B). Philatelists are stamp collectors, but that's not relevant here. Choice (A) is what you'd choose if you missed the key word, **replaced**.

2. It can be inferred from the passage that the author chose to begin referring to the gypsy moth by its scientific name because the author

   (A) is suggesting that Goldschmidt began to fall in love with his favored laboratory organism.
   (B) bemoans the disappearance of more emotionally resonant approaches to the natural world.
   (C) rejects Nabokov's more literary treatment of lepidopterology.
   (D) desires to highlight the analogy between a creature noted for its pestilent nature and Goldschmidt's internment in an American prison camp.
   (E) wanted to reflect and reinforce the shift from nineteenth-century natural history to twentieth-century biology.

This is a question of style and rhetoric. First, focus on the "when"—the switch from common name to scientific name occurs in the paragraph that describes the shift from nineteenth-century natural history to twentieth-century biology. Therefore, using the scientific name emphasizes the shift from collecting and classifying to experimentation and laboratory equipment like the compound microscope: choice E.

Guided Practice Answers

1. *exculpatory,* or that which removes (the "ex-" word part) "culpability"—or guilt. (Think of other "culp" words, like "culprit" and "culpable" and "culparooni"—oh, wait, I made that up. You see how the word-part stuff comes in handy, right?) The "-atory" part just morphs the word into the proper part of speech.
2. *cowed* and *obviate*.

CHAPTER 4
The Math Section

See *Appendix B: Math References* for added support.

FORM AND FUNCTION

The official name for this section of the GRE is "Quantitative Reasoning." The second word matters: The key is not blind calculation (you'll have a calculator, after all) but *reasoning*. There are four "content areas": algebra, arithmetic, geometry, and data "analysis"—or basic algebra, a limited number of arithmetic rules and features, basic geometry, and graph- and chart-reading with things like mean, median, mode, probability, etc. Don't worry. We'll cover everything you need!

You'll be dealing with three main item types:

- **quantitative comparison**, in which you compare the magnitude of two quantities (hereafter, **QC**);

- "normal" **problem-solving**-type items, featuring multiple-response, multiple-choice, as well as fill-ins, like the Verbal section (hereafter, **PS**);

- **data analysis** items, in which you are asked to interpret or analyze data that is given in a table, graph, or other data presentation. These questions are usually grouped together and could be multiple choice or numeric entry (hereafter, **DA**).

Here are some typical items you saw in the Diagnostic Test:

A **QC**:

A certain pasta sauce recipe requires $4\frac{1}{2}$ teaspoons of olive oil to make enough sauce for 6 servings.

Quantity A	Quantity B
The number of teaspoons of olive oil required for the same recipe to make enough sauce for 8 servings.	6 teaspoons

- Ⓐ Quantity A is greater.
- Ⓑ Quantity B is greater.
- Ⓒ The two quantities are equal.
- Ⓓ The relationship cannot be determined.

A **PS**:

What is the slope of the line whose equation is $4x - 8y = 36$?

- (A) 8
- (B) 4
- (C) 2
- (D) $\frac{1}{2}$
- (E) $\frac{1}{9}$

And a **DA**:

Question 1 is based on the following data.

Three rock bands—Alfa, Bolus, and Core—were ranked relative to each other at a music-fan site on three different occasions. Additionally, each band's sales were tracked as shown.

Date	RANKINGS BAND		
	Alfa	Bolus	Core
June 2011	1	3	2
Sept 2011	3	2	1
May 2012	2	1	3

RETAIL OUTLET	AVERAGE NUMBER OF SONG DOWNLOADS/DAY JUNE 2011–MAY 2012 Band		
	Alfa	Bolus	Core
StoreMart	7.2	9.1	4.2
E-Toon'z	9.3	7.3	3.8
otto's	2.2	6.5	2.7
izone	1.5	2.7	8.2
Impax	6.8	5.4	2.1

What is the ratio of the sum of the averages of Alfa's song downloads from all outlets to its rank in the May 2012 survey?

$$\frac{\boxed{}}{\boxed{}}$$

MATH CONTENT REVIEW

ETS has done a very good thing. Credit where credit is due!

If you're shaky on math definitions, conventions, and so on, please go to *http://www.ets.org/s/gre/pdf/gre_math_conventions.pdf* to familiarize yourself. It's a free, 10-page PDF that covers every convention used on the test. (In the unlikely event that changes, just go to *http://www.ets.org* and search for "GRE Math Conventions.") Also, see Appendix B for basic math reference material.

In what follows, I'll present the content you need in a format different from most test-prep books. Rather than present each math factoid randomly, I'll highlight the connections among the factoids. You'll thus:

- learn the factoids less painfully;

- see the factoids that form the basis for connections between and among many items on the test; and

- be "pre-adapted" to absorb the subsequent step-methods, which mix up various "content areas," as you'll see.

If you prefer to review your math factoids in the traditional way, ETS provides a free file—*http://www.ets.org/s/gre/pdf/gre_math_review.pdf*. It presents the material traditionally. Please feel free to take a look at it. (Again, in the unlikely event the URL changes, just go to *http://www.ets.org* and search for "GRE Math Review.") Just do whatever works. ☺ In fact, you can either take a look at that file first, and then read what follows or you can read what follows now and then look at that file. Or you can do both! Between the traditional presentation and mine, you should cover all bases.

OK. Let me take you on a tour through GRE math. Just sit back and read along.

Don't sit back entirely, though: in what follows, I'll refer to ideas you'll have to visualize. I'm purposely **not** including pictures, diagrams, etc. I want you to sketch them on scrap paper as we go, just as you'll have to do on the actual computer-based GRE.

Since all math factoids are inter-related on the GRE, and since we'll cover everything, we can dip in anywhere. So let's start with geometry formulas.

Please note: You'll have several formulas. Most deal with figures that have either zero, one, two, or three dimensions. That is, they deal with points, length of lines, area of 2-D shapes, or volumes of 3-D shapes.

You get the point about points. They have zero dimension. Lines have one dimension—extension, or "lengthiness." Technically, lines extend forever in opposite directions. That's why you see the arrowheads you'll see on number lines, for example. In contrast, line segments are limited: They start at x and end at y. Lines that never intersect are parallel. Lines at right angles (i.e., 90° angles) to each other are perpendicular.

It gets more interesting when you intersect one or more lines. Draw on your scrap paper the capital letter X. You've formed four line segments, and four angles. The angles opposite to each other are equal. The angles adjacent to each other are supplementary—meaning they add to 180°, the degree measurement of a straight line.

Because you drew your X like a capital letter X, and not a multiplication sign, you have two angles greater than 90° and two less than 90°. Those less than 90° are called "acute angles"—as in, "Look, acute little angle!"—the former are called obtuse. Unfortunately I have no good pun-mnemonic for them (fortunately?).

Finally, get a fresh piece of paper and draw two horizontal lines with plenty of space between them, like a big equals sign (=). Now draw a slanted line through them so that you have something like a "not-equals" sign (≠).

Well, all the acute angles in that figure are equal to each other, all the obtuse angles are equal to each other, and every pair of acute-and-obtuse angles is supplementary, meaning 180°.

Enough with the lines. Let's move on to circles.

The amazing thing about circles is the number π. Yes, this is a number—since it can't be accurately written out as anything but an approximation, we just use this Greek letter, but it's not a variable. Take any length you like—a micron, a light year, two feet—and double it. Then, multiply that result by this weird π thing and you'll get a perfect circle. No wonder certain Greeks worshiped this number! It's pretty close to magical that this indeed works.

The catch is that the length you took must form the "radius" of the circle—the distance from the center of the circle to any point on the edge of the circle. The "diameter" of a circle, by the way, is like the equator of the Earth: it's twice the radius, or a line that goes through the circle's center from one end to the other. Any other line that connects two points along the edge of a circle—that is, doesn't go through the center—is a "chord." And, finally, any line outside the circle that shares one point with the circle is tangent to that circle. Draw a circle and show a radius, a diameter, a chord, and a line tangent to the circle.

Back to what impressed the Greeks. Here's what we have so far:

Shape	Length
Circle	Circumference = $2\pi r$

Note that since $2r = d$, another form of circumference is $C = \pi d$.

The circumference is thus pretty much the distance around the edge of the circle—like the pizza pie crust. Circumference is pretty much the perimeter for circles, and it's a length. Remember there are no exponents in the formula. You'll never confuse it with the area of a circle again! (The radius r is to the first power. We don't write it as r^1—we don't write any first-power variables that way or we'd have tons of 1-exponents cluttering everything. That's why we don't write "$1x$." Coefficients of 1 carry no information, because 1 is the identity of multiplication. Multiply any number by 1 and you get that number.)

In fact, let's add perimeter into the mix:

Shape	Length
Circle	Circumference = $2\pi r$
Square	Perimeter = $4s$
Rectangle	Perimeter = $2l + 2w$
Quadrilateral	Perimeter = "Add the lengths of all four sides"
Polygon	Perimeter = "Add the lengths of all the sides"

Back to circles. Carrying forward our pizza analogy, what if we want to know the amount of cheese we need to cover the pizza? That's the area of the crust, as opposed to its length, which is its circumference.

To find that answer, take the same length, r, and instead of doubling it, square it. Then you multiply that result by π. Yes, "pizza π" is an awful pun that will help you remember these formulas!

This is about as close to magic as the real world gets. You can see why Pythagoras based a whole religion on mathematics. Let's add this to our chart:

Shape	Length	Area
Circle	Circumference = $2\pi r$	$A = \pi r^2$
Square	Perimeter = $4s$	
Rectangle	Perimeter = $2l + 2w$	
Quadrilateral	Perimeter = "Add the lengths of all four sides"	
Polygon	Perimeter = "Add the lengths of all the sides"	

Now, what if I want to find the length of one slice of pizza, not the whole pie? In the real world, if there are eight slices of equal size, you'd just divide the circumference by eight. It's the same here, except what we'd find is an "arc." An "arc" is a fraction of the circumference:

Shape	Length	Area
Circle	Circumference = $2\pi r$ Arc = $\dfrac{2\pi r}{n}$	$A = \pi r^2$
Square	Perimeter = $4s$	
Rectangle	Perimeter = $2l + 2w$	
Quadrilateral	Perimeter = "Add the lengths of all four sides"	
Polygon	Perimeter = "Add the lengths of all the sides"	

Very nice, you say. But how do I find n? It's easy. How many degrees are in a circle? Three hundred sixty. If the noted angle is, say, 90°, how many of those are there in a circle? Well, $\dfrac{360}{90} = 4$. In that case, n is 4. Note that we're *reasoning* things out here, not just memorizing!

Remember if you cut a circle in half through the center, you've not only formed the diameter of the circle, but you've also proven why a line is 180°. It's half a circle from one end of the line to the other.

How about finding the area of that slice, as opposed to the length of the fraction of circumference (meaning crust) of that slice? That area is called a "sector."

Unlike life, math is comfortably predictable. If arc is a fraction of circumference, then sector is a fraction of area, and you can determine it in the same way you determine arc:

Shape	Length	Area
Circle	Circumference = $2\pi r$ Arc = $\dfrac{2\pi r}{n}$	$A = \pi r^2$ Sector = $\dfrac{\pi r^2}{n}$
Square	Perimeter = $4s$	

Shape	Length	Area
Rectangle	Perimeter = 2*l* + 2*w*	
Quadrilateral	Perimeter = "Add the lengths of all four sides"	
Polygon	Perimeter = "Add the lengths of all the sides"	

Let's pause for a second and review. You've learned or re-learned the following:

- Formulas for the circumference, arc, area, and sector of circles
- A family of related formulas for perimeters
- How to distinguish between length and area formulas for circles so that you never have to worry about confusing the two
- How to reason your way through math rather than brute-force rote memorizing
- How to translate real-world, word-problems like pizza-crust length into abstract mathematical formulas

And it wasn't so hard, was it? Let's continue.

You'll notice that we call anything raised to the second power a "square." We do that because of the actual shape known as "square." Get a load of this: Take any length and square it, and you get the area of a square. Note the relationship between geometry and algebra. They're the same thing. Let's add that to our chart:

Shape	Length	Area
Circle	Circumference = $2\pi r$ Arc = $\dfrac{2\pi r}{n}$	$A = \pi r^2$ Sector = $\dfrac{\pi r^2}{n}$
Square	Perimeter = 4*s*	s^2
Rectangle	Perimeter = 2*l* + 2*w*	
Quadrilateral	Perimeter = "Add the lengths of all four sides"	
Polygon	Perimeter = "Add the lengths of all the sides"	

It's uncanny how that squaring applies to shapes other than squares. We've already seen that in the area of a circle.

Let's pause and consider what "squaring" is. Think of a line segment—a length—as composed not of an infinite number of points, which it is, but of, say, 10 points. Let's say the points are heads of several lettuce in a garden. If you have ten rows of ten lettuces per row, you have ways of figuring how many lettuces you have:

1. Count all the lettuces. This is pretty inefficient but will work.

2. Count all the lettuces in one row and multiply it by the number of rows. Better.

3. Since the number of lettuces per row equals the number of rows, just square the number of lettuces. Best!

Method 1 is pretty much addition. If Og has two rocks and he brings them over to his sister Gog, who has three, they can just set them down and count them to get five. After a few times, even the densest cave-person will realize that two of anything grouped with three of anything is five of anything. Thus abstraction, the basis of math and science, was born. Og and Gog really rocked.

This is most likely how math started! When people are taught math, they're usually taught as if these abstractions dropped out of the sky from the gods. Some respond to that, others don't.

Method 2 is multiplication. Multiplication is a shortcut to addition, just as addition is a shortcut to counting everything. If you're dealing with 50,000 lettuces, you can see how that would get boring and time-consuming.

Method 3 uses exponents. Powers, or exponents, are a shortcut to multiplication. We'll return to this story when we get to the rules for working with exponents, another sometimes troublesome math factoid. And note that this example could be easily altered to deal with the reciprocal operations—subtraction for addition; division for multiplication, and roots for exponents. But let's return to our chart.

Let's say our lettuce rows are more than 10—say, 35. You're now dealing with a rectangular garden plot, not a square one. The formula is clear:

Shape	Length	Area
Circle	Circumference = $2\pi r$ Arc = $\dfrac{2\pi r}{n}$	$A = \pi r^2$ Sector = $\dfrac{\pi r^2}{n}$
Square	Perimeter = $4s$	s^2
Rectangle	Perimeter = $2l + 2w$	lw
Quadrilateral	Perimeter = "Add the lengths of all four sides"	
Polygon	Perimeter = "Add the lengths of all the sides"	

Wait a minute. Why isn't there a 2-exponent in the rectangular area formula?

That's a good question! And it gives us a good opportunity to get into the rules of exponents. Note that when determining the area of a square, $s \times s = s^2$. Thus, although we never write it, $s^1 \times s^1 = s^2$. Recall that multiplication is a shortcut to adding. When you **multiply** bases, you **add** the exponents. You then go "down" a shortcut-step. Here's a graphic:

Bases	Exponents
Multiply	Add

But what happens when we raise a power to a power, though, as in $(x^2)^3$? Well, if we **added** exponents when we **multiplied** the bases, then if we're raising a base that is already raised to a given power to yet another power, what do you predict the rule should be?

Exactly. Multiply the exponents. It's always one step "down":

Bases	Exponents
Multiply	Add
Raised to a power	Multiply

Now what if we're just adding bases?

Bases	Exponents
Add	?
Multiply	Add
Raised to a power	Multiply

Well, reading the chart from the bottom, if you went from a power (base) to multiplication (exponent) to multiplication (base) to addition (exponent), where *can* you go from addition (base)? Correct, you go nowhere:

Bases	Exponents
Add	Nothing doing
Multiply	Add
Raised to a power	Multiply

Let's put this in mathspeak:

Bases	Exponents
$x^a + x^b$	Nothing doing. That is, find what the first term equals. Then find what the second term equals. Then add the results. For example: $$2^2 + 2^3 = 4 + 8 = 12$$ $$2^2 + 2^3 \neq 2^5 = 32$$ It's the same whether the bases are the same or different or whether the exponents are the same or different: If you're adding, you must do it this way or no way at all.

Bases	Exponents
Same bases, different power: $x^a x^b =$	x^{a+b}
Different bases, same power: $x^a y^a =$	$(xy)^a$
$(x^a)^b =$	x^{ab}

But what's all that got to do with the area of a rectangle? Well, since the formula is $A = lw$, and both l and w have an unwritten exponent of 1, and since you're multiplying the bases, you add the exponents to get 2. So it is indeed a two-dimensional (i.e., area) equation or function. ☺

Here's another little contextualization. The reciprocal operations for exponents will be exactly the same, and entirely predictable. Write it for yourself on a separate sheet of paper. There's one catch: recall that the reciprocal operation for raising to a power is taking a root—square root reverses squaring, for example.

Here's a key: roots are simply fractional exponents: $\sqrt{x} = x^{\frac{1}{2}}, \sqrt[n]{x} = x^{\frac{1}{n}}$. Here's another key: whereas any fractional power is a root, any negative power is the inverse of that positive power. Say what? It's easier in mathspeak: $x^{-n} = \frac{1}{x^n}$.

This clarifies the rules for roots. They should be, and are, just like those for exponents.

Let's consider another situation. You're wrapping a present. The present is in a box. Like pretty much all boxes, this one is a rectangular solid. How much wrapping paper will you need? You're being asked about the "surface area" of the rectangular solid. Think it through—better yet, draw a rectangular solid on scrap paper. Don't worry about labeling lengths. Make it look like a stick of butter.

OK, how many faces do you have? Six. Which are the same? Well, since it's a stick of butter, the two ends are the same, and the four other "side faces" are the same. If you found the area of one end and multiplied it by two, and then found the area of one side face and multiplied that by four—and then added the two results, you'd have the answer.

We just invented the formula for surface area, right? Let's add it in:

Shape	Length	Area
Circle	Circumference = $2\pi r$ Arc = $\dfrac{2\pi r}{n}$	$A = \pi r^2$ Sector = $\dfrac{\pi r^2}{n}$
Square	Perimeter = $4s$	s^2
Rectangle	Perimeter = $2l + 2w$	lw Surface area of rectangular solid = $2lh + 2lw + 2wh$
Quadrilateral	Perimeter = "Add the lengths of all four sides"	
Polygon	Perimeter = "Add the lengths of all the sides"	

The variables l, h, and w stand for "length," "height," and "width." Note that according to the rules of exponents, we're still dealing with a square function—area.

But how much butter do we have? Ah, now we must add a new dimension—the *third dimension*. It gets scary sometimes.

As with "square," the term "cube," which we use with powers of three, has a geometric meaning. Take that square and multiply it by another side of equal length and you get s^3. Put it on the chart:

Shape	Length	Area	Volume
Circle	Circumference = $2\pi r$ Arc = $\dfrac{2\pi r}{n}$	$A = \pi r^2$ Sector = $\dfrac{\pi r^2}{n}$	
Square	Perimeter = $4s$	s^2	Cube = s^3
Rectangle	Perimeter = $2l + 2w$	lw Surface area of rectangular solid = $2lh + 2lw + 2wh$	
Quadrilateral	Perimeter = "Add the lengths of all four sides"		
Polygon	Perimeter = "Add the lengths of all the sides"		

What about the circle-volumes? Well, there are two: a sphere and a right circular cylinder. I'll include the former for completeness, but it's not on the GRE. The latter is. For reasons you don't need to know, the formula for the volume of a sphere is $\dfrac{4}{3}\pi r^3$. It's the same for circumference and area. Take a length. In this case cube it, multiply by a factor, and then multiply by π. Let's put it in the chart:

Shape	Length	Area	Volume
Circle	Circumference = $2\pi r$ Arc = $\dfrac{2\pi r}{n}$	$A = \pi r^2$ Sector = $\dfrac{\pi r^2}{n}$	Sphere = $\dfrac{4}{3}\pi r^3$
Square	Perimeter = $4s$	s^2	Cube = s^3

(*continued*)

Shape	Length	Area	Volume
Rectangle	Perimeter = $2l + 2w$	lw Surface area of rectangular solid = $2lh + 2lw + 2wh$	
Quadrilateral	Perimeter = "Add the lengths of all four sides"		
Polygon	Perimeter = "Add the lengths of all the sides"		

OK, now the "can"—a.k.a., the right circular cylinder. Think it through. What's the base? Yes, a circle. Do we need the circumference or area of that circle? Well, if we want volume, we'll need to have the area on the bottom at least, so:

$$A = \pi r^2$$

Think of that bottom area as a poker chip or coin. Stack a bunch of chips or coins, and you have a right circular cylinder. How do you refer to how many chips or coins you've stacked? By height. So, the formula must be:

$$V = \pi r^2 h$$

And it is. Note that if you add the 2-exponent of the r to the unwritten 1-exponent of the h, you get 3. That's a cube function, which is what volume has to be. (What would the formula be to find the **surface area** of a right circular cylinder? Try it. Then compare it to this footnote—don't peek![1])

---

[1] Well, you have two circles of equal area, so use $2\pi r^2$ for that. What about the sides of the "can"? If you take off the circles at the top and bottom, and then cut the tube left over longitudinally and lay the resulting shape flat on the table, you have a rectangle? So one dimension of that rectangle is the height of the cylinder. What's the other? The length around the circles on the ends. What's that length? Yes, it's the circumference. So, in this case, $lw = 2\pi rh$. The whole formula is: $2\pi r^2 + 2\pi rh$. Note that memorizing this fact is nowhere near as helpful as reasoning it out first. We'll add it to the chart now.

Let's add it:

Shape	Length	Area	Volume
Circle	Circumference = $2\pi r$ Arc = $\dfrac{2\pi r}{n}$	$A = \pi r^2$ Sector = $\dfrac{\pi r^2}{n}$ Surface area of a right circular cylinder = $2\pi r^2 + 2\pi rh$	Sphere = $\dfrac{4}{3}\pi r^3$ Right circular cylinder = $\pi r^2 h$
Square	Perimeter = $4s$	s^2	Cube = s^3
Rectangle	Perimeter = $2l + 2w$	lw Surface area of rectangular solid = $2lh + 2lw + 2wh$	
Quadrilateral	Perimeter = "Add the lengths of all four sides"		
Polygon	Perimeter = "Add the lengths of all the sides"		

The volume of a rectangular solid? For reasons analogous to that of the area of a rectangle, it must be length times width times height. Add that.

Shape	Length	Area	Volume
Circle	Circumference = $2\pi r$ Arc = $\dfrac{2\pi r}{n}$	$A = \pi r^2$ Sector = $\dfrac{\pi r^2}{n}$ Surface area of a right circular cylinder = $2\pi r^2 + 2\pi rh$	Sphere = $\dfrac{4}{3}\pi r^3$ Right circular cylinder = $\pi r^2 h$
Square	Perimeter = $4s$	s^2	Cube = s^3

(continued)

Shape	Length	Area	Volume
Rectangle	Perimeter = $2l + 2w$	lw Surface area of rectangular solid = $2lh + 2lw + 2wh$	Rectangular solid = lwh
Quadrilateral	Perimeter = "Add the lengths of all four sides"		
Polygon	Perimeter = "Add the lengths of all the sides"		

All that's left are the areas and volumes of quadrilaterals (that aren't either squares or rectangles) and polygons. The good news is that you won't see the volumes on the GRE. So they're out. But we do need to delve into triangles to fill those in. The GRE loves triangles. So let's get into them.

First, how many degrees are in a triangle? Yes, 180°. A plain triangle will have 180°, just as any circle has 360°. The perimeter of a triangle would be the sum of all three sides. Let's add that:

Shape	Length	Area	Volume
Circle	Circumference = $2\pi r$ Arc = $\frac{2\pi r}{n}$	$A = \pi r^2$ Sector = $\frac{\pi r^2}{n}$ Surface area of a right circular cylinder = $2\pi r^2 + 2\pi rh$	Sphere = $\frac{4}{3}\pi r^3$ Right circular cylinder = $\pi r^2 h$
Square	Perimeter = $4s$	s^2	Cube = s^3
Rectangle	Perimeter = $2l + 2w$	lw Surface area of rectangular solid = $2lh + 2lw + 2wh$	Rectangular solid = lwh

Shape	Length	Area	Volume
Triangle	Perimeter = "Sum of all three sides"		
Quadrilateral	Perimeter = "Add the lengths of all four sides"		
Polygon	Perimeter = "Add the lengths of all the sides"		

But can the three sides of any triangle be just any length? There's a limit. Any side of a triangle must be less than the sum of the other two sides.

Let's say a triangle has a side length of 8 and a side length of 3. If the length of the third side were 11, there'd be no triangle, would there? Since 8 + 3 = 11, if the other side is merely 11, the 8 and 3 sides will just flop down on the 11 side—no triangle. Given a side of length 11, any two sides whose lengths sum to larger than 11 will make a triangle. That's the triangle inequality theorem.

What's the area of a triangle? Well, let's reason it out. First, take a square. Cut the square in half diagonally. What's left? Well, you have two triangles that share a hypotenuse. What is the area of a square? Correct, s^2. So the area of a triangle must be half of s^2. And it is—for that special triangle, a right isosceles triangle, about which we'll talk more soon. For other triangles, say, ones formed in the same fashion from a rectangle, the area would be half of lw. In triangle terms, l is the "base," b, and w is the "height," h. Add that to the chart:

Shape	Length	Area	Volume
Circle	Circumference = $2\pi r$ Arc = $\dfrac{2\pi r}{n}$	$A = \pi r^2$ Sector = $\dfrac{\pi r^2}{n}$ Surface area of a right circular cylinder = $2\pi r^2 + 2\pi rh$	Sphere = $\dfrac{4}{3}\pi r^3$ Right circular cylinder = $\pi r^2 h$

(continued)

Shape	Length	Area	Volume
Square	Perimeter = 4s	s^2	Cube = s^3
Rectangle	Perimeter = 2l + 2w	lw Surface area of rectangular solid = 2lh + 2lw + 2wh	Rectangular solid = lwh
Triangle	Perimeter = "Sum of all three sides"	$A = \frac{1}{2}bh$	
Quadrilateral	Perimeter = "Add the lengths of all four sides"		
Polygon	Perimeter = "Add the lengths of all the sides"		

Note that this is still a square function. What would the volume of a triangular solid (a.k.a., "prism") be? Well, if you take a triangle, whose area we now know, and extend its "depth" in the third dimension, you'll see that it has to be $V = \frac{bhl}{2}$, where l is what we referred to as the depth. Here it's called the "length" of the prism. Add it.

Shape	Length	Area	Volume
Circle	Circumference = $2\pi r$ Arc = $\frac{2\pi r}{n}$	$A = \pi r^2$ Sector = $\frac{\pi r^2}{n}$ Surface area of a right circular cylinder = $2\pi r^2 + 2\pi rh$	Sphere = $\frac{4}{3}\pi r^3$ Right circular cylinder = $\pi r^2 h$
Square	Perimeter = 4s	s^2	Cube = s^3

Shape	Length	Area	Volume
Rectangle	Perimeter = $2l + 2w$	lw Surface area of rectangular solid = $2lh + 2lw + 2wh$	Rectangular solid = lwh
Triangle	Perimeter = "Sum of all three sides"	$A = \frac{1}{2}bh$	Volume of a prism = $\frac{bhl}{2}$
Quadrilateral	Perimeter = "Add the lengths of all four sides"		
Polygon	Perimeter = "Add the lengths of all the sides"		

For any polygon, in theory you could break the figure into triangles and/or rectangles and squares, find the area of each, and be done with it. We'll add that, too:

Shape	Length	Area	Volume
Circle	Circumference = $2\pi r$ Arc = $\frac{2\pi r}{n}$	$A = \pi r^2$ Sector = $\frac{\pi r^2}{n}$ Surface area of a right circular cylinder = $2\pi r^2 + 2\pi rh$	Sphere = $\frac{4}{3}\pi r^3$ Right circular cylinder = $\pi r^2 h$
Square	Perimeter = $4s$	s^2	Cube = s^3
Rectangle	Perimeter = $2l + 2w$	lw Surface area of rectangular solid = $2lh + 2lw + 2wh$	Rectangular solid = lwh

(continued)

Shape	Length	Area	Volume
Triangle	Perimeter = "Sum of all three sides"	$A = \frac{1}{2}bh$	Volume of a prism = $\frac{bhl}{2}$
Quadrilateral	Perimeter = "Add the lengths of all four sides"		
Polygon	Perimeter = "Add the lengths of all the sides"	"Break the figure into triangles and/or squares and rectangles; find those areas; add them up"	

You can break any polygon into $(n - 2)$ triangles, where n is the number of sides in the polygon. Try to disprove that. Since a triangle has 180°, you can find the number of degrees in any polygon by subtracting 2 from the number of sides and multiplying that by 180: $(n - 2)180°$.

Two quadrilaterals are left to worry about: parallelograms and trapezoids. You don't really need a formula for either—the polygon area method just added will do since either shape can be broken into triangles and squares/rectangles. But if you *must* have two more formulas, just think about it.

For a parallelogram, if you were to break the figure into its component triangles and rectangle, and then find the areas, you'd need a base and height for the triangle and a length and width for the central rectangle. Luckily, the width of the rectangle is the height of the triangle. That helps.

I'll now just give you the formula. The key is knowing what the height is, and now you know:

Shape	Length	Area	Volume
Circle	Circumference = $2\pi r$ Arc = $\frac{2\pi r}{n}$	$A = \pi r^2$ Sector = $\frac{\pi r^2}{n}$ Surface area of a right circular cylinder = $2\pi r^2 + 2\pi rh$	Sphere = $\frac{4}{3}\pi r^3$ Right circular cylinder = $\pi r^2 h$

Shape	Length	Area	Volume
Square	Perimeter = 4s	s^2	Cube = s^3
Rectangle	Perimeter = 2l + 2w	lw Surface area of rectangular solid = 2lh + 2lw + 2wh	Rectangular solid = lwh
Triangle	Perimeter = "Sum of all three sides"	$A = \frac{1}{2}bh$	Volume of a prism = $\frac{bhl}{2}$
Quadrilateral	Perimeter = "Add the lengths of all four sides"	Parallelogram = bh	
Polygon	Perimeter = "Add the lengths of all the sides"	"Break the figure into triangles and/or squares and rectangles; find those areas; add them up"	

Now consider the trapezoid. Think of a trapezoid as a triangle with the tip cut off. That's what it is. To find the area of a triangle, you need the height and the base. It's the same with a trapezoid, but you have two bases—two horizontal lengths. Since you can now visualize what I mean, here's the formula without further ado:[2]

$$A = h\left(\frac{b_1 + b_2}{2}\right)$$

[2] You'll see I used h for height, whereas usually the term is a for altitude. They're the same. I changed it to height for clarity and to emphasize the relationship between this formula and the one for the area of a triangle.

Let's complete the chart!

Shape	Length	Area	Volume
Circle	Circumference = $2\pi r$ Arc = $\dfrac{2\pi r}{n}$	$A = \pi r^2$ Sector = $\dfrac{\pi r^2}{n}$ Surface area of a right circular cylinder = $2\pi r^2 + 2\pi rh$	Sphere = $\dfrac{4}{3}\pi r^3$ Right circular cylinder = $\pi r^2 h$
Square	Perimeter = $4s$	s^2	Cube = s^3
Rectangle	Perimeter = $2l + 2w$	lw Surface area of rectangular solid = $2lh + 2lw + 2wh$	Rectangular solid = lwh
Triangle	Perimeter = "Sum of all three sides"	$A = \dfrac{1}{2}bh$	Volume of a prism = $\dfrac{bhl}{2}$
Quadrilateral	Perimeter = "Add the lengths of all four sides"	Parallelogram = bh Trapezoid = $h\left(\dfrac{b_1 + b_2}{2}\right)$	
Polygon	Perimeter = "Add the lengths of all the sides"	"Break the figure into triangles and/or squares and rectangles; find those areas; add them up"	

Some of the toughest geometry problems are "multiple figure," such as a triangle inscribed within a circle or a circle circumscribing a square. The GRE can pile multiple figures all it likes: The rules never change.

Let's return to triangles. There's a bit more to go over. First, let's review some types of triangles:

- *The equilateral triangle.* "Equi-" means "equal," and "lateral" means "sides." So this is a triangle with three equal sides. Since the length of a side of a triangle is proportional to the size of the angle opposite that angle—as the length of the side gets bigger, the angle opposite it gets bigger, and vice versa—and we have three equal sides, what is the degree measurement of each of the three angles?

    Start with what you know: a triangle has 180°. Three equal sides means three equal angles, which means divide 180 by 3 to get 60. Done.

- *The isosceles triangle.* "Iso-" means "the same" and "celes" is derived from the Greek word "skelos," which means "legs." This triangle has two equal sides and one side unequal to the other two.

- *The right triangle.* This triangle has a right angle. The other two angles must add to 90°, since that's the measure of a right angle.

- *The right isosceles triangle.* This triangle has one right angle and two equal sides. Since those sides are equal, and the angles opposite those sides are also equal, each of the other two angle measurements must be 45°.

Let's linger on the right triangle.

First, consider the right isosceles triangle. If the side opposite one of the 45° angles is x, what's the length of the side opposite the other 45° angle? Yep: x. But what's the length of the side opposite the 90° angle—the hypotenuse? Well, that happens to be $x\sqrt{2}$. I could prove it, but just take it on faith so that we can move on. ☺ This "45:45:90" triangle is both a half of a square—and thus any square's diagonal is the side of the square times the square root of 2. This is good to know and is a shortcut to the Pythagorean theorem, which allows you to find an unknown side of a right triangle given two of the other sides. We'll get there in a moment. But the 45:45:90 triangle ratios let you find two unknown sides if given just one and provide proof that you're dealing with a right isosceles triangle. If given two sides, this is a good shortcut to the Pythagorean theorem.

There are three other so-called special right triangles:

1. *The 3:4:5 triangle.* The longest side is the hypotenuse. This triangle relates sides, not angles. It so happens that every so often you get a "Pythagorean triplet" like this—a triangle with integer sides. This is another shortcut to the Pythagorean theorem.

2. Another "triplet": *the 5:12:13 triangle.* Again, the longest side, as you know, is the hypotenuse.

3. *The 30:60:90 triangle.* As with the 45:45:90 triangle, the degree measurements correspond to a ratio among the three sides. Here's a handy little chart:

The 45:45:90, right isosceles triangle	Angle measurement	45	45	90
	Length of side **opposite** the angle measurement	x	x	$x\sqrt{2}$
The 30:60:90 triangle	Angle measurement	30	60	90
	Length of side **opposite** the angle measurement	x	$x\sqrt{3}$	$2x$

And now here's a handy mnemonic—the special right triangle with the "root 2" is the one that has 2 of the same angle measurements, whereas the special right triangle with the "root 3" is the one that has a 30° angle.

If you take an equilateral triangle and "drop a vertical" from the top vertex to the base (i.e., draw the height, which is perpendicular to the base and reaches the highest point of the triangle), you split the equilateral triangle into two component triangles. What kind of triangles are they? Draw it out to see! Note that you'll need special right triangles (or, in other cases, the Pythagorean theorem) to find heights to find triangle areas.

Let's pause a moment to talk about those colons in 45:45:90. The colons denote a ratio. A ratio can be expressed in several ways—as 45:90 or $\frac{45}{90}$, or "45 to 90," if speaking. So insight No. 1 is that a ratio is a fraction is a ratio is a fraction. By convention, we reduce fractions to their lowest terms, so $\frac{45}{90} = \frac{45 \times 1}{45 \times 2}$. Since $\frac{45}{45} = 1$, we can just cancel out the 45s to get $\frac{1}{2}$.

By similar logic, the ratio 45:45 = $\frac{45}{45} = \frac{1}{1}$. Both reduced fractions mean, "for every numerator you get whatever is in the denominator," or, in the case of $\frac{1}{2}$, it means, "for every one degree in that angle of the triangle, you get two degrees in the right angle."

Forget the triangle for a moment. Let's say a grocer will give you two apples for every three oranges you buy. What's that ratio? Two apples for every three oranges = 2 apples: 3 oranges = $\frac{2\ apples}{3\ oranges}$. Note that every two-term ratio implies a third. If I get two apples free for every three oranges I buy, for every three oranges I buy, I'll get 2 apples + 3 oranges = 5 pieces of fruit. Note further, that if the grocer would give you five total pieces of fruit for every three oranges you buy and that the only non-orange fruit the grocer has is apples, well, you could have deduced the other part of the ratio. Lots of GRE problems revolve around such deductions.

If you set a ratio equal to another ratio, you've got yourself a proportion. These come up constantly, and you can solve them with cross-multiplication. Let's say you have a recipe that calls for 2 cups of sugar for every 3 cups of flour. How many cups of flour would I need if I have 34 cups of sugar? I want to keep the recipe *proportional*. So I set up a proportion:

$$\frac{2\ cups\ of\ sugar}{3\ cups\ of\ flour} = \frac{34\ cups\ of\ sugar}{x\ cups\ of\ flour}$$

Notice that I kept the units in the set-up. I'll drop them when we cross-multiply, but the main way to mess up proportions is by not having the same units in the two numerators and the same units in the two denominators. Always write in the units to save yourself from an avoidable error. So:

$$\frac{2}{3} = \frac{34}{x}$$

Cross-multiply to get:

$$2x = 102$$

Divide both sides by 2 to get:

$$x = 51$$

OK. Let's get back to the triangles and that Pythagorean theorem. We'll use this to bring in a little more algebra.

Check it out: More than 2,500 years ago, Pythagoras found that for any right triangle, the square of the hypotenuse equals the sum of the squares of the other two sides. In mathspeak:

$$c^2 = a^2 + b^2$$

I can prove it to you. Let's take that 3:4:5 triangle:

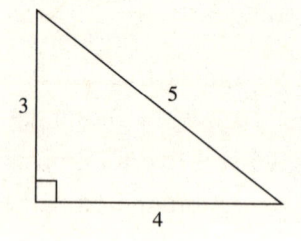

Well, does the Pythagorean theorem hold?

$$c^2 = a^2 + b^2$$

$$5^2 = 3^2 + 4^2$$

$$25 = 9 + 16$$

$$25 = 25$$

We're using squares, aren't we? Yes, and this theorem has its geometric analog:

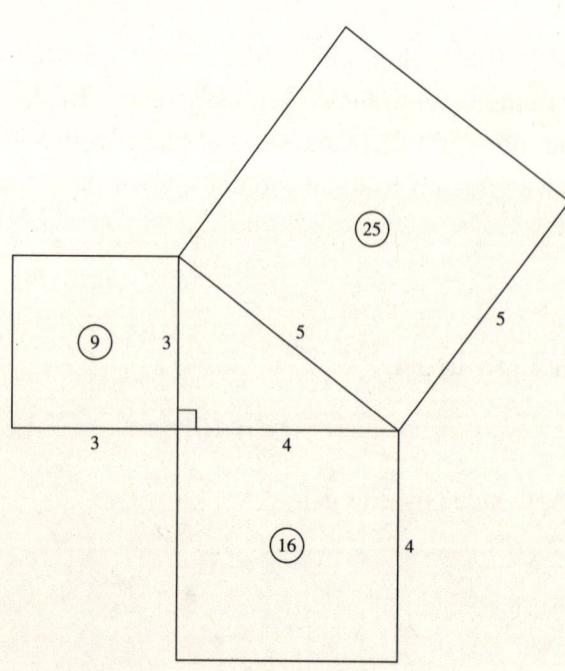

That geometric analog is almost certainly how this formula was discovered. Neat, isn't it? And you'll never forget the Pythagorean theorem now, either.

Let's say you know that $c = 6$ and $a = 4$. What is b? This is where we give major credit to medieval Arab culture for giving us algebra. The word itself is Arabic, from *al-jabr*, meaning "restoration." It's a good name, because algebra has two main rules:

1. Whatever you do to one side of the equation, you must do to the other side. The equation symbol is like the fulcrum of an old-fashioned scale or balance. Each side of the equation is a pan. The "weights" must always be the same.

2. You reverse the order of operations to isolate the variable on one side of the equation, and always do the same to both sides (see No.1).

That's it. The rest are details. They're important but still details all the same. ☺

Order of operations? Yes, that's the old **PEMDAS** thing, or, "Please Excuse My Dear Aunt Sally." When doing arithmetic, you always start with whatever's inside the Parentheses. Then you deal with Exponents. Next, from right to left, comes Multiplication and Division; finally, from right to left, comes Addition and Subtraction.

Algebra is simply a way to do arithmetic—same rules—when you have one or more unknowns. We use letters to stand in for variables—the unknown quantity.

Let's see this in action by setting up and solving the previous problem: Let's say that for a given right triangle, you know that $c = 6$ and $a = 4$. What is b?

1. Set up the equation; use the right formula.	$c^2 = a^2 + b^2$
2. Sub in what you know.	$6^2 = 4^2 + b^2$
3. Do the arithmetic you can.	$36 = 16 + b^2$

(continued)

4. Isolate the variable by reversing PEMDAS. In this case, you want b. That variable is "hidden" by two relationships: It is squared and it is added to 16. Reversing PEMDAS would mean dealing with the Addition first. How do you "negate" addition? By subtraction. Do that—but do it to both sides.	$36 = 16+b^2$ $\dfrac{-16}{20} = \dfrac{-16}{b^2}$
5. Now, isolate the variable by reversing the square. How do you do that? Yes, by taking the square root. And do it to both sides.	$\sqrt{20} = \sqrt{b^2}$ $\sqrt{20} = b$

You can simplify that radical by finding a "perfect square" in the factors of 20. Here are the factors of 20: 1×20, 2×10, and 4×5. Which of those is a perfect square—meaning, which of those is the result of squaring an integer? Alternatively, which of those numbers could be the area of a square that has sides that are integers? Only 4 fits the bill. Therefore:

$$\sqrt{20} = \sqrt{5} \times \sqrt{4} = \sqrt{5} \times 2 = 2\sqrt{5}$$

Note that you need to know reciprocal operations—what operation negates what? Addition reverses subtraction, and vice versa; multiplication reverses division, and vice versa; and raising to a power reverses taking a root, and vice versa. That's it! There's of course more to algebra, and we'll stick in the highlights as we move along in our whirlwind tour of GRE math. Next stop, coordinate geometry.

Give a shout-out to Descartes, the seventeenth-century French philosopher and scientist who married algebra and geometry for all time with his Cartesian coordinate plane. This led directly to calculus, modern science, and the rest.

The Cartesian plane really is a kind of latitude-longitude scale superimposed on a plane (i.e., a flat surface). This is a simple but powerful idea. It's really just two number lines at right angles to each other. Take the familiar number line. Draw one on your scratch paper. Put zero in the middle, and hatch marks for, say, -5 through 5. Label the right-hand arrow x.

Now, at a right angle to that line, draw another number line exactly like the one you just drew: you already have a zero; just put in the hatch marks and number from -5 to 5. Label the top arrow y.

You've got yourself a coordinate plane. You can now give us any point (x, y) with $-5 \leq x \leq 5$ and $-5 \leq y \leq 5$. You can even eyeball halves, like 4.5, and theoretically you could accurately graph any of the infinite values in those ranges for x and y. That's power.

Your coordinate plane's axes—the x and y lines—separate your plane into four square-ish sections. Ask yourself something: can the upper-right-hand section—we'll call it a quadrant—have any negative values for either x or y? It's not possible. Well, that quadrant is always $(+, +)$. The lower-right-hand quadrant? Must be $(+, -)$. The lower-left-hand? Must be $(-, -)$. And the upper-left-hand? Must be $(-, +)$.

Now, take your pencil or pen and line it up along the y-axis with the lead or ink end (the "point") pointing up, and about half of the pencil/pen above zero, half below. Rotate the point clockwise until you return to the original position. You've just swept a circle. And circles are 360°. Take this next bit on faith, but the equation of that circle is $x^2 + y^2 = r^2$ where r is the radius, and the center of the circle is at the origin, $(0, 0)$.[3]

Moreover, you've swept through all four quadrants. In so doing, you've swept through the four possible values for the slope of a line.

Slope—What's that? Well, let's start with the equation of a line. This equation is really just a little engine whose function is to take an input—say, values for x—and spit out an output—say, values for y. Inputs and outputs can be reversed, but each equation is like a recipe. Here's the recipe for a straight line:

$$y = mx + b$$

In this equation, m is the slope of the line and b is the "y-intercept"—where the line will cross the vertical y-axis. The slope is simply how steep the angle of the line is. As when you hike up a mountain, you want to know how much "vertical" you have to climb for every "horizontal" step forward. That's why a 10-mile walk in Kansas is nothing compared to a 10-mile walk in the Himalayas. In Kansas, you're basically walking on a flat surface—or, along the x-axis. Is there a slope? Nope. Mathematically, you determine slope by taking two points, (x_1, y_1) and (x_2, y_2) comparing them like this:

$$m = \frac{y_2 - y_1}{x_2 - x_1}$$

---

[3] What if the center of the circle is not at the origin? If the center is any point (h, k), then the equation is $(x - h)^2 + (y - k)^2 = r^2$.

If you've been walking on a flat surface, your *x* values will change, but your *y* values will always be zero. Therefore, you'll have:

$$m = \frac{0}{x_2 - x_1}$$

Whatever your *x*'s, *m* will always have to be zero because, if you solve for 0, *m* times the *x*'s has to equal 0. Therefore, any line parallel to the *x*-axis has a slope of zero.

If you were rock climbing a cliff at a right angle to the ground, however high you climb, your *x* values will never change. Therefore, you'll have:

$$m = \frac{y_2 - y_1}{0}$$

But you can't divide by zero! This slope is "undefined" or "infinite."

The only other possibilities are lines sloped like this: / or like this: \. The former must have a positive value; the latter, a negative. Try it with some points. Keep your sub-1s and sub-2s straight. The only way to screw up slope is to mix up your *x*'s and *y*'s.

So, your rotating writing implement starts at an undefined slope (overlapping the *y*-axis), and, moving clockwise, starts as very positive, increasingly getting less positive until it overlaps the *x*-axis, when the slope is zero, and then becomes negative, getting increasingly more negative until it overlaps the *y*-axis again. You can see how the rest of the rotation will mirror what you've just seen. But let's think about that *y*-intercept, *b*, in the equation of a line we've just gone over.

So far, your pencil has been anchored at the origin, (0, 0). If you hold the pencil at a 45° angle to each axis, so that the pencil bisects quadrant I (the upper-right-hand quadrant) and quadrant III (the lower-left-hand quadrant), you'll have a line with a slope of 1 that crosses the *y*-axis at 0. So if $b = 0$, so far, your line equation is:

$$y = mx$$

Let's find *m*. Take (0, 0) and (1, 1) as your two points:

$$m = \frac{1 - 0}{1 - 0}$$

Since we never write coefficients of 1, it looks as if your equation is:

$$y = x$$

But it's positive—note that. What would $y = -x$ look like? What happens if you slide your $y = x$ line up so that it crosses the y-axis at 2? Well, your equation is now $y = x + 2$.

Play around with this to see how the equation of a line can locate any possible line with total precision on the coordinate plane. Neat, huh?

It's also neat that if you're given any three of the variables—x, y, m, and/or b—you can find the missing variable. Given any point you're sure is on the line and either m or b, you can find either b or m, respectively.

Let me throw a couple of slope factoids at you. One is obvious: parallel lines have the same slope. One is less obvious: The slope of a line perpendicular to a given line is the negative reciprocal of the slope of the given line. If the slope of line No. 1 is 4, the slope of line No. 2, which is perpendicular to line No. 1, is $-\frac{1}{4}$.

You need to know a few more "moves" in algebra. We'll start with factoring and FOILing. These are reciprocal operations, and they're nothing more than doing arithmetical operations with unknowns (a.k.a., variables). In arithmetic, you factor, say, 12 by finding the integers that give 12 as a product: 1×12, 2×6, 3×4. If you want the prime factorization of a number, you take it all the way down to factors that are prime—that have only themselves and 1 as factors. In the case of 12, no matter which of the three sets of factors you choose, you'll end up with $3 \times 2 \times 2$. If you want to "get back to 12," you just multiply the factors, prime or not, together.

It's the same in algebra, but variables make it less obvious. Take these two factors:

$$(x - 2)(x + 2)$$

There is literally nothing different in principle between those two factors and 3×4. We just don't know what x is, so we can't give a numerical value for the two bracketed quantities. So what do we do? Remember distribution? You know, it's when you have something like this:

$$4(x + 9)$$

All you do is multiply 4 and x to get $4x$ and then 4 and 9 to get 36:

$$4(x + 9) = 4x + 36$$

"Distribution" is just how you do multiplication with variables. If x above had been 3, by distributing you'd get the value 48. When we know the value, we just follow PEMDAS, of course, adding 3 and 9 to get 12, and then multiplying by 4 to get 48. We have no such option with variables, of course.

Back to the $(x - 2)(x + 2)$ example. In this case, we don't have a nice number like 4 to distribute. What can we do? We distribute in a way that you can take on faith works every time. The recipe is known by the acronym **FOIL: Firsts, Outers + Inners, Lasts**. It's easier to understand when you watch it happen:

Firsts	Multiply the first terms in each bracketed quantity	$(\mathbf{x} - 2)(\mathbf{x} + 2)$ $x \times x = x^2$
Outers	Multiply the two outer terms	$(\mathbf{x} - 2)(x + \mathbf{2})$ $x \times 2 = 2x$
Inners	Multiply the two inner terms	$(x - \mathbf{2})(\mathbf{x} + 2)$ $-2 \times x = -2x$
Add Outers and Inners	What column one said	$2x + (-2x) = 0$
Lasts	Multiply the two last terms in each bracketed quantity	$(x - \mathbf{2})(x + \mathbf{2})$ $-2 \times 2 = -4$
What are you left with?	Write it from left to right	$x^2 - 4$

Note that I bolded the terms **with their signs**. Since we don't put +'s in front of positive terms, you have to remember that convention. Otherwise, realize that an easy way to mess up FOIL—and much of algebra—is to mess up the signs. The calculator won't know if you entered the wrong number—remember that 2 and -2 are as distant from each other on the number line as 2 and 6 or -2 and -6.

What about factoring? That's called "reverse FOILing" for a reason. Let's start with a different example:

"Break up" the first term to set up the factoring. "Break up" means "take the square root of" when the first term is a square, and so on.	$x^2 - 4x + 4$ $(x\ \ )(x\ \ )$
Now that you have your Firsts, you have to figure your Lasts—but you must do so in a way that the resulting Outers + Inners also work out. Factor the numerical term and start trying factors. In this case, your options are 4×1 and 2×2. You can't multiply 1 and 3 to get 4—the Last—so the Lasts must be 2 and 2.	$(x\ \ 2)(x\ \ 2)$
Figure out the signs. You need to have a $+4$. That means you must have either $+2 \times +2$ or -2×-2. Either set of numbers will get you $+4$. But which will get you $-4x$? That is, which of the two options, when added to each other, will give you -4? Only $-2+(-2)=-4$.	$(x - 2)(x - 2)$

It's really just a puzzle that can be fun. Try this one on scrap paper:

$$x^2 + 4x + 4$$

Turn the page when you're done.

Done. It turned out to be $(x + 2)(x + 2)$.

You've not only given FOILing and factoring/reverse FOILing a whirl, but you've also worked out the three useful "identities" that can help you when you're in an algebraic bind. These are classics; you can bet you'll see them on the GRE. Knowing them will save time:

1. $(x + y)(x + y) = (x + y)^2 = x^2 + 2xy + y^2$

2. $(x + y)(x − y) = x^2 − y^2$, a.k.a., "the difference of two squares"

3. $(x − y)(x − y) = (x − y)^2 = x^2 − 2xy + y^2$

Extra credit: What would $(x − y)^3$ equal? See the footnote for the answer.[4]

But what if you can't FOIL and can't get a nice integer value, like in this example:

$$x^2 + 2x − 5 = 0$$

You can try all day but you need the quadratic formula to figure it. These expressions with a power of 2 are called "quadratic." Quadratic has "quad-" in it, which refers, as in "quadrilateral," to something "square-ish"—though a square is just one special kind of quadrilateral. There's a reason to this madness.

Here's the quadratic formula, and this one is for memorization. Don't go nuts deriving it. It's just a condensed version in mathspeak of what we've been doing:

$$x = \frac{-b \pm \sqrt{b^2 - 4ac}}{2a}$$

where the general form of the quadratic equation is $ax^2+bx+c=0$. The variable a is the coefficient of x^2; b is the coefficient of x.

So, for

$$x^2 + 2x − 5 = 0$$

---

[4]First, $(x − y)^3 = (x − y)(x − y)(x − y)$. You know that $(x−y)(x−y) = x^2 − 2xy + y^2$. So you're left with $(x − y)(x^2 − 2xy + y^2)$. Do it just as you'd do any other distribution: Multiply each term in $(x^2 − 2xy + y^2)$ first by x and then by $−y$. You'll get $x^3 − 2x^2y + xy^2 − x^2y + 2xy^2 − y^3$. Combine like terms, and you'll get $x^3 − 3x^2y + 3xy^2 − y^3$.

you just plug and chug. This will be a good review of algebra rules. I'll take you through it:

First, sub in all the values:

$$x = \frac{-2 \pm \sqrt{2^2 - 4(1)(-5)}}{2(1)}$$

PEMDAS. No parentheses, aside from the conventional use to signify multiplication. So work the stuff under the radical sign. Remember roots are fractional exponents and count as E in PEMDAS.

Do the square first:

$$x = \frac{-2 \pm \sqrt{4 - 4(1)(-5)}}{2(1)}$$

Then do what's under the radical sign:

$$x = \frac{-2 \pm \sqrt{4 + 20}}{2}$$

Now complete what's underneath the radical sign:

$$x = \frac{-2 \pm \sqrt{24}}{2}$$

Now look for a perfect square in 24—6 × 4 will do:

$$x = \frac{-2 \pm (\sqrt{6})(\sqrt{4})}{2}$$

Get the numerical value of that perfect square:

$$x = \frac{-2 \pm (\sqrt{6})(2)}{2}$$

Now look to factor out a common factor. The denominator gives you a clue. If you could get a 2 outside the parentheses in the numerator, you'd have $\frac{2}{2} = 1$. That is, you could cancel them:

$$x = \frac{2(-1 \pm \sqrt{6})}{2}$$

Cancel to kill the denominator and you're done.

$$x = -1 \pm \sqrt{6}$$

That's a lot more algebra than you'll probably have to do on the GRE, but it's like swinging two bats in the on-deck circle. Follow that algebra and you're golden for the GRE.

Finally, you may get a question or two that require you to solve a system of two equations with two variables. Here's an example:

(1) $14x + 2y = 10$

(2) $7x - 2y = 5$

There are two ways to do this. The faster and better way is by combining the two equations such that one variable drops out. This is often the case. So let's try it. If you add equations (1) and (2) combining like with like, as per usual, the $+2y$ and $-2y$ cancel—that is, add to zero. Watch:

$$14x + 2y = 10$$
$$+7x - 2y = 5$$
$$\overline{21x = 15}$$
$$x = \frac{15}{21} = \frac{5}{7}$$

Now sub that value of x into either equation to get y:

$$14\left(\frac{5}{7}\right) + 2y = 10$$
$$2(5) + 2y = 10$$
$$10 + 2y = 10$$
$$2y = 0$$
$$y = 0$$

That's nice and fast! The second, slower, and worse way is to use substitution: Solve for one variable, sub that into the other equation, solve for the other variable. We'll use the same equations:

Solve (1) for y:

$$14x + 2y = 10$$
$$-14x \qquad -14x$$
$$\frac{2y = 10 - 14x}{2 \qquad\quad 2}$$
$$y = \frac{10 - 14x}{2}$$
$$y = \frac{2(5 - 7x)}{2}$$
$$y = 5 - 7x$$

OK. Now sub that into equation (2):

$$7x - 2(5 - 7x) = 5$$
$$7x - 10 + 14x = 5$$
$$21x = 15$$
$$x = \frac{15}{21} = \frac{5}{7}$$

And sub that value of x as in the previous example.

You'll note that I haven't shown you any inequalities. The rules are the same for them, with one important exception: If you ever divide by a negative while solving the inequality, you **must** flip the sign. If you have a "whatever" $\geq$ "something else" and you divide by a negative, you have to flip the sign to $\leq$. Same goes for $>$ and $<$.

You'll note that I haven't mentioned functions. They're no big deal—just another notational form. You can write most any equation as a function.

Here's an example. If you see the equation—

$$y = 4x - 8$$

—you know that means, "To generate a bunch of y values, take a bunch of x values and multiply each of them by 4. Then, for each of them, subtract 8 from that product. Those are your y values."

So, to borrow a T-chart from the Essay section:

x value	y value
0	−8
1	−4
2	0
−1	−12
−2	−16

You can graph that on the Cartesian plane and get the graph of that line. (The slope is 4 and the *y*-intercept, as you can see, is −8.)

That's the same as:

$$f(x) = 4x - 8$$

All that functional notation does for you is emphasize the rules for generating what in the former equation were *y* values. Here, all *f(x)* means is "for every *x* value, apply the following functions, or set of rules, to generate what we're not calling *y* values but is the same thing." So the *x*'s are the inputs, and the *f(x)*'s are the outputs.

In the previous example, the "domain" of the function—so to speak, "where the graph of the function can 'live' on the Cartesian plane"—is all the real numbers. Sometimes, you'll be given limitations on the domain—on what can legitimately be inputted to the function. Sometimes, instead of *f*, you'll see *g* or *h*. Don't worry. It's all conventional. The rules don't change.

The last thing you need to know—yes, it's almost over!—is a little bit about data analysis.

The overarching rule is: Read the column headings, titles, and labels in any given chart or graph. These DA's are as much reading tests as "quantitative," and several items test whether you can read raw data off a not-too-complex chart without looking at the wrong cell, row, or column. You could see several types of charts and graphs, almost certainly all familiar to you. But if you'd like to see examples, please refer to the GRE Math Review PDF at *http://www.ets.org/s/gre/pdf/gre_math_review.pdf*.

Next, you need to be familiar with a few arithmetic procedures that may not be so familiar.

First, measures of central tendency: mean (or average), median, and mode.

The mode is the term that shows up the most in a set. Thus, for {3,5,5,7,94}, the mode is 5. If there were also two 7s, there would be two modes, 5 and 7. If no element is repeated, there is no mode.

The median is the middle term in a set when put in numerical order. Thus, for {2,5,7,24,98}, the median is 7. If you have an even number of elements in a set, the median is the average of the two middle terms.

The average is the arithmetic mean of a set of numbers. Take the just-mentioned set, {2,5,7,24,98}. To find the average of that set, add all the elements and divide by the number of elements:

$$Average = \frac{Sum}{Number}$$

$$Average = \frac{2 + 5 + 7 + 24 + 98}{5}$$

$$Average = \frac{136}{5} = 27.2$$

Next you have what are called "measures of position"—determinations of where elements are located in a set. You need to be concerned with two: quartiles and percentiles. Quartiles divide a set into four approximately equal groups using medians. Here's an example:

Take the set {1,2,2,3,3,3,5,5,6,6,6,6,7,7,8,8,8,9,9,9}. There are 20 elements. So split it into two sets of 10:

(I) {1,2,2,3,3,3,5,5,6,6}

(II) {6,6,7,7,8,8,8,9,9,9}

The "second quartile" is just the median of the set—in this case 6. The first quartile is the median of Set (I), or 3; the third quartile is the median of Set (II), or 8.

Percentiles do the same thing quartiles do but at a much finer level of resolution. As previously noted, there are three quartiles, which are referred to as

Q_1, Q_2, and Q_3. There are 99 percentiles, and the key to remember is that $Q_1 = P_{25}$, $Q_2 = P_{50}$, $Q_3 = P_{75}$.

Another question is about that 20-element set with the "frequency distribution" of all its elements, or "how many times each element appears in the set." Check this out:

Element	Frequency
1	1
2	2
3	3
4	0
5	2
6	4
7	2
8	3
9	3

Thus, 1 appears once, 7 appears twice, 9 appears thrice, and so on. You can also describe the frequency in terms of percentages, but I'll show you that later, when I deal with percentages. ☺

Finally, you have "measures of dispersion," which tell you how far apart the elements are from each other. The most basic measure of dispersion is the range, which you find by subtracting the lowest value in a set from the highest value in a set. For that 20-element set above, the range would be $9 - 1 = 8$.

Then there's the "interquartile range." Don't let the big name scare you. Here's how you determine it: it's the difference between the third quartile and the first quartile. In the previous example, the third quartile was 8 and the first quartile was 3. Therefore, the interquartile range is 5.

You may see what are called "box-and-whisker plots" that display some of the previous information in one picture:

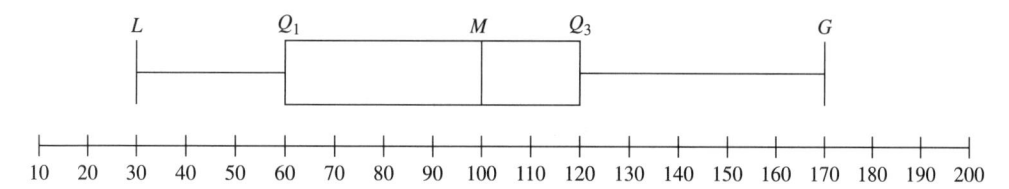

In that diagram, L is the lowest value, Q_1 is the first quartile, M is the median, Q_3 is the third quartile, and G is the greatest value.

Finally, there is the standard deviation. If your set has n values, you find the standard deviation by:

1. Finding the mean of the n values.

2. Finding the difference between that mean and each of the n values.

3. Squaring those differences.

4. Finding the mean of the squared differences.

5. Taking the non-negative square root of the mean squared difference.

It makes more sense with an example:

The set will be: {2,5,7,24,98}.

1. The mean is 27.2, as we found.

2. and 3. $(27.2-2)^2, (27.2-5)^2, (27.2-7)^2, (27.2-24)^2, (27.2-98)^2 =$ 635.04, 492.84, 408.04, 10.24, 5012.64

4. 1311.76

5. 36.22, roughly

Since the mean is 27.2, one standard deviation above the mean is $27.2 + 36.22 = 63.42$. It's unusual, but not impossible, to have a standard deviation greater than the mean. It just means your values were highly dispersed. One standard deviation below the mean would be $27.2 - 36.22 = -9.02$. To find the two or three deviations above or below the mean, add or subtract the standard deviation accordingly: twice for two deviations, and thrice for three.

You may be asked to find how many standard deviations—in decimals—a given value is, given also a standard deviation and a mean. Use this formula:

$$\frac{x - m}{d}$$

In that formula, x is the given value, m is the given mean, and d is the given standard deviation.[5] For example, if we wanted to know how many standard deviations above the mean the value 98 in the previous set was:

$$\frac{98 - 27.2}{36.22} \approx 1.95$$

Or just below two standard deviations above the mean.

You need to know a few counting principles.

First, if you have n items that can be arranged in m ways, there are $n \times m$ possible arrangements. For example, if you have three campsites, *A*, *B*, and *C*, and between *A* and *B* there are 4 possible hiking paths, and between *B* and *C* there are 5 possible hiking paths, there are $4 \times 5 = 20$ possible hikes from *A* to *C*.

However, you can't always just multiply the possibilities. Let's say you have 6 chairs in a row, and you want to find out how many ways you can seat 6 people in those chairs. The answer is not 36. Think about it. When you seat someone in the first chair you've used one person, and thus have 5 left for the second chair. Here's how it works:

Chair	Number of People Left to Seat
A	6
B	5
C	4
D	3
E	2
F	1

---

[5]This is not the official formula, but it'll work!

You have 6 × 5 × 4 × 3 × 2 × 1 = 720 options. That's a "factorial" and is symbolized as 6.

Most GRE "counting" items have to do with factorials or simple multiplication. Every so often, you'll see a tough permutations or combinations item.

- Permutations: The number of ways to select **and put into some kind of order** k elements out of n elements.

  Here's the formula: $P = \dfrac{n!}{(n-k)!}$

  Here's an example: How many distinct (means: different) three-digit integers can you make using the digits 4, 5, 6, and 7 if each digit can only appear once in the three-digit integer?

  Well, $n = 4$ (i.e., you have four digits to work with/choose from), and $k = 3$ (i.e., "three-digit integers"). Plug and chug:

  $$P = \dfrac{4!}{(4-3)!}$$

  $$P = \dfrac{4 \times 3 \times 2 \times 1}{1}$$

  There are 24 different ways to do it.

- Combinations: The number of ways to select k elements from a set of n elements **without worrying about putting the k elements into any kind of order**.

  Here's the formula: $C = \dfrac{n!}{k!(n-k)!}$

Here's an example: You are an eccentric intellectual who never wears the same color socks. You have a drawer filled with 20 socks, and each is a different color. Since you are an eccentric, you want to find out how many pairs of different socks you can sport at the local coffee shop while you play chess and read *Finnegans Wake*.

Well, $n = 20$ (20 socks from which to choose) and $k = 2$ ("pairs"). It doesn't matter which foot you put a sock on. Unlike the previous example, order doesn't matter here.

Plug and chug:

$$C = \frac{20!}{2!(20-2)!}$$

$$C = \frac{20!}{2!(18)!}$$

$$C = \frac{20 \times 19}{2 \times 1}$$

Whoa, what happened? Think about it: if 20! = 20 × 19 × 18 × 17 × ... × 2 × 1, and 18! = 18 × 17 × ... × 2 × 1, everything but 20 × 19 in the numerator will cancel out.

$$C = \frac{380}{2} = 190$$

We have just two more things to cover: probability and percents. Let's take percents first.

Just as the word suggests, "percents" are a form of a fraction that means "something out of 100"—or per *cent*. You can even see the 100 in the conventional percent symbol: %. There's the 1 and the two 0s.

Any fraction can be expressed as a percent. An easy way to do this is by setting up a proportion:

$$\frac{4}{5} = \frac{x}{100}$$

Cross-multiply and solve for *x*:

$$5x = 400$$

$$x = 80\%$$

Decimals are easy to convert to percents: use the place value. For example, 0.49 is $\frac{49}{100}$ or 49%. Similarly, 1.49 is $\frac{149}{100}$ or 149%.

Remember that 20-item set and the frequency distribution? Well, we can show the "relative frequency distribution" of all the elements. It's "relative" because it's not an absolute number of appearances—twice for 5, for example—but rather a ratio of appearances of each element to the total number of elements (in this case, 20), which is then converted (as above) into a percentage:

$$\{1,2,2,3,3,3,5,5,6,6,6,6,7,7,8,8,8,9,9,9\}$$

Element	Relative Frequency
1	5%
2	10%
3	15%
4	0%
5	10%
6	20%
7	10%
8	15%
9	15%

Note that it all adds to 100%.

I'll quickly run through some typical percent problems. Use this method if you're not comfortable with percents. In my experience, people learn a lot of different but equivalent ways to work with percents. If you have something that works, don't fix it.

To answer percent problems, translate English to math as in the following example: "What percent of 180 is 39?"

English	What	percent	of	180	is	39?
Math	x	%	×	180	=	39
	$\frac{x}{100}$		×	180	=	39
	$\left(\frac{x}{100}\right)180 = 39$					

Now solve for x:

$$\frac{180x}{100} = 39$$

$$\frac{18x}{10} = 39$$

$$18x = 390$$

$$x = 21\frac{2}{3}\%$$

Here's another example: "54 is 12% of what number?"

English	54	is	12%	of	what number?
Math	54	=	$\frac{12}{100}$	×	x
	\multicolumn{5}{c}{$54 = \frac{12x}{100}$}

Solve for x:

$$5400 = 12x$$

$$450 = x$$

You can also do percent increase and percent decrease problems in this translational fashion.

Example: "A clothing store ran a sale consisting of 30% off all items. If the sale price of a pair of pants was $60, what was its original price before the discount?"

First, change this into a more math-translatable sentence: "60 is 30% off of what number?"

English	60	is	30% off	of	what number?
Math	60	=	70%	×	x
	60	=	$\frac{70}{100}$	×	x
	\multicolumn{5}{c}{$60 = \frac{70x}{100}$}

Solve for *x*:

$$6000 = 70x$$

$$\$85.71 \cong x$$

Example: "The value of a stock increased by 15% in one year. If a share of the stock was worth $150 at the beginning of the year, what was its value at the end of the year?"

Translate to: "What is 15% greater than $150?"

English	What	is	15% greater than	150?
Math	x	=	115%	150
	$x = \dfrac{115}{100}(150)$			

Solve for *x*:

$$x = 172.50$$

Alternatively, you could find 15% of 150 (22.50) and add that to 150.

The key is to *reason* your way through the problems.

And finally—probability. I'm going to keep it simple. For more detail, see the GRE Math Review. But I'd wait on that—do some practice tests before you dive into that level of detail. Most of which is way too much in my opinion.

The key bits are:

- The probability of an event is the number of outcomes of that event divided by the number of all possible events.

Example: In a sock drawer there are 50 socks, 13 of which are brown. What is the probability that a sock picked at random will be brown? Well, you have 13 outcomes of that event, the picking of a brown sock, of 50 possible events, including picking a brown sock and picking a non-brown sock. In mathspeak: $\dfrac{13}{50}$. Note that you could also say that there is a 26% chance of picking a brown sock.

- If two events are mutually exclusive, the probability that they both occur is the sum of the probabilities of both events.

Example: What is the probability of rolling either an odd or an even number with a six-sided die?

These are mutually exclusive events—you can't roll both an odd and an even number. So, you must add the probabilities: for an even number, it's $\frac{3}{6} = \frac{1}{2}$. And for an odd number, it's $\frac{3}{6} = \frac{1}{2}$. Add those together to get 1. I know this was not a surprising result. You have a 100% chance of rolling either an even or an odd number with a six-sided die! Note that 1 is a 100% probability, 0 is a 0% probability, and all other probabilities are between 0 and 1.

- If two events are independent of each other, the probability that they both occur is the product of the probabilities of both events.

Example: "What is the probability of getting heads four times in a row when flipping a coin?"

Well, you have a $\frac{1}{2}$ chance every time, and these events are independent of each other—getting a head on flip 1 has no effect on whether you get a head or tail on flip 2. So, you must multiply the probabilities: $\frac{1}{2} \times \frac{1}{2} \times \frac{1}{2} \times \frac{1}{2} = \frac{1}{16}$.

Speaking of mutual exclusion, keep in mind a very handy technique for working out a typical GRE problem: the Venn diagram. An example will serve best:

27 students are taking three classes: Math, English, and Art. None of the 27 students are taking any other classes; all of the 27 students are taking at least one of the three classes. Furthermore:

- 18 are taking Math
- 12 are taking English
- 15 are taking Art
- No one is taking all three classes
- 3 are taking both English and Art
- 4 are taking both English and Math

How many students are taking both Math and Art?

If this kind of problem makes you nauseated, I understand! But drawing it out with a Venn diagram, the greatest diagram ever invented, in my humble opinion, Dramamines that feeling away!

Before we draw, let's think a little. First, if there are 27 students, but 18 + 12 + 15 = 45 taking Math, English, and Art, well, you know that some students are taking more than one class; and you're even told a bit about that.

Let's draw. A Venn diagram always consists of overlapping circles inside a big rectangle, like so:

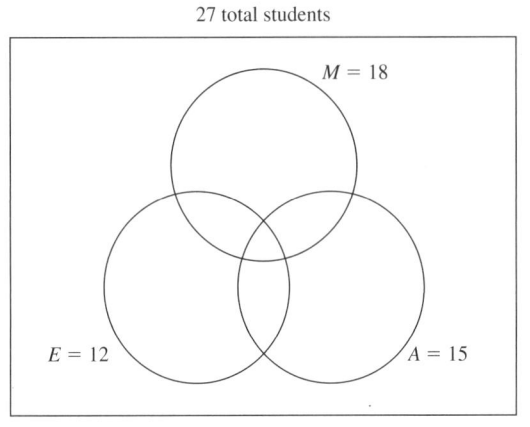

27 total students

$M = 18$

$E = 12$ $A = 15$

We're letting M stand for Math, E for English, and A for art. Each circle represents the number of students taking each of those classes. Reproduce this drawing on scrap paper. Fill in info as we go.

Note the overlaps. The triple overlap in the middle stands for those students taking all three classes. We were told no one is doing that, so enter a zero there. We're also told that 3 students are taking both English and Art, so fill in that number in the relevant overlap—where circle E and circle A overlap, but not the triple overlap. That's already filled in, and represents only those taking all three courses (i.e., nobody). We're told also that 4 students are taking both English and Math. So fill in that number in the relevant overlap—that of circles E and M. Note that the overlap between M and A is what you're asked about.

OK, now that you've filled in what you know, what's next? Well, focus on the English circle, E. If there are 12 students taking English, you've already accounted for 7 of them (the 4-overlap with Math and the 3-overlap with Art). Therefore, you can fill in a 5 in the part of the E circle outside of the two overlaps.

Next, you know there are 18 students taking Math. You've accounted for 4 of those already, so everything inside the Math circle but outside of the

118 | CHAPTER 4
The Math Section

Math-English overlap, must equal 14. Similarly, you know 15 students are taking Art, 3 of whom you've accounted for. So everything inside the Art circle but outside the Art-English overlap, must equal 12. Let x represent the Math-Art overlap. Then $14 - x$ represents the Math-only section and $12 - x$ represents the Art-only section.

Just to make sure we're on the same page, check out my diagram:

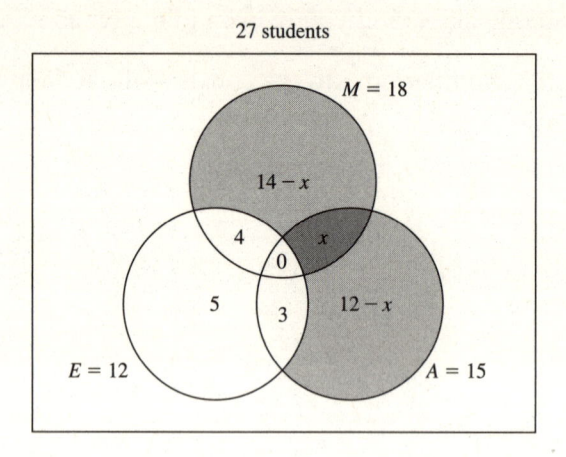

27 students

$M = 18$
$14 - x$
4
x
0
5
3
$12 - x$
$E = 12$
$A = 15$

Are we stuck? No. You can use the total number of students to deduce the Math-Art overlap. If you add 14 (the shaded parts of the Math circle), 12 (the shaded parts of the Art circle) and 12 (the sum of the English circle), you get 38. Well, you only have 27 students; subtract that from 38, and you know that the overlap between Math and Art is 11. Why? Because there must be 11 "double-counted" students, and since all other overlaps are already accounted for, they all must be math-and-art students! Fill the 11 in.

Finally, note that if that overlap is 11, there are only $18 - 11 - 4 = 3$ students taking Math only and, similarly, $15 - 11 - 3 = 1$ student taking Art only. All areas are now accounted for, and you are now familiar with the venerable Venn diagram. It's a beautiful thing, and it previews a key math strategy: When in doubt, draw it out!

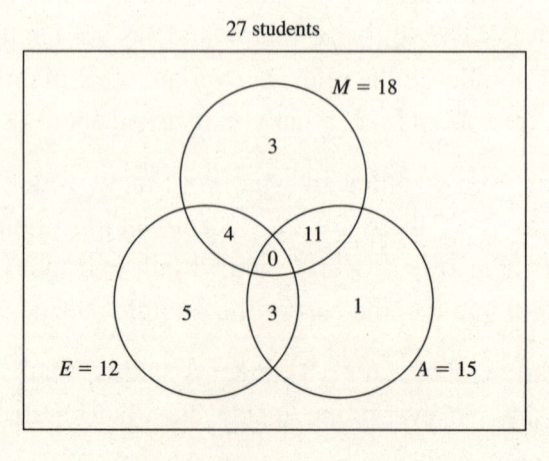

27 students

$M = 18$
3
4
11
0
5
3
1
$E = 12$
$A = 15$

Remember that relative-frequency chart? Well, you can also write that chart as a "probability distribution" simply by listing the percentages as decimals. Remember, for example, 15% probability is equal to a 0.15 probability because $15\% = \frac{15}{100} = 0.15$. Check this out:

$$\{1,2,2,3,3,3,5,5,6,6,6,6,7,7,8,8,8,9,9,9\}$$

Element	Probability Frequency
1	0.05
2	0.10
3	0.15
4	0.00
5	0.10
6	0.20
7	0.10
8	0.15
9	0.15

Note that the probabilities add to 1.

One final note—and it's apt, considering you're studying for a standardized test. The "normal distribution" is shaped like a bell curve. Draw one on scrap paper. If you don't know how, Google "bell curve." Note a few things:

1. The mean, median, and mode are pretty much the same: right in the visual middle.

2. The curve is symmetrical: cut it in half vertically and the pieces mirror each other.

3. About 68% of the represented data will be within one standard deviation; about 95% will be within two standard deviations.

This curve is pretty much how a whole bunch of GRE scores for, say, a year will look if you plot them. That's at least the goal.

Any distribution that doesn't look "normal" will have interesting changes in the three features noted in the previous list. Some of the toughest GRE items can touch on these changes. If you don't understand that stuff, putting in a ton of time to learn it is probably a waste of effort. Most likely, you'll never see it, as your performance on the first quantitative section won't lead to a tougher second section. If you do understand that stuff you don't need *my* help! However, please see the aforementioned GRE Math Review PDF for a full discussion. But be warned: It's in technical mathspeak! ☺

That's enough of *that*!

We're going to jump into the strategies now and show you how all this content knowledge can best be deployed against the GRE math items.

QUANTITATIVE COMPARISON (QC) STRATEGIES

All **QC**s have the same answer choices:

Ⓐ Quantity A is greater
Ⓑ Quantity B is greater
Ⓒ The two quantities are equal
Ⓓ The relationship cannot be determined

The key thing with **QC**s is to *compare*. If you find yourself doing a lot of calculations, you're almost certainly off-base. Do only as much calculation as is necessary to make an apples-to-apples comparison.

The "Normal" Way

Here's the step-method you should follow when doing **QC**s:

Step 1: Determine what you know.

Step 2: Determine where you need to go.

Step 3: Change one or both of the quantities to make an apples-to-apples comparison.

Step 4: Make the comparison.

Let me show you an item you've seen from the diagnostic:

A certain pasta sauce recipe requires $4\frac{1}{2}$ teaspoons of olive oil to make enough sauce for 6 servings.

Quantity A	**Quantity B**
The number of teaspoons of olive oil required for the same recipe to make enough sauce for 8 servings.	6 teaspoons

Step 1: Determine what you know.

You know that you have a ratio here: $\frac{4.5 \text{ teaspoons of olive oil}}{6 \text{ servings}}$.

Step 2: Determine where you need to go.

You must determine how many teaspoons of olive oil you'll need to make 8 servings. Thus, you need to set up a proportion.

Step 3: Change one or both of the quantities to make an apples-to-apples comparison.

$$\frac{4.5 \text{ teaspoons of olive oil}}{6 \text{ servings}} = \frac{x \text{ teaspoons of olive oil}}{8 \text{ servings}}$$

$$\frac{4.5}{6} = \frac{x}{8}$$

Cross-multiply and solve for *x*:

$$6x = 36$$
$$x = 6$$

Step 4: Make the comparison.

Nothing to it! It's C.

It's your turn! We'll lay a new one on you.

Guided Practice

The equation $x^2 + kx - 32 = 0$ has a root of 8, and k is a constant.

Quantity A	Quantity B
The value of k	5

Step 1: Determine what you know.

Compare what you came up with to this footnote.[6]

Step 2: Determine where you need to go.

Step 3: Change one or both of the quantities to make an apples-to-apples comparison.

Show your work in the following space.

Compare your response to this footnote.[7]

Step 4: Make the comparison.

Since –4 is less than 5, B is the answer.

Now we'll turn you loose on some **QC**s all by your lonesome!

---

[6]You have a quadratic you'll need to factor. Do what you can now: $(x +)(x -)$. You know you need opposite signs to get a –32. Note that one factor is 8. That means that one of the factors must be $x - 8$ because when you set that to zero—$x - 8 = 0$—you get $x = 8$.
[7]The other factor must be $(x + 4)$.

Independent Practice

Work these out on scrap paper, as you would for the actual GRE.

1. $p^2 + 2pq + q^2 = 16$

Quantity A	Quantity B
$p + q$	4

Ⓐ Quantity A is greater.
Ⓑ Quantity B is greater.
Ⓒ The two quantities are equal.
Ⓓ The relationship cannot be determined.

2. On a number line, the distance between a and 0 is 5.

Quantity A	Quantity B
The distance between a and 5 on the number line	0

Ⓐ Quantity A is greater.
Ⓑ Quantity B is greater.
Ⓒ The two quantities are equal.
Ⓓ The relationship cannot be determined.

3. The average (arithmetic mean) final exam score in Biology 101 is 92. The average final exam score in Chemistry 207 is 87.

Quantity A	Quantity B
The average final exam score of both Biology 101 and Chemistry 207	89.5

Ⓐ Quantity A is greater.
Ⓑ Quantity B is greater.
Ⓒ The two quantities are equal.
Ⓓ The relationship cannot be determined.

Independent Practice: Explanations

1. $p^2 + 2pq + q^2 = 16$

Quantity A	Quantity B
$p + q$	4

Ⓐ Quantity A is greater.
Ⓑ Quantity B is greater.
Ⓒ The two quantities are equal.
Ⓓ The relationship cannot be determined.

Well, you have to work with the material in the center to get to something like Quantity A. So factor that:

$$p^2 + 2pq + q^2 = 16$$
$$(p + q)(p + q) = 16$$
$$(p + q)^2 = 16$$

Use Quantity B to help push you in the right direction. But 16 has two square roots, namely +4 and −4. Then $p + q = 4$ or $p + q = -4$.

Choice D is correct.

2. On a number line, the distance between a and 0 is 5.

Quantity A	Quantity B
The distance between a and 5 on the number line	0

Ⓐ Quantity A is greater.
Ⓑ Quantity B is greater.
Ⓒ The two quantities are equal.
Ⓓ The relationship cannot be determined.

Remember a number line goes in two directions—positive to the right and negative to the left. The number *a* could be 5 units away from 0 because it's 5—*or because it's* –5. If *a* is 5, the distance from 5 is 0 units, but if *a* is –5, the distance from 5 is 10 units.

Choice D is correct.

3. The average (arithmetic mean) final exam score in Biology 101 is 92.
   The average final exam score in Chemistry 207 is 87.

Quantity A	**Quantity B**
The average final exam score of both Biology 101 and Chemistry 207	89.5

   Ⓐ Quantity A is greater.
   Ⓑ Quantity B is greater.
   Ⓒ The two quantities are equal.
   Ⓓ The relationship cannot be determined.

Well, what do you know here? You have two averages. What is the formula for an average? $Average = \frac{Sum}{Number}$. You have a problem: You don't know how many people were in either class, nor do you know what the sum of all points gained by all test-takers was for either exam. In other words, you have two unknowns in each case. You know the averages, but you don't know the sums or the numbers for either class. If there were the same number of students in each class, the average isn't weighted, and the answer is 89.5. If there weren't the same number of students in each class, then the average will not be 89.5. You can't determine that, so the answer is choice D.

Reverse Engineering

You should always feel free to pick numbers to make a comparison easier. Make sure you adhere to any requirements in the information above the quantity columns.

For example:

$$n > 3$$

Quantity A	Quantity B
$\dfrac{2n + 3}{3}$	n

   Ⓐ Quantity A is greater.
   Ⓑ Quantity B is greater.
   Ⓒ The two quantities are equal.
   Ⓓ The relationship cannot be determined.

First, although it's outside the allotted range, try $n = 3$. You'll see why. We're establishing a pattern:

Quantity A	Quantity B
$\dfrac{2(3) + 3}{3}$	3

Quantity A equals 3, and thus equals Quantity B.

Now try 4:

Quantity A	Quantity B
$\dfrac{2(4) + 3}{3}$	4

Quantity A is $\dfrac{11}{3}$. Pretty close to 4, but less than 4, whereas Quantity B is 4; that is, larger than A.

Try 5 to see if this pattern continues:

Quantity A	Quantity B
$\dfrac{2(5) + 3}{3}$	5

Quantity A is $\dfrac{13}{3}$ whereas Quantity B is 5, that is, larger than A.

You're not mathematically sure that the answer is B, but you're pretty close. Try 1000:

Quantity A	Quantity B
$\dfrac{2(1000) + 3}{3}$	1000

Quantity A is about 668; Quantity B is 1000. You're done! Choice B it is.

Another good strategy applies to geometry **QC**s: When in doubt, draw it out. Since figures may not be to scale, this is particularly useful.

For example:

Point *E* is the center of the circle.

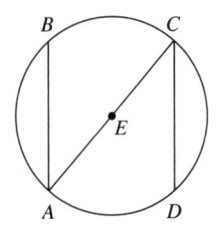

Quantity A	Quantity B
$\overline{AB}$	$\overline{CD}$

This isn't to scale, and none of these **QC** diagrams are necessarily to scale. So don't assume it has to be just how it looks. What you know for sure is that $\overline{AB}$ and $\overline{CD}$ are chords and $\overline{AC}$ is a diameter, since it goes through the center *E*.

Points *A* and *C* are fixed by being at the ends of the diameter. But where does point *B* have to be? All we know, geometrically, is that this is a chord. In fact, $\overline{AB}$ and $\overline{CD}$ can be anything but diameters, but what's preventing them from looking like this? . . .

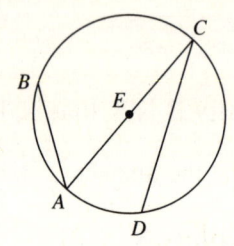

Or like this? . . .

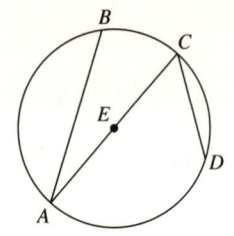

You've got a choice D on your hands. Drawing out other options based on what you know to be true, and nothing else, can help a lot.

If you're given a geometric problem without a figure, you know what to do! Yes. When in doubt, draw it out.

PROBLEM SOLVING (PS) STRATEGIES

PS items test the same material as **QC**s but in a different format. Most **PS** items are multiple-choice; some are multiple-response. You'll sometimes get a fill-in. The Normal Way for all three is about the same, but there is no way to reverse engineer a **PS** fill. You have no answer choices with which to work!

The "Normal" Way in Slow Motion

Here's the step method for PS items:

Step 1: Cover the answer choices.

Step 2: Determine what you know.

Step 3: Determine where you need to go.

Step 4: Start your calculations; uncover the answer choices.

Step 5: As you work, eliminate wrong answer choices.

Let's run through an item from the diagnostic to show this strategy.

Step 1: Cover the answer choices.

The idea here is not to be swayed by what's written. It's not as crucial as in Verbal, but it still helps to ignore the answer choices and concentrate on the stem:

What is the slope of the line whose equation is $4x - 8y = 36$?

Step 2: Determine what you know.

This is an equation of a line, but I can't just read off the slope because it's in the wrong form.

Step 3: Determine where you need to go.

I need to put this in the slope-intercept form, $y = mx + b$ by solving for y.

Step 4: Start your calculations. Uncover the answer choices.

Step 5: As you work, eliminate wrong answer choices.

(A) 8   (B) 4   (C) 2   (D) $\frac{1}{2}$ (E) $\frac{1}{9}$

Let's get to it:

$$4x - 8y = 36$$

(continued)

The "Normal" Way in Slow Motion (Continued)

Subtract 4x from both sides:

$$-8y = -4x + 36$$

Divide both sides by –8 but note that non-fractions won't work. Eliminate A, B, and C. If you were pressed for time, you could bail now and guess either D or E. But we'll finish:

$$y = \frac{1}{2}x - \frac{9}{2}$$

Choice D is correct.

Now let's see how you do on another one from the diagnostic exam.

Guided Practice

Work this one on scratch paper.

> **The lengths of two sides of a triangle are 8 and 4. Which of the following could be the length of the third side?**
>
> **Include all such measures.**

Step 1: Cover the answer choices.

Done for you.

Step 2: Determine what you know.

What is it about the sides of triangles that you need to know? (Hint: Is there a limitation on the length of the third side of the triangle, given the lengths of the other two sides?)

Step 3: Determine where you need to go.

Once you have the mathematical relationship, work it out.

Step 4: Start your calculations; uncover the answer choices.

Step 5: As you work, eliminate wrong answer choices.

- (A) 4
- (B) 6
- (C) 8
- (D) 10
- (E) 12

Which can you eliminate?

Well, since two sides of the triangle are 4 and 8, 12 must go. Also, if the third side were 4, then the two 4-sides would equal the third side, 8. That's no good. Eliminate 4, too. The other ones are good: B, C, and D are the answers.

It's your turn! I'm going to give you two toughies.

Independent Practice

1. R, S, and T are three triangles. The base of triangle R is 15% less than that of triangle S. The height of triangle R is 20% greater than that of triangle S. The base of triangle T is 20% less than that of triangle S, and the height of triangle T is 15% greater than that of triangle S. Which of the following is the positive difference between the area of triangle R and the area of triangle T?

$$\boxed{} bh$$

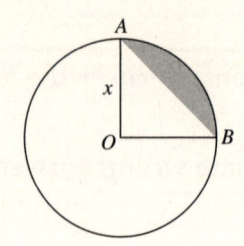

2. In the circle above, point O is the center of the circle. What is the perimeter of the shaded region?

(A) $\dfrac{\pi x^2}{4} - \dfrac{x^2}{2}$

(B) $\dfrac{\pi x^2}{4} + \dfrac{x^2}{2}$

(C) $x\sqrt{2} + \dfrac{\pi x}{2}$

(D) $x\sqrt{3} + \dfrac{\pi x}{2}$

(E) $x\sqrt{2} + \dfrac{\pi x^2}{4}$

Independent Practice: Explanations

1. R, S, and T are three triangles. The base of triangle R is 15% less than that of triangle S. The height of triangle R is 20% greater than that of triangle S. The base of triangle T is 20% less than that of triangle S, and the height of triangle T is 15% greater than that of triangle S. Which of the following is the positive difference between the area of triangle R and the area of triangle T?

$$\boxed{}\,bh$$

This is a toughie. Assume you've skipped this hard one and have now come back to it.

First, what do we know? Well, we're dealing with triangles and the area of triangles. That's $A = \dfrac{1}{2}bh$.

The bases and heights of triangles R and T are both related to those of S. So let's work out what triangle R's base and height are, even if we don't know where we're going yet.

- R base is 15% less than S base. Or: R base is 85% of S base: $0.85b$.
- R height is 20% more than S height: $1.2h$.

So the area of R is $\frac{1}{2}(0.85b)(1.2h) = \frac{1.02bh}{2} = 0.51bh$.

Do the same for T:

- T base is 20% less than S base; T base is 80% of S base: $0.8b$.
- T height is 15% greater than S height: $1.15h$.

So the area of T is $\frac{1}{2}(0.8b)(1.15h) = \frac{0.92bh}{2} = 0.46bh$.

The positive difference between the two areas is $0.05bh$.

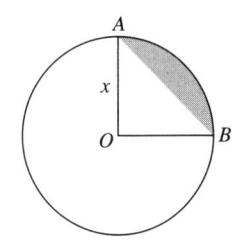

2. In the circle above, point O is the center of the circle. What is the perimeter of the shaded region?

    Ⓐ $\frac{\pi x^2}{4} - \frac{x^2}{2}$

    Ⓑ $\frac{\pi x^2}{4} + \frac{x^2}{2}$

    Ⓒ $x\sqrt{2} + \frac{\pi x}{2}$

    Ⓓ $x\sqrt{3} + \frac{\pi x}{2}$

    Ⓔ $x\sqrt{2} + \frac{\pi x^2}{4}$

What do we know? Lots. We have a right isosceles triangle circumscribed by a circle. The radius of the circle, which is also the length of each of the legs of the right isosceles triangle, is *x*. We're looking for the perimeter of the shaded area. That means we need to find the hypotenuse of the triangle and add that to the arc formed by the right angle, arc *AB*.

First, the hypotenuse. Since this is a right isosceles triangle, it's a 45:45:90 triangle. That means the hypotenuse is $x\sqrt{2}$. You can eliminate all but C and E now. You need to find the arc, which is a fraction of circumference. Note that E has the formula for area in the second term.

C is the correct choice. Only do as much math as you need. Time is of the essence. (A quarter of $2\pi x$ will give the second term in choice C.)

Reverse Engineering

There is one very powerful reverse-engineering strategy. When you can't do the algebra, pick numbers. By making the abstract concrete, you not only save time but it might also be your only shot to get to the answer.

One key is you can't apply this strategy mindlessly. You still have to *reason* your way through problems. Sometimes the numbers you pick can be anything; other times, the logic of the problem limits the numbers you can pick.

Let's take a look at a tough problem from the diagnostic test:

Muhammad has *b* bags of candy, each containing 20 pieces of candy. After he gives out *c* pieces of candy to each of his friends, he has *x* pieces of candy left over. Which of the following represents the number of friends Muhammad has?

(A) $\dfrac{20b - x}{c}$

(B) $\dfrac{20b + x}{c}$

(C) $\dfrac{20b}{c} - x$

(D) $\dfrac{20c - x}{b}$

(E) $\dfrac{20c + x}{b}$

Assign some easy-to-work-with numbers to the variables:

- There are 10 bags of candy ($b = 10$)

- Muhammad gives out 5 pieces of candy to each of his friends ($c = 5$); and

- He has 40 pieces of candy left over ($x = 40$)

If he starts out with 10 bags × 20 pieces of candy/bag = 200 total pieces, and gives 5 to each friend, 40 is a good and reasonable number to have left.

OK, then. Muhammad started with 200 pieces of candy. He ended up with 40. That means he gave away 160 pieces. If he gave those away in 5-piece batches to each of his friends, he has 160 ÷ 5 = 32 friends.

That 32 is your target value. Given the numbers you picked—which changed this from algebra to arithmetic—32 should come out. Now that you've found one possible answer, all you need to do is to plug in your values for b, c, and x to each of the answer choices. The one that spits out 32 is the right one:

$\dfrac{20b - x}{c}$	$\dfrac{20(10) - 40}{5}$ $\dfrac{200 - 40}{5}$ $\dfrac{160}{5} = 32$ (A) was right! You're done.
$\dfrac{20b + x}{c}$	
$\dfrac{20b}{c} - x$	
$\dfrac{20c - x}{b}$	
$\dfrac{20c + x}{b}$	

You won't always get as lucky as we just did and find the right answer on the first try! But one of the choices will be right. The more you eliminate, the better your chances of guessing correctly, even if you run out of time for that item. The calculations, also, usually go pretty fast, and you're picking numbers because you couldn't do it algebraically.

Now you try one—another from the diagnostic.

Guided Practice

I'll give you some hints. Work this out on scratch paper.

Rate is given by the equation $r = \dfrac{d}{t}$, where d is distance and t is time. If the distance traveled remains the same and the rate increases by 25 percent, then the amount of time elapsed must decrease by what percent?

(A) 20
(B) 25
(C) 60
(D) 80
(E) 125

First, pick a number for d.

Now pick a number for the first rate, r.

Plug your values into $r = \dfrac{d}{t}$ to find your t value.

Think about it. You have a value for t, given your first rate, r. The problem, however, is asking how much t will decrease—by what percentage, that is—if r goes up by 25%.

Well, pick a number that's 25% more than your first rate, r. That's your second rate—call it what you will. ☺

Now you have a second t value. Compare that to the first value to determine the percent decrease.

OK. Turn the page to see how I did it.

Let's say:

- $d = 100$ (miles, inches, parsecs; it matters not)
- the first rate, r, will be 20

    Plug in your values:

    $$r = \frac{d}{t}$$

    $$20 = \frac{100}{t}$$

    Now, divide both sides by 100:

    $$\frac{20}{100} = \frac{1}{t}$$

    Flip both sides:

    $$5 = t$$

Hold that thought.

The stem tells you that the rate is then increased by 25%. Well, 25% is one-fourth and 20 divided by 4 is 5. Add 5 to the original rate you picked, 20, and the new rate is now 25. You're thus following the recipe in the problem.

    Now, plug in your values:

    $$r = \frac{d}{t}$$

    $$25 = \frac{100}{t}$$

    Now, divide both sides by 100:

    $$\frac{25}{100} = \frac{1}{t}$$

> Flip both sides:
>
> $$4 = t$$
>
> Finally, you have to figure the percent decrease from 5 to 4. If this is obvious to you, you're done. If not, check this out:
>
> Subtract 4 from 5 to get 1. Then we write the fraction $\frac{1}{5}$ and just convert to a percent. This is done as follows: $\left(\frac{1}{5}\right)(100\%) = 20\%$. What does this mean? It means that if you started with 5 and went down to 4, you went down 20%.

DATA ANALYSIS (DA) STRATEGIES

These items come in sets: you'll have a couple of related charts or graphs with a few questions that ask you to interpret the data.

Don't bother studying the charts and graphs in detail. Read the titles, the column headings, and the labels. Get a feel for what's going on in the graphs—as you would with a long reading passage you're skimming. All graphical representations are to scale, and you can trust them. As with reading passages, don't bring in any outside knowledge. Everything you need is in front of you. ☺

The "Normal" Way

Here's the method, already touched upon:

1. Skim and scan the charts and graphs, noting titles, headings, and labels.
2. For each item, focus on what's asked; ignore the rest.
3. Make sure you're answering the question.

Let's run through one item from a set you saw during the diagnostic:

Questions x–y are based on the following data.

Three rock bands—Alfa, Bolus, and Core—were ranked relative to each other at a music-fan site on three different occasions. Additionally, each band's sales were tracked as shown.

RANKINGS

Date	Alfa	Bolus	Core
June 2011	1	3	2
Sept 2011	3	2	1
May 2012	2	1	3

Band

AVERAGE NUMBER OF SONG DOWNLOADS/DAY JUNE 2011–MAY 2012

RETAIL OUTLET	Alfa	Bolus	Core
StoreMart	7.2	9.1	4.2
E-Toon'z	9.3	7.3	3.8
otto's	2.2	6.5	2.7
izone	1.5	2.7	8.2
Impax	6.8	5.4	2.1

Band

(continued)

140 | CHAPTER 4
The Math Section

The "Normal" Way (Continued)

x. What is the ratio of the sum of the averages of Alfa's song downloads from all outlets to its rank in the May 2012 survey?

$$\frac{\boxed{}}{\boxed{}}$$

Select each box and type a number. Backspace to erase.

1. Skim and scan the charts and graphs, noting titles, headings, and labels.

What's going on? You have three bands ranked by fans on the left and some information on song downloads per day for each band at five different retail outlets. Both charts cover June 2011 to May 2012. At this point, ignore all the numbers.

2. For each item, focus on what's asked. Ignore the rest.

Read the stem.

This is just a graph-reading exercise with minimal math. Home in on what you're asked. Ignore the rest.

First, find the average number of song downloads for Alfa. That's in column one under "Band" in the song download chart. Add that column. You'll get 27. Enter that value in the numerator.

Second, find the ranking for Alfa in May 2012. It's in the rankings chart and it's 2. Enter that value in the denominator.

3. Make sure you're answering the question.

You don't want to enter the 2 in the numerator or 27 in the denominator, for example, let alone entering the wrong cell's information because you were careless! If it helps to use your fingers on the computer screen, do so!

The key challenge is finding the right information while remaining undistracted, so whatever focuses your attention is worthwhile.

Try the next one.

Guided Practice

Three rock bands—Alfa, Bolus, and Core—were ranked relative to each other at a music-fan site on three different occasions. Additionally, each band's sales were tracked as shown.

Date	RANKINGS BAND Alfa	Bolus	Core
June 2011	1	3	2
Sept 2011	3	2	1
May 2012	2	1	3

AVERAGE NUMBER OF SONG DOWNLOADS/DAY JUNE 2011–MAY 2012

RETAIL OUTLET	Alfa	Bolus	Core
StoreMart	7.2	9.1	4.2
E-Toon'z	9.3	7.3	3.8
otto's	2.2	6.5	2.7
izone	1.5	2.7	8.2
Impax	6.8	5.4	2.1

142　CHAPTER 4
The Math Section

y. The sum of the average number of Bolus's song downloads per retail outlet is approximately what percentage greater than that of Core's?

(A) 15%　(B) 45%　(C) 55%　(D) 70%　(E) 87%

Click on your selection.

1. Skim and scan the charts and graphs, noting titles, headings, and labels.

Already done for the last one.

2. For each item, focus on what's asked. Ignore the rest.

This is the key step. Focus, focus, focus.

Write down what you need to look for on scrap paper. Compare your response to this footnote.[8]

3. Make sure you're answering the question.

What did you get? Compare your response to the following:

There's a little more math here, but you still have to find the raw data without getting messed up. Go to the song download chart. The sum of the average number of Bolus's song downloads is found in column two under "Band." Add those to get 31.

Column three under "Band" will give you the analogous data for Core. Add those up to get 21.

Now the math part, addition aside: Bolus's number is **approximately** what percentage **greater** than that of Core?

---

[8] First, you need to add the average number of Bolus's song downloads per retail outlet. Then, you need to add Core's. When you've done that, compare the two.

Translate that sentence into math, dropping the "approximately" and the "greater." We'll return to those when we get an answer:

Bolus's sum	is	what	percentage	of	Core's sum?
31	=	x	$\frac{something}{100}$	×	21

Write the math properly:

$$31 = \left(\frac{x}{100}\right)21$$

Do the distribution on the right side of the equation:

$$31 = \frac{21x}{100}$$

Now multiply both sides by 100 to get rid of the denominator:

$$3100 = 21x$$

Divide both sides by 21:

$$147.6 \cong x$$

We threw in a little approximation there with that little squiggly above the equals sign, and we'll throw in some more, legitimately, of course.

First, note that 100% of anything is the thing itself, because 100% = 1. So, whatever remains above 100 must be the **greater** thing we're seeking. In this case, it's about 47.6%. The closest value—more approximation—is 45%. Choice B is correct.

Try one on your own.

Independent Practice

Three rock bands—Alfa, Bolus, and Core—were ranked relative to each other at a music-fan site on three different occasions. Additionally, each band's sales were tracked as shown.

RANKINGS			
Date	BAND		
	Alfa	Bolus	Core
June 2011	1	3	2
Sept 2011	3	2	1
May 2012	2	1	3

AVERAGE NUMBER OF SONG DOWNLOADS/DAY JUNE 2011–MAY 2012			
RETAIL OUTLET	Band		
	Alfa	Bolus	Core
StoreMart	7.2	9.1	4.2
E-Toon'z	9.3	7.3	3.8
otto's	2.2	6.5	2.7
izone	1.5	2.7	8.2
Impax	6.8	5.4	2.1

x. If the average number of downloads per day for all three bands at StoreMart held true for 1000 days, what would be the total number of Alfa, Bolus, and Core song downloads from StoreMart during that time?

(A) 11,400   (B) 12,400   (C) 14,300   (D) 20,400   (E) 20,500

Independent Practice: Explanations

Three rock bands—Alfa, Bolus, and Core—were ranked relative to each other at a music-fan site on three different occasions. Additionally, each band's sales were tracked as shown.

Date	\multicolumn{3}{c}{RANKINGS}		
	\multicolumn{3}{c}{BAND}		
	Alfa	Bolus	Core
June 2011	1	3	2
Sept 2011	3	2	1
May 2012	2	1	3

AVERAGE NUMBER OF SONG DOWNLOADS/DAY JUNE 2011–MAY 2012

RETAIL OUTLET	Alfa	Bolus	Core
StoreMart	7.2	9.1	4.2
E-Toon'z	9.3	7.3	3.8
otto's	2.2	6.5	2.7
izone	1.5	2.7	8.2
Impax	6.8	5.4	2.1

x. If the average number of downloads per day for all three bands at StoreMart held true for 1000 days, what would be the total number of Alfa, Bolus, and Core song downloads from StoreMart during that time?

(A) 11,400   (B) 12,400   (C) 14,300   (D) 20,400   (E) 20,500

First you have to figure what is asked. That's really the main challenge. Think it through:

1. Each band has an average download/day at StoreMart. I can find that in the relevant chart.

2. "Held true" means that the average would be mathematically accurate for that thousand-day period.

3. We want the total number of all three bands' song downloads during that period.

4. I know that $Average = \dfrac{Sum}{Number}$. I know the average, and I know the number of days: I'm looking for the sum of all songs downloaded.

Find the StoreMart row. First, you'll need to add up the individual average downloads per day for the three bands: 7.2 + 9.1 + 4.2 = 20.5. You know that the number of days is 1000. Fill in your equation:

$$20.5 = \dfrac{Sum}{1000}$$

Multiply both sides by 1000 to get the sum: 20,500. Choice E is correct.

CHAPTER 5
The Analytical Writing Section

INTRODUCTION TO THE ESSAYS

This section is also known as the "the essays." You have two writing tasks: to construct an argument ("analyze an issue") and to evaluate an argument ("analyze an argument"). My tasks are to:

- show you that the two essays require pretty much the same process;

- help you maximize your current command of Standard Written English.

The essays are graded according to a pretty generous and straightforward scoring rubric. Since this is writing-under-pressure, you will not be crushed for a few stray infelicities of grammar. The emphasis is on the construction and clarity of the argument, though sentence variety and word usage do play a subordinate role.

If you practice and master the method I'll present to you and still feel you need to improve your language facility, you can do no better for additional review than to borrow or buy *The Elements of Style* by Strunk, White, and Angell. This book is the most concise, lucid, and efficient path to improvement. The key is *if* you feel you need it: Don't assume you do.

The scoring rubric is pretty much as follows. You're graded on:

1. How extensive and sophisticated your analysis/argument is;

2. How well-supported your assertions are;

3. The degree to which your writing is focused and organized;

4. The degree of sentence variety and aptness of word usage.

The emphasis is on your ability to think critically and write clearly, not on perfect grammar and spelling. The writing is a problem only if it gets in the way of the reader's appreciation of your argument.

The scale is 0 to 6 in half-point increments. Scores are determined by how well you achieve the four points above. Of course, you must fully understand and answer the prompt, but that will come automatically when you follow the step-method that's coming right about . . . now.

The One-and-Only Way

Unlike other sections, essays really require that you stick to one method. There's no need to reinvent the wheel here and no need for much experimentation. Trust me on this. Trust me and every English or composition teacher you've had. All I'm setting forth is garden-variety writing advice here. You must break down the writing task into separate sub-tasks; you will **not** simply start writing. That's the analog of having no prediction for a multiple-choice or multiple-response item and just jumping into the nasty, distracting answer choices!

Step 1: Read the prompt carefully.

Step 2: Brainstorm your answer by creating a T-chart.

Step 3: Put your ideas in order with an outline.

Step 4: Then, and only then, write, concentrating on clear diction and syntax.

Step 5: Edit.

Let's discuss these steps a bit. First, you'll want to give a minute or two to step 1. You really do want to make sure you understand the prompt. As you'll see, when you analyze an argument, you'll spend a bit more time on the prompt. Relax; it will all make sense. Second, spend a few minutes brainstorming and outlining. If you have around 20 minutes to write, that's more than enough. Quality, not quantity, is the goal. Finally, don't cut corners by failing to give your essay a quick proofreading! This extra effort could bump you up a half- or even a full point.

Note that by reading the prompt carefully, you ensure avoiding a low score, which is in part given for missing the point of the prompt. Furthermore, by investing the time in brainstorming and outlining, you're isolating the organizational feature of your essay for specific attention. Here's where you'll actually get the bulk of your score—remember, you're graded more on your critical thinking than on your polished writing. Your outline will almost always follow this tried-and-true pattern:

i. Introduction, in which I present the thesis and introduce the main supporting points.

ii. Main supporting point 1, and its support.

iii. Main supporting point 2, and its support.

iv. Main supporting point 3, and its support.

v. Conclusion that wraps it up nicely.

If you have two big supporting points, each of which has rich supporting argumentation, four paragraphs are fine.

When you have the outline, when you actually begin to write, you then have a roadmap to follow when you write. *Now* you can concentrate on varying the syntax and being as clear as you can. Finally, spending a couple of minutes at the end to edit will help bolster your language/clarity "grade." While not the main point, this can indeed gain you, well . . . points. ☺

A final note. If you're used to making something other than an outline—say, a concept map—please continue to do so. Step 3 requires some handy organizational tool: A hierarchical list is fine, but so is a map or flowchart. If you don't usually take this step of organizing your ideas before you start an essay in your real-world writing, I urge you to make an exception when you write your GRE essay and in preparing for it. If you're not the "prewriting" type, I'd at least compose a simple outline because of the importance of organization in the rubric for evaluating a GRE essay. A few minutes spent putting your ideas in order can save a half hour of wheel-spinning when you write the GRE essay. An outline won't hurt your essay, and it's likely to help it. Trust me on this one. OK?

Let's run through the process with an Issue essay—the one you saw on the diagnostic:

> As an increasing portion of humanity connects to the Internet, global harmony will increase.
>
> To what extent do you agree or disagree with the previous statement? Explain your reasoning, and as you develop your argument, consider ways in which the statement may or may not be valid and explain how your position is affected by those considerations.

Step 1: Read the prompt carefully.

Focus on the relationship: as *x* increases, *y* increases. That's really the whole "structure"; the rest is "content." So will *y* go up as *x* goes up? Could *y* go down as *x* goes up? Or perhaps *x* and *y* are really unrelated? Those are the options. To keep it simple, consider these pro–con questions, yes or no. That brings us to. . . .

Step 2: Brainstorm your answer by creating a T-chart.

Place pro arguments on one side, con arguments on the other. Start filling in both sides as things occur to you. You must be free and easy at this here. Don't do any "editing." Let your ideas flow. Your position is whichever side of the chart is longer, "thicker," or just better, that's your position.

Pro	Con
Greater connections and info flow will allow people to learn about each other, break down prejudice	Greater connections and info flow will highlight problems and foment dissent
Immediate connection will increase natural human empathy	Internet gatekeepers will tend to edit, consciously or not, images of the "Other" to pre-existing taste
More information means more knowledge means more widely distributed power	More information means more confusion which means even greater fodder for stubborn irrationalities
A "flattened" hierarchy of knowledge-sharing must inevitably lead to greater democracy, which will lead to greater harmony	A "flattened" hierarchy of knowledge-sharing must lead to anarchy, which will lead to greater disharmony
[and so on . . .]	[and so on . . .]

Note that you could have answered this any way you liked. All prompts are designed in this fashion. The readers don't care *what* position you take, as long as it's well-supported and clearly expressed. They also don't care what kind of support you choose, as long as it's truly supportive. There's no need to stick in a highfalutin reference to Foucault or Einstein. As with $10 vocabulary words, unless they're entirely apt, they'll stick out and hurt your score. Keep it simple; write in an appropriate but authentic voice.

Step 3: Put your ideas in order with an outline.

Here's one outline based on the pro side, which is what we'll run with. Note how we focus on the links in the argument, not the details. Remember, for Issue prompts, you're creating an argument; for Argument prompts, you're analyzing an argument.

Note the mention of counterarguments. They're important to anticipate and deal with reasonably. Doing a T-chart helps anticipate them, of course!

For teaching purposes, this is written "telegraphically" but much more formally than you would do it "for real."

i. Agree: More Internet means more global harmony, b/c:

   1. More Internet = more immediate contact with the "Other" = more empathy.

   2. More Internet = more knowledge; more knowledge = more power (Bacon quote).[1]

   3. Since Internet is a "flat" hierarchy, more Internet = more democracy; more democracy = greater harmony.

ii. More Internet = more immediate contact with the "Other" = more empathy

   1. Harder to "diffuse responsibility" when your actions stare you in the face.

   2. Harder to suppress natural empathy when you "get to know people" via social media sites, blogs, etc.

   3. Internet connectivity is like traveling (w/o moving) which usually broadens perspectives.

iii. More Internet = more knowledge; more knowledge = more power (Bacon quote)

   1. Despite a ton of garbage online, as there always is in any medium (books, oral traditions, etc.), knowledge exists in abundance. With proper education, more knowledge can only be a good thing.

   2. Francis Bacon: "Knowledge is power." True then, true today. Foundation of European modernity. Only other option is letting the Guardians rule, and trusting them to be "nice" and "fair." Bad track record for that.

   3. All democratic theorists agree that an uneducated populace kills democracy.

iv. Since Internet is a "flat" hierarchy, more Internet = more democracy; more democracy = greater harmony

   1. The nature of the free Internet—non-hierarchical, low barrier to entry, etc.—encourages discussion, debate, and peer-to-peer relationships and confidence needed for true democracy. Example of Robin Lane Fox email; others.

---

[1] Which will be apt, not "decorative!" ☺

2. While Internet can be monitored (everywhere, but good e.g. are US and UK, home of civil liberties in many ways), controlled (China, for example) or even shut down (Egypt in January 2011), it's very hard to permanently maintain total closure—truth will out. There's always a technical way 'round.

v. Conclusion: Iranian, Tunisian, Egyptian, et al. revolts all organized via Internet. QED. ☺

Step 4: Then, and only then, write, concentrating on clarity and language.

OK. Here's a good, 5-ish-level essay. Keep in mind that this was spat out as you will spit yours out—in a limited amount of time. Luckily, the GRE isn't a martinet looking to downgrade you for some errors. It's probably longer than yours was or would be because I type fast. That's not necessarily a benefit. This could be cut down a bit more—and I did do the final, important step of editing! But it's probably a 5; maybe a 5.5; *certainly* a 4.5.

The more people who connect to the Internet, the more likely those ramifying interconnections among people will lead to global harmony, though the cause and effect is neither immediate nor simple. First, it's well known that increased contact with the "Other," though not a panacea, does tend to lead to greater understanding, unlocking the natural empathy humans often suppress. Second, the Internet is a vast library, a vast repository of knowledge that must lead to greater awareness, and thence to more informed choices. "Knowledge is power," said Francis Bacon nearly half a millennium ago; he was right then and he's right now. Third, since the Internet is by definition quite "flat"—there is far less of a hierarchy of authority in this free and open medium than in, say, traditional book-or article-publishing—that peer-to-peer structure fosters democratic values. And the more democracy there is—the more people are actually in control of their own destinies—the greater global harmony will be.

Anyone who's seen the prologue to *2001: A Space Odyssey* has to bitterly laugh at how familiar the battle over the water hole between the two tribes of pre-humans is. It's the archetypal us-versus-them situation, in which limited resources lead to overemphasis on tribal affiliations. Had the pre-humans in that film considered themselves all to be members of one tribe, one family, sharing, not fighting, would have ensued. All humans seem to construct Others based on a wide variety of differences, both real and imagined, suppressing the seemingly innate drive toward the Golden Rule—or, natural empathy. It's harder to suppress that natural empathy when you actually get to know, and even see, former Others on a nearly daily basis via social networks, blogs, and the like. Furthermore, while no sane person would pass by a starving child without giving it some food, most quite sane people can easily ignore vaguely understood but not immediately witnessed suffering. That's harder to do when you see live pictures of terrible suffering—again, natural empathy usually trumps tribal feelings. The Internet actually allows anyone with a connection to travel more widely than any person ever has physically travelled. Though no guarantee, of course, usually the more one travels, the more one's perspective and empathy broadens.

But the Internet doesn't just provide opportunity for moral and emotional growth. It also provides a giant "Alexandrian library" of information. Bacon's dictum was spot on—the more knowledge you have, the more power you have. While the negative implication of Bacon's dictum is surely clear—nuclear weapons, anyone?—humans will have to think their way out of their massive predicaments, and that requires knowledge. Yes, there is a ton of garbage online—as there has always been in any medium, from oral traditions to cylinder seals to books. But there is clearly a limitless amount of knowledge available to anyone on Earth with an internet connection and cell phone. With proper education, people can find their way to the wheat while ignoring the chaff. In fact, the only other option is to let some elite Guardian class get all the knowledge and education and then hope that they will use their power justly. This method of human social organization doesn't have the best track record, to say the least. Democracy, direct or representative, is widely agreed to depend crucially on an informed and educated populace. There's no guarantee that having an informed and educated populace will solve all problems—or even save the species. But at least a well-informed, educated populace living in a global democracy can destroy itself through a majority vote, so to speak. One must assume that the more democracy there is, the more harmony there will be.

The educative effects of what one finds online is not the only buttress for democratic development. The precise way in which one interacts with others on the Internet itself supports democratic development. The Internet is a mostly "flat" hierarchy: there's almost no barrier to entry and no real gatekeepers (as of yet in most of the West). This flat hierarchy encourages democratic debate by making everyone a potential peer to everyone else. That builds confidence and erodes needless fears about not being "expert" enough to run one's own life and contribute to the collective running of all our lives—a.k.a., "democracy." For example, I recently read Robin Lane Fox's *Alexander the Great*. I loved it, but had a few questions. I Googled Fox, got an e-mail address, asked my questions, and less than 24 hours later, got a nice and illuminating reply. That's education in action! While the Internet can be monitored, as is currently being done in the US and UK despite a strong tradition of civil liberties in both countries, controlled, as in China and elsewhere, or even shut down, as happened in Egypt in January 2011, it's very hard to maintain total discipline in such a gigantic, complex, and ever-ramifying system. The truth will always out; there's always a way around censorship, sooner or later.

Speaking of Egypt, that revolt, like the one in Tunisia, an earlier one in Iran, was organized and fostered via the Internet. Other forms of media, like satellite television, played a role, but the role of social networking sites both to lay the educative groundwork, increase emotional ties of solidarity among proto-revolutionaries and their international supporters, and organize the minute-by-minute demonstrations, were, regardless of the ultimate outcomes, pure democracy in action. Again, no guarantees ever obtain in human life except death, but it's very hard to see the rise of Internet connectivity among human beings as anything but betokening our last, best hope for global democracy and harmony.

Where's step 5, you ask? Oh, I spent a minute or two editing. So should you!

Guided Practice

OK. It's your turn. We'll use an Argument prompt, and I'll note the slight differences as we work through it together.

> The following is an email from the senior vice president of human resources at National Investment Company (NIC).
>
> "Several recent high-profile studies have shown that salary level is among the weakest predictors of job satisfaction at Fortune 500 companies. Therefore, in the interest of maintaining and improving the productivity of our workforce, NIC should not attempt to outbid other firms for new hires but rather should highlight non-salary benefits of joining the NIC team. Although we may lose some of the more salary-motivated applicants, we will gain loyal, happy, motivated employees."
>
> Write an essay in which you provide specific evidence to strengthen the argument given in the passage above. Make sure to explain how the evidence you provide would support the argument.

We're now analyzing a given argument, not creating one. But it doesn't make a lot of difference. You need to create an argument to analyze an argument. In this case, the specific directions tell you to strengthen only.

Step 1: Read the prompt carefully.

This is the main difference between Issue and Argument essays—you *really* need to parse this prompt word-for-word. Give it a try below. Make a chart. Use bullets. Do whatever works:

I'll write my parsing here at greater length than you would or should on the actual test for teaching purposes only. I'm bolding key terms to be discussed below.

1. **Many** studies show salary level is one of the weakest predictors of job sat. **at F-500**.

    Thus:

2. to **maintain** and **improve productivity**

    NIC shouldn't

3. outbid **other companies**

    but rather should

4. highlight **non-salary bennies**

    By doing so, NIC will

5. lose some salary-motivated employees

    but

6. gain **loyal, happy, well-motivated employees**

Now, whether you were going to strengthen or weaken this argument, you'd first have to identify the missing links. If you're intention is to weaken, you exploit and exacerbate them; if you're intention is to strengthen, you account for and ameliorate them. Either way, you must first identify them.

Step 2: Brainstorm your answer by creating a T-chart.

Line up the key terms or parts of the claim on the left of the T-chart provided on the following page and place strengthenings on the right:

CHAPTER 5
The Analytical Writing Section

Key terms, claims	"Strengthenings"

My version follows. A less elaborate, jotted version of this is just fine for the real thing. This takes time to *read*, and you won't *write* anything so elaborate. However, it takes little time to *think* it up as you scribble down far more incomplete jottings than what follows.

I scribbled this on paper in about three minutes. You can do the same. Trust me.

Missing link	**"Strengthenings"**
Many	Dive in on these quasi-quantifications. If many is good, the vast majority is better! Invent freely—you're strengthening an argument here, not recounting your years of research. Plausible is all that matters. I'm going to say, "the vast majority of meta-analyses of two decades of studies both in the US and abroad."
Fortune 500	Well, NIC better be in that cohort or this is all beside the point. I'll do it one better: NIC is in the Fortune 100, and the higher on that list you go, the more the trend holds.
maintain/improve	Account for both states. Not only will de-emphasis on salary level not reduce *x* (we'll deal with *x* itself in a moment), it will actually raise *x*.
productivity	Note that the argument jumps from salary level being weakly related to **(1) job satisfaction** to lowered salary level leading to increased **(2) productivity**. You have to connect 1 to 2. How about arguing that lots of studies show a very high level of correlation between job satisfaction and productivity. One can't assume anything on AWAs! Make the case!

(continued)

Missing link	"Strengthenings"
other companies	Perhaps we should add that a very high percentage of applicants to NIC are also applicants to other Fortune 500 companies, whereas a low percentage of NIC applicants actually apply to non-Fortune-500 companies. Just to keep the comparison as tight as possible, we'll keep the cohort as monolithic as possible. (Those who end up at F500s may be preadapted to think salary is the lowest driver of job satisfaction. Maybe they "learn" to feel that way once at an F500—but why not strengthen it up?)
non-salary benefits	Be as wide-ranging as possible. Account for the obvious counterargument—don't businesspeople want to make as much dough as possible?—by discussing the pecuniary but non-salary benefits: say, a defined benefit pension plan (we can be somewhat fictional, as long as we're plausible!); a stock-sharing program; excellent medical benefits that are obviously a cost savings (100% lifetime coverage for all, paid for at a high percentage by NIC); health-savings accounts that aren't use-it-or-lose-it; European-style vacation benefits that take advantage of NIC-purchased discounts in airfare, hotels, etc. Just pile up the possibilities, in your head or scribbled on paper.
loyal, happy, and well-motivated employees	Why not refer to studies that show an inverse relationship between salary-motivated employees and loyal, happy, well-motivated employees? Implication: the salary-motivated ones are mercenary. Can't trust them: disloyal.

Missing link	"Strengthenings"
loyal, happy, and well-motivated employees (*continued*)	Invent freely: perhaps the salary-motivated ones have been shown in studies (based on surveys, whatever) to be the most likely to jump from company to company? Perhaps the salary-motivated ones are simply ignorant of what really would make them happy? Like decent benefits, etc., as well as a caring, creative, challenging corporate culture. We emphasized cash-value bennies; but fun has a value, too! As does true freedom in and recognition of one's work; you could bring in the joy-producing benefits of NIC's unusual, organization and suchlike. Finally, define "motivated"—link job satisfaction to productivity through motivation via non-salary bennies.

Step 3: Put your ideas in order with an outline.

OK. Now we need to work a bit of an outline. Here's the good news. The list you made is fine for an outline.

A couple of notes before you dive in: your intro paragraph will always take the form of naming what the key gaps are. Your subsequent paragraphs attack each one, and the best way to organize is to go in order of how they come up in the prompt. Your conclusion is *very* conclusion-y, as you'll see below in the 5-ish essay provided.

Step 4: Then, and only then, write, concentrating on clarity and language.

OK. Go for it! Use the following lined pages to write your sample essay. And don't forget:

Step 5: Edit.

Here's what I came up with—a 5-ish level essay to which you can compare yours:

While it may well be the case that the level of salary is among the weakest predictors of job satisfaction at Fortune 500 companies, it's a bit of a jump from "job satisfaction" to "increased productivity." That is only the most glaring weakness in the presented argument; others will be dealt with as they arise: each weakness will be strengthened in the order in which it arose in the argument.

First, one would like to see a quantification of "many" with reference to the number of studies that found salary level to be not very much related to job satisfaction. Is "many" greater or less than 50 percent of the studies? How many studies are we talking about here, anyway? Is this a particularly well-studied phenomenon? Furthermore, a little more information about the nature of the studies would be helpful, too—one would like to see statistically significant, well-constructed, scientific studies, of course. Were it the case, something like "the vast majority of meta-analyses of two decades of studies both in the US and abroad" would bolster the argument. Also, one should note that NIC is a Fortune 500 company—and one would expect that it is, given the citation of studies of Fortune 500 companies. If NIC is not a Fortune 500 company, one would need to see some argumentation that shows why the studies apply to a non-Fortune-500 company.

Second, and most important, is the jump from job satisfaction to productivity. That's a gaping hole in the argument. How about showing that lots of studies show a very high level of correlation between job satisfaction and productivity? Anything that bridges the gap will very much improve and strengthen the case being made. More specifically, one would like to see first exactly how low salary levels in particular jobs or "business functions" (e.g., program managers in training and learning) can go before job satisfaction is affected, and, further, how job satisfaction correlates to productivity in a similarly segmented manner. Additionally, one would have to show how productivity is not only unaffected negatively by job satisfaction levels but also *improved* by job satisfaction levels, since the interest is in "maintaining and improving" productivity.

Third, assuming that NIC is indeed a Fortune 500 company, it would further bolster the argument to show that the "other companies" against which NIC competes for talent are also largely (or perhaps nearly exclusively?) Fortune 500 companies. That would mean that NIC and its competitors are seeking talent from the very cohort examined in the cited studies, the cohort supposedly less interested in salary level than one might have expected. If it were the case that the studies showed an even lower correlation between salary level and job satisfaction in, say, Fortune

100 companies, then if NIC and most of its competitors for talent were Fortune 100 companies, that would further buttress the argument.

Fourth, another fairly big hole in the argument is the nature of the non-salary benefits. A common-sense objection to the cited studies is that business people want to make as much money as possible. Common sense isn't necessarily correct, but accounting for that counter-argument would strengthen the case. Non-salary benefits can be either pecuniary in some fashion or not. In the first category one might find any of the following (among other possibilities):

- a defined benefit pension plan;

- a stock- or profit-sharing program;

- excellent medical benefits that are obviously a cost savings (e.g., 100% lifetime coverage for all, paid for at a high percentage by NIC);

- health-savings accounts that aren't use-it-or-lose-it per annum;

- European-style vacation benefits that take advantage of NIC-purchased discounts in airfare, hotels

In the second category, especially if NIC is indeed a Fortune 500 (or 100) company, would be the prestige and social capital of employment at a top company. It's also possible that NIC has a "Google-like" corporate culture in which people have fun as they work, are trusted with an unusually high level of autonomy, a real emphasis on collaboration rather than competition among employees, and suchlike.

Which brings us to the last hole in the argument: one would like to see evidence of an inverse relationship between salary-motivated employees and "loyal, happy, and well-motivated" employees. Clear evidence in wide-ranging, accurate studies of the relevant cohort would be helpful; independent studies of the non-pecuniary non-salary category of benefits just described would also bolster the case, especially if it could be shown how NIC provides such an environment. Studies of NIC's employees' loyalty, happiness, motivation, productivity, job satisfaction and so forth, compared to other sufficiently NIC-like corporations, would do the trick.

In conclusion, one is certainly ready to accept the assertions in this argument, even if some are at first glance counterintuitive. However, as in any good argument, hidden assumptions need to be uncovered and dealt with; unnecessary leaps in logic need to be acknowledged and bridged. The given argument features too many gaps over which even sympathetic audience members will stumble.

Again, it's a bit wordy, given my ability to type quickly and despite my doing a quick edit at the end, that all-too-often-skipped step! A few errors, too—especially, to my eye, the nearly mixed metaphor at the end. Can you stumble over a gap on a path—i.e., a hole—as opposed to over an obstacle—i.e., some bulky thing jutting out above the level of the path? But surely a 5, I would think.

Remember you don't have to follow your outline fanatically. The main points should be sacrosanct, but you can tinker with minor points as you write. And bulleted lists are OK, too! They often are helpful on Argument tasks.

You'll have plenty of opportunity to apply your newfound essay-writing-algorithm in the practice tests. If you require more practice, ETS provides a ton of official prompts online. I'll give you the URL if you *promise* me that you won't go nuts and write dozens of essays! That would be over-preparation, and it would detract from your other GRE prep, not to mention the rest of your responsibilities. You want to have a method you can apply to every prompt—and you do. You don't want to waste time working through more than a handful of each. But by all means, do *read* all the prompts! And feel free to sketch out some T-charts and such. Just don't go nuts. OK?

Here are the links:

- *http://www.ets.org/gre/revised_general/prepare/analytical_writing/issue/pool*
- *http://www.ets.org/gre/revised_general/prepare/analytical_writing/argument/pool*

SUMMING UP

Well, you have certainly learned a lot! We've been through all three sections—Verbal Reasoning, Quantitative Reasoning, and Analytical Writing. You've reviewed not only the diagnostic, in large part, but also a ton of verbal and math content. You've learned and practiced a variety of methods, both the "normal," forward way and the reverse-engineering, backward way. You have a lot of tools in your toolbox.

Now it's time to practice some more. Work through the rest of the tests in this book and online. One trick that's helped my GRE students is to make sure never to do any work on the paper-based tests you use for practice. Force yourself to work on scratch paper, even if you're working on paper.

Please note that REA's online diagnostic test is not "section-adaptive." As you learned, section-adaptivity mostly focuses your rough score, but for perfect testlikeness, download the free PowerPrep software from *http://www.ets.org/gre*.

I would save the whole PowerPrep package for last. Not only are the scores as accurate as can be, but also PowerPrep's testing interface is what you'll see on test day. REA's testing engine has all the functionality of the actual testing interface but it will look slightly different. It's not a big deal, but you might as well practice in the real interface!

No matter how long you've been prepping—a few months or a few days—do yourself a big favor and don't study the day before your test. It won't do any good, and could do plenty of harm. You need, above all, to be as sharp as possible for test day. Relax the day before. Don't do anything too stressful.

On that note: get a lot of sleep as you approach your test date! I know, I know: just do it. The more sleep deprived you are, the worse off you'll be.

Be prepared for test day. In fact, go to *http://www.ets.org/gre/general/test_day* and read it! There are a lot of policies and procedures; be familiar and prepared.

Some final motherly doting from me:

- Put all your stuff in your bag so you don't have to scramble.

- If you're not intimately familiar with your testing center, do yourself a favor and drive out there a week before, just so you know where it is, where your room is, what traffic or construction there may be, and so on.

- Eat a good meal!

- Unless the roof caved in or something astronomical happened, do not cancel your scores! By the time you get to the test, you'll have taken so many practice tests, between REA and ETS, that you'll pretty much know what you'll be getting. So, chill!

Now, on to practice.

Paper-and-Pencil Test 1

SECTION 1

Analytical Writing: Analyze an Issue
30 Minutes

You will be given a short statement that presents or implies a general interest issue. Write a response in which you discuss the extent to which you agree or disagree with the statement and explain your reasoning for the position you take. In developing and supporting your position, describe specific circumstances in which the statement would or would not be true and explain how these examples shape your position.

Issue Topic

To improve the United States educational system, school districts should be controlled by a federal governing body that standardizes all curricula, hiring standards, and teacher contracts, with little control by local districts.

SECTION 2

Analytical Writing: Analyze an Argument
30 Minutes

You will be given a short passage that presents an argument. Write a response in which you discuss what specific evidence is needed to evaluate the argument and explain how the evidence would weaken or strengthen the argument.

Argument Topic

The following is a news release from the prime minister of the country of Almafa.

"Recently a group of anti-government activists working for the University of Almafa has claimed that the increase in the number of deaths of lake-dwelling birds is a direct result of corporations emptying sewage into Lake Barshir, and that the government is ultimately responsible for these avian deaths because it has failed to impose restrictions on waste disposal for corporations. This is patently false. Data collected by these activists themselves shows that the lake-dwelling birds go through a five-year cycle of increased births followed by increased deaths, so the increased deaths are a natural part of this cycle. Additionally, corporations have the option not to empty their sewage into Lake Barshir whether regulations forbid it or not."

NO TEST MATERIAL ON THIS PAGE

SECTION 1

Verbal Reasoning

25 Questions

35 Minutes

Questions 1 to 3 are based on the following reading passage.

Although it is viewed today largely as an instrument played for religious ceremonies, the pipe organ has been an enormously popular instrument for centuries, and a variety of secular music has been composed specifically to be played on it. Before the Baroque era, music was composed to be played on any keyboard instrument, whether pipe organ or harpsichord. However, the beginning of the Baroque era began an emphasis on composing for specific instruments. Composers in the Classical era preferred the greater dynamic range of the piano, so composing for the pipe organ waned in popularity. But by the beginning of the nineteenth century, pipe organs came into fashion again and were liberated from their positions in churches and cathedrals. Organ-makers were commissioned to build pipe organs in concert halls and other secular venues, and compositions for orchestra increasingly included parts for pipe organs. By the beginning of the twentieth century, pipe organs became even more firmly secular as accompaniment for movie pictures.

> For the following question, consider each of the choices separately and select all that apply.

1. Which of the following can be inferred from the passage regarding the pipe organ before the Baroque period?

    A Pipe organs were built primarily in churches and cathedrals.
    B The harpsichord and pipe organ did not sound alike.
    C Pipe organs were out of fashion.

2. Select the sentence in the passage in which the author introduces the differences between the pipe organ and the piano.

3. In the context in which it appears, "liberated" most nearly means

    Ⓐ emancipated.
    Ⓑ exhilarated.
    Ⓒ freed.
    Ⓓ popularized.
    Ⓔ disowned.

GO ON TO NEXT PAGE →

> Question 4 is based on the following reading passage.

Conventional wisdom holds that the best way to burn fat is to do aerobic (cardio) exercises at a consistent rate of intensity for an hour a day. **However, new research shows that shorter workouts of varied intensity could burn far more fat than longer, slower workouts can.** This research shows that forcing the heart to work at a high rate of intensity in short bursts followed by periods of recovery strengthens the heart and stimulates the body's metabolism. Increased metabolism results in a higher resting rate of caloric burn and increased fat loss.

4. In the passage above, the portion in boldface plays which of the following roles?

   (A) It introduces an idea that is consistent with the introductory sentence of the passage.
   (B) It introduces an idea that contradicts the introductory sentence of the passage.
   (C) It provides evidence that supports the thesis in the introductory sentence of the passage.
   (D) It asks a critical question that has not been asked before.
   (E) It confirms an opinion previously expressed by the author.

> For Questions 5 to 8, select one entry for each blank from the corresponding column of choices. Fill all blanks in the way that best completes the text.

5. Although inherently (i) _____ about the whims of her audience, Sarah Bernhardt professed to care little what others thought of her, creating a public image of a(n) (ii) _____ woman.

Blank (i)
(A) unconcerned
(B) adroit
(C) instinctual

Blank (ii)
(D) unconstrained
(E) craven
(F) aloof

6. In her seminal novel *A Room of One's Own*, Virginia Woolf posited the radical notion that women craved _____ of thought and were not satisfied only with work toward a familial or communal goal.

   (A) rigor
   (B) discipline
   (C) autonomy
   (D) radicalism
   (E) novelty

7. In many parts of the United States, different strains of cuisine have become so (i)_____ that it is difficult to ascertain which portions are (ii)_____ to the region.

Blank (i)	Blank (ii)
Ⓐ homogenized	Ⓓ analogous
Ⓑ hybridized	Ⓔ irrelevant
Ⓒ robust	Ⓕ native

8. The naturalistic beauty of a blooming flower may look random, but the petals grow and open in a(n) _____ spiral preordained by the genetic code of the flower's particular species.

Ⓐ candid
Ⓑ voluptuous
Ⓒ stigmatized
Ⓓ assorted
Ⓔ ordered

Questions 9 to 12 are based on the following reading passage.

It has been posited that Chinese immigrants to the United States separated themselves and refused to assimilate into the larger American society out of loyalty to their home country and contempt for their new country. However, the lack of assimilation of Chinese immigrants to the United States in the nineteenth and early twentieth centuries had little to do with the desires of the immigrants themselves. Men came over to work in the mining and railroad industries, but American whites saw them as a "yellow peril" and decried them as "cheap Chinese labor." The same groups who protested their presence in the country were able to deny them naturalization or citizenship, so they had no rights under the Constitution. Eventually, public outcry from political and labor organizations led to the passage, in 1882, of the Chinese Exclusion Act, which prevented new immigrants from entering the United States from China for 10 years.

Because of the Chinese Exclusion Act, men who had come to the United States with the intention of working for several years and then bringing their families over from China to live with them were unable to bring over their wives and children for an entire decade. Not only did this strain their marriages and family ties severely, but it also prevented them from enjoying family life in the United States. Single Chinese men could not bring over Chinese women to marry, nor were they allowed to marry white American women because of miscegenation laws. They were alone and isolated, a group with no rights or voice in the country they lived and worked in.

A combination of exclusion from public life and exclusion from family life propelled these Chinese immigrants to band together for mutual support, and by the beginning of the twentieth century the majority of the Chinese-American population lived in Chinatowns in major urban areas. They had their own banks, grocery stores, and other services necessary to function in society. Because they were so concentrated and isolated, they were able to live traditional Chinese lives even though they were not in China. In essence, they were a completely separate society from larger American culture, not by choice but because they had no other alternative.

9. The primary purpose of the passage is to

   (A) question the prevailing opinion about the reasons for Chinese immigration to the United States before the passage of the Chinese Exclusion Act.

   (B) compare the groups of immigrants to the United States from China that arrived before the passage of the Chinese Exclusion Act with those who arrived after the Chinese Exclusion Act was passed.

   (C) discuss ways in which Chinese immigrants to the United States could have assimilated into the larger culture if they had been interested in assimilating.

   (D) manage expectations of Chinese nationals who are interested in immigrating to the United States and are concerned about assimilating.

   (E) explain how an idea about the reasons Chinese immigrants did not assimilate into the larger American culture in the late nineteenth century is not the correct perception of their motivations for not assimilating.

> For the following question, consider each of the choices separately and select all that apply.

10. The passage implies that single Chinese men who had immigrated to the United States before the Chinese Exclusion Act was passed in 1882 probably did which of the following?

    [A] Stayed single rather than marry African-American women or other ethnic minorities
    [B] Started their own businesses in rural areas
    [C] Were able to find work in large cities

11. Select the sentence in the passage that explains how it was possible logistically for Chinese immigrants to function as a separate society from the larger American society.

> For the following question, consider each of the choices separately and select all that apply.

12. It can be inferred from the passage that, compared to other groups of immigrants, Chinese immigrants who arrived in the United States in the nineteenth and early twentieth centuries were which of the following?

    A They were more skilled than other immigrant groups were.
    B They were more easily identified visually as immigrants than other groups were.
    C They were more apt to strike out into professions that were not typical of their immigrant group than other immigrants were.

Question 13 is based on the following reading passage.

The expanding popularity of the Internet has resulted in an ever-increasing number of retail websites from which consumers can purchase goods of all types and origins, including many products a given consumer would never have had access to purchase before the Internet existed. Paradoxically, the plethora of choices of both products to purchase and websites to purchase from leaves some consumers confused and unable to buy anything, a dilemma called "option paralysis."

13. Which of the following best summarizes the problem described in the passage above?

    Ⓐ The Internet has made it possible for consumers who are paralyzed and cannot shop in physical stores to purchase products.
    Ⓑ The increased choices offered by the Internet can confuse some shoppers so that they are unable to choose what to purchase.
    Ⓒ A paradox has created an abundance of products from which consumers can choose to purchase on the Internet.
    Ⓓ Because the Internet is everywhere, consumers are now exposed to products which would not have been available to them before and which they will not purchase.
    Ⓔ Internet shopping has expanded so that consumers now have access to a wider variety of products than ever before.

GO ON TO NEXT PAGE →

For Questions 14 to 17, select one entry for each blank from the corresponding column of choices. Fill all blanks in the way that best completes the text.

14. The lack of progress in converting more members of the executive committee was bewildering to the chair of the committee, who did not understand that humans are often as _____ by emotional reasons as they are by mere facts.

    (A) confused
    (B) detracted
    (C) influenced
    (D) competitive
    (E) insured

15. Without intending to, the alderman alienated a segment of his constituency by talking _____ about the results of the project that had been promoted and backed by those constituents.

    (A) astutely
    (B) mechanically
    (C) plaintively
    (D) ritualistically
    (E) derisively

16. The cartoonist's (i)_____, expressed through imprecise shading and open facial expressions on the characters, was the trademark of a style that disguised (ii) _____ social justice and political consciousness.

Blank (i)	Blank (ii)
(A) artistic discipline	(D) an aversion to
(B) carefree ease	(E) an indifference to
(C) glib manipulation	(F) a deep commitment to

17. Among the challenges of navigating an employment system that privileges experience over talent is the (i) _____ of getting a job in the first place. Without an extensive employment history, it is virtually impossible to get a foot in the door of the organization, but how can an applicant begin to accrue (ii) _____ without being able to win a first job? This trap (iii) _____ many talented individuals who would love to enter the field but can't find an opening, so they give up and choose a different career.

Blank (i)	Blank (ii)	Blank (iii)
Ⓐ conundrum	Ⓓ a record of employment	Ⓖ spurs
Ⓑ clarity	Ⓔ the correct skills	Ⓗ anticipates
Ⓒ redaction	Ⓕ a natural affinity	Ⓘ thwarts

Questions 18 to 20 are based on the following reading passage.

Although the activity has existed for many years, geocaching has grown in popularity since the advent of inexpensive GPS (Global Positioning Systems), which allow more people—even families with young children—to participate. Whereas once it was known as "letterboxing," and required the laborious use of compasses and maps to locate small wood boxes in obscure places, the GPS now allows for a more streamlined adventure. A typical cache is a small, waterproof container stashed in a remote location, along with a logbook which is signed by each of the cache's finders. Geocaches are found in over 100 countries and all seven continents, providing reassurance that the globe still holds some secrets, even if they have been wrought by humans. Geocaching allows all participants to be Columbus, Cornado, or Magellan, if only for a few hours.

Select only one answer choice:

18. This passage chiefly addresses which of the following ideas about the appeal of geocaching?

Ⓐ How it is tied to a growing sense of globalism
Ⓑ How it provides a sense of adventure with the aid of technology
Ⓒ That it is an inexpensive activity for children in an age of cheap technology
Ⓓ That it satisfies the basic human desire to complete tasks and gain accomplishments
Ⓔ As it is not a recent appearance in human culture, it provides a sense of continuing a tradition

> **Consider each of the three choices separately and select all that apply:**

19. The passage suggests that being a successful geocacher requires

    A an innate sense of adventure.
    B an ability to traverse terrain not accessible by vehicle.
    C funds to purchase a variety of technological instruments.

20. Select the sentence that most clearly indicates the part of the culture of geocaching that involves a sense of discovery.

> **Select the two answer choices that, when used to complete the sentence, fit the meaning of the sentence as a whole and produce completed sentences that are alike in meaning.**

21. Although the applicants were concerned because the assessment was _____ in its scope, they ultimately found support for continuance of their project from the assessor.

    A oblique
    B resolute
    C exigent
    D stringent
    E convert
    F mitigated

22. Julia Child's extensive contributions to the codification and popularity of French cooking techniques _____ her culinary beginnings, as she was raised by a mother who did not cook well.

    A assumed
    B belied
    C engaged
    D contradicted
    E surmised
    F renewed

23. The process of developing a standard code of conduct for stem cell researchers has been delayed because instead of focusing on purely ethical issues, policymakers have been forced to address _____ concerns first.

- [A] concrete
- [B] hypothetical
- [C] theoretical
- [D] economic
- [E] moral
- [F] fiduciary

24. At the opening of her solo show, the artist displayed photographs featuring her award-winning _____ with light and shadow.

- [A] proficiency
- [B] insensitivity
- [C] unfamiliarity
- [D] difference
- [E] alliance
- [F] adeptness

25. After years of collecting data in frigid swamps and murky bogs to push forward their study, the research team was _____ the increased funding to expand the project to another county.

- [A] exhausted by
- [B] intrigued by
- [C] curious about
- [D] alert to
- [E] overjoyed at
- [F] excited for

STOP. This is the end of Verbal Reasoning Section 1.

NO TEST MATERIAL ON THIS PAGE

SECTION 2

Verbal Reasoning

25 Questions

35 Minutes

For Questions 1 to 4, select the two answer choices that when used to complete the sentence, fit the meaning of the sentence as a whole and produce completed sentences that are alike in meaning.

1. With the departure of the long-time artistic director, the theater company was _____ able to alter the downward trend of ticket sales by attracting new audience members.

   A momentarily
   B finally
   C concisely
   D ultimately
   E frankly
   F succinctly

2. Although the institute was famous for producing creative risk-takers, it was precisely the _____ of the program that allowed students to achieve the mastery of their field necessary to be able to experiment.

   A mediation
   B complicity
   C regularity
   D arbitration
   E manifestation
   F uniformity

3. At the press conference, the mayor's aide read a statement to the media that was so _____ that the reporters could barely follow along and were not sure what the mayor's position on the issue was.

   A pithy
   B abstract
   C germane
   D unstructured
   E regular
   F complicit

GO ON TO NEXT PAGE →

4. Never perturbed, the bus driver took the lesser peccadilloes of traffic as a necessary but _____ feature of the job.

A unwelcome
B grievous
C blatant
D pleasant
E dangerous
F disagreeable

Questions 5 and 6 are based on the following reading passage.

"Sleep apnea" actually refers to any of three forms of a breathing disorder characterized by abnormally low breathing, or pauses in breathing, during sleep. The three forms—obstructive sleep apnea (OSA), central sleep apnea (CSA), and mixed sleep apnea—are all diagnosed with a "sleep study," in which the subject spends the night in a laboratory. During the sleep study, the subject is hooked up to sensors to track breathing, heart rate, and other physiological changes. Once the subject is equipped, he or she performs a normal nightly routine and goes to sleep in the bed in the laboratory. Researchers track breathing changes throughout the night as the subject sleeps to discover if the subject has breathing problems because of obstructions in the nasal passage or because of low respiratory effort.

For the following question, consider each of the choices separately and select all that apply.

5. It can be inferred from the passage that which one of the following statements is true about sleep apnea?

A Sleep apnea cannot be treated without surgery.
B Researchers studying sleep apnea have knowledge of respiratory science.
C Sleep apnea may be caused by more than one health issue.

6. It can be inferred that the author of the passage mentions "low respiratory effort" primarily in order to

Ⓐ mention a reason, aside from blockage, that could cause sleep apnea.
Ⓑ explain who sleep apnea affects.
Ⓒ discuss one of three types of sleep apnea.
Ⓓ indicate the difference between pauses in breathing and low breathing.
Ⓔ question why a subject needs to be monitored so closely.

The rat problem in Harborville is increasing. Over the last 18 months, researchers estimate that the population of wild rats has increased by 40 percent. City officials are convinced that the rodenticide the city sprays once a month has become ineffective, but an outside group claims that cuts in city garbage pickup is providing more food for the rats, and that this is the cause of the increase in population.

7. Which of the following, if true, most strengthens the argument of the outside group?

   (A) The rodenticide is being manufactured by a different company now than it was two years ago.
   (B) The rat population is up higher in neighborhoods that have had deeper cuts in garbage pickup, and the rat population is not up as high in neighborhoods that have maintained frequent garbage pickup.
   (C) The rat population is up more in the downtown area of Harborville than in residential neighborhoods.
   (D) Rodenticide is not used in Harborville's closest neighboring town.
   (E) Garbage pickup occurs less frequently since the cuts, but occurs at regular intervals during the week.

Questions 8 and 9 are based on the following reading passage.

"Manifest destiny" refers to various beliefs held by some, essentially stating that the United States of America was destined to expand from the Atlantic Ocean to the Pacific Ocean. Specifically, the term meant that Anglo-Saxon America needed to control the continent. The general logic behind manifest destiny was that Anglo-Saxon America meant progress and modernity, and that progress was necessary against the savage societies of the Native Americans and Mexicans who inhabited what are now the Western states. As such, it was used by some to justify the Mexican-American War (1846–1848), which ultimately forced Mexico to sell the northern parts of its country to the United States. Manifest destiny fell out of favor, and was largely discredited in the second half of the nineteenth century.

For the following question, consider each of the choices separately and select all that apply.

8. Which of the following statements about manifest destiny can be inferred from the passage?

   [A] Manifest destiny, for some, included an element of racism.
   [B] Manifest destiny ended only when the United States gained all the territory proponents of the belief wanted.
   [C] Manifest destiny was not favored by everyone in the United States.

9. Select the sentence that describes a practical result of the belief described in the passage.

> For Questions 10 to 13, select one entry for each blank from the corresponding column of choices. Fill all the blanks in the way that best completes the text.

10. Appropriately, the councilwoman who headed the oversight committee with such (i) _____ was equally (ii) _____ about her own personal finances, doing an in-depth review of all accounts and expenditures every month.

Blank (i)
Ⓐ robustness
Ⓑ lassitude
Ⓒ pedantry

Blank (ii)
Ⓓ vigilant
Ⓔ profligate
Ⓕ mendacious

11. Although the Minority Leader found the personal views of the Majority Whip to be (i) _____, she was able to work with the Whip and the rest of the Majority leadership to craft a bill that both sides could (ii) _____. While neither side could (iii) _____, passing the bill allowed both sides to take credit for bipartisan leadership and "getting past our differences" for the good of the constituency.

Blank (i)
Ⓐ sensible
Ⓑ reprehensible
Ⓒ well-worn

Blank (ii)
Ⓓ support
Ⓔ oppose
Ⓕ commingle

Blank (iii)
Ⓖ plead ignorance
Ⓗ claim victory
Ⓘ give clemency

12. While the astronomer's ideas about the temperature of the planet Mercury were widely accepted, the committee debated over whether to _____ her theory of gravitational change or to reject it.

Ⓐ stalk
Ⓑ edify
Ⓒ resolve
Ⓓ refute
Ⓔ adopt

13. Adjustments to the train schedule left commuters bewildered and angry, and as more passengers were left stranded on the platform the collective level of _____ rose quickly.

    (A) foreboding
    (B) ire
    (C) passiveness
    (D) alacrity
    (E) velocity

Questions 14 to 16 are based on the following reading passage.

When Gloria Munson started as a union organizer in 1962, she never expected it to become her career and the passion of her life. At the time, she was merely pitching in with her secretarial skills to the cause of workers' rights, not thinking long term about what she would be gaining and losing. But over the years, as she continued to choose organizing over other careers, over her marriage, and over family life, it became apparent that this was Munson's calling. In hindsight, perhaps she would have been more hesitant to jump into this life had she known how all-consuming it would be.

14. Which of the following can be inferred from the passage about Gloria Munson?

    (A) Gloria Munson organized unions for different industries throughout her long career.
    (B) Gloria Munson went to secretarial school so that she could become a secretary for the union.
    (C) Gloria Munson had a personal life that did not include a family or a stable marriage.
    (D) Gloria Munson did not look back on her career until she was almost through with it.
    (E) Gloria Munson asked herself if she should work as a union organizer before she took her first job with the union.

15. In the second sentence ("At the time ... losing."), the author of the passage is most likely suggesting that

    (A) choosing a family life is more important than having a long career.
    (B) unions were not active in their present state in 1962.
    (C) Munson knew what she was doing when she took the first job organizing a union in 1962.
    (D) it is better to have a sense of perspective and planning when one embarks upon a new career.
    (E) Munson was not fully aware of what taking her first job with the union could lead to.

GO ON TO NEXT PAGE →

16. Which of the following best describes the main idea of the passage?

   A) Unions needed organizers in the 1960s who were willing to dedicate their lives to the cause.
   B) Women were able to create satisfying careers with unions as early as the 1960s.
   C) Gloria Munson and her family dedicated their lives to organizing for unions.
   D) Gloria Munson did not realize how extensive and absorbing her union organizing career would be when she began it.
   E) Gloria Munson was a secretary for a union who never had a family.

For Questions 17 to 20, select one entry for each blank from the corresponding column of choices. Fill all the blanks in the way that best completes the text.

17. As long as we have music, no language barriers, whether deliberate or accidental, can prevent children from sharing _____.

   A) a forgotten dream
   B) a common emotion
   C) a new word
   D) an official goal
   E) an ancient discovery

18. The relationship between funding available to the schools from local taxes and enrichment offered to students by the schools has always been (i) _____. Although it might seem that money coming in should equal money going out, the reality has not always been so (ii) _____.

Blank (i)	Blank (ii)
A) complex	D) comprehensible
B) simple	E) direct
C) costly	F) prepared

19. I find the music of Manhoff and Tweedy to be surprisingly (i) _____ for the genre. In a field crowded by strong beats and aggressive, almost dehumanized bass lines, they have created an almost (ii) _____ experience for the listener.

Blank (i)	Blank (ii)
(A) austere	(D) energetic
(B) subtle	(E) puzzling
(C) wan	(F) ephemeral

20. When going into a negotiation, it is important to prepare (i) _____. Without properly projecting all contingencies and outcomes of the exchange, it is too easy to be lured into a false sense of confidence and to overlook (ii) _____ details that could (iii) _____ affect the case.

Blank (i)	Blank (ii)	Blank (iii)
(A) quietly	(D) cognizant	(G) barely
(B) harmoniously	(E) vital	(H) adversely
(C) adequately	(F) existing	(I) judiciously

For Questions 21 to 25, select one answer choice unless otherwise instructed.

Although they have branded themselves as "the Twin Islands," Marshalle and Bartiki are wildly different from each other. The government of Marshalle has outlawed development on the beaches of the island except in a designated hotel and restaurant area, so the beaches are protected lands, open to the public for "non-disruptive" activities such as sunbathing and kayaking. In contrast, Bartiki is almost completely developed and is a party island, attracting students on vacation from all over the world. They spend more per visit than visitors to Marshalle do, although the Marshalle vacationers tend to have higher incomes than the Bartiki vacationers. This has caused an increase both in population and in annual income for the residents of Bartiki, who work primarily in tourism.

21. According to the passage, visitors to Bartiki have a higher rate of which of the following than visitors to Marshalle do?

   (A) Income
   (B) Spending
   (C) Education
   (D) Vacation length
   (E) Kayaking

GO ON TO NEXT PAGE →

Because of the growth of the Internet, it is now possible for a designer to create a new font or typeface, publish it instantaneously to the whole world, and sell it to any Internet users with a credit card. This capability has resulted in an explosion of available fonts in the last 15 years. The vast majority of computer users, however, even the ones engaged in publishing, _____.

22. Which of the following most logically completes the passage?

    Ⓐ continue to use the 30 or so fonts available in most word processing programs
    Ⓑ design their own fonts but never sell them to anyone else
    Ⓒ prefer a sans serif font because they are easier to read than are serif fonts
    Ⓓ are extremely particular about the fonts they use, having come from design backgrounds
    Ⓔ ask an art director to choose the fonts they use in their publications and documents

Questions 23 to 25 are based on the following reading passage.

Scientists who study the migratory patterns of birds are waiting to see what the effects of global climate change will be on birds' migratory patterns. One camp feels that the birds can't help but to change patterns as the temperatures and weather patterns around the world change. Another camp feels that the birds' patterns may not change, because while temperatures are changing, the times of year at which the seasons change has not been significantly altered. Summers may be hotter, and winters may have more storms and more precipitation, but the weeks during the year in which the seasons change have largely remained the same. Still another camp feels that temperatures will affect actual migration times little, if at all, but that the biggest effect of climate change on birds will be changes in their food supply. It may be decades before the effects begin to form a pattern solid enough to discover which of the camps has made the correct prediction.

For the following question, consider each of the choices separately and select all that apply.

23. The passage indicates that researchers who study birds would likely agree with which of the following statements about the migration of birds?

    A Bird migration is exactly the same now as it was decades ago.
    B As the global climate changes, patterns of bird migration will inevitably change.
    C The possible effects of global climate change on bird migration patterns hasn't been established yet.

24. Select the sentence that discusses an effect of global climate change that does not directly affect birds' migratory times.

25. In the passage, the author is primarily concerned with

- Ⓐ summarizing a hypothesis.
- Ⓑ advancing one point of view.
- Ⓒ asking an easy question.
- Ⓓ discussing three theories.
- Ⓔ analyzing evidence.

STOP. This is the end of Verbal Reasoning Section 2.

NO TEST MATERIAL ON THIS PAGE

SECTION 1

Quantitative Reasoning

1.

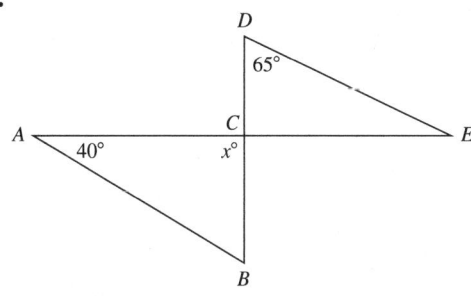

$\overline{AB}$ is parallel to $\overline{DE}$.

Quantity A	**Quantity B**
x	90

Ⓐ Quantity A is greater.
Ⓑ Quantity B is greater.
Ⓒ The two quantities are equal.
Ⓓ The relationship cannot be determined from the information given.

2. $0 < y < x < 12$

Quantity A	**Quantity B**
$x - y$	$\dfrac{1}{x} - \dfrac{1}{y}$

Ⓐ Quantity A is greater.
Ⓑ Quantity B is greater.
Ⓒ The two quantities are equal.
Ⓓ The relationship cannot be determined from the information given.

GO ON TO NEXT PAGE →

3. *x* is an even integer.
   y is an odd integer.

Quantity A	**Quantity B**
The probability that $(x + y)^2$ is odd	The probability that $x^2 + y^2$ is odd

- Ⓐ Quantity A is greater.
- Ⓑ Quantity B is greater.
- Ⓒ The two quantities are equal.
- Ⓓ The relationship cannot be determined from the information given.

4. $x = \dfrac{1}{3}$

Quantity A	**Quantity B**
$\dfrac{1}{x - \dfrac{1}{x - \dfrac{1}{x}}}$	1

- Ⓐ Quantity A is greater.
- Ⓑ Quantity B is greater.
- Ⓒ The two quantities are equal.
- Ⓓ The relationship cannot be determined from the information given.

5.

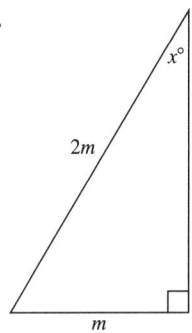

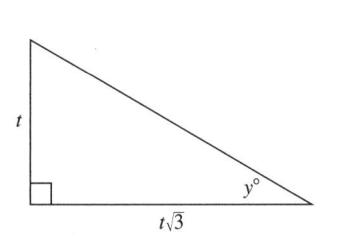

Quantity A	Quantity B
x	y

(A) Quantity A is greater.
(B) Quantity B is greater.
(C) The two quantities are equal.
(D) The relationship cannot be determined from the information given.

Quantity A	Quantity B
6. $2^{111} + 2^{111} + 2^{112} + 2^{113} + 2^{114}$	2^{115}

(A) Quantity A is greater.
(B) Quantity B is greater.
(C) The two quantities are equal.
(D) The relationship cannot be determined from the information given.

7. $m > 3$

Quantity A	Quantity B
The number of minutes in $3m + 1$ hours	The number of hours in $7m + 4$ days

(A) Quantity A is greater.
(B) Quantity B is greater.
(C) The two quantities are equal.
(D) The relationship cannot be determined from the information given.

GO ON TO NEXT PAGE →

8. $3x + y = 9$
   $3y + x = 7$

Quantity A	Quantity B
$2x + 2y$	10

   - Ⓐ Quantity A is greater.
   - Ⓑ Quantity B is greater.
   - Ⓒ The two quantities are equal.
   - Ⓓ The relationship cannot be determined from the information given.

9. Thirty percent of the students at Smalltown University attend the first football game. Sixty percent of those attending are male, the remaining ninety people attending are female.

Quantity A	Quantity B
The student population of Smalltown University	800

   - Ⓐ Quantity A is greater.
   - Ⓑ Quantity B is greater.
   - Ⓒ The two quantities are equal.
   - Ⓓ The relationship cannot be determined from the information given.

Each of questions 10 through 25 has one of four different formats:

- If the question is followed by answer choices A through E, each enclosed in a circle, then there is only one correct answer.

- If the question is followed by a number of answer choices, each enclosed in a box, then there is at least one correct answer.

- If the question is followed by a single box, then you must enter a numerical answer. This answer may be either integer or decimal. It may also be negative. Do not enter a fraction.

- If the question is followed by two boxes in the form of a fraction, then you must enter a fraction for the answer. You must enter an integer in each box. If the answer is negative, you may enter the negative sign in either box.

QUANTITATIVE REASONING | 203
Section 1

For the following question, enter your answer in the boxes.

10. $a_1, a_2, a_3, a_4, \ldots a_n, \ldots$

In the sequence above, each term is defined by $a_n = \dfrac{1}{2^n}$ for each integer value of n, $n \geq 1$. What is the sum of the first six terms of the sequence?

Give your answer as a fraction.

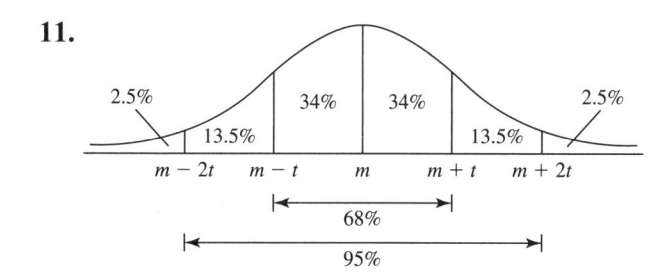

$$\text{Sum} = \frac{\boxed{}}{\boxed{}}$$

11.

The mean of a normally distributed set of data is 60 and the standard deviation is 4. Within which one of the following intervals do approximately 95 percent of the data lie?

Ⓐ 60–64
Ⓑ 56–64
Ⓒ 56–58
Ⓓ 52–68
Ⓔ 48–72

GO ON TO NEXT PAGE→

12. If $\left(\dfrac{\frac{1}{2^{-8}}}{\frac{1}{8^{-4}}}\right)^{-1} = 4^x$, what is the value of x?

(A) −3
(B) −2
(C) −1
(D) 2
(E) 3

13. In the xy-coordinate plane, the coordinates of the vertices of $\triangle NJL$ are $N(-2, 2)$, $J(5, 2)$, and $L(7, 5)$. What is the area of $\triangle NJL$?

(A) 7.5
(B) 10.5
(C) 12.5
(D) 20
(E) 21

14. A 10-sided polygon has how many distinct diagonals?

(A) 32
(B) 33
(C) 34
(D) 35
(E) 36

15.

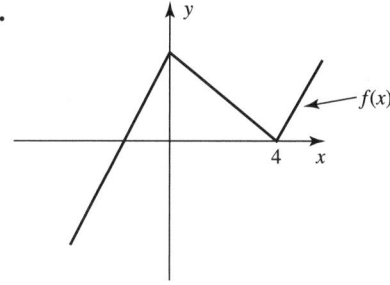

In the standard xy-coordinate plane, the graph above displays the function f. Which one of the following graphs represents f(x − 2)?

A

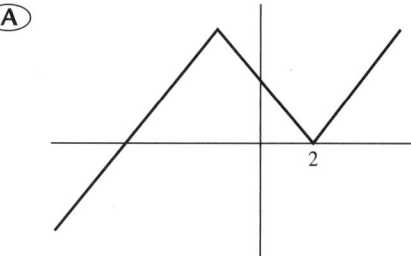

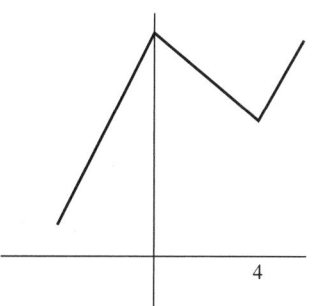

B

C

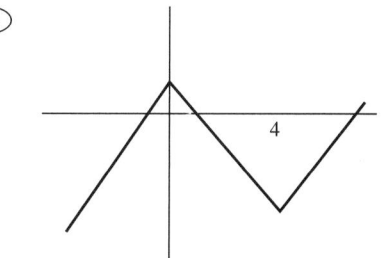

D

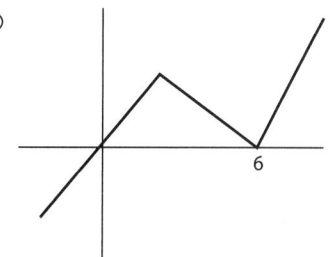

E

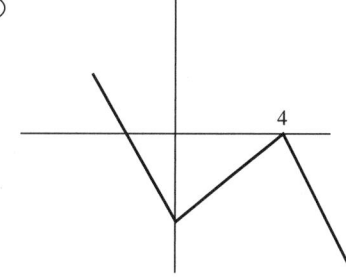

For the following question, select all the answer choices that apply.

16. A taxi in Normville charges $2 for the first $\frac{1}{4}$ mile and $0.50 for each additional $\frac{1}{4}$ mile or part thereof. Josh paid a fare of $4, not including tip. Which amount could represent the distance Josh traveled in the taxi?

Indicate <u>all</u> such distances.

- [A] 1 mile
- [B] 1.1 miles
- [C] 1.2 miles
- [D] 1.3 miles
- [E] 1.4 miles

Questions 17 to 20 are based on the following data.

For city *x*, marital status of the population age 65 and over, by age group and sex, 2004

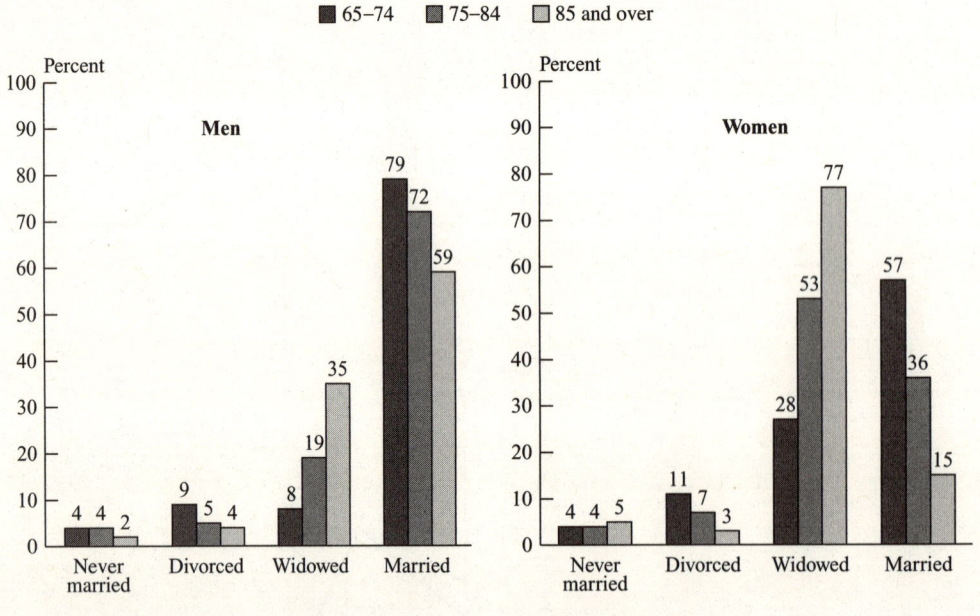

Legend: ■ 65–74   ■ 75–84   □ 85 and over

Men (Percent)

Category	65–74	75–84	85 and over
Never married	4	4	2
Divorced	9	5	4
Widowed	8	19	35
Married	79	72	59

Women (Percent)

Category	65–74	75–84	85 and over
Never married	4	4	5
Divorced	11	7	3
Widowed	28	53	77
Married	57	36	15

Source: U.S. Census Bureau, Current Population Survey, Annual Social and Economic Supplement.

For city *x*, Percent of Total Population by Age Group and Gender, 2004

Age Group	Men	Women
85 and older	$\frac{1}{2}$%	$1\frac{1}{2}$%
75–84	6%	9%
65–74	15%	18%
Below 65	25%	25%

Total population of city *x* in 2004 is 200,000.

17. For city *x* in 2004, how many more men than women are between ages 75–84 and married?

[   ] men

18. If the population in 2005 for city *x* increased to 220,000 and all the percents in the data remained the same, what was the increase in widowed men age 85 and over?

- Ⓐ 30
- Ⓑ 35
- Ⓒ 40
- Ⓓ 45
- Ⓔ 50

19. For city *x* in 2004, what is the total amount of people never married and ages 65–74?

- Ⓐ 2,380
- Ⓑ 2,480
- Ⓒ 2,540
- Ⓓ 2,640
- Ⓔ 2,740

20. For city *x* in 2004, if a person is chosen at random, what is the probability that the person is male or below age 65?

- Ⓐ 25 percent
- Ⓑ 38.7 percent
- Ⓒ 71.5 percent
- Ⓓ 74.2 percent
- Ⓔ 77.9 percent

GO ON TO NEXT PAGE →

21. If 3 plus x percent of 3 is equal to 6 plus y percent of 6, express x in terms of y.

- (A) $y + 50$
- (B) $y + 100$
- (C) $2y + 50$
- (D) $2y + 100$
- (E) $2y$

For the following question, select all the answer choices that apply.

---

22. Given the line $2x + 3y = 9$, which of the following MUST be true?

Select all that apply.

- [A] The slope of the line is $-\frac{2}{3}$.
- [B] The y-intercept of the line is $\frac{9}{2}$.
- [C] The line $y = -\frac{2}{3}x + 6$ is parallel to the given line.
- [D] The line $2x = 8 - 3y$ is parallel to the given line.

23. If $\dfrac{(24!)(22!)}{(23!)(21!)} = n(n-2)$, what is the positive value of n?

- (A) 24
- (B) 23
- (C) 22
- (D) 21
- (E) 20

For the following question, enter your answer in the box.

---

24. Three flowers are randomly selected from a vase containing four pink flowers, three yellow flowers, and five white flowers. In how many ways is it possible to select three flowers of the same color?

☐ possibilities

25. If, $y = \dfrac{x+1}{x-1}$ express x in terms of y. ($x \neq 1$)

Ⓐ $\dfrac{y+1}{y-1}$

Ⓑ $\dfrac{y-1}{y+1}$

Ⓒ $\dfrac{y+1}{1-y}$

Ⓓ $\dfrac{1-y}{1+y}$

Ⓔ $1 + \dfrac{1}{y}$

STOP. This is the end of Quantitative Reasoning Section 1.

NO TEST MATERIAL ON THIS PAGE

SECTION 2

Quantitative Reasoning

Quantity A

1. The area of a non-rectangular parallelogram with adjacent sides of 10 and 8

Quantity B

The area of a rectangle with sides of 4 and 20.

Ⓐ Quantity A is greater.
Ⓑ Quantity B is greater.
Ⓒ The two quantities are equal.
Ⓓ The relationship cannot be determined from the information given.

2. $\frac{1}{2} < x < 1$

$\frac{1}{2} < y < 1$

Quantity A

xy

Quantity B

$x + y$

Ⓐ Quantity A is greater.
Ⓑ Quantity B is greater.
Ⓒ The two quantities are equal.
Ⓓ The relationship cannot be determined from the information given.

Quantity A

3. $8^{40} + 27^{40}$

Quantity B

$4^{60} + 9^{60}$

Ⓐ Quantity A is greater.
Ⓑ Quantity B is greater.
Ⓒ The two quantities are equal.
Ⓓ The relationship cannot be determined from the information given.

GO ON TO NEXT PAGE →

4. In the standard xy-coordinate plane, let the point (a, b) represent the coordinates where the graphs of $y = 2x + 1$ and $y = -x + 4$ intersect.

Quantity A	Quantity B
a	b

Ⓐ Quantity A is greater.
Ⓑ Quantity B is greater.
Ⓒ The two quantities are equal.
Ⓓ The relationship cannot be determined from the information given.

5. n is a prime number greater than 2

Quantity A	Quantity B
The number of distinct positive factors of $49n^2$	7

Ⓐ Quantity A is greater.
Ⓑ Quantity B is greater.
Ⓒ The two quantities are equal.
Ⓓ The relationship cannot be determined from the information given.

6. All lines intersect at right angles

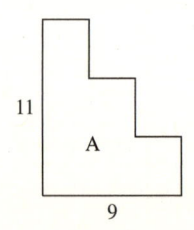

Note: Figures not drawn to scale.

Quantity A	Quantity B
The perimeter of figure A	The perimeter of figure B

Ⓐ Quantity A is greater.
Ⓑ Quantity B is greater.
Ⓒ The two quantities are equal.
Ⓓ The relationship cannot be determined from the information given.

7. $x, y \neq 0, x \neq y$

Quantity A　　　　　　　**Quantity B**
$(x + y)^2 - 8$　　　　　　$(x - y)^2 + 24$

Ⓐ Quantity A is greater.
Ⓑ Quantity B is greater.
Ⓒ The two quantities are equal.
Ⓓ The relationship cannot be determined from the information given.

8. $f(x) = x - 1$

$g(x) = x^2$

$h(x) = f(x + 2) - g(2x)$

Quantity A　　　　　　　**Quantity B**
$h(3)$　　　　　　　　　　　0

Ⓐ Quantity A is greater.
Ⓑ Quantity B is greater.
Ⓒ The two quantities are equal.
Ⓓ The relationship cannot be determined from the information given.

9. Of 300 people, 40 percent are women and there are 240 golf players.

Quantity A　　　　　　　**Quantity B**
The greatest number of　　　The least number of men
women golf players　　　　　golf players

Ⓐ Quantity A is greater.
Ⓑ Quantity B is greater.
Ⓒ The two quantities are equal.
Ⓓ The relationship cannot be determined from the information given.

GO ON TO NEXT PAGE →

10.

x	1	3	7
$f(x)$	m	8	n

The chart above represents several values for a linear function f. What is the value of $n + 2m$?

(A) 8
(B) 12
(C) 16
(D) 24
(E) 30

11.

Name	Round 1	Round 2
Mickey	10	20
Gavi	60	100
Yoel	20	30
Adina	70	90
Leora	50	80

The chart above reflects the scores resulting from playing a board game. Two rounds were played and the scores posted. Which player had the greatest percent increase in his or her score from round 1 to round 2?

(A) Mickey
(B) Gavi
(C) Yoel
(D) Adina
(E) Leora

12. $a_1, a_2, a_3, a_4 \ldots a_n, \ldots$

In the sequence above, each term after the first is defined by $a_n = a_{n-1} + d$, where d is a constant and n takes on integer values greater than 1. If $a_2 + a_4 = 30$ and $a_3 + a_6 = 42$, what is the value of the constant d?

(A) 2
(B) 2.5
(C) 3
(D) 3.5
(E) 4

For the following question, select all the answer choices that apply.

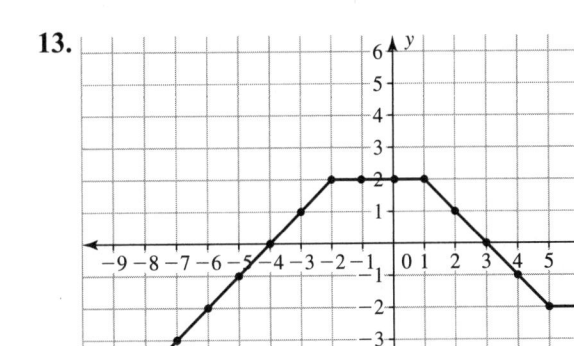

13.

In the xy-coordinate plane, the figure above represents the function f from $-8 \leq x \leq 10$. If $f(a) = f(2)$, what is the value of a if $a \neq 2$?

Indicate all such values.

A -3
B -2
C 1
D 2
E 9

14.

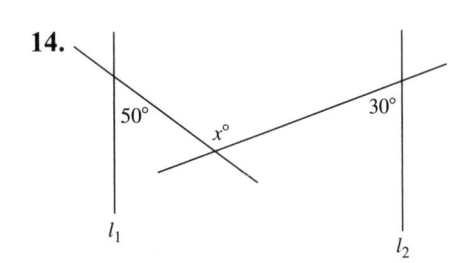

In the figure above, line l_1 is parallel to line l_2. What is the value of x?

A 80
B 90
C 100
D 110
E 120

For Questions 15 and 16, enter your answers in the boxes.

15. If gasoline costs $ $3.29\frac{9}{10}$ per gallon, what is the cost in dollars of 20 gallons of this gasoline? Omit the dollar sign when marking your answer.

Give your answer in the form xx.xx.

☐ dollars

16. If $x - \sqrt{5} = 1$, what is the value of $x^2 - 2x + 1$?

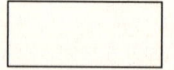

☐

Questions 17 to 20 are based on the following graph.

Sales Revenue and Advertising Cost for the NJL Company (in millions of dollars)

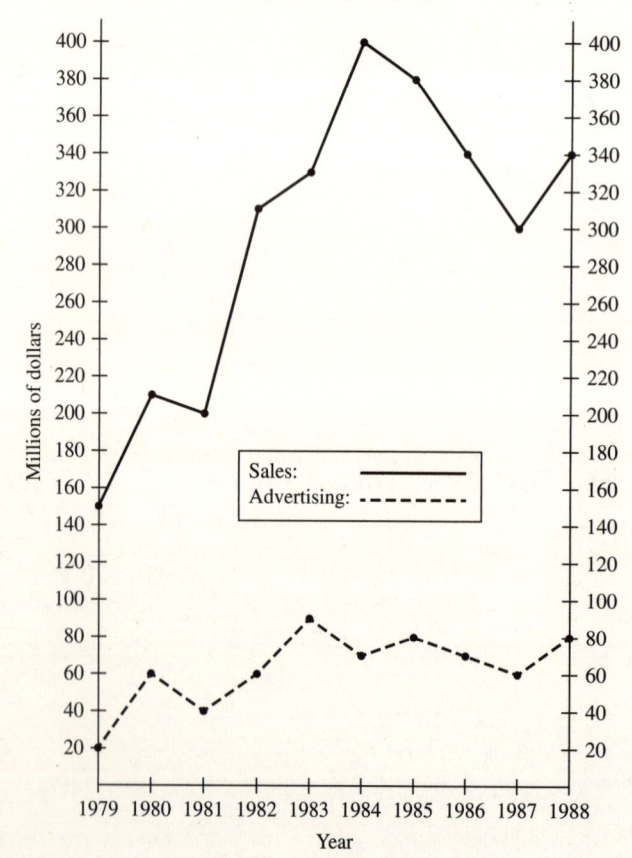

17. If the 1984 sales figure was revised to be 10 percent lower, then the average of the sales figures over the 10-year period 1979–1988 would be approximately how much lower?

   Ⓐ $4 million
   Ⓑ $6 million
   Ⓒ $10 million
   Ⓓ $20 million
   Ⓔ $40 million

18. Select all that apply.

   For which of the years 1980–1985 inclusive did the sales exceed the advertising cost by more than $200 million?

   Indicate all such years.

   ☐ A 1980
   ☐ B 1981
   ☐ C 1982
   ☐ D 1983
   ☐ E 1984
   ☐ F 1985

19. For the year 1981, the sales were approximately what percent greater than the advertising cost?

   Ⓐ 25%
   Ⓑ 75%
   Ⓒ 100%
   Ⓓ 300%
   Ⓔ 400%

20. Between which two consecutive years from 1979–1986 was the rate of sales growth the greatest?

   Ⓐ 1979–1980
   Ⓑ 1981–1982
   Ⓒ 1982–1983
   Ⓓ 1983–1984
   Ⓔ 1987–1988

21. Machine A can produce 30 gallons of glup in $\frac{1}{4}$ hour. Machine B can produce 20 gallons of glup in $\frac{1}{3}$ hour and machine C can produce 15 gallons of glup in $\frac{1}{2}$ hour. At this rate, if all three machines work concurrently, how many <u>minutes</u> does it take to produce 280 gallons of glup?

(A) 50
(B) 55
(C) 60
(D) 70
(E) 80

For the following question, enter your answer in the boxes.

22. A committee of five is to be chosen from six juniors and eight seniors. What is the probability that the committee will include two juniors and three seniors?

Give your answer as a fraction.

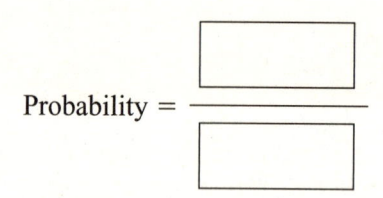

Probability = $\frac{\boxed{}}{\boxed{}}$

23. If each dimension of a rectangular prism (a box shape) can be expressed in the form $4n - 1$ where n is a positive integer, which one of the following <u>cannot</u> be a possible value for the volume of the prism?

(A) 27
(B) 63
(C) 125
(D) 147
(E) 231

24. Which number line below represents the solution set to the inequality

$$\frac{-3(2-x)}{4} \geq \frac{-2(3-x)}{2} ?$$

Ⓐ 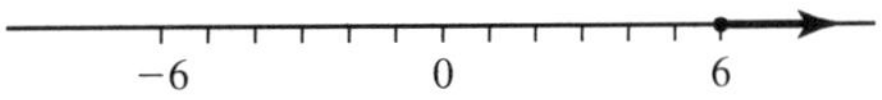

Ⓑ 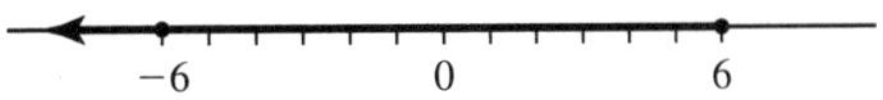

Ⓒ 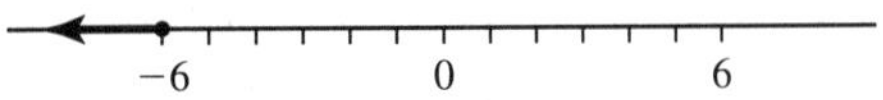

Ⓓ 

Ⓔ 

25. In the standard *xy*-coordinate plane, if a line through the points (1, 3) and (4, 7) is perpendicular to a line through the points (−2, 1) and (5, *y*), what is the value of *y*?

Ⓐ $-\frac{17}{4}$

Ⓑ -4

Ⓒ $-\frac{11}{4}$

Ⓓ $-\frac{9}{4}$

Ⓔ -3

STOP. This is the end of Quantitative Reasoning Section 2.

Answer Key: Verbal Reasoning Section 1

Question Number	Correct Answer
1.	A and B
2.	Composers in the Classical era preferred the greater dynamic range of the piano, so composing for the pipe organ waned in popularity.
3.	C
4.	B
5.	B and D
6.	C
7.	A and F
8.	E
9.	E
10.	A and C
11.	They had their own banks, grocery stores, and other services necessary to function in society.
12.	B
13.	B
14.	C
15.	E
16.	B and F
17.	A, D, and I
18.	B
19.	A and C
20.	Geocaches are found in over 100 countries and all seven continents, providing reassurance that the globe still holds some secrets, even if they have been wrought by humans.
21.	C and D
22.	B and D

ANSWER KEY: VERBAL REASONING
Section 1

Question Number	Correct Answer
23.	D and F
24.	A and F
25.	E and F

Answer Key: Verbal Reasoning Section 2

Question Number	Correct Answer
1.	B and D
2.	C and F
3.	B and D
4.	A and F
5.	B and C
6.	A
7.	B
8.	A and C
9.	As such, it was used by some to justify the Mexican-American War (1846–1848), which ultimately forced Mexico to sell the northern parts of its country to the United States.
10.	A and D
11.	B, D, and H
12.	E
13.	B
14.	C
15.	E
16.	D
17.	B
18.	A and E
19.	B and F
20.	C, E, and H

Question Number	Correct Answer
21.	B
22.	A
23.	C
24.	Still another camp feels that temperatures will affect actual migration times little, if at all, but that the biggest effect of climate change on birds will be changes in their food supply.
25.	D

Answer Key: Quantitative Reasoning Section 1

Question Number	Correct Answer
1.	B
2.	A
3.	C
4.	A
5.	C
6.	C
7.	A
8.	B
9.	B
10.	$\frac{63}{64}$
11.	D
12.	D
13.	B
14.	D
15.	D
16.	B and C
17.	2,160
18.	B
19.	D
20.	C
21.	D
22.	A, C, and D
23.	A
24.	15
25.	A

Answer Key: Quantitative Reasoning Section 2

Question Number	Correct Answer
1.	B
2.	B
3.	C
4.	B
5.	A
6.	A
7.	D
8.	B
9.	C
10.	D
11.	A
12.	E
13.	A and E
14.	A
15.	65.98
16.	5
17.	A
18.	C, D, E, and F
19.	E
20.	B
21.	E
22.	$\frac{840}{2,002}$
23.	C
24.	B
25.	A

Answer Explanations

Analytical Writing: Section 1
Analyze an Issue

Sample of a Level 5 Essay

The idea to give a federal governing body control over curricula, hiring standards, and teacher contracts for schools is an excellent one. Giving federal control to schools and teachers would eliminate or reduce most of the problems with our current educational system. The main advantages would be in standardization of curriculum, ability to equalize spending across districts, and ability to hire excellent teachers and keep them.

Over the last decade there has been an effort to test students across the country to see what they know and how they perform relative to other students. While the impetus behind this drive for testing makes sense—find the students that are having problems and help them learn what they don't know yet—the very real difficulty comes from the fact that individual states have radically different sets of standards of what students should be learning in the classroom at each grade level. This means that a child in one state could be studying hard, paying attention in class, and passing tests with flying colors but still be behind students in another state who are not trying as hard or performing as well on tests, simply because the second state required more things to be taught to students that year. Centralizing curriculum would at the very least solve the problem of inequalities in standards, so the standardized tests given could now be given to all students across the country to see where their weaknesses and strengths lie.

A second seemingly insurmountable problem is the fact that local school districts get the money they spend on students in their district from tax money paid in their districts. This means that there is more money to spend per student in wealthier districts and far less in poorer districts. With unequal money, there is no way to give children the same education. If control over schools was centralized, the federal department of education could take in tax money from across the country and allot the exact same dollar value for each student across the country, so that all students were on an equal playing field once they arrived at school each morning. This would not allow for inequalities outside of school and in their communities, of course, but it would give kids from poorer districts a fighting chance inside school.

An issue stemming from the inequalities in available funds for schools is the wide variance in teacher hiring practices and salaries. Although most public school teachers have unions to help advocate for them, this still does not ensure that teachers with the same amount of experience and education are compensated fairly. A centralized department could set teacher salaries at steady levels for the amount of experience and education they have attained, adjusting for costs of living differences across the country, and pay teachers an equalized salary. This would eliminate politics and wrangling from district to district and allow teachers to focus on teaching.

In conclusion, centralizing control of schools would be a good thing for students, teachers, and administrators. It would provide a clearer picture of how our students are doing by creating the same expectations for all students. It would give all schools, teachers, and students the same financial resources to work with. And it would pay teachers what they were worth, regardless of what district they taught in. This plan should be considered by our elected officials.

Answer Explanations

Analytical Writing: Section 2
Analysis of an Argument

Sample of a Level 5 Essay

The statement released by the prime minister of Almafa, while strong in tone, contains several logical errors that render it incomplete. Without giving evidence to close up these gaps in logic, the statement cannot be taken seriously, and further investigation into the government's responsibility for the deaths of birds on Lake Barshir should be conducted.

The prime minister states that the activists who study birds have collected data showing a five-year cycle of increased births followed by increased deaths for the birds, and that this proves that the deaths of birds on Lake Barshir is a normal part of this cycle. However, she never provides evidence that the deaths are in proportion to this natural cycle. If the number of birds who died is similar to the number of birds who always die in this part of the cycle, then the prime minister's assertion is likely to be correct. However, if the number of deaths is significantly higher, then the normal cycle would not at all account for the deaths of the birds. The prime minister needs to prove that the bird deaths are in proportion to the normal number of deaths seen.

The prime minister goes on to hedge by stating that even if the deaths were caused by pollution in Lake Barshir, the government had no responsibility for this, as companies could choose not to pollute the lake without a directive from the government. However, it is a basic principle of economics that corporations will maximize profits by cutting corners unless they are discouraged from doing so. By not enacting laws and penalties to discourage and penalize corporate pollution in the lake, the government is, in fact, encouraging it just by virtue of not enacting a penalty. The prime minister cannot escape the basic principles of economics and corporate behavior.

The prime minister's statement would be strengthened if she could demonstrate that the deaths of the birds were in proportion to the expected number of deaths, and provide some evidence to show that government inaction did not actually act as a de facto encouragement to companies to pollute. Without strengthening the argument in this way, the prime minister's statement is not valid, and further investigation into the government of Almafa's responsibility for the bird deaths should be conducted.

Answer Explanations
Verbal Reasoning: Section 1

1. A and B

The answers are A and B. The passage states that pipe organs were liberated from churches and cathedrals in the nineteenth century, so they must have been in churches and cathedrals before the Baroque period, choice A. The passage also states that music was written for pipe organ and harpsichord interchangeably before the Baroque period, but that afterward it was written for specific instruments, so the two instruments could not sound similar enough to be written for together, choice B. The passage says that composing for the pipe organ lost popularity in the Classical era, so it must have been more popular in earlier times, so choice C may or may not be true.

2. ANSWER:

Composers in the Classical era preferred the greater dynamic range of the piano, so composing for the pipe organ waned in popularity.

This sentence talks about what composers preferred about the piano, which means that the pipe organ did not have those characteristics.

3. C

The answer is C. The passage indicates that pipe organs had been built in churches and cathedrals but were now being built in secular locations, so this means they were being freed from their former locations, choice C. Emancipated means "freed from constraint or control," so choice A is incorrect. Choices B and E make no sense in the context of the sentence. Choice D is a different meaning of "liberated" that is not correct in this context.

4. B

The answer is B. The bold sentence states an idea that contrasts with the first sentence of the passage. Choices A, C, and E state the opposite role. Choice D indicates that it is a question, when it is actually a statement.

5. B and D

The answers are B and D. For the first blank, the word "although" indicates that the answer needs to be the opposite of "care little what others thought of her" with regard to her audience. Thus, choice A is eliminated. Choice C, while giving the right general idea, does not indicate her skill as strongly as choice B does. For the second blank, choice E makes no sense in the context of the sentence. Choice F gives the correct tone, but the sentence does not indicate that she was unfeeling; rather, she was unfettered, which is choice D.

6. C

The answer is C. The word in the blank needs to indicate "individual" thought. The best choice is C. Choices A and B are too similar and do not mean "individual." Choice D goes too far, and choice E is not serious enough.

7. A and F

The answers are A and F. In the first blank, the sentence gives the idea that the cuisines have become mixed. This immediately eliminates choice C. Choice A means mixed, whereas choice B means genetically engineered to be something new, which is not right for this sentence. In the second blank, the sentence gives the idea that it is hard to tell which cuisines originally come from a region. Choice D gives the correct tone, but is a comparison, not an indication of "originally from." Choice E makes no sense in the context of the sentence. Choice F means originally from.

8. E

The answer is E. The blank needs to be the opposite of "random." Choices A and D are too close to "random." Choices B and C have nothing to do with the context of the sentence. Choice E means the opposite of "random."

9. E

The answer is E. The passage discusses the reasons Chinese immigrants could not assimilate, not that they specifically chose not to, as some have thought. Choice E is closest to this. Choices A and B do not discuss assimilation. Choice C is the opposite of what the passage does. Choice D discusses current immigration.

ANSWER EXPLANATIONS
Verbal Reasoning: Section 1

10. A and C

The answers are A and C. The passage states that Chinese men were not allowed to marry white women, and then discusses that they stayed single, so they must not have married anyone else. It also states that most of the Chinese immigrant population lived in large cities, so they must have been able to find work. The passage does not discuss their starting their own businesses, or living in rural areas.

11. ANSWER:

They had their own banks, grocery stores, and other services necessary to function in society.

The answer explains that Chinese immigrants had their own services to support daily life, so they did not have to interact with the larger culture.

12. B

The answer is B. The passage states that Chinese immigrants were discriminated against and could not blend in, so they must have been able to be visually identified. The passage gives no information about their skills or professions.

13. B

The answer is B. The passage presents two ideas. The first is that people can buy more things now on the Internet than they ever could before. The second is that because of all of these choices, some consumers become confused and cannot decide what to buy. Choice B is the only option that expresses both ideas. Choice E expresses the first but not the second idea. Choice A confuses the word "paralysis" in the last sentence with physical paralysis. Choice C falsely attributes the ability to create products to a paradox. Choice D only explores the idea that consumers have access to products they wouldn't have had access to in pre-Internet days.

14. C

The answer is C. The word in the blank needs to mean "swayed." Choice C is the best match. Choices A and B are negative, so they don't match. Choices D and E do not make sense in the sentence.

15. E

The answer is E. The word in the blank needs to mean "negatively." Choice E is the best match. Choices A, B, and D are neutral. Choice C has too much of an added "sad" meaning to be the best match.

16. B and F

The answers are B and F. The word in the first blank needs to mean "looseness." The best match is choice B. Choice A means the opposite, and choice C is negative. The word in the second blank needs to mean "being in favor of." Choice F is the best match. Choice D is the opposite, and choice E is neutral.

17. A, D, and I

The answers are A, D, and I. The word in the first blank needs to mean "problem." The best match is choice A. Choice B is the opposite, and choice C makes no sense in the sentence. The word in the second blank needs to mean "experience." The best match is choice D. Choice E talks about skills, not experience, and choice F talks about affinity, not experience. The word in the third blank needs to mean "stops." The best match is choice I. Choice G is the opposite, and choice H makes no sense in the sentence.

18. B

The answer is B. Choice A confuses the word "global" in GPS with globalism. Choice C takes a small part of the passage and inflates it. Choice D talks about motive when the passage did not address motive. Choice E takes a small part of the passage and inflates it.

19. A and C

The answers are A and C. The passage indicates that geocaching has always required a desire to have an adventure and discover new things, which is choice A. Nothing in the passage indicates that inaccessible terrain is a prime feature of geocaching, so choice B is eliminated. The passage discusses the uses of various instruments, from compasses to GPS systems, for geocaching, so choice C is true.

20. ANSWER:

Geocaches are found in over 100 countries and all seven continents, providing reassurance that the globe still holds some secrets, even if they have been wrought by humans.

The phrase "the globe still holds some secrets" implies that geocachers can discover these secrets.

21. C and D

The answers are C and D. Eliminate choices B and F, as they have no synonyms. Choices A and E are synonyms, as are C and D. Of the two choices, only C and D fit the idea of the sentence that the assessment would be rigorous.

22. B and D

The answers are B and D. The word in the blank needs to mean "were in opposition to." The best matches are choices B and D. Choices A and E have the opposite meanings. Choices C and E do not make sense in the sentence.

23. D and F

The answers are D and F. This is a tricky question because the sentence itself doesn't tell us exactly what word needs to go in the blank. However, we know that the word should not mean something similar to "ethical," and that we need two words with the same meaning. Choices D and F have the same meaning, as do choices B and C. Choice E is too similar to "ethical." Choice A could work, but it has no match. Choices B and C are too close to "ethical," while choices D and F both mean "having to do with money," so the best matches for the blank are D and F.

24. A and F

The answers are A and F. The word in the blank needs to mean "ability." Choices A and F are the best matches. Choices B, C, and D are all opposites. Choice E means "friendship" more than "ability."

25. E and F

The answers are E and F. The word in the blank needs to mean "happy about." Choices E and F are the best matches. Choice A is the opposite. Choices B and C indicate a questioning that doesn't make sense in the sentence. Choice D doesn't make sense in the sentence and does not have a match.

Answer Explanations
Verbal Reasoning: Section 2

1. B and D

The answers are B and D. The word in the blank needs to mean "at last." The best matches are choices B and D. Choices C and F do not make sense in the sentence. Choice A could fit in the sentence but has no matching answer choice. Choice E makes no sense in the sentence.

2. C and F

The answers are C and F. The word in the blank needs to mean "solidness." Choices C and F are the best matches. The other pair of choices, A and D, do not make sense in the sentence. Neither choice B nor choice E make sense in the sentence, either.

3. B and D

The answers are B and D. The word in the blank needs to mean "wandering." The best matches are B and D. The other pair, choices A and C, are the opposite. Choice E is the opposite meaning. Choice F makes no sense in the sentence.

4. A and F

The answers are A and F. The word in the blank needs to mean "unpleasant." Choices A and F are the best matches. Choices B and E are too extreme. Choice C makes no sense in the sentence. Choice D is the opposite.

5. B and C

The answers are B and C. The passage does not discuss methods of treatment for sleep apnea. Although it mentions blockage, that does not indicate that the only treatment is surgery. Choice B is correct because the description of the sleep study discusses changes in respiration, so the researchers need to understand them. Choice C is correct because the passage discusses two different causes: blockage and low respiratory effort.

6. A

The answer is A. The passage mentions low respiratory effort as one of two reasons for sleep apnea that could be discovered during a sleep study. As such, it is a reason other than blockage, and choice A is correct. Choice B is incorrect because subjects are not described. Choice C is incorrect because the three types are not discussed in this part of the passage. Choice D discusses a different part of the passage. Choice E misrepresents the passage.

7. B

The answer is B. If the rat population is up where the garbage sits longer, this indicates that the rats are finding food in the garbage, which is contributing to their increase in population. Choice A would support the city officials' position. Choice C doesn't tell us anything without knowing about garbage pickup in those neighborhoods. Choices D and E are irrelevant to the argument.

8. A and C

The answers are A and C. Choice A is supported because the passage states that Anglo-Saxon America was seen as better than the "savage" societies of the Native Americans and Mexicans. Choice B is not supported by the passage, which simply says that manifest destiny "fell out of favor." Choice C is supported because the passage says that "some" supported it.

9. ANSWER:

As such, it was used by some to justify the Mexican-American War (1846–1848), which ultimately forced Mexico to sell the northern parts of its country to the United States.

This sentence describes the use of the idea of manifest destiny as a support for a multi-year war between the United States and Mexico.

10. A and D

The answers are A and D. The word in the first blank needs to mean "strength." Choice A is the best match. Choice B is the opposite. Choice C is too extreme, and has a negative connotation, which is not indicated in the sentence. The word in the second blank needs to mean "strong." Choice D is the closest match. Choice E is the opposite, as is choice F.

11. B, D, and H

The answers are B, D, and H. The word in the first blank needs to mean "bad." Choice B is the closest match. Choice A is the opposite, and choice C makes no sense in the sentence. The word in the second blank needs to mean "agree on." Choice D is the best match. Choice E is the opposite, and choice F makes no sense in the sentence. The word in the third blank needs to mean "say they won." Choice H is the best match. Choice G gives the wrong idea, and choice I makes no sense in the sentence.

12. E

The answer is E. The word in the blank needs to mean "accept." The best match is choice E. Choices A, B, and C do not make sense in the sentence. Choice D is the opposite.

13. B

The answer is B. The word in the blank needs to mean "anger." Choice B is the best match. Choice A is close but not exactly the correct meaning. Choice C is the opposite. Choices D and E do not make sense in the sentence.

14. C

The answer is C. The passage states that she chose her career over family life and a marriage, so choice C is supported. There is no information about different industries, so choice A is not supported. There is no information about secretarial school, so choice B is not supported. The passage does not tell us when or whether Gloria Munson looked back on her career, so choice D is not supported. Choice E is contradicted by the passage.

15. E

The answer is E. The passage says that Munson did not know that her first job would lead to such a long career, which supports choice E. Choices A and B are not supported at all in the passage. Choice C is the opposite of what the passage says. Choice D is not supported, as the passage does not make a value judgment.

16. D

The answer is D. The passage discusses union organizer Gloria Munson and how she took her first job in the union not knowing how extensive her career would be, which supports choice D. Choices A and B may be true, but they are not supported by the passage. Choice C mentions Gloria Munson's family, which the passage says she did not have. Choice E is true, but it is not the focus of the passage, so it is not the best answer.

17. B

The answer is B. The phrase in the blank needs to mean "something in common." The best match is choice B. Choice A is not supported because there is nothing to indicate than anything has been forgotten. Choice C is not indicated in the passage, nor are choices D or E.

18. A and E

The answers are A and E. Choose the second blank first. The word in the second blank needs to mean "simple." Choice E is the best match. Choice D is close, but not exactly it. Choice F makes no sense in the sentence. Now go to the first blank. The word in the first blank, since the second blank is "direct," needs to mean "complicated." The best match is choice A. Choice B is the opposite, and choice C is not as strong a match as is choice A.

19. B and F

The answers are B and F. The word in the first blank needs to mean "not strong and aggressive." The best match is choice B. Choice A is the wrong meaning, and choice C is too extreme. The word in the second blank needs to mean "not strong and aggressive." The best match is choice F. Choice D does not fit the meaning. Choice E makes no sense in the sentence.

20. C, E, and H

The answers are C, E, and H. The word in the first blank needs to mean "well." The best match is choice C. Choices A and B do not really make sense in the sentence. The word in the second blank needs to mean "important." The best match is choice E. Choice D does not make sense in the sentence. Choice F is not strong enough. The word in the third blank needs to mean "poorly." The best match is choice H. Choice G is the opposite meaning. Choice I is also the opposite meaning.

21. B

The answer is B. The passage states the visitors to Bartiki spend more per visit than visitors to Marshalle do, which supports choice B. None of the other answer choices are supported by the passage; in fact, choice A is contradicted by the passage.

22. A

The answer is A. The passage discusses the huge number of fonts available and then sets up the contrast with the word "however," so the correct answer needs to show an idea that not all the fonts are in use. Choice A is the best match. Choice B does not make sense, as we know logically that most computer users do not design their own fonts. Choice C is not supported by the passage. Choices D and E are not supported by the passage, either.

23. C

The answer is C. The passage discusses three theories of what global climate change might do to bird migration, but does not come to a conclusion. This supports choice C. Choices A and B are contradicted by the passage, which makes no definite conclusions.

24. ANSWER:

Still another camp feels that temperatures will affect actual migration times little, if at all, but that the biggest effect of climate change on birds will be changes in their food supply.

This sentence discusses the effect that birds' food supplies may change with global climate change.

25. D

The answer is D. The passage discusses three theories about the possible effects of global climate change on bird migration. The best match is choice D. Choices A and B are not supported because they only discuss one idea. Choice C is eliminated because the passage does not ask just one question. Choice E is not supported because it does not have evidence to analyze.

Answer Explanations
Quantitative Reasoning: Section 1

1. B

> Note: Figure not drawn to scale.
>
> Note: If two lines are parallel, the alternate interior angles are equal.

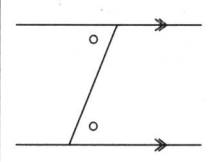

STEP 1 Since $\overline{AB}$ is parallel to $\overline{DE}$, the measure of angle A = the measure of angle E and the measure of angle D = the measure of angle B.

STEP 2 The sum of the angles of a triangle is 180.

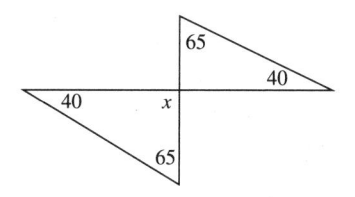

$40 + 65 + x = 180$

$x = 75$

Quantity B > Quantity A

2. A

STEP 1 In Quantity A, since $x > y$, $x - y$ is always positive.

In Quantity B, use the common denominator of xy, and subtract.

STEP 2 $\dfrac{1}{x} - \dfrac{1}{y} = \dfrac{y}{xy} - \dfrac{x}{xy} = \dfrac{y-x}{xy}$

STEP 3

$y - x$ is always negative.

xy is always positive.

$\therefore \dfrac{y - x}{xy}$ is always negative.

Quantity A $>$ Quantity B

3. C

STEP 1

$$x = \text{even}$$
$$y = \text{odd}$$
$$\overline{x + y \text{ is always odd.}}$$
$$\overline{(x + y)^2 \text{ is always odd.}}$$
$$\text{Probability}\left((x + y)^2 \text{ is odd}\right) = 1$$

STEP 2

$$x = \text{even}$$
$$y = \text{odd}$$
$$\overline{x^2 \text{ is always even.}}$$
$$y^2 \text{ is always odd.}$$
$$\overline{x^2 + y^2 \text{ is always odd.}}$$
$$\text{Probability}\left(x^2 + y^2 \text{ is odd}\right) = 1$$

Quantity A $=$ Quantity B

4. A

> Note: Begin from the bottom upward.

STEP 1 $\dfrac{1}{x - \dfrac{1}{x - \dfrac{1}{\left(\dfrac{1}{3}\right)}}} = \dfrac{1}{x - \dfrac{1}{x - 3}}$

ANSWER EXPLANATIONS | 241
Quantitative Reasoning: Section 1

STEP 2 $\dfrac{1}{x-\dfrac{1}{\dfrac{1}{3}-3}} = \dfrac{1}{x-\dfrac{1}{\dfrac{-8}{3}}} = \dfrac{1}{x+\dfrac{3}{8}}$

STEP 3 $\dfrac{1}{\dfrac{1}{3}+\dfrac{3}{8}} = \dfrac{1}{\dfrac{17}{24}} = \dfrac{24}{17}$

Quantity A > Quantity B

5. C

Note: Figures not drawn to scale.

These triangle relationships should be memorized (Special right triangles).

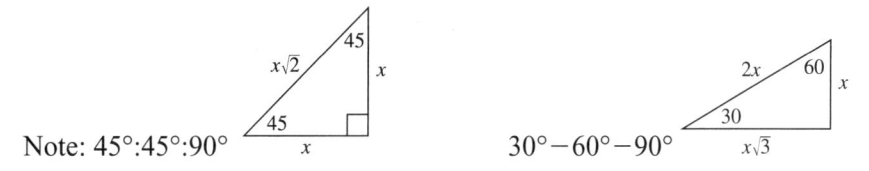

Note: 45°:45°:90°   30°−60°−90°

STEP 1 Based on the 30°−60°−90° relationships, $x = 30°$ and $y = 30°$.

6. C

Note:
$x^a \times x^b = x^{a+b}$
$\left(x^a\right)^b = x^{ab}$

STEP 1 Factor 2^{111} out of the sum in Quantity A.

$2^{111} + 2^{111} + 2^{112} + 2^{113} + 2^{114} = 2^{111}(1 + 1 + 2^1 + 2^2 + 2^3)$

$= 2^{111}(1 + 1 + 2 + 4 + 8)$

$= 2^{111}(16)$

$= 2^{111}(2^4) = 2^{115}$

Quantity A = Quantity B

7. A

STEP 1 Each hour is 60 minutes:

$$\therefore 3m + 1 \text{ hours} = 60(3m + 1) \text{ minutes}$$

STEP 2 Each day is 24 hours:

$$\therefore 7m + 4 \text{ days} = 24(7m + 4) \text{ hours}$$

STEP 3 $60(3m + 1)$ vs $24(7m + 4)$

$180m + 60$ vs $168m + 96$

> Note:
>
> If $m = 3$, Quantity A = 600 vs Col B = 600.
>
> If $m > 3$, Quantity A always has greater values.

Quantity A > Quantity B

8. B

STEP 1 Consider adding or subtracting the equations to create the desired calculation.

Try adding the equations:

$$\begin{aligned} 3x + y &= 9 \\ x + 3y &= 7 \\ \hline 4x + 4y &= 16 \end{aligned}$$

STEP 2 Divide by 2: $2x + 2y = 8$

Quantity B > Quantity A

9. B

STEP 1 If 60 percent of those attending are male, then 40 percent are female.

STEP 2 Let x = number of students attending the football game: 40 percent of x = 90.

STEP 3 Solve for x: $\frac{40}{100}(x) = 90$

$x = 225$ students attended

ANSWER EXPLANATIONS | 243
Quantitative Reasoning: Section 1

STEP 4 Let p = total student population

30 percent of p = 225

STEP 5 Solve for p: $\frac{30}{100}(p) = 225$

$p = 750$

Quantity B > Quantity A

10. $\frac{63}{64}$

STEP 1 $a_1 = \frac{1}{2^1} = \frac{1}{2}$

$a_2 = \frac{1}{2^2} = \frac{1}{4}$

$a_3 = \frac{1}{2^3} = \frac{1}{8}$

$a_4 = \frac{1}{2^4} = \frac{1}{16}$

$a_5 = \frac{1}{2^5} = \frac{1}{32}$

$a_6 = \frac{1}{2^6} = \frac{1}{64}$

STEP 2 $a_1 + a_2 + a_3 + a_4 + a_5 + a_6 = \frac{1}{2} + \frac{1}{4} + \frac{1}{8} + \frac{1}{16} + \frac{1}{32} + \frac{1}{64} = \frac{63}{64}$

or equivalent fraction

11. D

> Note: For a normal distribution:
> Let m = mean
> Let t = a standard deviation

(All percentages are approximate.)

STEP 1 Overlay the actual data on the normal curve.

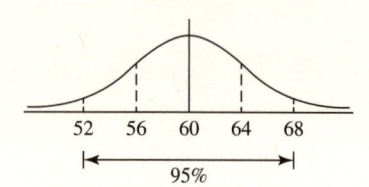

STEP 2 We expect that 95 percent of the data will be within 2 standard deviations about the mean.

$$60 \pm 2(4) \begin{cases} 60 + 8 = 68 \\ 60 - 8 = 52 \end{cases}$$

[Normal distribution curve with values 52, 56, 60, 64, 68 marked; 95% range indicated from 52 to 68.]

Thus, the correct interval is 52–68.

12. D

Note: $x^{-a} = \dfrac{1}{x^a} \quad \dfrac{x^a}{x^b} = x^{a-b}$

STEP 1 Distribute the $^{-1}$ power

$$= \left(\dfrac{\frac{1}{2^{-8}}}{\frac{1}{8^{-4}}} \right)^{-1} = \dfrac{\frac{1}{2^8}}{\frac{1}{8^4}} = \dfrac{8^4}{2^8}$$

STEP 2 State the equation in base 2 and solve: $\dfrac{8^4}{2^8} = 4^x$

$$\dfrac{(2^3)^4}{2^8} = (2^2)^x$$

$$\dfrac{2^{12}}{2^8} = 2^{2x}$$

$$2^4 = 2^{2x}$$

$$2x = 4$$

$$x = 2$$

13. B

Note: In an obtuse triangle, the height used to calculate the area is outside the triangle.

STEP 1 Draw a rough sketch.

STEP 2 Use the horizontal side of the triangle as the base.
$NJ = 7$ (from $x = -2$ to $x = 5$).

ANSWER EXPLANATIONS | 245
Quantitative Reasoning: Section 1

STEP 3 The corresponding height, marked h, is 3 (from $y = 2$ to $y = 5$).

STEP 4 Area = $\frac{1}{2}(7)(3) = \frac{21}{2} = 10.5$

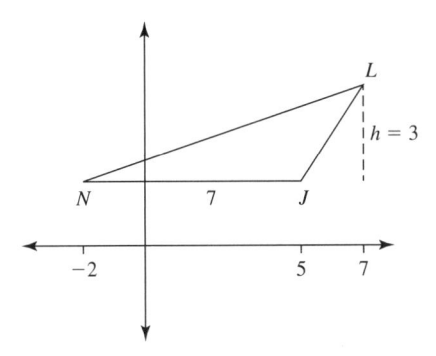

14. D

Note:
- The number of distinct diagonals in an n-sided polygon = $(_nC_2) - n$
- $_nC_2 = \dfrac{n!}{2!(n-2)!}$

STEP 1 The number of diagonals in a 10-sided polygon is: $_{10}C_2 - 10$.

STEP 2 $_{10}C_2 = \dfrac{10!}{2!8!} = \dfrac{10 \cdot 9 \cdot \cancel{8!}}{2! \cancel{8!}} = \dfrac{90}{2} = 45$

STEP 3 $_{10}C_2 - 10 = 45 - 10 = 35$

15. D

STEP 1 The notation $f(x - 2)$ denotes that the graph moves 2 spaces to the RIGHT.

16. B and C

Note: The expression "or part thereof" means that you pay for the whole next unit no matter how little of it you use.

STEP 1 Organize the information: $2.00 = 0.25$ miles

$0.50 = 0.25$ miles

$0.50 = 0.25$ miles

$\dfrac{0.50}{3.50} = \dfrac{0.25 \text{ miles}}{1 \text{ mile}}$

246 Paper-and-Pencil Test 1

STEP 2 The expression "or part thereof" implies that you pay the $0.50 for the next 0.25 miles or any part of it.

More simply stated, you pay the full $0.50 for any distance traveled greater than 1 mile, up to and including the full 0.25 miles.

STEP 3 You pay $4.00 to travel any distance greater than 1 mile and less than or equal to 1.25 miles.

17. 2,160

STEP 1 Determine the number of men and women ages 75 to 84.

men: 6 percent of 200,000 = (0.06)(200,000) = 12,000

women: 9 percent of 200,000 = (0.09)(200,000) = 18,000

STEP 2 In the age group, 72 percent of the men are married and 36 percent of the women are married.

Number of men (75–84 and married) = 12,000 × 72% = 8,640

Number of women (75–84 and married) = 18,000 × 36% = 6,480

STEP 3 Difference is 8,640 − 6,480 = 2,160

18. B

STEP 1 Calculate the number of men ages 85 and over in 2004 and 2005.

2004: $\frac{1}{2}$% of 200,000 = (0.005)(200,000) = 1,000

2005: $\frac{1}{2}$% of 220,000 = (0.005)(200,000) = 1,100

STEP 2 35 percent of the numbers in step 1 represent widowed men ages 85 and over.

2005: 35% of 1,100 = 0.35(1,100) = 385

2004: 35% of 1,000 = 0.35(1,000) = 350

STEP 3 Increase was 385 − 350 = 35.

ANSWER EXPLANATIONS | 247
Quantitative Reasoning: Section 1

19. D

STEP 1 Calculate the number of men and women ages 65–74.

men: 15% of 200,000 = 30,000
women: 18% of 200,000 = 36,000

STEP 2 The percent in this age group that never married is 4 percent for each of men and women.

men: 4 percent of 30,000 = 1,200
women: 4 percent of 36,000 = 1,440
Total 2,640

20. C

Note: $P(A \text{ or } B) = P(A) + P(B) - P(A \text{ and } B)$

STEP 1 Probability (male)

$\frac{1}{2}$ percent + 6 percent + 15 percent + 25 percent = $46\frac{1}{2}$ percent

Probability (age is below 65) = 50 percent

Probability (male AND below age 65) = 25 percent

STEP 2 Probability (male or below age 65) =

$P(\text{male}) + P(\text{below age 65}) - P(\text{male AND below age 65})$

Probability (male or below age 65)

= $46\frac{1}{2}$ percent + 50 percent − 25 percent

= 71.5 percent

21. D

STEP 1 Write the example algebraically.

$3 + \frac{x}{100}(3) = 6 + \frac{y}{100}(6)$

STEP 2 Solve for x:

$100\left[3 + \frac{x}{100} = 6 + \frac{y}{100}(6)\right]$

$300 + 3x = 600 + 6y$

$3x = 300 + 6y$

$x = 2y + 100$

22. A, C, and D

> Note:
> - When written as $y = mx + b$, m = slope, b = y-intercept
> - If two lines are parallel they have equal slopes and different y-intercepts.
> - The y-intercept occurs at $x = 0$.

STEP 1 Rearrange the given equation

$$2x + 3y = 9$$

$$3y = -2x + 9$$

$$y = -\frac{2}{3}x + 3$$

$\boxed{A}$ The slope is $-\frac{2}{3}$, this choice is TRUE.

$\boxed{B}$ The y-intercept is $\frac{9}{2}$, this choice is NOT true.

$\boxed{C}$ $y = -\frac{2}{3}x + 6$ has the same slope and a different y-intercept than the given line. This choice is TRUE.

$\boxed{D}$ Rearranging $2x = 8 - 3y \Rightarrow y = -\frac{2}{3}x + \frac{8}{3}$

This line is also parallel to the given line, this choice is TRUE.

23. A

> Note: $n! = n(n-1)!$

STEP 1 $\dfrac{(24!)(22!)}{(23!)(21!)} = \dfrac{(24)(\cancel{23!}) \cdot (22)(\cancel{21!})}{(\cancel{23!})(\cancel{21!})} = 24(22) = n(n-2)$

STEP 2 By observation $24(22) = n(n-2)$

$$n = 24$$

24. 15

> Note:
> - r items can be selected from a group of n items in $_nC_r$ ways.
> - $_nC_r = \dfrac{n!}{r!(n-r)!}$

ANSWER EXPLANATIONS
Quantitative Reasoning: Section 1

STEP 1 Selecting 3 flowers of the same color could either be 3 pink, 3 yellow, or 3 white.

STEP 2 3 pink can be selected from a group of 4 in $_4C_3 = 4$ ways.
3 yellow can be selected from a group of 3 in only 1 way.
3 white can be selected from a group of 5 in $_5C_3 = 10$ ways.

STEP 3 The possible number of ways to get flowers of the same color is $4 + 1 + 10 = 15$.

25. A

STEP 1 Cross-multiply and distribute.

$$\frac{y}{1} = \frac{x+1}{x-1}$$

$$y(x-1) = 1(x+1)$$

$$xy - x = y + 1$$

STEP 2 Rearrange with any term containing x on the left side and all the terms not containing an x on the right of the equal sign.

$$xy - x = y + 1$$

STEP 3 Factor out the x, and divide by $y - 1$.

$$x(y-1) = y + 1$$

$$x = \frac{y+1}{y-1}$$

Answer Explanations
Quantitative Reasoning: Section 2

1. B

Note: Area of a rectangle = $b \times h$

Area of parallelogram = $b \times h$

STEP 1 Find the area of the rectangle.

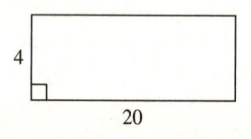

$A = bh = 4(20) = 80$

STEP 2 Draw the parallelogram.

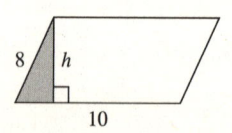

Observe that the shaded area is a right triangle, the hypotenuse is 8, the leg h must be less than the hypotenuse. Therefore, h is less than 8. Consequently: Area is less than 80.

Quantity B > Quantity A

2. B

STEP 1 x and y are each positive proper fractions greater than $\frac{1}{2}$

$x + y$ must be greater than 1

STEP 2 $x \times y$ is the product of two proper fraction which must be less than 1

Quantity B > Quantity A

ANSWER EXPLANATIONS
Quantitative Reasoning: Section 2

3. C

Note:
- To compare the two columns, try to make them appear similar (same bases).
- $(X^a)^b = X^{ab}$

STEP 1

$$8^{40} = (2^3)^{40} = 2^{120}, \quad 27^{40} = (3^3)^{40} = 3^{120}$$

$$4^{60} = (2^2)^{60} = 2^{120}, \quad 9^{60} = (3^2)^{60} = 3^{120}$$

STEP 2

Quantity A: $2^{120} + 3^{120}$

Quantity B: $2^{120} + 3^{120}$

Quantity A = Quantity B

4. B

Note: The graphical intersection of two graphs is analogous to solving simultaneous equations for the solution set.

STEP 1 Solve $y = 2x + 1$ and $y = -x + 4$ simultaneously

STEP 2 $y = 2x + 1 = -x + 4$

$2x + 1 = -x + 4$

$3x = 3$

$x = 1$

STEP 3 If $x = 1$, $y = -x + 4$

$= -1 + 4$

$y = 3$

$\therefore a = 1$ and $b = 3$

Quantity B > Quantity A

5. A

STEP 1 $49n^2 \to 7 \times 7 \times n \times n$

STEP 2 $7 \times 7 \times n \times n$ is divisible by:

1	7×7	$7 \times 7 \times n$	$7 \times 7 \times n \times n$
7	$7 \times n$	$n \times n \times 7$	
n	$n \times n$		

$$\underbrace{\qquad\qquad\qquad\qquad\qquad\qquad}_{9 \text{ factors}}$$

Quantity A $>$ Quantity B

6. A

STEP 1

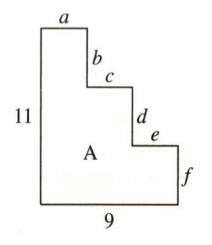

$a + c + e = 9$
$b + d + f = 11$

The perimeter of figure A is
$2(11) + 2(9) = 40$

STEP 2

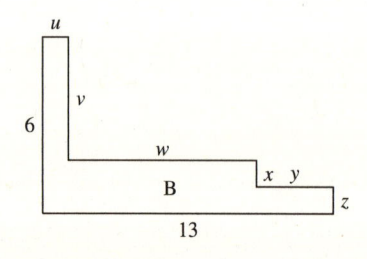

$u + w + y = 13$
$v + x + z = 6$

The perimeter of figure B is
$2(6) + 2(13) = 38$

Quantity A $>$ Quantity B

7. D

STEP 1 Expand:

Quantity A: $(x + y)^2 - 8 = (x + y)(x + y) - 8 = x^2 + 2xy + y^2 - 8$
Quantity B: $(x - y)^2 + 24 = (x - y)(x - y) + 24 = x^2 - 2xy + y^2 - 24$

ANSWER EXPLANATIONS
Quantitative Reasoning: Section 2

STEP 2 Compare the answers, ignoring the x^2 and y^2 terms which are common to both.

$$2xy - 8 \text{ vs } -2xy + 24$$

STEP 3 If $xy = 8$ then $2xy - 8 = -2xy + 24$} Quantity A = Quantity B

If $xy \neq 8$ then $2xy - 8 \neq -2xy + 24$} Quantity A ≠ Quantity B

The relationship cannot be determined.

8. B

STEP 1 $h(x) = f(x + 2) - g(2x)$

$h(3) = f(3 + 2) - g(2 \cdot 3)$

$= f(5) - g(6)$

STEP 2

$f(x) = x - 1$	$g(x) = x^2$
$f(5) = 5 - 1 = 4$	$g(6) = 6^2 = 36$

STEP 3 $h(3) = 4 - 36 = -32$

Quantity B > Quantity A

9. C

Note: A diagram is helpful.

STEP 1 Construct a diagram.

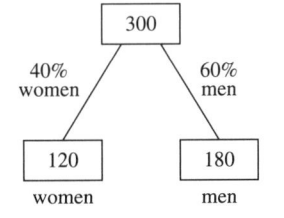

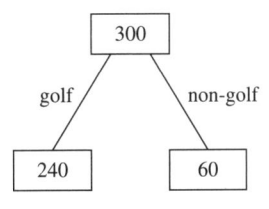

```
        300                           300
       /   \                         /    \
    40%    60%                   golf    non-golf
   women   men                   /          \
    /       \                  240           60
  120      180
 women     men
```

STEP 2 There are 120 women. The greatest number of women who are golf players is 120.

STEP 3 There are 240 golf players and only 120 women. At least 120 men must play golf. The least number of men who are golf players is 120.

Quantity A = Quantity B

10. D

> Note:
> - Slope $= \dfrac{\Delta y}{\Delta x} = \dfrac{y_2 - y_1}{x_2 - x_1} = \dfrac{f(x_2) - f(x_1)}{x_2 - x_1}$
> - A linear function has a constant slope.

STEP 1 Calculate the slope using the values (1, m) and (3, 8).

$$\text{Slope} = \dfrac{\Delta y}{\Delta x} = \dfrac{8 - m}{3 - 1} = \dfrac{8 - m}{2}$$

STEP 2 Calculate the slope using the values (3, 8) and (7, n).

$$\text{Slope} = \dfrac{\Delta y}{\Delta x} = \dfrac{n - 8}{7 - 3} = \dfrac{n - 8}{4}$$

STEP 3 Equate the slopes, cross-multiply, and rearrange the terms.

$$\dfrac{8 - m}{2} = \dfrac{n - 8}{4} \Rightarrow 4(8 - m) = 2(n - 8)$$

$$32 - 4m = 2n - 16$$

$$2n + 4m = 48$$

$$n + 2m = 24$$

11. A

> Note: Percent change $= \dfrac{\text{Change}}{\text{Original}} \times 100$

STEP 1 Calculate the percent change for each player.

(A) Mickey: $\dfrac{20 - 10}{10} \times 100 = 100$ percent

(B) Gavi: $\dfrac{100 - 60}{60} \times 100 = 66\dfrac{2}{3}$ percent

(C) Yoel: $\dfrac{30 - 20}{20} \times 100 = 50$ percent

(D) Adina: $\dfrac{90 - 70}{70} \times 100 = 28\dfrac{4}{7}$ percent

(E) Leora: $\dfrac{80 - 50}{50} \times 100 = 60$ percent

ANSWER EXPLANATIONS | 255
Quantitative Reasoning: Section 2

12. E

STEP 1 The sequence can be viewed in the following manners:

View 1: $\dfrac{a_1}{1} \dfrac{a_2}{2} \dfrac{a_3}{3} \dfrac{a_4}{4} \dfrac{a_5}{5} \dfrac{a_6}{6} \ldots$

View 2: $\dfrac{a_1}{1} \dfrac{a_1+d}{2} \dfrac{a_2+d}{3} \dfrac{a_3+d}{4} \dfrac{a_4+d}{5} \dfrac{a_5+d}{6} \ldots$

View 3: $\dfrac{a_1}{1} \dfrac{a_1+d}{2} \dfrac{a_1+2d}{3} \dfrac{a_1+3d}{4} \dfrac{a_1+4d}{5} \dfrac{a_1+5d}{6} \ldots$

STEP 2

$a_2 + a_4 = 30$ $\qquad\qquad$ $a_3 + a_6 = 42$

$(a_1 + d) + (a_1 + 3d) = 30$ $\qquad$ $(a_1 + 2d) + (a_1 + 5d) = 42$

$2a_1 + 4d = 30$ $\qquad\qquad$ $2a_1 + 7d = 42$

STEP 3 Solve simultaneously by subtracting $2a_1 + 4d = 30$ from $2a_1 + 7d = 42$.

$$\begin{array}{r} 2a_1 + 7d = 42 \\ -2a_1 + 4d = 30 \\ \hline 3d = 12 \\ d = 4 \end{array}$$

13. A and E

> Note: $f(a) = b$
>
> means: for an x-value of a, the function y value is b.
>
> means: the point $x = a, y = b$ is on the function.
>
> means: a is the input to the function, $f(a)$ or b is the output value of the function.

STEP 1 Analyze $f(2)$. The input x-value is 2. The corresponding y-value is 1.

$f(2) = 1$

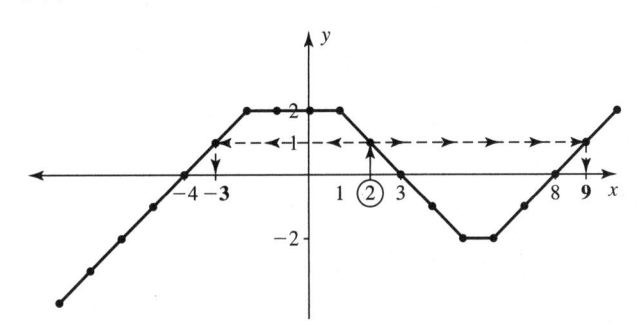

STEP 2 Analyze $f(a) = f(2) = 1$

This asks what value of x has an output or y-value of 1. From the graph we can see that both $x = -3$ and $x = 9$ have y values of 1.

$\therefore a = -3$ or $a = 9$

14. A

Note: Figure not drawn to scale.

STEP 1 The best approach is to draw a line parallel to l_1 and l_2 as shown below.

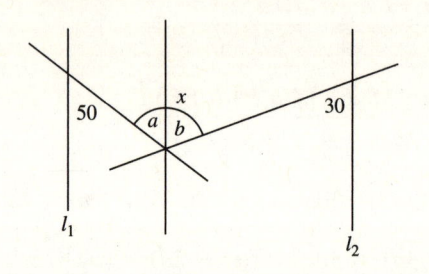

STEP 2 By alternate interior angles $a = 50$ and $b = 30$ ∴ $x = 80$

15. 65.98

STEP 1 $3.29\dfrac{9}{10} = 3.299$

STEP 2 $(20)(3.299) = 65.98$

16. 5

STEP 1 Rather than solving for x and substituting, there is a more clever way to find the solution.

Observe that $x^2 - 2x + 1 = (x - 1)^2$.

STEP 2 Observe that $x - \sqrt{5} = 1$ can be changed to $x - 1 = \sqrt{5}$.

STEP 3 $x^2 - 2x + 1 = (x - 1)^2 = \left(\sqrt{5}\right)^2 = 5$

ANSWER EXPLANATIONS | 257
Quantitative Reasoning: Section 2

17. A

STEP 1 The original 1984 sales figure was $400 million.
10 percent lower would be $400 − $40 = $360 million.

STEP 2 The average of the 10-year period $= \dfrac{\text{Sum of the 10 sales figures}}{10}$

STEP 3 The sum of the sales figures for the 9 years that were not changed remains the same.

STEP 4 Note: The question asks for a comparison of the averages, not the actual average.

STEP 5 Let S = The sum of the 9 unaffected sales figures.

Original average $= \dfrac{\text{Sum of the 9 unaffected sales figures} + 400}{10} = \dfrac{S + 400}{10}$

Revised average $= \dfrac{\text{Sum of the 9 unaffected sales figures} + 360}{10} = \dfrac{S + 360}{10}$

The difference is: $\left(\dfrac{S + 400}{10}\right) - \left(\dfrac{S + 360}{10}\right) = \dfrac{40}{10} = \$4$ million.

18. C, D, E, and F

STEP 1 For each year, the data can be read directly from the graph. The difference was more than $200 million for years 1982, 1983, 1984, and 1985.

19. E

Note: Percent change $= \dfrac{\text{Change}}{\text{Original}} \times 100$

STEP 1 Locate the values for 1981 sales = $200 million.

Advertising = $40 million

STEP 2 The question asks for a comparison of the difference between sales and advertising as compared to advertising expressed as a percent.

$\dfrac{(\text{sales} - \text{advertising})}{\text{advertising}} \times 100$

$= \dfrac{200 - 40}{40} \times 100 = 400$ percent

20. B

> Note: Rate of change can be evaluated by looking at the slope.

STEP 1 In effect, the question is asking between which two consecutive years was the positive slope of the graph the steepest. It is steepest from 1981 to 1982.

21. E

STEP 1 Find the production of each machine for a common time period.

Machine A can produce 120 gallons in 1 hour.

Machine B can produce 60 gallons in 1 hour.

Machine C can produce 30 gallons in 1 hour.

Working simultaneously, the three machines produce 210 gallons in 1 hour.

STEP 2 Establish a proportion of gallons to minutes.

$$\frac{\text{Gallons}}{\text{Minutes}} : \frac{210}{60} = \frac{280}{x} \Rightarrow \frac{7}{2} = \frac{280}{x}$$

STEP 3 Cross-multiply and solve for x: $7x = 2(280)$

$$x = 80$$

22. $\dfrac{840}{2,002}$

> Note: The number of different ways r items can be selected from a group of n items is ${}_nC_r = \dfrac{n!}{r!(n-r)!}$.

STEP 1 2 juniors can be selected from a group of 6 in ${}_6C_2$ ways.

${}_6C_2 = 15$

STEP 2 3 seniors can be selected from a group of 8 in ${}_8C_3$ ways.

${}_8C_3 = 56$

STEP 3 5 people can be selected from a group of 14 people in ${}_{14}C_5$ ways.

${}_{14}C_5 = 2,002$

STEP 4 The probability of 2 juniors and 3 seniors

$$= \frac{({}_6C_2)({}_8C_3)}{{}_{14}C_5} = \frac{15(56)}{2,002} = \frac{840}{2,002} \text{ or an equivalent fraction.}$$

ANSWER EXPLANATIONS
Quantitative Reasoning: Section 2

23. C

> Note: Given any integer n, $4n$ is always even.
> $\left.\begin{array}{l}4n - 1 \\ 4n + 1\end{array}\right\}$ are always odd.

STEP 1 $4n - 1$, where n is a positive integer that takes on the values
$4(1) - 1 = 3, 4(2) - 1 = 7, 4(3) - 1 = 11$

STEP 2

$3(3)(3) = 27$

$3(3)(7) = 63$

$3(7)(7) = 147$

$3(7)(11) = 231$

There is no way to create the value 125.

24. B

> Note: When multiplying or dividing an inequality by a negative number, the direction of the inequality reverses.

STEP 1 Cross-multiply $\dfrac{-3(2 - x)}{4} \geq \dfrac{-2(3 - x)}{2}$

$-6(2 - x) \geq -8(3 - x)$

STEP 2 Distribute.

$-12 + 6x \geq -24 + 8x$

$12 \geq 2x$

STEP 3 Solve for x.

$6 \geq x$

or

$x \leq 6$

25. A

> Note:
> - If two lines are perpendicular, their slopes are negative reciprocals.
> - If two lines are perpendicular, their slopes multiply to -1.
> - $m = \text{Slope} = \dfrac{\Delta y}{\Delta x} = \dfrac{y_2 - y_1}{x_2 - x_1}$

STEP 1 Calculate the slope of the line through the points $(1, 3)$ and $(4, 7)$.

$$m_1 = \frac{\Delta y}{\Delta x} = \frac{7 - 3}{4 - 1} = \frac{4}{3}$$

STEP 2 Calculate the slope of the line through the points $(-2, 1)$ and $(5, y)$.

$$m_2 = \frac{\Delta y}{\Delta x} = \frac{y - 1}{5 - (-2)} = \frac{y - 1}{7}$$

STEP 3 For the lines to be perpendicular, the product of their slopes is -1.

$$m_1 \cdot m_2 = \left(\frac{4}{3}\right)\left(\frac{y - 1}{7}\right) = \frac{4y - 4}{21} = -1$$

STEP 4 Solve for y:

$$4y - 4 = -21$$
$$4y = -17$$
$$y = -\frac{17}{4}$$

Paper-and-Pencil Test 2

SECTION 1

Analytical Writing: Analyze an Issue
30 Minutes

Write a response in which you discuss the extent to which you agree or disagree with the statement and explain your reasoning for the position you take. In developing and supporting your position, describe specific circumstances in which the statement would or would not be true and explain how these examples shape your position.

Issue Topic

Telling the truth is more important than sparing others' feelings.

SECTION 2

Analytical Writing: Analyze an Argument
30 Minutes

Write a response in which you discuss what specific evidence is needed to evaluate the argument and explain how the evidence would weaken or strengthen the argument.

Argument Topic

The Deputy Mayor of Actontown released the following statement to the press:

"Despite the recent statement by the Fleet Street Merchants' Union protesting the proposed street construction on the eight-block stretch of Fleet Street between Foster Street and Andrews Avenue, the city council has decided to go forward with the plan to widen the street. The demolition and reconstruction are expected to take 11 months, and the business owners will not have to pay for the remodeling of their storefronts that will be part of the widening. While it is true that each storefront will end up with less square footage after the street widening, the businesses will become more profitable because of the increased traffic on the widened street. We are doing this for the good of the merchants themselves, so they should support the project wholeheartedly."

NO TEST MATERIAL ON THIS PAGE

SECTION 1

Verbal Reasoning

25 Questions
35 Minutes

Questions 1 to 4 are based on the following reading passage.

Before computer software is released for download by the public, it undergoes an extensive and strenuous process of testing called Quality Assurance (QA). **The QA process is tightly structured and organized to expose any errors, or bugs, in the software.** Human testers follow checklists of operations to perform on the software—pressing every button, clicking every icon, inputting different types of information—to see how the software will react and to determine if there are any faulty sequences. When a bug is discovered, the tester logs it in another computer program called a bug tracker, which allows programmers to test the bug, fix it, and then record that they fixed it and what actions they took, so the QA team can retest the functionality. Only by following this process can the developers ensure that they test every operation an end-user could perform and that the software runs correctly under real-life conditions.

For the following question, consider each of the choices separately and select all that apply.

1. Which of the following can be inferred from the passage about the Quality Assurance process?

    A Bugs are mistakes in the programming of software that can be fixed.
    B An error in software programming might not be evident unless a certain sequence of actions is performed.
    C Errors in software are a result of the user's clicking an incorrect icon.

2. Select the sentence in the passage in which the author explains the process of accounting for and fixing errors in a software program.

3. In the context in which it appears, "end-user" most nearly means

    A tracking software.
    B error.
    C person who uses the software.
    D person who tests the software.
    E developer.

GO ON TO NEXT PAGE →

4. In the passage above, the portion in boldface plays which of the following roles?

  (A) It discusses the job functions that occur in the QA process.
  (B) It asks a question about why the QA process is necessary.
  (C) It establishes that the QA process is specific and regimented.
  (D) It describes the steps of the QA process.
  (E) It explains why the QA process is necessary.

> For Questions 5 to 8, select one entry for each blank from the corresponding column of choices. Fill all blanks in the way that completes the text.

5. Without knowing the (i) _____ of the position, the applicant could not determine how to most effectively represent her past experience or education to demonstrate that she was the (ii) _____ candidate.

Blank (i)	Blank (ii)
(A) units	(D) hapless
(B) requirements	(E) enervated
(C) advantages	(F) optimal

6. The rock star's (i) _____ contained so many references to the other musicians she had played with, been married to, and been arrested with that it became difficult for the reader to remember which artist was a former lover and which was a (ii) _____.

Blank (i)	Blank (ii)
(A) memorabilia	(D) co-conspirator
(B) concert film	(E) devotee
(C) memoir	(F) composer

7. The (i) _____ of Henry David Thoreau as a misanthrope has obscured the more (ii) _____ elements of his writing.

Blank (i)	Blank (ii)
(A) delineation	(D) humanitarian
(B) characterization	(E) humanistic
(C) discerning	(F) sympathetic

8. To be termed scientific, a method of inquiry must be based on gathering observable, _____, and measurable evidence subject to specific principles of reasoning.

Ⓐ theoretical
Ⓑ natural
Ⓒ empirical
Ⓓ independent
Ⓔ hypothetical

Questions 9 to 12 are based on the following reading passage.

While the popular perception of Mars may be that of a "dead" planet, the sand dunes that surround the edge of the planet's North Pole offer compelling evidence of geological, if not biological, life. High-resolution images from NASA's Mars Reconnaissance Orbiter show that the dark basalt dunes are in near-constant flux. Researchers have four years' worth of images to study, which show the changes in the landscape. Winter on Mars is a particularly tempestuous season for weather, as a blanket of dry ice covers the dunes and loosens the sand, causing avalanches.

The images sent back from the Orbiter are even more precious because the instrument has lasted beyond its proposed expiration date, allowing a far richer and more complex look at the planet than originally expected. Launched from Earth in August of 2005, the Orbiter reached and entered Mars' orbit in March of 2006. It was tasked to orbit for one full Martian year (the equivalent of two Earth years), and end its mission in December of 2010. Yet it remains intact as it circles the red planet, capable, NASA says, of sending images for another five years.

NASA seeks further funding to maintain the hard-working Orbiter, but debate over the continuation of exploring Mars centers on the high costs of such instruments. The Orbiter cost over $720 million, with $180 million of that sum going to mission operations. A NASA instrument circling in space has no "off" switch; the Orbiter will continue to send images as it is programmed to do. The question is one of funding here on Earth—will the mission be deemed important enough to subsidize scientists who can receive, review, and understand the images the Orbiter faithfully sends? This question crystallizes a central issue in twenty-first-century space exploration: the machines humans build to plunge into the depths of space are proving to be sturdier than humans' will to continue the exploration for which they were created.

9. The primary purpose of the passage is to

  A describe the remarkable findings of the Mars Reconnaissance Orbiter.
  B compare the expected capabilities of the Orbiter with the actual work it has done.
  C persuade readers to support further funding for NASA's programs, such as the Orbiter.
  D question the feasibility of continuing the Orbiter program.
  E use the example of the Orbiter program to illuminate a dichotomy in the space exploration program—the instruments built are sturdier than the public interest in what is discovered.

10. The passage implies that

  A NASA's engineers built the Orbiter only to operate for five years, with a minimum of care.
  B the Orbiter's discovery that Mars' sand dunes are in near-constant flux justifies the expense of the instrument.
  C the variability of public interest in NASA's programs makes funding them at a consistent level difficult.

11. Select the sentence in the passage that most clearly shows the author's purpose in using the example of the Mars Reconnaissance Orbiter.

For the following question, consider each of the choices separately and select all that apply.

---

12. It can be inferred from the passage that the cost of the Orbiter

  A is, in the author's opinion, justifiable by the complexity of information it has returned to Earth.
  B leads some to question if the information received is important enough to justify the expense.
  C will most likely be a point of debate when the project is submitted for further funding.

> **Question 13 is based on the following reading passage.**

In the past five years, the public's understanding of nutritional information has greatly increased. Purchased food is sold in containers with clearly presented nutritional information that is less deceptive. Additionally, in several major cities in the United States, restaurants must clearly display the calorie count for all foods and beverages that they serve. Nonetheless, obesity remains a major and growing epidemic in the country, with 25 percent of the country overweight.

13. Which of the following, if true, best reconciles the apparent discrepancy presented in the passage?

    (A) While people are presented with ever-increasing nutritional information about the foods they consume, few are able to interpret such information in a way that informs their food choices.
    (B) Additional nutritional information is helpful, but does not address existent obesity.
    (C) Obesity can be passed genetically, regardless of the food a person consumes.
    (D) In the past five years, there have been improvements in nutritional information from both food manufacturers and restaurants.
    (E) Not every major city requires the posting of nutritional information by restaurants.

> **For Questions 14 and 15, select the two answer choices that, when used to complete the sentence, fit the meaning of the sentence as a whole and produce completed sentences that are alike in meaning.**

14. Following the _____ of the refugees during the conflict, the non-governmental agency workers found it difficult to make an accurate count of the number of members of the minority group no longer residing in the country.

    [A] fleecing
    [B] diaspora
    [C] extradition
    [D] slaughter
    [E] suppressing

GO ON TO NEXT PAGE →

15. The author's heavy hand with _____ created a work full of allusions and double meanings, but kept the essential theme too obscure for readers to discern.

   A alliteration
   B foreshadowing
   C allegory
   D symbolism
   E irony

> For Questions 16 to 17, select one entry for each blank from the corresponding column of choices. Fill all blanks in the way that best completes the text.

16. The uprising was (i) _____; yet, the (ii) _____ of the people soon supplanted the staging with actual defiance.

Blank (i)	Blank (ii)
A rebellious showboating	D resolve
B political grandstanding	E earnestness
C insincere spectacle	F chance

17. The doctor's quest to find a cure for the disease was considered (i) _____ by most, but few could doubt her resolve. After many years of painstaking research, she was able to locate the primary cause of the disease, although a cure remained (ii) _____. Although the doctor felt regret that her discovery was not that which she had worked for, there was a sense of (iii) _____ from the result.

Blank (i)	Blank (ii)	Blank (iii)
A unlikely	D allusive	G gratification
B quixotic	E elusive	H sufficiency
C visionary	F effusive	I irritation

Questions 18 to 20 are based on the following reading passage.

The ubiquity of social media in the urban areas of the United States may give the false impression that the vast majority of the country's citizens primarily communicate through this form. In fact, it is the very characteristics that define urban living—including large populations, the physical location of news organizations, and the reality of mass transit—that create the need for social media. In less populated areas, a car radio is often sufficient entertainment for the commuter, and the idea of chatting online seems laughable when one's neighbor waits across the street with a fresh pot of coffee and homemade cookies. Most telling, however, is the difference in the pace of life. City dwellers are used to a breakneck lifestyle, in which the most commodious means of communicating with one's community is a tweet; in the country, however, such rapid updates are preposterous. No one needs a tweet to alert them that the grass is growing.

18. The argument presented by the author of the passage

    (A) makes a factual case for a slower-paced lifestyle.
    (B) asserts that the presence of national news organizations is obtrusive to rural life.
    (C) is limited by overgeneralizations about residents of urban and rural areas, indulging in stereotypes of both.
    (D) specifies the locations depicted to create a specific argument.
    (E) provides support of the notion that most social media is inherently feverish.

19. Which of the following statements about urban life is supported by the passage?

    (A) Urban dwellers live a chaotic lifestyle in which social communities must be built ad hoc.
    (B) Urban dwellers benefit from having the major news outlets located in their proximate location, allowing them an insider's perspective.
    (C) The necessary commutes on mass transit for most urban dwellers has given rise to the popularity of social media that can be pursued during that time.

20. In the context in which it appears, "preposterous" most nearly means

    (A) ludicrous.
    (B) impossible.
    (C) incredible.
    (D) irrational.
    (E) needless.

GO ON TO NEXT PAGE →

For Questions 21 to 25, select the two answer choices that, when used to complete the sentence, fit the meaning of the sentence as a whole and produce complete sentences that are alike in meaning.

21. By deviating from the planned schedule, the delivery service caused a(n) _____ in which the elevator was unavailable to residents during the evening rush hour.

    A vehicle
    B logjam
    C carrier
    D blockage
    E agenda
    F onus

22. Although a portrayal of a troubled marriage, Dickens' novel preceded the _____ of his own divorce within the decade.

    A attainment
    B precognition
    C prescience
    D actuality
    E investigation
    F scrutiny

23. With the Senate having great difficulty resolving the finer points of the bill, passage will _____ on the ability of congressional legislative aides to construct a compromise.

    A repose
    B rely
    C hinge
    D reside
    E founder
    F loll

24. Without warning, the cellist chose a brisker tempo for her solo than what she had set in rehearsal, leaving the rest of the orchestra _____ to match her.

   A usurped
   B stupefied
   C stumped
   D lagging
   E hastening
   F scrambling

25. Because she had traveled abroad without noticeable jet lag, the woman felt confident that she would be able to present at a conference immediately after her arrival. Therefore, her disorientation was _____.

   A perplexing
   B distracting
   C complicating
   D systematic
   E perturbing
   F questionable

STOP. This is the end of Verbal Reasoning Section 1.

NO TEST MATERIAL ON THIS PAGE

SECTION 2

Verbal Reasoning

25 Questions
35 Minutes

> For Questions 1 to 4, select the two answer choices that, when used to complete the sentence, fit the meaning of the sentence as a whole and produce completed sentences that are alike in meaning.

1. Turning a blind eye to the mismanagement and financial incompetence that crippled the company, the CEO _____ pursued licensing their trademark characters for a quick cash infusion.

   A animatedly
   B blithely
   C unobtrusively
   D morosely
   E lightheartedly
   F vivaciously

2. The Battle of Gettysburg remains one of the most memorable conflicts of the American Civil War, not just because it was a noted turning point and a lengthy clash, but also for the remarkable _____ of soldiers fighting for both factions.

   A initiative
   B sincerity
   C zeal
   D efficiency
   E readiness
   F fervor

GO ON TO NEXT PAGE →

3. Given that the estate refuses to release its grip on the copyright of the famed author's last work, the only way for readers to enjoy it is by locating a(n) _____ version.

- [A] unauthorized
- [B] abridged
- [C] mass-produced
- [D] draft
- [E] unwarranted
- [F] pirated

4. Well-known to be fiercely private, he did make an exception and share _____ details about his personal life occasionally through a friendly journalist's online column.

- [A] clandestine
- [B] discreet
- [C] sequestered
- [D] quarantined
- [E] reserved
- [F] magnified

Questions 5 and 6 are based on the following reading passage.

As a stage of normal emotional and cognitive development in children, the term "separation anxiety" is somewhat of a misnomer. The term "separation anxiety" describes the effect, which is that a child, often quite close to the age of 24 months, is unwilling to be separated from one or two special caregivers, and often the primary caregiver. The child becomes anxious and fearful when required to separate from this caregiver. However, the root cause cognitively of this stage is not, in fact, a matter of separating from the caregiver, but stems from the new recognition that the child is a separate entity from others. Because the child suddenly feels separate and untethered to another person, the loss of that person becomes frightening. In effect, it is the beginning of independence that creates an immediate need for dependence.

> **For the following question, consider each of the choices separately and select all that apply.**

5. It can be inferred from the passage that separation anxiety involves which of the following elements?

- [A] Behavior indicating fear or anxiety when the primary caregiver is not in the vicinity
- [B] A strong desire to be close to the primary caregiver physically
- [C] Being tethered physically to the primary caregiver

6. It can be inferred that the author of the passage mentions the phrase "root cause" primarily in order to

(A) show that because this behavior occurs at such a young age, it must be controlled or else it will continue into adulthood.
(B) denote an organic process that forms from the child's fears and anxiety.
(C) hypothesize that separation anxiety is a maladaptive behavior.
(D) discuss the ways in which a primary caregiver should be acting to eliminate separation anxiety.
(E) establish that there is something underlying separation anxiety that we do not immediately see in the child's behavior.

Question 7 is based on the following passage.

Precipitation has been increasing for the month of October over the last 12 years in the highlands region of Mondova. Researchers have noticed that the lizard population of the highlands has increased by 64 percent over that same time period. They feel that the increased moisture in the region is increasing the rate at which the lizards breed and reproduce, and that this is causing the increase in the lizard population.

7. Which of the following, if true, most strengthens the researchers' argument?

(A) The increased rain has caused a decrease in the population of the wild dogs that are the lizards' biggest predator.
(B) The increased precipitation is probably a result of the weather systems called El Nino and several years of warmer weather in the spring months.
(C) The lizards come to full maturity more quickly in moister environments, and the females lay eggs more frequently in moister environments.
(D) In wetter weather the lizards' reproductive systems slow down and they mate less frequently than they do in drier conditions.
(E) The research on lizard breeding habits was financed by a grant from the government of Mondova.

Questions 8 and 9 are based on the following reading passage.

The game of Prisoner's Dilemma, in which the actions of two people who have committed a crime but are being examined separately by the police, is a classic exercise of logic. During the examination by the police, each person has the chance to implicate the other person or to accept some of the blame, and there is no evidence to support or disprove any of the assertions. The lengths of the sentences each prisoner gets varies by whether or not they implicate themselves or each other. As we work out the possible outcomes of the testimony, we discover the complexity involved in both the decisions made and in the decision-making process for both prisoners.

> For the following question, consider each of the choices separately and select all that apply.

8. Which of the following statements about Prisoner's Dilemma can be inferred from the passage?

   A Prisoner's Dilemma is played on a standard chess board using one piece from each team.
   B Doing well at Prisoner's Dilemma involves being able to accurately predict what the other prisoner will do.
   C The challenge of Prisoner's Dilemma lies in working out the different outcomes to determine what the best path for a prisoner to take is in the examination.

9. Select the sentence that describes what the prisoners are asked by the police during the examination.

> For Questions 10 to 13, select one entry for each blank from the corresponding column of choices. Fill all the blanks in the way that best completes the text.

10. With (i) _____, the scientist approached the delicate task of sorting through the physiological structure, but in time found that a(n) (ii) _____ hand was, in fact, his best tool.

Blank (i)	Blank (ii)
A misapprehension	D immovable
B comprehension	E unfaltering
C appending	F regular

11. Commonly, Charlotte Brontë's classic novel *Jane Eyre* is remembered for its overarching theme of (i) _____ ideas. Yet Brontë saw her work as a way to make (ii) _____ use of her own childhood memories of the cruel boarding school where she and her sisters attended. Of course, Brontë wrote the novel not only as a means of (iii) _____ those demons, but also as a way to improve her family's meager finances.

Blank (i)	Blank (ii)	Blank (iii)
A realistic	D pragmatic	G purging
B romantic	E sober	H cleansing
C utopian	F idealistic	I revitalizing

12. With the author's noted expertise in phylogeny, her attendance at the biological sciences conference was considered a _____.

- (A) favor
- (B) gratuity
- (C) boon
- (D) benevolence
- (E) compliment

13. Meteorology, once derided as a science of prediction instead of fact, has been greatly _____ by the rise of complex computer modeling programs that allow much more accurate predictions about the paths and severity of weather events.

- (A) enhanced
- (B) intensified
- (C) enlarged
- (D) focused
- (E) exacerbated

Questions 14 to 16 are based on the following reading passage.

Italo Calvino's seminal novel *Se una notte d'inverno un viaggiatore* (*If on a winter's night a traveler*) is a labyrinthine exploration of the folly and misguided efforts of literary criticism. Calvino skewers various forms of literary criticism popular at the time, everything from numerical analysis of the frequency of words in a text to symbolism to meta-symbolism. Intercalated with the chapters criticizing—in story form—criticism are chapters that form a running story celebrating reading for the pleasure of reading. The complexity of the novel is both a declaration of triumph from Calvino at writing a criticism that is almost too thick to be criticized, and a love note from Author to unencumbered Reader.

14. Which of the following can be inferred from the passage regarding Calvino's *If on a winter's night a traveler*?

- (A) *If on a winter's night a traveler* is a book written for children.
- (B) At the time in which Calvino wrote *If on a winter's night a traveler* literary criticism was more popular than it is today.
- (C) *If on a winter's night a traveler* is rarely taught in university courses because it is too complex to be understood.
- (D) *If on a winter's night a traveler* contains at least two different stories that alternate throughout the book.
- (E) Calvino wrote *If on a winter's night a traveler* as a response to criticism of one of his earlier books.

GO ON TO NEXT PAGE →

15. In the fourth sentence ("The complexity of the novel ... Reader."), the author of the passage is most likely suggesting that

    (A) *If on a winter's night a traveler* is too complex for anyone to analyze.
    (B) Calvino prefers those who read books because they like them to those who read books to analyze them.
    (C) Calvino's need to criticize those who criticize novels is a result of his inability to read for pleasure.
    (D) the desire for pleasure is greater than the desire to criticize.
    (E) a reader who can read the novel solely for pleasure will never understand the criticism Calvino levels.

16. Which of the following best describes the central issue with which the passage is concerned?

    (A) Italo Calvino's belief that literary criticism is a worthless exercise, as expressed in *If on a winter's night a traveler*
    (B) Italo Calvino's masterful use of the conventions of literary criticism to criticize his own novel *If on a winter's night a traveler*
    (C) The sweet simplicity of the love story Italo Calvino writes in *If on a winter's night a traveler*
    (D) The two parallel stories in Italo Calvino's *If on a winter's night a traveler*
    (E) The dual sides of Italo Calvino's novel *If on a winter's night a traveler*: one a criticism and one a story

> For Questions 17 to 20, select one entry for each blank from the corresponding column of choices. Fill all the blanks in the way that best completes the task.

17. The meeting was nearly _____ by the board members' insistence on reaching a unanimous consensus before proceeding with the implementation of the plan.

    (A) thwarted
    (B) hindered
    (C) broadsided
    (D) derailed
    (E) ridiculed

18. The Civil Rights Movement and the Equal Rights Movement of the twentieth century did not (i) _____ in entirely similar circumstances, yet the overall (ii) _____ of each was similar in spirit.

Blank (i)
(A) prevail
(B) coalesce
(C) subsist

Blank (ii)
(D) mission
(E) unfaltering
(F) intent

19. The reviewer commented on the play's (i) _____, but I was struck by the (ii) _____ of the work: indeed, it resembled nothing I'd seen before.

Blank (i)
(A) obscurity
(B) conventionality
(C) ordinariness

Blank (ii)
(D) off-kilter tone
(E) nonconformity
(F) ingenuity

20. Smith's message is that polio, once considered (i) _____, still threatens. Particularly (ii) _____ are impoverished countries that have not thoroughly vaccinated their populations. Therefore, the threat of the devastating illness still (iii) _____.

Blank (i)
(A) extinguished
(B) reduced
(C) lessened

Blank (ii)
(D) susceptible
(E) impressible
(F) predisposed

Blank (iii)
(G) looms
(H) approaches
(I) brews

Question 21 is based on the following reading passage.

The antibacterial properties of honey are commonly known to beekeepers. Outside the world of apiary science, honey is known only as a sweet, delicious treat. In reality, however, honey has many other properties aside from edibility and sweetness, including the ability to seal and disinfect wounds. It works not only on wounds in which the skin has been abraded or punctured, but also to soothe and heal burns. These properties of honey would not be obvious to the casual observer, as bees themselves do not have skin like human skin, nor do they experience burns the same way we do. Why, then, is the substance they produce so perfectly fitted to fixing problems experienced by a totally different species?

21. According to the passage, honey has properties that provide healing for

   (A) the skin of bees.
   (B) the skin of humans.
   (C) the skin of dogs.
   (D) a different species of bee.
   (E) pollen-producing flowers.

Question 22 is based on the following reading passage.

Ergonomic design attempts to solve problems of poor positioning and repetitive stress injuries by designing workspaces that allow the user to sit, stand, or move in positions that are better for body fluidity and movement. Companies that have invested in furniture and redesigned workspaces to maximize ergonomics have discovered that their employees are more efficient, experience less pain and fatigue, and have fewer health problems than they did with non-ergonomic furniture. Thus, investing in ergonomic workspaces can actually be _____.

22. Which of the following most logically completes the passage?

   (A) a cost savings for the company by increasing employee output and decreasing employee downtime
   (B) a luxury only some companies can afford
   (C) something that benefits the employees more than it benefits the company
   (D) a long process without one definite best answer for each job function in the company
   (E) a good addition to an employee health program that emphasizes healthy eating and increased exercise

Questions 23 to 25 are based on the following reading passage.

Emperor penguins, like other birds, mate for a breeding season to incubate and hatch their egg together, once the female has laid it. Unlike other birds, however, the penguins do not build a nest for their egg, and it is not the female that incubates the egg until it hatches. Instead, the female lays the egg, then rolls it quickly over the ice to the male, who nestles it on top of his feet and covers it with a flap of skin on his belly. His feet protect the egg from the frigid cold of the ice, and the egg is warm and safe inside the pouch formed by the skin flap. Once the egg is settled with the male, the female begins the long trek over several miles to the water's edge to find food for herself and for the baby penguin that will hatch out of the egg. Only after several weeks when she returns and feeds the hatchling will the male finally be able to go off to find food for himself.

VERBAL REASONING
Section 2

> For the following question, consider each of the choices separately and select all that apply.

23. The passage indicates that penguins who mate to breed do which of the following?

    A Become partners for life
    B Divide the responsibilities of caring for the egg
    C Return to the same spot to breed year after year

24. Select the sentence that discusses what happens after the female returns with food for the hatchling.

25. In the passage, the author is primarily concerned with

    A hypothesizing about an outcome.
    B asking a question.
    C weighing two theories.
    D describing a process.
    E analyzing two criticisms.

STOP. This is the end of Verbal Reasoning Section 2.

NO TEST MATERIAL ON THIS PAGE

SECTION 1

Quantitative Reasoning

25 Questions
40 Minutes

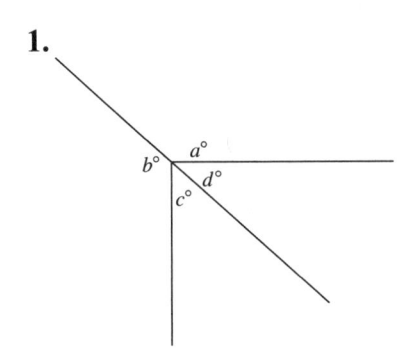

1.

$a = 1.5b$, $b = 2c$, and $c = 2.5d$

Quantity A	Quantity B
c	60

Ⓐ Quantity A is greater.
Ⓑ Quantity B is greater.
Ⓒ The two quantities are equal.
Ⓓ The relationship cannot be determined from the information given.

2. A fence is supported by equally spaced fence posts. The distance from the first fence post to the tenth fence post is 80 ft.

Quantity A	Quantity B
The distance in feet from the third fence post to the fifth fence post	16

Ⓐ Quantity A is greater.
Ⓑ Quantity B is greater.
Ⓒ The two quantities are equal.
Ⓓ The relationship cannot be determined from the information given.

GO ON TO NEXT PAGE →

3. $x^2 = y^2 = z^2$ ($xyz \neq 0$)

Quantity A	Quantity B
$\dfrac{x}{y}$	$\dfrac{y}{z}$

- (A) Quantity A is greater.
- (B) Quantity B is greater.
- (C) The two quantities are equal.
- (D) The relationship cannot be determined from the information given.

4. The ratio of the numerical value of the area of a circle to the numerical value of its circumference is 4:5

Quantity A	Quantity B
The diameter of the circle	3

- (A) Quantity A is greater.
- (B) Quantity B is greater.
- (C) The two quantities are equal.
- (D) The relationship cannot be determined from the information given.

5. Triangle NJL is isosceles, with $JN = 10$ and $JL = 4$.

Quantity A	Quantity B
The perimeter of $\triangle NJL$	24

- (A) Quantity A is greater.
- (B) Quantity B is greater.
- (C) The two quantities are equal.
- (D) The relationship cannot be determined from the information given.

6. There are six students studying for an exam.

Quantity A	Quantity B
The number of different two-person study groups that could be formed	The number of different four-person study groups that could be formed

- (A) Quantity A is greater.
- (B) Quantity B is greater.
- (C) The two quantities are equal.
- (D) The relationship cannot be determined from the information given.

QUANTITATIVE REASONING | **289**
Section 1

7. $x \neq 2, y \neq 3, v \neq 4, m \neq 5$

Quantity A

$$\frac{x-2}{2-x} + \frac{3-y}{y-3}$$

Quantity B

$$\frac{4-v}{v-4} + \frac{m-5}{5-m}$$

Ⓐ Quantity A is greater.
Ⓑ Quantity B is greater.
Ⓒ The two quantities are equal.
Ⓓ The relationship cannot be determined from the information given.

8. A group of 10 students plans to equally share the cost of a graduation gift for their friend. If two additional people join the group and contribute equally for the gift, the individual contribution decreases by $3.

Quantity A

The cost of the gift in dollars

Quantity B

150

Ⓐ Quantity A is greater.
Ⓑ Quantity B is greater.
Ⓒ The two quantities are equal.
Ⓓ The relationship cannot be determined from the information given.

9. Towns A, B, and C are all on the same straight road. The distance from town A to town B is 11 and the distance from town B to town C is 9.

Quantity A

The distance from town A to town C

Quantity B

20

Ⓐ Quantity A is greater.
Ⓑ Quantity B is greater.
Ⓒ The two quantities are equal.
Ⓓ The relationship cannot be determined from the information given.

GO ON TO NEXT PAGE →

Each of questions 10 through 25 has one of four different formats:

- If the question is followed by answer choices A through E, each enclosed in a circle, then there is only one correct answer.

- If the question is followed by a number of answer choices, each enclosed in a box, then there is at least one correct answer.

- If the question is followed by a single box, then you must enter a numerical answer. This answer may be either integer or decimal. It may also be negative. Do not enter a fraction.

- If the question is followed by two boxes in the form of a fraction, then you must enter a fraction for the answer. You must enter an integer in each box. If the answer is negative, you may enter the negative sign in either box.

For the following question, enter your answer in the box.

10.

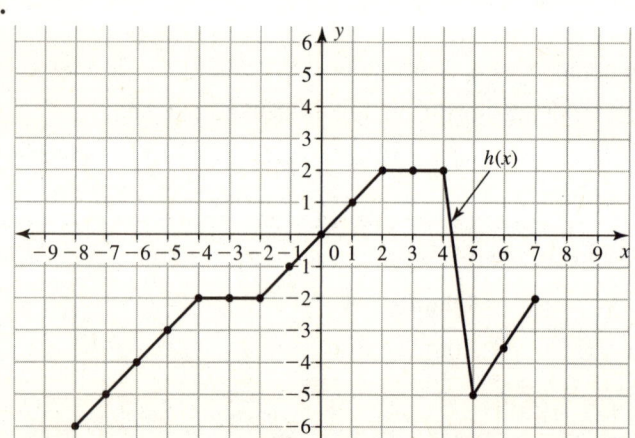

In the xy-coordinate plane, the figure above represents the function h from $-8 \leq x \leq 7$. What is the value of $h(h(5))$?

$h(h(5)) = $ ☐

11.

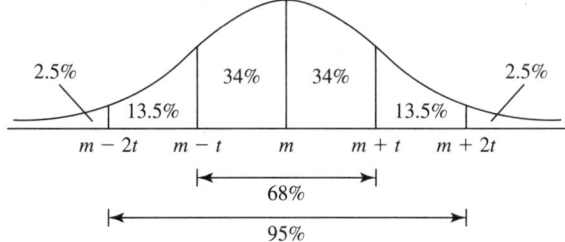

The scores on a test approximate a normal distribution with a mean of 80 and a standard deviation of 5. Approximately what percent of the scores are below 70?

- (A) 2.5
- (B) 13.5
- (C) 16
- (D) 36.5
- (E) 47.5

12. If one of the roots of the quadratic function $f(x) = 10x^2 + kx - 3$ is $\frac{1}{5}$, what is the value of the constant k?

- (A) 7
- (B) 9
- (C) 11
- (D) 12
- (E) 13

13. The average of four numbers is two more than the average of the three numbers after one of the numbers is removed. If the number removed was 7, what is the average of the three numbers that remain?

- (A) −3
- (B) −2
- (C) −1
- (D) 1
- (E) 3

14. Given the equation $\frac{1}{2^x} + \frac{3}{2^x} = 2^a$, solve for x in terms of a.

   (A) $4 + a$
   (B) $4 - a$
   (C) $a - 2$
   (D) $a + 2$
   (E) $2 - a$

For the following question, select all the answer choices that apply.

---

15. Which of the following will NEVER change the median of nine different numbers? Indicate all such statements.

   [A] Increasing the lowest of the numbers
   [B] Decreasing the greatest of the numbers
   [C] Increasing each number by 2
   [D] Increasing the greatest of the numbers
   [E] Decreasing the lowest of the numbers

16. In a group of people, $\frac{1}{3}$ are male. Two-fifths of the females in the group are students. If there are 30 non-student females in the group, how many males are in the group?

   (A) 15
   (B) 17
   (C) 20
   (D) 25
   (E) 30

Questions 17 to 20 are based on the following data.

Contribution to Federal Candidates for Office by Source, 2006

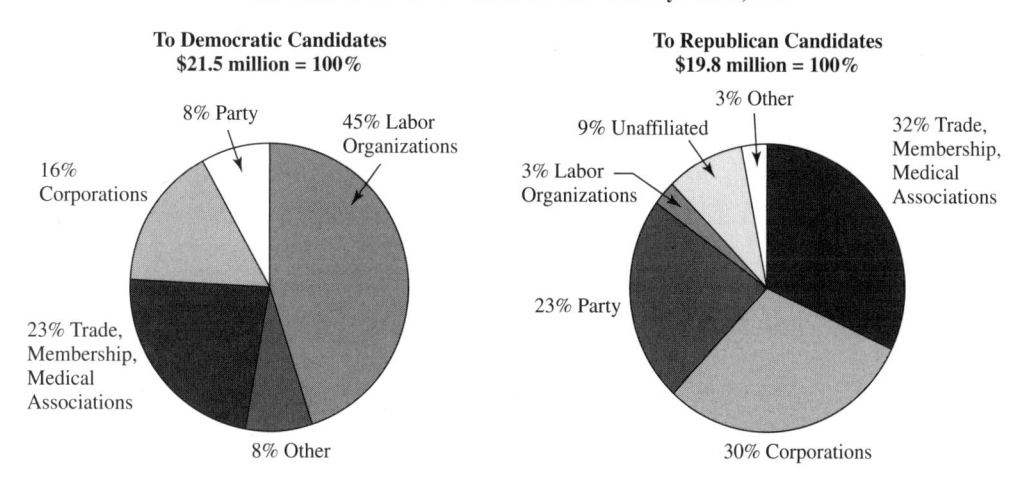

To Democratic Candidates
$21.5 million = 100%

- 8% Party
- 45% Labor Organizations
- 16% Corporations
- 23% Trade, Membership, Medical Associations
- 8% Other

To Republican Candidates
$19.8 million = 100%

- 3% Other
- 9% Unaffiliated
- 32% Trade, Membership, Medical Associations
- 3% Labor Organizations
- 23% Party
- 30% Corporations

17. For 2006, what was the total dollar support to Democratic and Republican candidates made by corporations expressed as a percent of total contributions from all sources? (Round to one decimal place.)

    (A) 21.2 percent
    (B) 21.7 percent
    (C) 22.1 percent
    (D) 22.7 percent
    (E) 23.1 percent

18. To construct an accurate pie chart for the data, what central angle should be used to represent the labor organizations' Democratic contribution?

    (A) 135°
    (B) 147°
    (C) 153°
    (D) 158°
    (E) 162°

19. If the total 2006 contribution to the Democratic candidates represents a 15 percent increase over the total they received in the previous election, what was the approximate amount received in the previous election?

(A) 18,700,000
(B) 18,500,000
(C) 18,300,000
(D) 18,100,000
(E) 17,900,000

20. The 2006 labor organizations' contribution to the Democrats was approximately what percent greater than the labor organizations' 2006 Republican contribution?

(A) 62 percent
(B) 127 percent
(C) 198 percent
(D) 407 percent
(E) 1,529 percent

For the following question, select all the answer choices that apply.

21. If g is a factor of f^2, but not a factor of f, then f and g could be which of the following? Indicate all possible choices.

[A] $f = 3, g = 4$
[B] $f = 8, g = 4$
[C] $f = 6, g = 3$
[D] $f = 10, g = 6$
[E] $f = 10, g = 4$

Question 22 is based on the following graph.

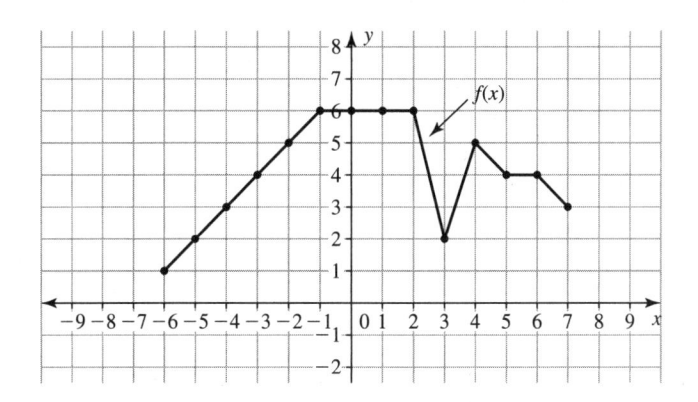

22. In the xy-coordinate plane, the figure above represents the function f from $-6 \leq x \leq 7$. If $f(7) = m$, what is the value of $f(m)$?

   (A) -4
   (B) 2
   (C) 3
   (D) 5
   (E) 6

Question 23 is based on the following table.

Number of Siblings	Frequency
0	5
1	12
2	10
3	8
4	5

For the following question, enter your answer in the box.

23. The table above provides the frequency distribution for a class survey about siblings. What is the mean of the distribution?

Mean = ☐

24. What is the sum of the increasing consecutive integers from −15 to 20?

(A) 90
(B) 110
(C) 220
(D) 380
(E) 460

For the following question, enter your answer in the box.

25. $a_1, a_2, a_3, a_4, \ldots a_n \ldots$

In the sequence above, each term is defined by $a_n = \dfrac{1}{2n-1} - \dfrac{1}{2n+1}$, for each integer value of n, $n \geq 1$. What is the sum of the first eight terms?
Give your answer as a fraction.

Sum = ☐/☐

STOP. This is the end of Quantitative Reasoning Section 1.

SECTION 2

Quantitative Reasoning

25 Questions
40 Minutes

1. $2x - 5y = 8$

   Quantity A

   $\dfrac{10y - 4x}{-3}$

   Quantity B

   5

   (A) Quantity A is greater.
   (B) Quantity B is greater.
   (C) The two quantities are equal.
   (D) The relationship cannot be determined from the information given.

2. Joan's second test score was 10 points higher than her first test score. Josh's second test score was 10 points higher than his first test score.

   Quantity A

   Joan's percent increase from her first test score to her second test score

   Quantity B

   Josh's percent increase from his first test score to his second test score

   (A) Quantity A is greater.
   (B) Quantity B is greater.
   (C) The two quantities are equal.
   (D) The relationship cannot be determined from the information given.

3. The length of one side of a rectangle is 8 and the length of its diagonal is 17.

   Quantity A

   The area of the rectangle

   Quantity B

   100

   (A) Quantity A is greater.
   (B) Quantity B is greater.
   (C) The two quantities are equal.
   (D) The relationship cannot be determined from the information given.

GO ON TO NEXT PAGE→

4. Alexia has a can containing 21 coins which are either nickels or quarters. The total value of the coins in the can is $3.05.

Quantity A

The number of nickels in the can

Quantity B

The number of quarters in the can

(A) Quantity A is greater.
(B) Quantity B is greater.
(C) The two quantities are equal.
(D) The relationship cannot be determined from the information given.

5. The ratio of male to female faculty at school A is 2:3. The ratio of male to female faculty at school B is 5:4. Each of the schools has the same number of total faculty.

Quantity A

The number of male faculty at school A

Quantity B

The number of female faculty at school B

(A) Quantity A is greater.
(B) Quantity B is greater.
(C) The two quantities are equal.
(D) The relationship cannot be determined from the information given.

6.

Quantity A

The average of 11 consecutive odd integers, if the middle integer is 23

Quantity B

The average of 11 consecutive integers, if the middle integer is 23

(A) Quantity A is greater.
(B) Quantity B is greater.
(C) The two quantities are equal.
(D) The relationship cannot be determined from the information given.

7. Data set A = 3, 4, 5, 6, 3, 4, 3, 4, 3, 3

Quantity A

The mode of data set A

Quantity B

The second quartile of the data set A

(A) Quantity A is greater.
(B) Quantity B is greater.
(C) The two quantities are equal.
(D) The relationship cannot be determined from the information given.

	Quantity A	**Quantity B**
8.	The numerical value of the volume of a cube with edge w	The numerical value of the surface area of a cube with edge w

- (A) Quantity A is greater.
- (B) Quantity B is greater.
- (C) The two quantities are equal.
- (D) The relationship cannot be determined from the information given.

9. Nathan can do a particular job alone in 4 days, Joshua can do it alone in 6 days, and Larry can do it alone in 10 days.

Quantity A	**Quantity B**
The number of days to do the particular job if Joshua and Larry work together	The number of days to complete the particular job if Nathan does it alone

- (A) Quantity A is greater.
- (B) Quantity B is greater.
- (C) The two quantities are equal.
- (D) The relationship cannot be determined from the information given.

For the following question, enter your answer in the box.

10. If the five designs shown above are to be placed in a linear arrangement with the condition that the square cannot be in the first, third, or fifth position, then how many different arrangements are possible?

[   ] arrangements

GO ON TO NEXT PAGE →

For the following question, select all the answer choices that apply.

11. If doubling a number *n* has the same value as halving the number, which of the following must be true?

    Indicate all such statements.

    A *n* is negative.
    B *n* is even.
    C *n* is zero.
    D *n* is not an integer.
    E *n* is odd.

Question 12 is based on the following graph.

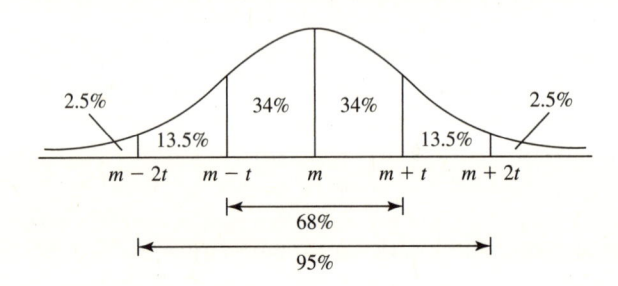

12. On a standardized test, the scores are normally distributed with a mean of 80 and a standard deviation of 5. If a student scored 92, which one of the following describes the percentile rank?

    A Below the 67th percentile
    B Between the 67th percentile and the 84th percentile
    C Between the 84th percentile and the 91st percentile
    D Between the 91st percentile and the 97th percentile
    E Above the 97th percentile

Question 13 is based on the following figure.

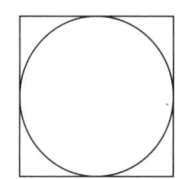

13. In the figure above, the circle is inscribed in the square. If the circumference of the circle is 5, what is the area of the square?

- (A) $\dfrac{5}{\pi}$
- (B) $\dfrac{5}{4\pi}$
- (C) $\dfrac{25}{\pi}$
- (D) $\dfrac{25}{\pi^2}$
- (E) $\dfrac{25}{4\pi^2}$

Question 14 is based on the following table.

Type of Salad	Number of Votes
Tuna	6
Egg	2
Pasta	4
Potato	1
Chicken	4
Garden	4
Cobb	12
Shrimp	7

14. The chart above shows the results of a survey in which 40 different students were asked to name their favorite type of salad. If this data were converted to a pie chart, the central angle representing egg salad would be how many degrees?

- (A) 10
- (B) 12
- (C) 14
- (D) 16
- (E) 18

15. If x and y are positive and $4^{2x+1} = 8^{3y-2}$, what is the value of $4x - 9y$?

- (A) -8
- (B) -6
- (C) -2
- (D) 0
- (E) 6

16. If the area of a square is $3x$, what is the length of its diagonal?

- (A) $\sqrt{3x}$
- (B) $\sqrt{6x}$
- (C) $x\sqrt{3}$
- (D) $x\sqrt{6}$
- (E) $3\sqrt{x}$

Questions 17 to 20 are based on the following data.

Dollars Spent in August 1998 by 50 State University Students for Textbooks (Organized by grade level of student)

	Freshman	Sophomore	Junior	Senior	Graduate
	$280	$258	$279	$266	$216
	295	291	294	289	253
	268	302	310	290	198
	284	273	303	257	221
	305	287	283	303	192
	308	312	277	271	218
	284	297	292	280	226
	278	281	269	264	214
	263	266	298	288	219
	296	280	304	270	196
Total	$2,861	$2,847	$2,909	$2,778	$2,153

Dollars Spent in August 1998 by 50 State University Students for School Incidentals (Organized by grade level of student)

	Freshman	Sophomore	Junior	Senior	Graduate
	$62	$65	$63	$77	$64
	59	63	65	69	60
	62	64	67	73	57
	64	65	74	73	76
	62	63	71	75	64
	64	61	69	66	60
	55	62	65	82	66
	60	64	67	76	67
	63	67	70	73	69
	63	66	69	77	69
Total	$614	$640	$680	$741	$652

17. Of all the grade levels, which group's data has the greatest range for money spent on school incidentals?

  (A) Freshman
  (B) Sophomore
  (C) Junior
  (D) Senior
  (E) Graduate

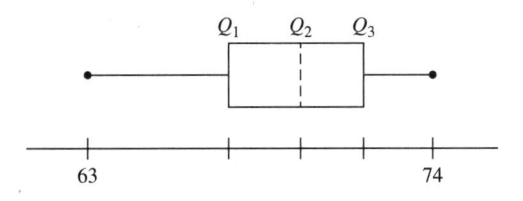

18. If the junior class data of dollars spent for school incidentals was displayed as the box-and-whisker plot shown above, what is the value associated with Q_2 (the second quartile)?

$Q_2 =$ ⬚

19. If the freshman class had 3,000 students in August 1998, which of the following is the best approximation in dollars for the total amount spent (textbooks + incidentals) by the entire freshman class in August 1998?

(A) 993,500
(B) 1,012,500
(C) 1,042,500
(D) 1,082,500
(E) 1,112,500

20. The average of the total expense (textbooks + incidentals) for seniors in August 1998 is approximately what percent greater than the average of the total expense for graduate students in August 1998?

(A) 24.75 percent
(B) 24.85 percent
(C) 24.95 percent
(D) 25.05 percent
(E) 25.45 percent

21. A four-digit number is to be formed which cannot begin with a zero or end in a seven. Assuming digits can be repeating, how many such numbers can be formed?

(A) 9^4
(B) $9^2 \times 10^2$
(C) 9×10^3
(D) $9^3 \times 10$
(E) $10 \times 9 \times 8 \times 7$

22. The average of $a + 2$, $b - 1$, and $c + 5$ is 10. What is the average of $a - 1$, $b + 7$, $c + 2$, and 8?

(A) 11
(B) 10
(C) 9
(D) 8
(E) 7

For the following question, select all the answer choices that apply.

23. $\dfrac{x}{y} = \dfrac{2}{5}$

    Which of the following MUST be true?
    Indicate all such answers.

    A $x = 2$
    B $5x = 2y$
    C $x^2 < y^2$
    D $y > x$

24. If $x + y = \sqrt{12}$, and $x - y = \sqrt{3}$, what is the value of $y^2 - x^2$?

    A -6
    B -4
    C -2
    D -1
    E 3

25. The product of $\sqrt{5(11)} \times \sqrt{a(b)} \times \sqrt{4(7)(11)}$ is an integer. If a and b are prime numbers, what is the sum of a^2 and b^2?

    A 52
    B 67
    C 74
    D 85
    E 117

STOP. This is the end of Quantitative Reasoning Section 2.

Answer Key: Verbal Reasoning Section 1

Question Number	Correct Answer
1.	A and B
2.	When a bug is discovered, the tester logs it in another computer program called a bug tracker, which allows programmers to test the bug, fix it, and then record that they fixed it and what actions they took, so the QA team can retest the functionality.
3.	C
4.	C
5.	B and F
6.	C and D
7.	B and E
8.	C
9.	E
10.	A and C
11.	The question is one of funding here on Earth—will the mission be deemed important enough to subsidize scientists who can receive, review, and understand the images the Orbiter faithfully sends?
12.	A, B, and C
13.	A
14.	B
15.	D
16.	C and D
17.	B, E, and G
18.	C
19.	C
20.	A
21.	B and D

ANSWER KEY: VERBAL REASONING
Section 1

Question Number	Correct Answer
22.	A and D
23.	B and C
24.	E and F
25.	A and E

Answer Key: Verbal Reasoning Section 2

Question Number	Correct Answer
1.	B and E
2.	C and F
3.	A and F
4.	B and E
5.	A and B
6.	E
7.	C
8.	C
9.	During the examination by the police, each person has the chance to implicate the other person or to accept some of the blame, and there is no evidence to support or disprove any of the assertions.
10.	A and E
11.	B, D, and G
12.	C
13.	A
14.	D
15.	B
16.	E
17.	D
18.	B and F
19.	B and F
20.	A, D, and G

ANSWER KEY: VERBAL REASONING
Section 2

Question Number	Correct Answer
21.	B
22.	A
23.	B
24.	Only after several weeks when she returns and feeds the hatchling will the male finally be able to go off to find food for himself.
25.	D

Answer Key: Quantitative Reasoning Section 1

Question Number	Correct Answer
1.	B
2.	A
3.	D
4.	A
5.	C
6.	C
7.	C
8.	A
9.	D
10.	-3
11.	A
12.	E
13.	C
14.	E
15.	D and E
16.	D
17.	D
18.	E
19.	A
20.	E
21.	E
22.	B
23.	1.9
24.	A
25.	$\dfrac{16}{17}$

Answer Key: Quantitative Reasoning
Section 2

Question Number	Correct Answer
1.	A
2.	D
3.	A
4.	A
5.	B
6.	C
7.	B
8.	D
9.	B
10.	48
11.	B and C
12.	E
13.	D
14.	E
15.	A
16.	B
17.	E
18.	68
19.	C
20.	E
21.	B
22.	B
23.	B and C
24.	A
25.	C

Answer Explanations

Analytical Writing: Section 1
Analyze an Issue

Sample of a Level 5 Essay

While some would say that telling the truth is more important than sparing others' feelings, telling the truth in all situations can cause more problems than it solves. In particular, if a person doesn't strictly need to know the truth, telling her something that will hurt her can be worse for her than never knowing. In the following essay I will use examples to show situations in which telling the truth would be worse than sparing someone's feelings.

One simple example in which telling the truth is counterproductive is in complimenting someone you love on something they've done for you. If your grandmother makes your favorite meal but does not cook it well, you could be honest and tell her it does not taste good to you. But this would hurt your grandmother's feelings, and there's no reason to do so. Eating a meal that doesn't taste good is a small price to pay to keep your grandmother happy and feeling like she's doing something good for you.

Another simple example is telling someone when he doesn't look good. Unless the problem with his appearance is something he can fix easily (such as having something in his teeth or a misbuttoned shirt), it serves no purpose to tell someone that he does not look good. It will only make him feel bad, and will also make him unhappy with you. Instead of preserving the relationship between you, you will introduce bad feelings for no reason.

A more serious situation in which telling the truth might not be the best policy would be discovering information someone is not aware of that could adversely affect the other person's life. For example, discovering that a friend's spouse is committing adultery is an almost impossible position to be in. If you tell your friend about the infidelity, your friend will probably not believe you initially, and will become extremely angry and will resent you. Even if the friend gets out of the relationship, the friend will likely never come back to you as a friend. In contrast, not saying anything and simply being there for your friend when the friend eventually finds out about the infidelity will preserve your relationship and allow you to be a support for the friend when the relationship ends.

In short, telling the truth in all situations can irreparably harm your relationship with the person to whom you tell the truth. It may be better, in some situations, to preserve the other person's good feelings if telling the truth doesn't have a clear purpose. Even if telling the truth seems obvious, you should think about whether telling the truth will strengthen or harm your relationship.

Answer Explanations

Analytical Writing: Section 2
Analyze an Argument

Sample of a Level 5 Essay

The argument made by the Deputy Mayor, that the merchants on the part of Fleet Street that will be widened will gain business because of the widening project, has too many flaws to be persuasive. If the Deputy Mayor could give evidence to support the assertions in the argument and could plug some of the holes in the argument, the argument would make sense. As it stands, however, the Deputy Mayor's statement is too flawed to convince readers.

The Deputy Mayor states that, despite losing square footage from their storefronts, the merchants will be more profitable because of increased street traffic. This assertion makes two huge assumptions that are not proven. The first is that widening the street will actually increase traffic. If other patterns do not change once the widening occurs, there may be no increase in traffic whatsoever. The Deputy Mayor did not provide any evidence that the traffic will definitely increase. In addition, what if the traffic increases but it is all through traffic that does not stop to make purchases from the merchants on Fleet Street? If the cars do not stop, then the merchants won't make any more money, and the increased traffic may even dissuade some of their current customers from stopping anymore.

The second assumption the Deputy Mayor makes is that, with less square footage, the merchants will still be profitable. What if a merchant needs exactly the amount of space they have currently to be able to properly serve customers? Reducing footage will reduce the number of tables a restaurateur can serve, the number of chairs a hairstyling salon can hold, and the counter space a bakery can hold. What if losing space makes it difficult or impossible for a merchant to provide the same level of service or to produce the best products? The Deputy Mayor has not given any research showing that less space is truly practicable for any, let alone all, of the merchants on that stretch of Fleet Street.

The Deputy Mayor's biggest assumption, however, is that having your business blocked or closed for 11 months will not cause you to lose business either during that time or after that time. If customers cannot enter your business for almost a year, or have to find an alternate route to get to your business, those customers may go somewhere else. And they might not come back, even after the construction is done and your business has reopened. The argument that the widening of the street will be good for business does not take into account the fact that the merchants may lose business during the project that will never come back.

If the Deputy Mayor could prove that his assertions are correct or plug the holes in the argument, the statement would make sense. As it stands, however, the statement is not persuasive, and the City Council should not enact the plan to widen the street without a true impact study.

Answer Explanations
Verbal Reasoning: Section 1

1. A and B

The answers are A and B. The passage discusses the process of finding and fixing bugs in software, so choice A is supported. The passage also discusses the QA process and how it tests everything that can be done with software methodically, so choice B is supported by the passage. Choice C is not supported by the passage, because the passage discusses clicking icons as a way to discover bugs, not as something that causes them.

2. ANSWER:

When a bug is discovered, the tester logs it in another computer program called a bug tracker, which allows programmers to test the bug, fix it, and then record that they fixed it and what actions they took, so the QA team can retest the functionality.

The correct sentence describes the use of a bug tracker program to log a discovered bug, fix it, and then document that it has been fixed so it can be retested.

3. C

The answer is C. Another word for "end-user" in the sentence is "operator of the software." The best match for this is choice C. Choices A and B do not identify an end-user as a person. Choice D confuses an end-user with a QA tester, and choice E confuses an end-user with a person who creates the software.

4. C

The answer is C. The bolded sentence explains that QA is a specific, organized process, which supports choice C. Choices A, D, and E are covered in other parts of the passage. Choice B is not supported because the passage doesn't ask a question.

ANSWER EXPLANATIONS
Verbal Reasoning: Section 1

5. B and F

The answers are B and F. The word in the first blank needs to mean "specifications." The best match is choice B. Choice A does not make sense in the sentence. Choice C is close, but does not fit with the candidate's need to represent herself best. The word in the second blank needs to mean "best." The best match is choice F. Choices D and E are both opposite of the meaning.

6. C and D

The answers are C and D. The word in the first blank needs to mean "story of her life." The best match is choice C. Choices A and B are similar, but the sentence refers to the "reader," which indicates a written text. The word in the second blank needs to mean "someone she got arrested with." The best match is choice D. Choice E is a fan, not someone she did something with. Choice F indicates a musical relationship.

7. B and E

The answers are B and E. The word in the first blank needs to mean "imagining." Choice B is the best match. Choice A is close but not close enough. Choice C is the opposite process. The word in the second blank needs to mean "human-loving." The best match is choice E. Choice D does not actually mean "human-loving" although it sounds like it does. Choice F is a positive word, but it does not indicate that Thoreau likes other people.

8. C

The answer is C. The word in the blank needs to mean "measurable." The best match is choice C. Choices A and E are the opposite. Choice B is not supported by the sentence. Choice D is not supported by the sentence, either.

9. E

The answer is E. The passage discusses the Orbiter program and how the Orbiter itself will outlive the mission humans created it for. This supports choice E. Choice A is not discussed. Choice B is partly true, but not the point of the passage. Choices C and D are not supported by the passage.

10. A and C

The answers are A and C. The passage discusses the Orbiter's original mission, which supports choice A. The passage discusses the sand dunes on Mars during winter, not the dunes at all times, so choice B is not supported. The passage says that there is debate at NASA about funding more Mars missions, so this supports choice C.

11. ANSWER:

The question is one of funding here on Earth—will the mission be deemed important enough to subsidize scientists who can receive, review, and understand the images the Orbiter faithfully sends?

The sentence shows that the Mars Orbiter is just one example of something that may or may not be worth funding, depending on the interest we now have in the data it gathers.

12. A, B, and C

The answers are A, B, and C. The author refers to the information sent from the Orbiter as "more precious," which supports choice A. The third paragraph of the passage examines the question of continuing funding, which supports choices B and C.

13. A

The answer is A. The passage states that people have increasing amounts of nutritional information available to them, but that the rate of obesity is increasing, so people must not be able to act on that information, which supports choice A. The passage does not mention existent obesity, so choice B is not supported. Choices C and D are not supported by the passage. Choice E is supported by the passage, but is not a discrepancy.

14. B

The answer is B. The word in the blank needs to mean "flight." The best match is choice B. Choices A, D, and E are far too negative. Choice C means the opposite.

15. D

The answer is D. The word in the blank needs to mean "confusing allusions." The best match is choice D. Choices A and B are not supported by the sentence. Choice C is close, but "allegory" doesn't involve allusions and double meaning as symbolism does. Choice E is not supported by the sentence.

ANSWER EXPLANATIONS 319
Verbal Reasoning: Section 1

16. C and D

The answers are C and D. Start with the second blank. The word in the second blank needs to mean "actual defiance." The best match is choice D. Choice E is very close, but "resolve" is stronger and leads to action whereas "earnestness" can be derailed more easily. Choice F is not close. Now work out the first blank. The word in the first blank needs to mean "staged." The best match is choice C. Choices A and B are not even close to staging.

17. B, E, and G

The answers are B, E, and G. The word in the first blank needs to mean "foolish." The best match is choice B. Choice A has a similar meaning, but does not contain the sense of stupidity for continuing. Choice C is the opposite. The word in the second blank needs to mean "difficult to find." The best match is choice E. Choice D is a homophone with a different meaning, and choice F sounds similar but also has the wrong meaning. The word in the third blank needs to mean "achievement." The best match is choice G. Choice H is not strong enough, and choice I is the opposite.

18. C

The answer is C. The passage is broad and paints stereotypes of both urban and rural dwellers, which supports choice C. Choices A and B are not supported by the passage. Choice D is not supported because the passage does not specify locations. Choice E does not make sense and is not supported by the passage.

19. C

The answer is C. The passage does not mention creating communities ad hoc in urban areas, so choice A is not supported. Choice B is not supported by the passage, which doesn't mention an insider's perspective. Choice C is supported when the passage says that mass transit gave rise to the need for social media.

20. A

The answer is A. Since the word means "ridiculous," the best match is choice A. None of the other choices come near to matching the meaning of the word.

21. B and D

The answers are B and D. The word in the blank needs to mean "obstruction." The best matches are choices B and D. Choices A and C do not make sense—how could a delivery service cause a vehicle or a carrier? Choice E is closer, but not exactly right, and has no other matching choice.

22. A and D

The answers are A and D. The word in the blank needs to mean "happening." The best matches are choices A and D. The other pair, choices B and C, would mean "foreknowledge," which doesn't make sense in the sentence. Choices E and F also do not make sense in the sentence.

23. B and C

The answers are B and C. The word in the blank needs to mean "depend." The best matches are choices B and C. Choices A and D do not give the idea of a dependent relationship. Choice E is too negative, and choice F does not make sense in the sentence.

24. E and F

The answers are E and F. The word in the blank needs to mean "hurrying up." The best matches are choices E and F. The other pair, choices B and C, do not mean "hurrying up." Choice A makes no sense in the sentence, and choice D is the opposite meaning.

25. A and E

The answers are A and E. The word in the blank needs to mean "upsetting and surprising." The best matches are choices A and E. Choice B is not supported, because we don't know if anyone else noticed her distraction. Choice C is too extreme. Choices D and F are not indicated in the sentence.

Answer Explanations
Verbal Reasoning: Section 2

1. B and E

The answers are B and E. The word in the blank needs to mean "without a care." The best matches are B and E. Choices A and F indicate an energy that isn't supported by the sentence. Choices C and D do not match each other, and they are both opposite.

2. C and F

The answers are C and F. The word in the blank needs to mean "passion." The best matches are choices C and F. Choice A does not describe emotion, nor do choices D and E. Choice B is too weak a feeling.

3. A and F

The answers are A and F. The word in the blank needs to mean "unofficial." The best matches are choices A and F. Choices B and C are not supported by the passage—how would those exist if they weren't released by the estate? Choice D is unlikely to exist. Choice E does not make sense in the sentence.

4. B and E

The answers are B and E. The word in the blank needs to mean "private." The best matches are choices B and E. Choice A gives the idea of deliberately secret, which is too extreme. Choices C and D both mean "hidden away from others," which is too extreme. Choice F is the opposite.

5. A and B

The answers are A and B. The passage states that the child "becomes anxious and fearful when required to separate from this caregiver," which supports both choices A and B. The passage does not mention being tethered physically to anyone, however, so choice C is not supported.

6. E

The answer is E. The passage mentions the phrase "root cause" when it switches from the discussion of the external signs of separation anxiety to the underlying cognitive reason, which supports choice E. The passage mentions nothing about separation anxiety continuing, so choice A is not supported. The passage does not say it is an organic process, so choice B is not supported. The passage states that separation anxiety is common, so choice C is not supported. The passage does not say that separation anxiety can be eliminated, so choice D is not supported.

7. C

The answer is C. Choice C provides the scientific reason why the population of lizards would increase in wetter conditions. Choice A is an alternate cause for the increase in the lizard population that would not support the researchers' argument. Choice B provides a reason for the increase in precipitation, but does not address the lizard population. Choice D provides a reason that the researchers' argument would be false. Choice E has nothing to do with the researchers' argument.

8. C

The answer is C. The last sentence of the passage says that the challenge is in working out the complexity of possible outcomes, which supports choice C. Chess boards are not mentioned in the passage, so choice A is not supported. Choice B assumes that the challenge of Prisoner's Dilemma is in being one of the prisoners, not in working out what the prisoners will do, so choice B is not supported.

9. ANSWER:

During the examination by the police, each person has the chance to implicate the other person or to accept some of the blame, and there is no evidence to support or disprove any of the assertions.

The sentence describes what the prisoners tell the police in the examination room.

10. A and E

The answers are A and E. The word in the first blank needs to mean "a lack of understanding." The best match is choice A. Choice B is the opposite. Choice C sounds similar to the best match, but is not the same in meaning. The word in the second blank needs to mean "steady." The best match is choice E. Choice D is similar, but means "not able to be moved," not "steady." Choice F is not strong enough.

11. B, D, and G

The answers are B, D, and G. The word in the first blank needs to conjure "love." The best match is choice B. Choice A is the opposite. Choice C ignores the love aspects of the book. The word in the second blank needs to mean "practical." The best match is choice D. Choice E is too extreme, and choice F is the opposite. The word in the third blank needs to mean "getting rid of." The best match is choice G. Choice H is not strong enough. Choice I is too positive.

12. C

The answer is C. The word in the blank needs to mean "lucky thing." The best match is choice C. Choice A does not indicate who the favor would be for. Choice B does not make sense in the sentence. Choices D and E are close, but have slightly different meanings.

13. A

The answer is A. The word in the blank needs to mean "helped." The best match is choice A. Choices B, C, D, and E are all too extreme.

14. D

The answer is D. The passage states that there is a story celebrating reading for the pleasure of reading intercalated with the chapters criticizing criticism, which supports choice D. Choices A, C, and E are not supported because the passage contains no information about the reading level of the book, university courses, or why Calvino wrote the book. Choice B is not supported because there is no mention in the passage of the popularity of literary criticism.

15. B

The answer is B. The passage states that the novel is a "love note" to those who love to read and a "triumph" at writing something that is almost impossible to criticize, which supports choice B. Choice A is not supported because it says "almost too thick to be criticized." There is nothing in the passage to support choice C. Choice D is far too broad and is not supported in the passage. There is nothing in the passage that supports choice E.

16. E

The answer is E. The passage discusses two contrasting parts of Calvino's novel, which supports choice E. Choices A, B, and C only discuss one aspect of the novel, so they are not supported. Choice D mentions the two parts, but only the stories, and assumes that the criticism half is only one story.

17. D

The answer is D. The word in the blank needs to mean "taken off course." The best match is choice D. Choices A and B give the idea that the meeting was stopped. Choice C does not make sense in the sentence, nor does choice E.

18. B and F

The answers are B and F. The word in the first blank needs to mean "come together." The best match is choice B. Choice A is too extreme, and choice C is too weak. The word in the second blank needs to mean "purpose." The best match is choice F. Choice D is too extreme, and choice E does not make sense in the sentence.

19. B and F

The answers are B and F. Start with the second blank. The word in the blank needs to mean "newness." The best match is choice F. Choice D is not supported by the sentence, and choice E is too negative. Now go back to the first blank. The word in the blank needs to mean "not-new-ness." The best match is choice B. Choice A is not supported by the sentence, and choice C is too weak.

20. A, D, and G

The answers are A, D, and G. The word in the first blank needs to mean "eradicated." The best match is choice A. Choices B and C are too weak. The word in the second blank needs to mean "vulnerable." The best match is choice D. Choice F does not make sense in the sentence, and choice E is too extreme. The word in the third blank needs to mean "threatens." The best match is choice G. Choice H is too weak, and choice I doesn't indicate that it is threatening.

21. B

The answer is B. The passage discusses the fact that a product produced by one species has healing properties for another species. This supports choice B, but not choices A, D, or E. Choice C is not supported because there is no mention of dogs in the passage.

22. A

The answer is A. The passage states that employees are more productive and less sick when using ergonomic workspaces, which supports choice A. Choice B is the opposite of the conclusion of the passage. Choice C is not supported, as the passage does not indicate if either group benefits more strongly from a redesign. Choice D is out of the scope of the passage. Choice E introduces an entirely new topic that may not be related to the ergonomic redesign.

23. B

The answer is B. The passage states that they mate for a breeding season, not for life, so choice A is not supported. The passage describes what the male does and what the female does while the egg is incubating, so choice B is supported. There is no evidence in the passage to support choice C.

24. ANSWER:

Only after several weeks when she returns and feeds the hatchling will the male finally be able to go off to find food for himself.

The last sentence describes that, after the female returns with food for the hatchling, the male goes out to look for food for himself.

25. D

The answer is D. The passage describes the process of breeding and hatching an egg, which is choice D. There is no hypothesis, question, theories, or criticisms, so there is no support for the other choices.

Answer Explanations
Quantitative Reasoning: Section 1

1. B

> Note: Figure not drawn to scale.
>
> Note: There are 360° in a circle.

STEP 1 Express each angle in terms of a single variable.

STEP 2 $a = 1.5b = (1.5)(2c) = 3c = (3)(2.5d) = 7.5d$

$b = 2c = 2(2.5d) = 5d$

$c = 2.5d$

$d = d$

STEP 3 Add the angles to 360° and solve for d.

$$a + b + c + d = 360$$

$$7.5d + 5d + 2.5d + d = 360$$

$$16d = 360$$

$$d = 22.5$$

STEP 4 $c = 2.5d = (2.5)(22.5) = 56.25$

Quantity B > Quantity A

2. A

STEP 1 Diagram the situation.

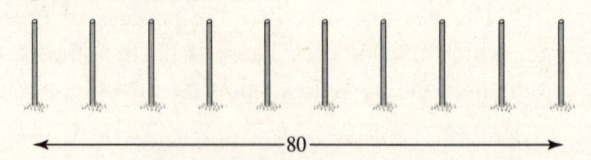

There are nine spaces, so the distance between fence posts is $\frac{80}{9}$ feet.

STEP 2 The distance from the third post to the fifth post includes two spaces.

$$2\left(\frac{80}{9}\right) = \frac{160}{9} > 16$$

Quantity A > Quantity B

3. D

Note: $x^2 = y^2 \Rightarrow x = \pm y$

STEP 1 $x^2 = y^2$ does NOT mean $x = y$. It means $x = \pm y$.

As an example if $x^2 = y^2 = z^2 = 4$

then: $\begin{cases} x \text{ could be } +2 \text{ or } -2 \\ y \text{ could be } +2 \text{ or } -2 \\ z \text{ could be } +2 \text{ or } -2 \end{cases}$

STEP 2 Using our example, since $x = \pm 2, y = \pm 2, z = \pm 2$

then $\frac{x}{y} = \pm 1$ and $\frac{y}{z} = \pm 1$.

The relationship cannot be determined.

4. A

Note: Circle: $A = \pi r^2$
$C = 2\pi r$

STEP 1 Establish an equation:

$$\frac{\pi r^2}{2\pi r} = \frac{4}{5}$$

STEP 2 Cross-multiply and solve for r.

$$5(\pi r^2) = 4(2\pi r)$$
$$5\pi r^2 = 8\pi r$$
$$r = \frac{8}{5}$$

STEP 3 Diameter = 2(radius) = $\frac{16}{5}$

Quantity A > Quantity B

5. C

> Note: The sum of the length of any two sides of a triangle must be greater than the length of the third side.

STEP 1 Since the triangle is isosceles, there must be two sides of equal length. The only options for side *NL* are 4 or 10.

STEP 2 Side *NL* cannot be 4, because the sum of *NL* + *JL* would not be greater than side *NJ* (4 + 4 is not greater than 10).

STEP 3 Side *NL* must be 10.

STEP 4 Perimeter of $\triangle NJL$ = 10 + 10 + 4 = 24

Quantity A = Quantity B

6. C

> Note:
> - $_nC_r$ represents the number of different groups of *r* items that can be formed from *n* items.
> - $_nC_r = \dfrac{n!}{r!(n-r)!}$

Method 1

$$\text{Quantity A} = {_6C_2} = \frac{6!}{2!(6-2)!} = \frac{6!}{2!(4!)} = 15$$

$$\text{Quantity B} = {_6C_4} = \frac{6!}{4!(6-4)!} = \frac{6!}{4!(2!)} = 15$$

Method 2 Try to diagram the situation.

Represent the students as A, B, C, D, E, F

Quantity A:
AB BC CD DE EF
AC BD CE DF
AD BE CF   } 15
AE
AF BF

Quantity B:
ABCD ABDE ABEF BCDE BDEF ACDE ACEF CDEF
ABCE ABDF   BCDF   ACDF   } 15
ABCF   BCEF   ACEF

Quantity A = Quantity B

ANSWER EXPLANATIONS | 329
Quantitative Reasoning: Section 1

7. C

Note: Assuming $x \neq a$: $a - x = -(x - a)$ and $\dfrac{a-x}{x-a} = \dfrac{x-a}{a-x} = -1$.

STEP 1 $\quad \dfrac{x-2}{2-x} + \dfrac{3-y}{y-3} = (-1) + (-1) = -2$

STEP 2 $\quad \dfrac{4-v}{v-4} + \dfrac{m-5}{5-m} = (-1) + (-1) = -2$

Quantity A = Quantity B

8. A

Note: Represent the situation algebraically.

STEP 1 Set $x = $ the cost of the gift.

STEP 2 If 10 people contribute equally, each pays $\dfrac{x}{10}$.

STEP 3 If 12 people contribute equally, each pays $\dfrac{x}{12}$.

STEP 4 Establish the equation: $\dfrac{x}{10} - \dfrac{x}{12} = 3$.

STEP 5 Find a common denominator and solve for x:

$$\dfrac{6x}{60} - \dfrac{5x}{60} = 3$$

$$\dfrac{x}{60} = 3$$

$$x = 180$$

Quantity A > Quantity B

9. D

Note: Use a diagram.

STEP 1 There are two possible diagrams.

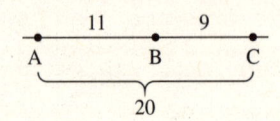

```
    11      9
•———————•———————•
A       B       C
⎣_____⎦
        20
```

Quantity A = Quantity B

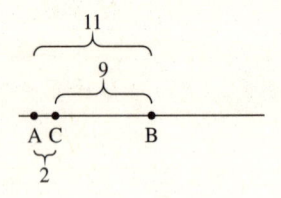

```
     11
  ⎤‾‾‾‾‾‾‾⎡
     9
  ⎤‾‾‾⎡
•—•————•————————
A C    B
⎣⎦
 2
```

Quantity B > Quantity A

The relationship cannot be determined.

10. −3

Note: $f(a) = b$

  means: for an x-value of a, the function y-value is b.

  means: the point $x = a, y = b$ is on the function.

  means: a is the input to the function, $f(a)$ or b is the output value of the function.

STEP 1 We begin the analysis of $h(h(5))$ at the inner $h(5)$.

The input x-value of 5 has an output y-value of −5.

$h(5) = -5$

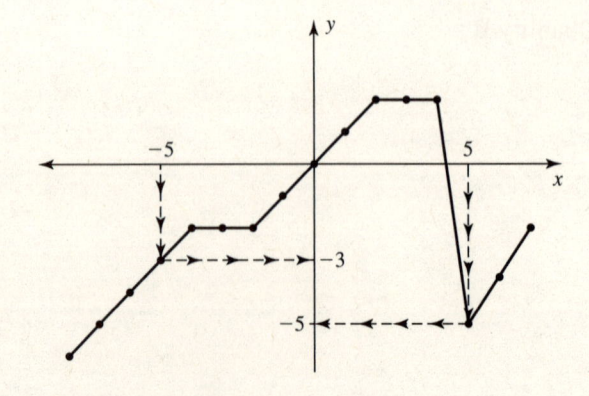

ANSWER EXPLANATIONS | 331
Quantitative Reasoning: Section 1

STEP 2 Analyze $h(h(5)) = h(-5)$.

The input x-value is now -5 and the corresponding y-value is -3.

$h(h(5)) = h(-5) = -3$

11. A

Note: For a normal distribution:
Let m = mean
Let t = a standard deviation

(All percentages are approximate.)

STEP 1 Overlay the actual data on the normal curve.

STEP 2 A score of 70 occurs 2 standard deviations below the mean. The labeled curve indicates that ~2.5 percent of the scores will be below 70.

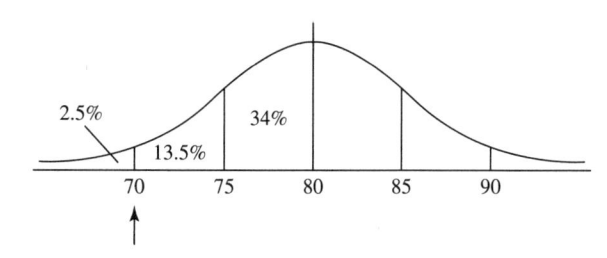

12. E

Note: Roots are the values of x that make a function equal zero.

STEP 1 Substitute $x = \dfrac{1}{5}$ and equate the function to zero.

$$10\left(\dfrac{1}{5}\right)^2 + k\left(\dfrac{1}{5}\right) - 3 = 0$$

STEP 2 Solve for k:

$$10\left(\dfrac{1}{25}\right) + k\left(\dfrac{1}{5}\right) - 3 = 0$$

$$\dfrac{2}{5} + \dfrac{1}{5}k - 3 = 0$$

$$\dfrac{1}{5}k = 3 - \dfrac{2}{5}$$

$$\dfrac{1}{5}k = \dfrac{13}{5}$$

$$k = 13$$

13. C

> Note: Let S = sum of the numbers
> A = average of the numbers
> n = the quantity of the number
> $\Big\}$ $A = \dfrac{S}{n}$ or $S = A \times n$

STEP 1 Express the data algebraically. Let w, x, y, and z represent the four numbers and let w be the number removed.

$$\frac{w + x + y + z}{4} = \frac{x + y + z}{3} + 2$$

STEP 2 Substitute $w = 7$, cross-multiply, and solve for $x + y + z$.

$$\frac{7 + x + y + z}{4} = \frac{x + y + z}{3} + \frac{6}{3}$$

$$\frac{7 + x + y + z}{4} = \frac{x + y + z + 6}{3}$$

$$3x + 3y + 3z + 21 = 4x + 4y + 4z + 24$$

$$x + y + z = -3$$

STEP 3 The average of x, y, z is $\dfrac{x + y + z}{3} = \dfrac{-3}{3} = -1$.

14. E

> Note: $\dfrac{x^a}{x^b} = x^{a-b}$. If $2^a = 2^b$, then $a = b$.

STEP 1 Combine the fractions on the left:

$$\frac{1}{2^x} + \frac{3}{2^x} = 2^a$$

$$\frac{4}{2^x} = 2^a$$

STEP 2 Replace 4 with 2^2 and divide: $\dfrac{2^2}{2^x} = 2^a$

$$2^{2-x} = 2^a$$

STEP 3 Solve for x: $2 - x = a$

$$x = 2 - a$$

ANSWER EXPLANATIONS
Quantitative Reasoning: Section 1

15. D and E

STEP 1 Visualize nine arbitrary different numbers whose median (middle number) we will arbitrarily say is 20.

1 2 3 4 20 21 22 23 24

STEP 2 Analyze each choice.

- $\boxed{A}$ If we increase the lowest number we can force it to the right of 20 and the median will change, such as increasing the 1 by 50 to 51.
- $\boxed{B}$ If we decrease the greatest number we can force it to the left of 20 and the median will change, such as decreasing the 24 by 50 to -26.
- $\boxed{C}$ Increasing each number by 2 will also increase the median by 2.
- $\boxed{D}$ Increasing the greatest number will not change the position of the 24; it will still be the last number. The median will NOT change.
- $\boxed{E}$ Decreasing the lowest number will not change the position of the 1; it will still be the first number. The median will NOT change.

16. D

STEP 1 Draw a diagram.

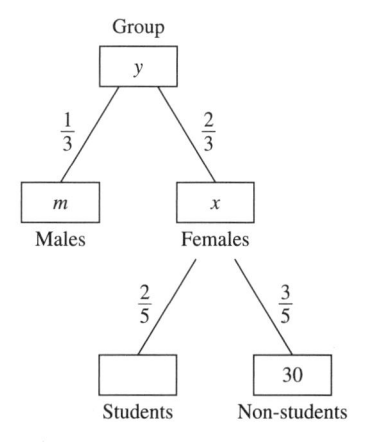

```
              Group
               y
              / \
           1/3   2/3
           /     \
          m       x
        Males   Females
                 / \
               2/5  3/5
               /     \
             [ ]     30
          Students  Non-students
```

STEP 2 Let x = number of females:

$$x\left(\frac{3}{5}\right) = 30 \Rightarrow x = 50$$

STEP 3 Since $\frac{1}{3}$ of the group are males and $\frac{2}{3}$ of the group are females, there are twice as many females as males.

STEP 4 There are 50 females and 25 males.

17. D

STEP 1 Find the dollar contributions for Democrats and Republicans.

Democrats: 16 percent of $21.5 million = 3,440,000
Republicans: 30 percent of $19.8 million = 5,940,000
$$\overline{9,380,000}$$

STEP 2 Express this data as a percent of total contributions:

$$\frac{9,380,000}{21,500,000 + 19,800,000} \times 100 = 22.71 \text{ percent} \approx 22.7\%$$

18. E

> Note: The percentage is out of 100.
> Central angles are out of 360°.

STEP 1 45 percent is 45 out of 100.

You should use 45 percent of 360° = 162°.

19. A

STEP 1 Let x = amount received in the previous election.

x + 15% of x = 2006 contribution

$x + 0.15x = 21,500,000$

$1.15x = 21,500,000$

$x \approx 18,695,652$

20. E

> Note: Percent greater = $\dfrac{\text{Larger} - \text{smaller}}{\text{Smaller}} \times 100$

STEP 1 Calculate the labor organizations' contribution.

Democrat: 0.45 (21,500,000) = 9,675,000
Republican: 0.03 (19,800,000) = 594,000

STEP 2 Percent greater = $\dfrac{9,675,000 - 594,000}{594,000} \times 100$

$\approx 1,529$ percent

ANSWER EXPLANATIONS | **335**
Quantitative Reasoning: Section 1

21. E

> Note: Factors of a number divide into the number without a remainder.

STEP 1 Try each set of answer choices.

$\boxed{A}$ $\dfrac{f^2}{g} = \dfrac{9}{4}$ ∴ g is NOT a factor of f^2. This choice is incorrect.

$\boxed{B}$ $\dfrac{f^2}{g} = \dfrac{64}{4} = 16$, $\dfrac{f}{g} = \dfrac{8}{4} = 2$ ∴ g is a factor of f. This choice is incorrect.

$\boxed{C}$ $\dfrac{f^2}{g} = \dfrac{36}{3} = 12$, $\dfrac{f}{g} = \dfrac{6}{3} = 2$ ∴ g is a factor of f. This choice is incorrect.

$\boxed{D}$ $\dfrac{f^2}{g} = \dfrac{100}{6}$ ∴ g is NOT a factor of f^2. This choice is incorrect.

$\boxed{E}$ $\dfrac{f^2}{g} = \dfrac{100}{4} = 25$, $\dfrac{f}{g} = \dfrac{10}{4} = \dfrac{5}{2}$. This choice is correct.

22. B

> Note: $f(a) = b$
> means: For an x-value of a, the function y-value is b.
> means: The point $x = a$, $y = b$ is on the function.
> means: a is the input to the function, $f(a)$ or b is the output value of the function.

STEP 1 Analyze $f(7)$.

The input $x = 7$ has a corresponding y-value of 3.

$f(7) = 3$ ∴ $m = 3$

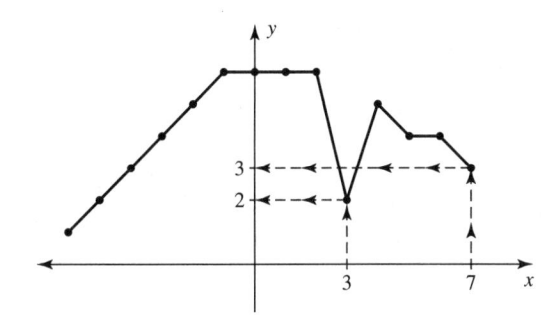

STEP 2 Analyze $f(m) = f(3)$.

The input $x = 3$ has a corresponding y-value of 2.

$f(3) = 2$

23. 1.9

> Note: The mean (arithmetic mean) is the average $= \dfrac{\Sigma x_i f_i}{\Sigma f_i}$

STEP 1 Mean $= \dfrac{5(0) + 12(1) + 10(2) + 8(3) + 5(4)}{5 + 12 + 10 + 8 + 5} = \dfrac{76}{40} = 1.9$

24. A

> Note: The sum of the consecutive increasing integers from $-a$ to $+a$ is 0.

STEP 1 Layout the problem.

$\underline{-15, -14, -13 \ldots\ldots 13, 14, 15,}$ 16, 17, 18, 19, 20

These add up to zero.

STEP 2 $0 + 16 + 17 + 18 + 19 + 20 = 90$

25. $\dfrac{16}{17}$

STEP 1 Develop the sequence.

$a_1 = \dfrac{1}{2(1) - 1} - \dfrac{1}{2(1) + 1} = \dfrac{1}{1} - \dfrac{1}{3}$ $\qquad a_5 = \dfrac{1}{2(5) - 1} - \dfrac{1}{2(5) + 1} = \dfrac{1}{9} - \dfrac{1}{11}$

$a_2 = \dfrac{1}{2(2) - 1} - \dfrac{1}{2(2) + 1} = \dfrac{1}{3} - \dfrac{1}{5}$ $\qquad a_6 = \dfrac{1}{2(6) - 1} - \dfrac{1}{2(6) + 1} = \dfrac{1}{11} - \dfrac{1}{13}$

$a_3 = \dfrac{1}{2(3) - 1} - \dfrac{1}{2(3) + 1} = \dfrac{1}{5} - \dfrac{1}{7}$ $\qquad a_7 = \dfrac{1}{2(7) - 1} - \dfrac{1}{2(7) + 1} = \dfrac{1}{13} - \dfrac{1}{15}$

$a_4 = \dfrac{1}{2(4) - 1} - \dfrac{1}{2(4) + 1} = \dfrac{1}{7} - \dfrac{1}{9}$ $\qquad a_8 = \dfrac{1}{2(8) - 1} - \dfrac{1}{2(8) + 1} = \dfrac{1}{15} - \dfrac{1}{17}$

STEP 2 The sum of a_1 through a_8 is:

$\left(1 - \dfrac{1}{3}\right) + \left(\dfrac{1}{3} - \dfrac{1}{5}\right) + \left(\dfrac{1}{5} - \dfrac{1}{7}\right) + \left(\dfrac{1}{7} - \dfrac{1}{9}\right) + \left(\dfrac{1}{9} - \dfrac{1}{11}\right) + \left(\dfrac{1}{11} - \dfrac{1}{13}\right) + \left(\dfrac{1}{13} - \dfrac{1}{15}\right) + \left(\dfrac{1}{15} - \dfrac{1}{17}\right)$

$= 1 + \left(\dfrac{1}{3} - \dfrac{1}{3}\right) + \left(\dfrac{1}{5} - \dfrac{1}{5}\right) + \left(\dfrac{1}{7} - \dfrac{1}{7}\right) + \left(\dfrac{1}{9} - \dfrac{1}{9}\right) + \left(\dfrac{1}{11} - \dfrac{1}{11}\right) + \left(\dfrac{1}{13} - \dfrac{1}{13}\right) + \left(\dfrac{1}{15} - \dfrac{1}{15}\right) - \dfrac{1}{17}$

$= 1 - \dfrac{1}{17} = \dfrac{16}{17}$ or equivalent fraction

Answer Explanations
Quantitative Reasoning: Section 2

1. A

STEP 1   Observe that $10y - 4x$ is related to the given $2x - 5y$.

STEP 2 $-2(2x - 5y) = -4x + 10y = 10y - 4x$

STEP 3 $10y - 4x = -2(2x - 5y) = -2(8) = -16$

STEP 4 $\dfrac{10y - 4x}{-3} = \dfrac{-16}{-3} = 5\dfrac{1}{3}$

Quantity A > Quantity B

2. D

> Note: Percent change $= \dfrac{\text{Change}}{\text{Original}} \times 100$

STEP 1   The percent change between two values is a function of the starting value as well as the amount of change.
  A 10-point increase between two test results can have varied percent changes depending on the first test score.

STEP 2   Assume Joan's score increased from 10 to 20.

Percent change $= \dfrac{20 - 10}{10} \times 100 = 100$ percent.

This is a 100 percent change.

Assume Joan's score increased from 50 to 60.

Percent change $= \dfrac{60 - 50}{50} \times 100 = 20$ percent.

This is a 20 percent change.

STEP 3   Neither Joan's nor Josh's initial test score is known. Hence, the percent change cannot be determined.

The relationship cannot be determined.

3. A

> Note: Area rectangle = (base)(height)
>
> [rectangle with height h and base b]
>
> Pythagorean theorem: $(\text{leg1})^2 + (\text{leg2})^2 = (\text{hypotenuse})^2$

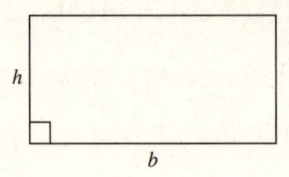

STEP 1 Draw a diagram.

Let x be the unknown side of the rectangle.

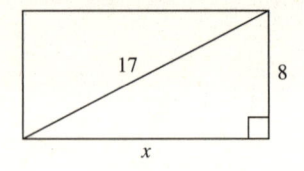

[rectangle with diagonal 17, right side 8, bottom x]

STEP 2 Use the Pythagorean theorem and solve for x.

$$x^2 + 8^2 = 17^2$$
$$x^2 + 64 = 289$$
$$x^2 = 225$$
$$x = \sqrt{225} = 15$$

STEP 3 Area = 8(15) = 120

Quantity A > Quantity B

4. A

STEP 1 Set up two equations.

Let n = number of nickels
q = number of quarters

$n + q = 21$
$5n + 25q = 305$

STEP 2 Solve $\dfrac{n + q = 21 \Rightarrow n = 21 - q}{5n + 25q = 305}$

$$5(21 - q) + 25q = 305$$
$$105 - 5q + 25q = 305$$
$$20q = 200$$
$$q = 10 \quad \therefore \quad n = 11$$

Quantity A > Quantity B

ANSWER EXPLANATIONS | **Quantitative Reasoning: Section 2** | **339**

5. B

> Note: If two items are in the ratio of 2:3, they can be represented as $2x$ and $3x$, respectively, and their total is $5x$.

STEP 1 Let t = total faculty at school A = total faculty at school B

STEP 2 At school A: male : female = 2 : 3 ⇒ male = $2x$
$$\frac{\text{female} = 3x}{\text{total} = 5x}$$

STEP 3 Set $5x = t$ ∴ $x = \dfrac{t}{5}$

The number of male faculty at school A is $2x = \dfrac{2t}{5}$.

STEP 4 At school B: male : female = 5 : 4 ⇒ male = $5y$
$$\frac{\text{female} = 4y}{\text{total} = 9y}$$

STEP 5 Set $9y = t$ ∴ $y = \dfrac{t}{9}$.

The number of female faculty at school B is $4y = \dfrac{4t}{9}$.

STEP 6 Since t is a positive number, $\dfrac{4t}{9} > \dfrac{2t}{5}$.

Quantity B > Quantity A

6. C

> Note: For any equally spaced group of data with an odd number of elements, the average is always the middle or center number.

STEP 1 "The average of 11 consecutive odd integers."

1. The integers are equally spaced
2. There is an odd number of elements
} the average = middle number = 23

STEP 2 "The average of 11 consecutive integers."

1. The integers are equally spaced
2. There is an odd number of elements
} the average = middle number = 23

Quantity A = Quantity B

7. B

> Notes:
>
> Mode: The most frequently occuring data value.
>
> Second quartile (Q_2): The median of the data.

STEP 1 List the data set in ascending order.

$$3, 3, 3, 3, 3, 4, 4, 4, 5, 6$$

STEP 2 The mode is 3 (it occurs most frequently).

STEP 3 The median (second quartile) for an even quantity of data items is the average (arithmetic mean) of the middle two data values when the data is arranged in ascending order 3, 3, 3, 3, 3, 4, 4, 4, 5, 6

$$\text{Median} = \frac{3+4}{2} = 3.5$$

Quantity B > Quantity A

8. D

> Note: Cube $\begin{cases} \text{Edge} = w \\ \text{Surface area} = 6w^2 \\ \text{Volume} = w^3 \end{cases}$

STEP 1 Surface area = $6w^2$

Volume = w^3

if $0 < w < 6$ $6w^2 > w^3$

if $w = 6$ $6w^2 = w^3$

if $w > 6$ $6w^2 < w^3$

The relationship cannot be determined.

9. B

STEP 1 We need to look at Joshua and Larry's rate.

Joshua can do the job in 6 days. He does $\frac{1}{6}$ of a job each day.

Larry can do the job in 10 days. He does $\frac{1}{10}$ of a job each day.

Together they do: $\frac{1}{6} + \frac{1}{10} = \frac{4}{15}$ of a job each day.

ANSWER EXPLANATIONS **341**
Quantitative Reasoning: Section 2

STEP 2 At the rate of $\frac{4}{15}$ of a job each day, it would take $\frac{15}{4}$ days to do the job.

$$\frac{15}{4} < 4$$

Quantity B > Quantity A

10. 48

STEP 1 View the layout of the five shapes as five dashes to be filled in.

— — — — —

STEP 2 Do the restrictions first.
If the square cannot be in the first position, the first position can be filled by any of four other shapes.

4 — — — —

STEP 3 The first spot has used one of the shapes. How many shapes are now available to be placed in the third position? Only three. We cannot use the square. 4 — 3 — —

STEP 4 The first and third positions have used two of the five shapes. How many shapes are now available for the fifth position. Only two. We cannot use the square. 4 — 3 — 2

STEP 5 The second position can be filled by any of the two remaining shapes (the square is now available) and the fourth position can only be filled by the one remaining shape. 4 2 3 1 2

STEP 6 The product 4(2)(3)(1)(2) = 48 represents the solution.

11. B and C

STEP 1 $2n = \frac{n}{2}$ ∴ $4n = n$ *This is only true if* $n = 0$.

STEP 2 $n = 0$ Note that zero is an even integer.

12. E

Note: For a normal distribution:
Let m = mean
Let t = a std deviation

(All percentages are approximate.)

STEP 1 Overlay the actual data on the normal curve.

STEP 2 A score of 92 is beyond 2 standard deviations to the right of the mean ∴ It is in the last 2.5 percent of the normal curve.

This means at least 97.5 percent of the data points are below this score.

The score of 92 is above the 97 percentile.

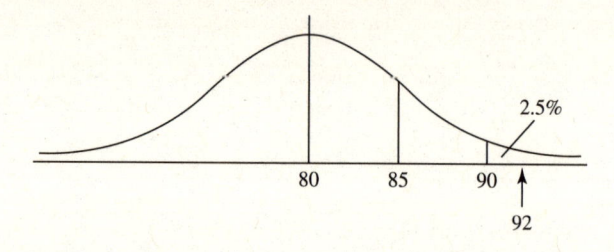

13. **D**

STEP 1 Since the radius of the circle is half the side of the square, we should first find the radius of the circle.

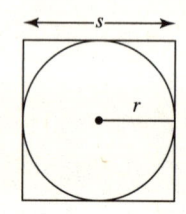

STEP 2 $C = 2\pi r$

$5 = 2\pi r \Rightarrow r = \dfrac{5}{2\pi}$

STEP 3 $s = 2r = 2\left(\dfrac{5}{2\pi}\right) = \dfrac{5}{\pi}$

STEP 4 Area of square $s^2 = \left(\dfrac{5}{\pi}\right)^2 = \dfrac{25}{\pi^2}$

14. **E**

Note: A pie chart is based on 360°.

STEP 1 Determine the fraction of the survey represented by egg salad.

$\dfrac{2}{40} = \dfrac{1}{20}$

STEP 2 The pie chart central angle should likewise be $\dfrac{1}{20}$ of 360° = 18°.

ANSWER EXPLANATIONS
Quantitative Reasoning: Section 2 | 343

15. A

> Note: $2^2 = 4$, $2^3 = 8$, $(x^a)^b = x^{ab}$

STEP 1 Express with a common base.
$$(2^2)^{2x+1} = (2^3)^{3y-2}$$
$$2^{4x+2} = 2^{9y-6}$$

STEP 2 Recall: If $2^a = 2^b \Rightarrow a = b$.
$$\therefore 2^{4x+2} = 2^{9y-6}$$
$$4x + 2 = 9y - 6$$
$$4x - 9y = -8$$

16. B

> Note:
> For a square with side $= s$ and diagonal $= d$,
> $$\text{Area} = s^2 \text{ or } \frac{d^2}{2}$$

STEP 1 Use the equation
$$\text{Area} = \frac{d^2}{2}$$

STEP 2 If $A = 3x$, substitute and solve for d.
$$3x = \frac{d^2}{2}$$
$$d^2 = 6x$$
$$d = \sqrt{6x}$$

17. E

> Note: Range is (highest value) − (lowest value).

STEP 1 Calculate the range for each grade level.

Grade Level	Highest Value	Lowest Value	Range
Freshman	64	55	9
Sophomore	67	61	6
Junior	74	63	11
Senior	82	66	16
Graduate	76	57	19

18. 68

> Note: Figure not drawn to scale.
>
> - The median of an even data quantity is the average (arithmetic mean) of the two middle numbers when the data is arrayed in ascending order.
>
> - The second quartile (Q_2) is the median.

STEP 1 Array the data in ascending order and locate the two middle numbers.

63 65 65 67 67 69 69 70 71 74

STEP 2 Median = Q2 = $\dfrac{(67 + 69)}{2}$ = 68

19. C

> Note: Average = $\dfrac{\text{Sum of items}}{\text{Quantity of items}}$

STEP 1 The best number to use to approximate the amount spent would be to use the average of the freshman class.

Sum of textbook + incidentals for freshmen = 2,861 + 614 = 3,475

Average expense = $\dfrac{3,475}{10}$ = 347.50

STEP 2 Total expense for 3,000 freshmen = 3,000(347.50) = $1,042,500

20. E

> Note: Average = $\dfrac{\text{Sum of the items}}{\text{Quantity of items}}$
>
> Percent greater = $\dfrac{\text{Greater value} - \text{Lesser value}}{\text{Lesser value}} \times 100$

STEP 1 Calculate the average total expense for the seniors and graduate students.

Average total expense for seniors = $\dfrac{2,778 + 741}{10}$ = 351.9

Average total expense for graduate students = $\dfrac{2,153 + 652}{10}$ = 280.5

STEP 2 Percent greater = $\dfrac{351.9 - 280.5}{280} \times 100 = 25.\overline{45}$ percent

ANSWER EXPLANATIONS **345**
Quantitative Reasoning: Section 2

21. B

STEP 1 View the number as four dashes to be filled in. __ __ __ __

STEP 2 Do the restrictions first:

If the number cannot begin with a zero, the first dash can be filled with any of nine other digits: $\underline{9}$ __ __ __

STEP 3 If the last digit cannot be a seven, the last dash can be filled with any of nine other digits: $\underline{9}$ __ __ $\underline{9}$

STEP 4 The middle two spaces can be filled with any of the 10 digits: $\underline{9}\ \underline{10}\ \underline{10}\ \underline{9}$

STEP 5 The product $9 \cdot 10 \cdot 10 \cdot 9 = 9^2 \cdot 10^2$ represents the solution.

22. B

STEP 1
$$\frac{(a+2)+(b-1)+(c+5)}{3} = 10$$
$$\frac{a+b+c+6}{3} = 10$$
$$a+b+c+6 = 30$$
$$a+b+c = 24$$

STEP 2
$$\frac{(a-1)+(b+7)+(c+2)+8}{4} = x$$
$$\frac{a+b+c+8+8}{4} = x$$
$$\frac{a+b+c+16}{4} = x$$

Recall from step 1 that $a+b+c = 24$. $\frac{24+16}{4} = \frac{40}{4} = 10$

23. B and C

STEP 1 $\frac{x}{y} = \frac{2}{5}$ does NOT mean $x = 2$ and $y = 5$; rather, it means x divided by y has the value $\frac{2}{5}$.

$\boxed{A}$ $x = 2$ could be true, but it is not a MUST-be true.

If $x = 4$ and $y = 10$, $\frac{x}{y} = \frac{4}{10} = \frac{2}{5}$.

$\boxed{B}$ By cross-multiplication $5x = 2y$. This is a MUST-be true.

[C] The absolute value of y is always greater than the absolute value of x; therefore, y^2 is always greater than x^2.

[D] If $x = -2$ and $y = -5$, then $\dfrac{x}{y} = \dfrac{-2}{-5} = \dfrac{2}{5}$. But -5 is smaller than -2.

This choice does NOT have to be true.

24. **A**

    STEP 1   Recall that: $y^2 - x^2 = (y - x)(y + x)$.

    STEP 2   We are given $x + y = \sqrt{12}$ ∴ $y + x = \sqrt{12}$.

                 We are given $x - y = \sqrt{3}$ ∴ $y - x = -\sqrt{3}$.

    STEP 3 $y^2 - x^2 = (y - x)(y + x) = \left(-\sqrt{3}\right)\left(\sqrt{12}\right) = -\sqrt{36} = -6$.

25. **C**

> Note: $\sqrt{a}\,\sqrt{b} = \sqrt{ab}$
>
> $\sqrt{a}\,\sqrt{a} = a$

    STEP 1   Combine the square roots:

$$\sqrt{5(11)} \cdot \sqrt{a(b)} \cdot \sqrt{4(7)(11)} = \sqrt{4(11)(11)(5)(7)(a)(b)}$$

$$= 2(11)\sqrt{5(7)(a)(b)}$$

    STEP 2   To obtain an integer, with the constraint that a and b are prime numbers, either $a = 5$ and $b = 7$ or $a = 7$ and $b = 5$.

    STEP 3   Either way, $a^2 + b^2 = 5^2 + 7^2 = 74$

Appendix A
Score Conversion Table

Score Conversion Table
Paper-and-Pencil Tests

| Verbal and Quantitative Sections || Essays ||
Number of Questions Correct	Final Score	Total Score for Both Essays	Final Score
0	130	0	0
1	131	1	0.5
2	132	2	1
3	132	3	1.5
4	133	4	2
5	134	5	2.5
6	135	6	3
7	136	7	3.5
8	136	8	4
9	137	9	4.5
10	138	10	5
11	139	11	5.5
12	140	12	6
13	140		
14	141		
15	142		
16	143		
17	144		
18	144		
19	145		
20	146		

Verbal and Quantitative Sections

Number of Questions Correct	Final Score	Number of Questions Correct	Final Score
21	147	36	159
22	148	37	160
23	148	38	160
24	149	39	161
25	150	40	162
26	151	41	163
27	152	42	164
28	152	43	164
29	153	44	165
30	154	45	166
31	155	46	167
32	156	47	168
33	156	48	168
34	157	49	169
35	158	50	170

Appendix B
Math Reference

Common Mathematical Symbols

Symbol	Example	Meaning
$=$	$y = 4$	y equals 4
$<$	$3 < 6$	3 is less than 6
$\leq$	$x \leq z$	x is less than or equal to z
$>$	$9 > 0$	9 is greater than 0
$\geq$	$8 \geq w$	8 is greater than or equal to w
$\approx$	$6.999 \approx 7$	6.999 is approximately equal to 7
$|\ |$	$|5|$	The absolute value of 5
$\pm$	7 ± 2	7 plus 2 or 7 minus 2
$\sqrt{\ }$	$\sqrt{10}$	The square root of 10
$\sqrt[3]{\ }$	$\sqrt[3]{27}$	The cube root of 27
$\angle$	$\angle A$	Angle A
$\triangle$	$\triangle ABC$	Triangle ABC
$\parallel$	$\overleftrightarrow{AB} \parallel \overleftrightarrow{CD}$	Line AB is parallel to line CD
$\perp$	$\overleftrightarrow{EF} \perp \overleftrightarrow{GH}$	Line EF is perpendicular to line GH
$\cong$	$\angle P \cong \angle Q$	Angle P is congruent to angle Q
$\sim$	$\triangle JKL \sim \triangle RST$	Triangle JKL is similar to triangle RST
$\in$	$2 \in A$	2 is an element of set A
$\notin$	$5 \notin B$	5 is not an element of set B

Symbol	Example	Meaning
$\cap$	$D \cap F$	The intersection of sets D and F
$\cup$	$H \cup J$	The union of sets H and J
$\subset$	$X \subset Y$	Set X is a proper subset of set Y
$\subseteq$	$R \subseteq N$	Set R is a subset of set N
!	$n!$	n factorial

Basic Geometric Figures

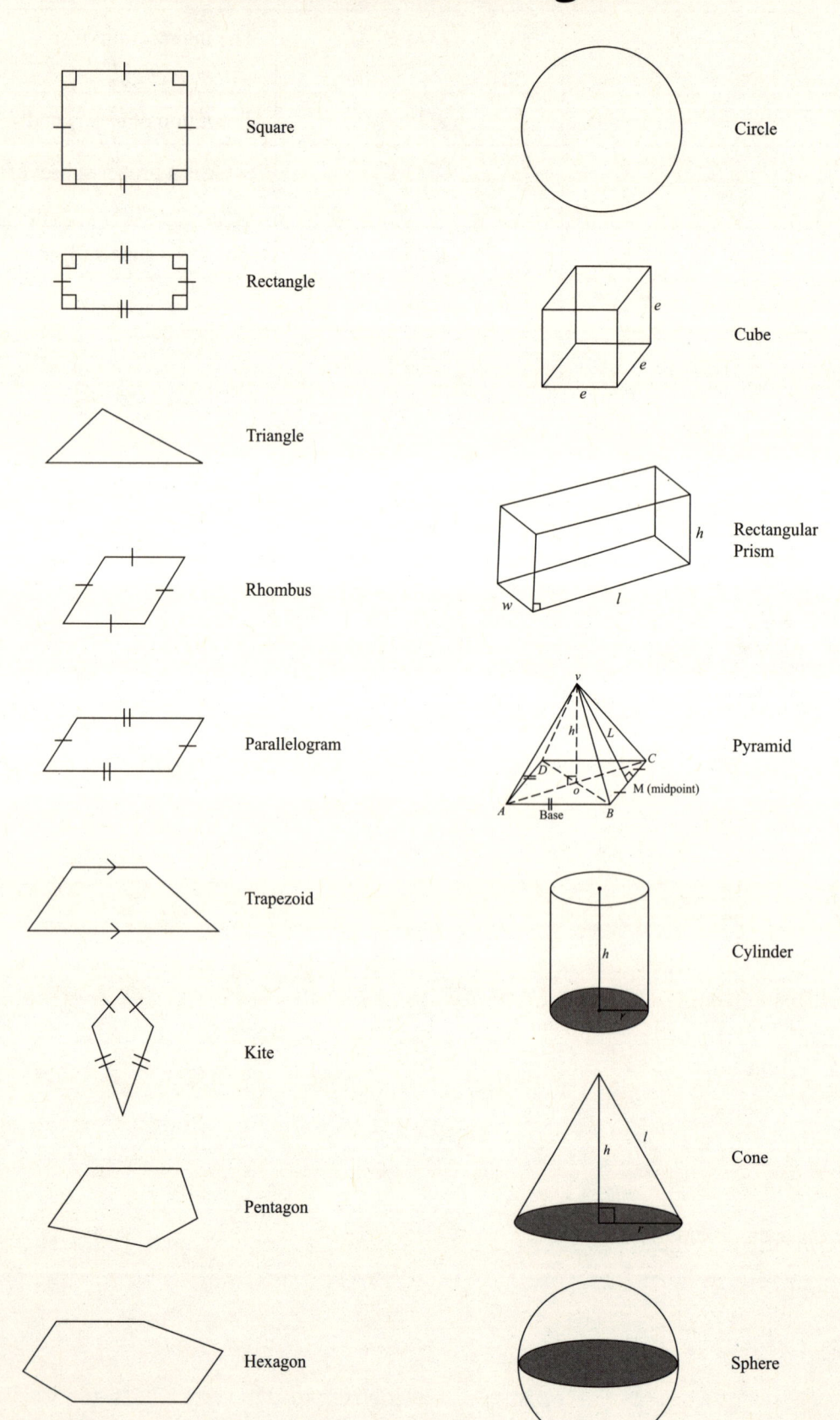

	Square		Circle
	Rectangle		Cube
	Triangle		Rectangular Prism
	Rhombus		
	Parallelogram		Pyramid
	Trapezoid		Cylinder
	Kite		Cone
	Pentagon		Sphere
	Hexagon		

GLOSSARY

Absolute value: The positive value of a nonzero number. Also, the distance of a number from zero on the number line.

Acute angle: An angle whose measure is less than 90°.

Angle bisector of a triangle: A line segment that extends from a vertex to the opposite side and divides the vertex angle into two congruent smaller angles.

Apothem: A line segment from the center of a polygon that is perpendicular to a side.

Base: A number that is raised to an exponent (see *exponent*).

Binomial: An algebraic expression that consists of two terms.

Box plot: A graphical way to display the main features of a data set, such as the median and the quartiles.

Central angle: An angle formed by two radii of a circle.

Chord: A line segment whose endpoints are points on a circle.

Circumference: Distance around a circle.

Complement of a set: The elements that are in the universal set but not in the given set.

Complementary angles: Two angles whose sum measures 90°.

Composite number: A number that contains at least three factors.

Concentric circles: Two circles of different sizes with the same center.

Cone: A three-dimensional figure with a circular base and a vertex.

Congruent: Two or more angles (or sides) with the same measure.

Congruent figures: Two or more figures with the same size and same shape.

Consecutive integers: Integers whose difference is 1.

Constant: A quantity that can assume only one value.

Cube: A three-dimensional figure, shaped like a box, for which all edges are equal in length.

Cylinder: A three-dimensional figure whose bases are two congruent circles and whose side is a curved rectangle.

Denominator: The lower part of a fraction.

Diameter: A chord of a circle that contains the center.

Domain: The values of the independent variable of a function.

Element: A member of a set.

Empty set: A set with no elements.

Equilateral triangle: A triangle in which the angles are congruent and the sides are congruent.

Exponent: A number attached as a superscript to a base. If the exponent is a positive integer, then it shows the number of times that a base is multiplied by itself. For example, in the number 3^5, 3 is the base and 5 is the exponent. 3^5 means $(3)(3)(3)(3)(3) = 243$.

Even number: An integer that is divisible by 2.

Face: A plane surface of a geometric solid.

Factors of a number: Integers that divide into a given number with no remainder.

Function: A set of ordered pairs for which there is only one range value for each domain value.

Greatest common factor: The largest integer that can divide into a given group of integers.

Hexagon: A six-sided figure.

Histogram: A graphical way to display data with adjacent rectangular bars.

Horizontal axis: The x-axis of a coordinate system.

Integer: A counting number, negative or positive, or zero.

Intersection of sets: The elements that are common to the given sets.

Irrational number: A number that cannot be expressed as the quotient of two integers.

Isosceles trapezoid: A trapezoid whose non-parallel sides are congruent.

Isosceles triangle: A triangle with at least two congruent sides.

Kite: A four-sided figure that contains two pairs of adjacent congruent sides.

Least common multiple: The smallest integer that can be divided by a given group of integers. Also known as the lowest common denominator.

Line graph: A graphical way to display data over a period of time.

Mean: The average of a group of numbers.

Median of a set of data: The middle number of a group of numbers arranged in numerical order, either ascending or descending.

Median of a trapezoid: The line segment that joins the midpoints of the two nonparallel sides.

Median of a triangle: A line segment that joins a vertex with the midpoint of the opposite side.

Midline: A line segment that joins the midpoints of two sides of a triangle.

Midpoint: A point on a line segment that lies halfway between the endpoints.

Mode: The number that occurs most frequently in a data set.

Monomial: An algebraic expression that contains only one term.

Natural number: A positive integer.

Numerator: The top part of a fraction.

Obtuse angle: An angle whose measure is more than 90°, but less than 180°.

Odd number: An integer that is not divisible by 2.

Origin: The point where the *x*- and *y*-axes intersect on a coordinate plane.

Parallel lines: Lines in the same plane that never intersect.

Parallelogram: A four-sided figure for which the opposite sides are parallel.

Pentagon: A five-sided figure.

Perpendicular lines: Lines that meet at a right angle.

Pi: The ratio of the circumference of a circle to its diameter. The symbol is π.

Pie graph: A pictorial way to display data using a circle that is subdivided into sections.

Polygon: Any closed geometric figure.

Polynomial: An algebraic expression that consists of terms.

Prime number: A number that consists of only two factors, itself and 1.

Product: The result of a multiplication.

Proportion: Two equal ratios.

Pyramid: A three-dimensional figure that contains a polygonal base, triangular sides, and a vertex.

Quadrilateral: A four-sided figure.

Quartile: A number that divides a data set into specific fourths.

Quotient: The result of a division.

Radius: One-half a diameter. Also, the distance between the center of a circle and a point on the circle.

Range of a data set: The difference between the highest and lowest values.

Range of a function: The values of the dependent variable of a function.

Ratio: A fractional comparison for two integers.

Rational number: A number that can be expressed as a ratio of two integers.

Reciprocal: The value of 1 divided by a given number.

Rectangle: A parallelogram that contains four right angles.

Rectangular prism: A three-dimensional figure, shaped like a box, which has six rectangular surfaces.

Reflection: A movement of a point or figure about a given line so as to produce a mirror image.

Regular polygon: A polygon in which all sides and all angles are congruent.

Rhombus: A parallelogram in which all sides are congruent.

Right angle: An angle that measures 90°.

Right circular cone: A three-dimensional figure containing a circular base and a vertex, for which the line segment connecting the vertex to the center of the base is perpendicular to the base.

Rotation: A circular movement of a point or figure about a given point.

Scalene triangle: A triangle that contains no congruent sides.

Scatterplot: A graphical way to display data as a series of points on an *xy*-coordinate plane.

Secant of a circle: A line that intersects the circle twice.

Similar figures: Two or more figures with the same shape, but not necessarily the same size.

Slope: The ratio of rise over run for a line.

Sphere: A three-dimensional figure that is shaped like a ball.

Square: A parallelogram in which all sides are congruent and all angles measure 90°.

Standard deviation of a data set: A measure of the dispersion of the data about the mean.

Straight angle: An angle whose measure is 180°.

Supplementary angles: Two angles the sum of whose measures is 180°.

Tangent to a circle: A line that touches the circle at only one point.

Translation: A movement of a point or figure either horizontally, vertically, or both.

Transversal: A line that intersects two given lines.

Trapezoid: A four-sided figure that contains exactly two non-congruent parallel sides.

Triangle: A three-sided figure.

Union of sets: The elements that exist in at least one of the given sets.

Universal Set: The set of all elements under consideration.

Variable: Any quantity that can assume more than one value.

Venn diagram: A representation of two or more sets that are displayed as circles within a universal set shown as a rectangle.

Vertex of a polygon: A point at which two sides intersect.

Vertical angles: Opposite angles formed by two intersecting lines.

Vertical axis: The y-axis of a coordinate system.

Whole number: Any positive integer or zero.

X-intercept: The point at which a graph crosses the x-axis.

Y-intercept: The point at which a graph crosses the y-axis.

FORMULAS AND RULES

Algebra

1. Consecutive integers: $n, n + 1, n + 2, n + 3,\ldots$

2. Consecutive odd integers or consecutive even integers: $n, n + 2, n + 4, n + 6,\ldots$

3. $x^{-m} = \dfrac{1}{x^m}$

4. $(x^m)(x^n) = x^{m+n}$

5. $\dfrac{x^m}{x^n} = x^{m-n}$

6. $\left(x^m\right)^n = x^{mn}$

7. $(x^m)(y^m) = (xy)^m$

8. $\left(\dfrac{x}{y}\right)^m = \dfrac{x^m}{y^m}$

9. For $ax + by = c$, the x-intercept is $\left(\dfrac{c}{a}, 0\right)$ and the y-intercept is $\left(0, \dfrac{c}{b}\right)$.

10. For $ax^2 + bx + c = 0$, $x = \dfrac{-b \pm \sqrt{b^2 - 4ac}}{2a}$.

11. For $ax^2 + bx + c = 0$, the sum of the roots $= -\dfrac{b}{a}$ and the product of the roots $= \dfrac{c}{a}$.

12. For $y = ax^2 + bx + c$, the x-coordinate of the vertex is $-\dfrac{b}{2a}$.

13. For $y = a(x - h)^2 + k$, the vertex is located at (h, k).

14. Slope of a line (m) through the points (x_1, y_1) and (x_2, y_2): $m = \dfrac{y_2 - y_1}{x_2 - x_1}$.

15. Midpoint of a line segment with endpoints (x_1, y_1) and (x_2, y_2): $\left(\dfrac{x_1 + x_2}{2}, \dfrac{y_1 + y_2}{2}\right)$.

16. Distance (d) between the points (x_1, y_1) and (x_2, y_2): $d = \sqrt{(x_2 - x_1)^2 + (y_2 - y_1)^2}$.

17. Given the point (x, y): (a) $(x, -y)$ is a reflection about the x-axis; (b) $(-x, y)$ is a reflection about the y-axis; (c) $(-x, -y)$ is a reflection about the origin.

18. Given the point (x, y), (a) $(y, -x)$ is a 90° clockwise rotation; (b) $(-y, x)$ is a 90° counterclockwise rotation.

19. Given the point (x, y), $(x + h, y + k)$ represents a horizontal shift of h units and a vertical shift of k units.

20. $a, a + d, a + 2d, a + 3d, \ldots$ represents an arithmetic sequence, where $a =$ first term and $d =$ common difference.

21. In an arithmetic sequence, the nth term is given by $a_n = a + (n - 1)(d)$ and the sum is given by $S = \dfrac{n}{2}[2a + (n - 1)d]$.

22. $a, ar, ar^2, ar^3, \ldots$ represents a geometric sequence, where $a =$ first term and $r =$ common ratio.

23. In a geometric sequence, the nth term is given by $a_n = ar^{n-1}$ and the sum is given by $S = \dfrac{a - ar^n}{1 - r}$.

24. The sum of an infinite geometric sequence in which $|r| < 1$ is $S = \dfrac{a}{1 - r}$.

25. For simple interest, $A = P + PRT$, where $A =$ amount, $P =$ principal, $R =$ rate, and $T =$ time.

26. For compound interest, $A = P\left(1 + \dfrac{r}{n}\right)^{nt}$, where $A =$ amount, $P =$ principal, $r =$ annual rate, $n =$ number of compounding periods per year, and $t =$ number of years.

Geometry

Two-dimensional Figure	Perimeter	Area
1. Triangle	Add the sides	$\frac{1}{2}bh$ or $\sqrt{s(s-a)(s-b)(s-c)}$
2. Square	$4x$	x^2
3. Rectangle	$2l + 2w$	lw
4. Parallelogram	$2l + 2w$	bh
5. Rhombus	$4x$	$\left(\frac{1}{2}\right)(d_1)(d_2)$
6. Trapezoid	Add the sides	$\left(\frac{1}{2}\right)(h)(b_1 + b_2)$
7. Regular polygon of n sides	Add the sides	$\frac{1}{2}(a_p)(p)$
8. Circle	$2\pi r$ or πD (circumference)	πr^2
9. Sector of a circle	$\left(\frac{n°}{360°}\right)(2\pi r) + 2r$	$\left(\frac{n°}{360°}\right)(\pi r^2)$

10. Arc length of a circle $(L) = \left(\frac{n°}{360°}\right)(2\pi r)$

11. Sum of the angles of a polygon $= (n - 2)(180°)$

12. Each interior angle of a regular polygon $= \frac{(n - 2)(180°)}{n}$

13. Sum of the measures of the exterior angles of a polygon $= 360°$

14. For a right triangle, $a^2 + b^2 = c^2$ (Pythagorean theorem)

<u>Legend:</u> a, b, c, x = side; a_p = apothem; b, b_1, b_2 = base; d_1, d_2 = diagonal; D = diameter; h = vertical height; l = length; n = number of sides; $n°$ = central angle measure, p = perimeter; r = radius; s = semi-perimeter; w = width.

Three-dimensional Figure	Surface Area	Volume
15. Cube	$6e^2$	e^3
16. Rectangular prism	$2lw + 2lh + 2wh$	lwh
17. Rectangular pyramid	$B + 4T$	$\frac{1}{3}Bh$
18. Cylinder	$2\pi rh + 2\pi r^2$	$\pi r^2 h$
19. Cone	$\pi r^2 + \pi r\sqrt{r^2 + h^2}$ or $\pi r^2 + \pi rL$	$\frac{1}{3}\pi r^2 h$
20. Sphere	$4\pi r^2$	$\frac{4}{3}\pi r^3$

21. Diagonal of a Rectangular Prism = $\sqrt{l^2 + w^2 + h^2}$

Legend: B = area of base; e = edge; h = vertical height; l = length; L = slant height; r = radius; T = area of lateral triangle; w = width.

Data Analysis

1. Mean of a list of data: Add the data and then divide the sum by the number of data.

2. Mean ($\bar{x}$ or μ) of a list of data with associated frequencies: Multiply each datum by its associated frequency, add these products, then divide by the total frequency of all data.

3. Median (Q_2) of a list of n data arranged in ascending order, where n is odd: The number located in the $\frac{n+1}{2}$ position.

4. Median (Q_2) of a list of n data arranged in ascending order, where n is even: The mean of the numbers located in the $\frac{n}{2}$ and the $\frac{n}{2} + 1$ positions.

5. First quartile (Q_1): The median of the lower half of the data.

6. Third quartile (Q_3): The median of the upper half of the data.

7. Interquartile range (*IQR*): $Q_3 - Q_1$.

8. Standard deviation: Subtract the mean from each data, square these differences, divide by the number of data, then take the square root of this quotient.

9. Standard score: Subtract the mean from the raw score and then divide by the number of data.

10. *n*! (*n* factorial): $(n)(n-1)(n-2)(n-3)(\cdots)(1)$.

11. Number of permutations of *n* objects taken *r* at a time ($_nP_r$): $\dfrac{n!}{(n-r)!}$.

12. Number of combinations of *n* objects taken *r* at a time ($_nC_r$): $\dfrac{n!}{(r!)(n-r)!}$.

13. Probability of event *A* [P(*A*)]: $\dfrac{\text{Number of successful outcomes}}{\text{Total number of outcomes}}$.

14. $P(\overline{A}) = 1 - P(A)$, where $\overline{A}$ is the complement of event *A*.

15. $P(A \text{ and } B) = P(A) \times P(B)$, if *A* and *B* are independent events.

16. $P(A \text{ and } B) = P(A) \times P(B|A)$, if *A* and *B* are dependent events, where $P(B|A)$ is the probability of B occurring, given that A has already occurred.

17. $P(A \text{ or } B) = P(A) + P(B) - P(A \text{ and } B)$, for any events *A* and *B*.

18. $P(A \text{ or } B) = P(A) + P(B)$, if A and B are mutually exclusive events.

19. Expected value of a random variable: Multiply each value of the variable by its associated frequency and then add these products.

AVOIDING COMMON PITFALLS

Arithmetic

- Zero is an integer, but it is neither positive nor negative.

- When doing a multiplication problem such as (5)(4)(3), you may multiply any two of these first, then multiply the resulting product by the third number. So, (5)(4)(3) = (20)(3) = (15)(4) = (5)(12). But do **not** calculate as (5)(4) + (5)(3).

- In adding or (subtracting) fractions, do not simply add (or subtract) denominators. Each fraction must be converted to a common denominator. For example, to compute $\frac{2}{3} - \frac{1}{5}$, change each fraction to a common denominator of 15. Then we have $\frac{10}{15} - \frac{3}{15} = \frac{7}{15}$.

- For any problem involving a percent change, be sure that you select the proper base. Thus, the percent increase from 10 to 15 is calculated by taking their difference, dividing by 10, then multiplying by 100 and attaching the percent sign; the result is 50%. But the percent decrease from 15 to 10 is found by taking their difference, dividing by 15 (not 10), then multiplying by 100 and attaching the percent sign; the result is $33\frac{1}{3}\%$.

- When multiplying numbers with equivalent bases, simply add the exponents. So, $3^4 \times 3^6 = 3^{10}$. Notice that the bases are not multiplied. Also, be sure not to multiply unlike bases. This means that $4^4 \times 2^3 \neq 8^7$. But, we can rewrite 4^4 as $\left(2^2\right)^4 = 2^8$. [Note that $\left(2^2\right)^4$ means $2^2 \times 2^2 \times 2^2 \times 2^2$.] Then $4^4 \times 2^3 = 2^8 \times 2^3 = 2^{11}$ or 2,048. If the bases cannot be made identical, evaluate each one first, then multiply. For example, $5^2 \times 7^3 = 25 \times 343 = 8{,}575$.

- The number 17 is prime because it has exactly two positive factors, namely 1 and 17. The number 15 is composite because it has more than two positive factors, namely 1, 3, 5, and 15. The number 1 is neither prime nor composite because its only positive factor is 1.

- You may divide zero by a nonzero number, but division by zero is not defined. Thus, $\frac{0}{3} = 0$, but each of $\frac{3}{0}$ and $\frac{0}{0}$ is undefined.

- A bar symbol that is placed over a decimal number indicates repetition only for the digits under the bar. Thus, $2.08\bar{3} = 2.083333\ldots$, but $2.\overline{083} = 2.083083083\ldots$

- $|5| + |4| = |9|$ and $|-5| + |-4| = |-9|$, but you **cannot** assume that $|a| + |b| = |a + b|$ for all a, b. If $a = 5$ and $b = -4$, $|5| + |-4| = 5 + 4 = 9$. But $|5+(-4)| = |1| = 1$.

- For any nonzero x, $x^0 = 1$. For example, $8^0 = 1$. However, 0^0 is undefined. The number zero raised to any positive integer has a value of zero. As an example, $0^4 = 0$.

- A negative exponent applied to any given number (base) means the reciprocal of that number raised to the additive inverse of the exponent. Thus,

$$5^{-1} = \frac{1}{5^1} = \frac{1}{5}, \; -3^{-2} = -\frac{1}{3^2} = -\frac{1}{9}, \text{ and } \left(\frac{1}{2}\right)^{-3} = \frac{1}{\left(\frac{1}{2}\right)^3} = \frac{1}{\left(\frac{1}{8}\right)} = 8.$$

But be extra careful whenever the given base is negative. As examples,

$$(-2)^{-4} = \frac{1}{(-2)^4} = \frac{1}{16} \text{ and } (-5)^{-3} = \frac{1}{(-5)^3} = -\frac{1}{125}.$$

- A ratio of 8 feet to 2 inches is not equal to 4 to 1. When the units are different, change them to a common unit. In this case, we can change 8 feet to $(8)(12) = 96$ inches. Then the correct ratio is 96 to 2, which reduces to 48 to 1. However, if we are solving a proportion, then we can mix units in each ratio. As an example, suppose that 2.5 inches represents 1 mile on a map. How many inches represent 3 miles? Let x represent the required number of inches. We can write the proportion $\frac{2.5}{1} = \frac{x}{3}$. The solution is found by cross-multiplying, which leads to $x = (2.5)(3) = 7.5$.

- Avoid taking averages of averages to arrive at an answer that requires an average. This is especially important in determining an average grade or an average speed.

  Example: Susan has test scores of 90, 80, and 88. What score does she need on her fourth test so that she will have an average of 89 on all four exams? A mistake would be to determine her average on the first three tests, which is $\frac{90 + 80 + 88}{3} = \frac{258}{3} = 86$, then determine her fourth exam to be 92. While it is true that $\frac{86 + 92}{2} = 89$, this approach is wrong. The correct way is to find her total on the first three tests, which is 258. In order for Susan to have an 89 average on all four tests, she needs a total of $(89)(4) = 356$ points. Thus, she would need a score of $356 - 258 = 98$.

Example: Jimmy averaged 40 miles per hour for 1 mile, then 60 miles per hour for the next mile. What was his average rate? A common error would be to simply find $\frac{40 + 60}{2} = 50$ miles per hour. This is incorrect. Remember that average rate multiplied by time equals distance. Thus, average rate means total distance divided by total time. In traveling 40 miles per hour, the time to go 1 mile is $\frac{60}{40} = 1.5$ minutes $= 0.025$ hours. In traveling 60 miles per hour, the time to go 1 mile is 1 minute $= 0.01\overline{6}$ hours. The total distance is 2 miles and the total time is 2.5 minutes $= 0.041\overline{6}$ hours. Therefore, the average rate is $\frac{2}{0.041\overline{6}} = 48$ miles per hour.

- If n is an odd integer, the next odd integer is represented by $n + 2$, **not** $n + 1$. Just as with consecutive even integers, consecutive odd integers are two numbers apart. Thus, a list of four consecutive odd integers, beginning with n is as follows: $n, n + 2, n + 4, n + 6$.

Algebra

- Remember that in adding (or subtracting) similar algebraic terms, only the coefficients are added (or subtracted). Thus, $7x + 3x = 10x$, **not** $10x^2$. Likewise $11x^2y - 2x^2y = 9x^2y$. Dissimilar terms such as mn^3 and m^3n may **not** be added or subtracted.

- For the evaluation of expressions such as $4 + 5x^3$, be sure that you first cube the value of x, then multiply by 5, and finally add 4. Thus, if $x = -2$, the value of $4 + 5x^3$ is $4 + 5(-2)^3 = 4 + (5)(-8) = 4 - 40 = -36$.

- An expression such as $\frac{x}{y + z}$ does **not** equal $\frac{x}{y} + \frac{x}{z}$. This can be easily checked with numbers. If $x = 1$, $y = 2$, and $z = 3$, then $\frac{x}{y + z} = \frac{1}{5}$, but $\frac{x}{y} + \frac{x}{z} = \frac{1}{2} + \frac{1}{3} = \frac{5}{6}$. However, we **can** state that $\frac{x + y}{z} = \frac{x}{z} + \frac{y}{z}$.

As an example, let $x = 2$, $y = 3$, and $z = 7$. Then $\frac{x+y}{z} = \frac{2+3}{7} = \frac{5}{7}$ and $\frac{x}{z} + \frac{y}{z} = \frac{2}{7} + \frac{3}{7} = \frac{5}{7}$.

- $\sqrt{x^2 + y^2} \neq x + y$, unless x or y equal zero. Since $(x + y)^2 = x^2 + 2xy + y^2$, the correct expression should be $\sqrt{x^2 + 2xy + y^2} = x + y$.

- $f(g(x))$ does not mean the same as $f(x) \times g(x)$. $f(g(x))$ is a composite function in which the rule of $f(x)$ is applied to the function $g(x)$. $f(x) \times g(x)$ means to find the product of the two functions. As an example, let $f(x) = x + 2$ and $g(x) = x^2$. Then $f(g(x)) = f(x^2) = x^2 + 2$, whereas $f(x) \times g(x) = (x + 2)(x^2) = x^3 + 2x^2$.

- In general, $f(2x) \neq 2f(x)$. For example, let $f(x) = 3x + 8$. Then $f(2x) = (3)(2x) + 8 = 6x + 8$, but $2f(x) = (2)(3x + 8) = 6x + 16$.

- Be aware that $(-x)^2 \neq -x^2$. On the left side of this inequality, we determine the opposite of x, then square it. On the right side, we square the number first, then take the opposite number. For example, $(-3)^2 = (-3)(-3) = 9$, whereas $-3^2 = -(3^2) = -9$. Consider the following expression: $18 - x^2$. If $x = -4$, the correct computation of the value of $18 - x^2$ would be $18 - (-4)^2 = 18 - (-4)(-4) = 18 - 16 = 2$.

- In using the quadratic formula $\frac{-b \pm \sqrt{b^2 - 4ac}}{2a}$, be certain that you calculate the **entire** numerator before dividing by $2a$. So, for the equation $2x^2 + 7x + 4 = 0$, the solutions are $x = \frac{-7 \pm \sqrt{49 - 4(2)(4)}}{4} = \frac{-7 \pm \sqrt{49 - 32}}{4} = \frac{-7 \pm \sqrt{17}}{4} \approx \frac{-7 + 4.12}{4}$ or $\frac{-7 - 4.12}{4}$. Then $x = -0.72$ or -2.78.

  As an extra caution, if your final answer appears as $\frac{6 \pm \sqrt{13}}{6}$, do **not** cancel the 6's. This will lead to a wrong answer of $1 \pm \sqrt{13}$.

- In dealing with the solutions of inequalities, the multiplication (or division) of a negative quantity requires a change in the direction of the inequality sign. For example, in solving $-3x > 15$, divide by -3 and switch the inequality sign to $<$. Thus, the solution is $x < -5$. But note that the solution to $4x < -24$ is $x < -6$; the inequality did not change direction because we divided by a positive 4.

- When reducing algebraic fractions, cancel out common factors, **not** individual common terms of the numerator and denominator. For example, the expression $\frac{x^2 + x - 2}{x^2 - 4}$ is **not** equivalent to $\frac{x-2}{-4}$. The correct procedure is to factor both numerator and denominator, then cancel like factors. Thus, $\frac{x^2 + x - 2}{x^2 - 4} = \frac{(x+2)(x-1)}{(x+2)(x-2)} = \frac{x-1}{x-2}$.

- An equation such as $x^2 = 36$ has two solutions, namely 6 and -6. But the symbol $\sqrt{36}$ represents just 6. An equivalent expression for -6 would be $-\sqrt{36}$.

Geometry

- When using the Pythagorean theorem to determine a missing side of a right triangle, remember that c represents the hypotenuse. Either of a or b can represent either leg. If the values of a and b are given, then $c = \sqrt{a^2 + b^2}$. But, if the values of a and c are given, then $b = \sqrt{c^2 - a^2}$.

- In a circle, a central angle has the same measure as its intercepted arc. But the measure of an inscribed angle is one-half the measure of its intercepted arc.

Data Analysis

- In a set, each element is only counted once. In a list, also called a data set, each element must be counted as many times as it occurs. Thus, to find the mean of the list 2, 5, 5, 8, 9, we must add these five numbers then divide by 5. The mean would be $\frac{29}{5} = 5.8$.

- In counting the number of possible outcomes of an event, be sure that you don't double count an outcome.

  Example: How many cards in a deck are clubs or kings? There are 13 clubs and 4 kings, but there are **not** 17 such cards. The actual number is 16 because the king of clubs was counted as both a club and a king.

- The distinguishing feature between a permutation and a combination of objects is the requirement of order. For a permutation, order matters; for a combination, order is irrelevant. As an example, given the numbers 1, 2, 3, the six permutations of two of these numbers are 12, 13, 21, 23, 31, and 32. But the three combinations of two of these numbers are simply 12, 13, and 23.

- In probability questions involving the selection of objects, pay close attention to whether replacement is permitted. For example, suppose a jar contains six marbles, three of which are red. The probability of selecting two red marbles, one at a time, **without** replacement is $\frac{3}{6} \times \frac{2}{5} = \frac{1}{5}$. But the probability of selecting two red marbles, one at a time, **with** replacement is $\frac{3}{6} \times \frac{3}{6} = \frac{1}{4}$.

Appendix C
GRE Vocabulary Enhancer

GRE VOCABULARY ENHANCER

You will encounter three types of questions in the Verbal Reasoning measure of the GRE revised General Test: Reading Comprehension, Text Completion, and Sentence Equivalence. The GRE has two Verbal Reasoning sections containing approximately 20 questions per section and you will have 30 minutes to answer those questions.

Your success on the GRE Verbal Reasoning Section begins with one fundamental insight: these questions have been written and designed to test your vocabulary. No matter which section you are working in, you will be expected to demonstrate that you have a good command of vocabulary. Because of this, you should focus on strengthening your vocabulary.

You may be feeling a bit intimidated right now because you may think your vocabulary skills aren't that great. But don't get discouraged. First, remember one of the most important strategies to beating the GRE: Don't be intimidated! Second, there are plenty of ways to build up your vocabulary skills before taking the GRE. The simplest and best way of improving your vocabulary is to read! It doesn't matter what you read—books, magazines, newspapers—as long as you read!

While you're reading, however, you have to pay attention. You should be asking yourself some questions while reading. These questions include:

- What is the main idea?

- What is the author's purpose?

- How does the author make his or her argument?

- What tone does the author use?

If you keep asking yourself these questions, you'll be surprised how much more you understand while reading. And understanding more will lead to a stronger vocabulary.

Unfortunately, you may not remember all of the words you read. That's why we've provided you with an extremely valuable tool to build your vocabulary: the Vocabulary Enhancer. The Vocabulary Enhancer includes a list of some of the most frequently appearing vocabulary words on the GRE verbal sections. In addition, the GRE Vocabulary Enhancer has lists of the most important prefixes, roots, and suffixes that you'll need to know to help you recognize more words on the GRE.

What Is the Vocabulary Enhancer?

Learning words requires a lot of time and concentration. It's easy to become overwhelmed by looking at the vast number of words that make up the English language. Instead of giving you a list of thousands and thousands of words, we've picked over 175 words that are guaranteed to help you on the GRE.

We've given you the words that appear most often on the GRE. Study and know these words and you *will* get a better score.

In addition to learning words, recognizing the most important prefixes, roots, and suffixes will give you the skills to understand words that you don't even know. Even though we've provided you with the words that appear the most on the GRE, you will encounter words that you don't know. Fortunately, most English words are based on Greek or Latin words. Studying the meanings of Greek and Latin words will help you "break down" unfamiliar English words so you can understand them. These Greek and Latin words have survived in modern English language as parts of words, such as prefixes, roots, and suffixes. The Vocabulary Enhancer teaches you to recognize these Greek and Latin meanings of prefixes, roots, and suffixes that are used in English so that you can unlock the meaning of unfamiliar words and thereby unlock the answers to the GRE.

How to Use the Vocabulary Enhancer

The Vocabulary Builder presents a group of words and then presents lists of prefixes, roots, and suffixes. The best way for you to use the Enhancer is to study it one section at a time. Turn to the group of vocabulary words and identify the ones that you don't know or that are defined in unusual ways. Write these words down on index cards with the word on one side and definition on the other. Study these cards and then test yourself by completing the drills that follow the list. Check your answers and review any words that you missed. Then go on to the next group of words.

Once you've gone through the groups of words, turn to the list of prefixes. Review the list and identify the prefixes that are not familiar to you. Write these prefixes on the front of an index card and their meanings on the back of the card.

Study the cards and test yourself by answering the drill questions that follow the list. Check your answers and review any prefixes that you missed. Move on to the roots list and repeat these steps. Then study the suffixes list.

The Vocabulary Enhancer will enable you to attack the GRE Verbal Reasoning measure with confidence that you never knew you could possess.

The GRE Vocabulary Enhancer

The most frequently tested words on the GRE		
Word	Part of Speech	Meaning
aberrant	adj.	abnormal; straying from the normal or usual path
abstemious	adj.	sparing in use of food or drinks
acerbic	1.–adj.	tasting sour or bitter
	2.–n.	harsh in language or temper
alacrity	n.	cheerful promptness or speed
allude	v.	to refer indirectly to something
allusion	n.	an indirect reference (often literary); a hint
altruism	n.	unselfish devotion to the welfare of others rather than self
amalgam	n.	a mixture or combination (often of metals)
amalgamate	v.	to mix, merge, combine
ameliorate	v.	to improve or make better
anachronism	n.	something out of place in time (e.g., an airplane in 1492)
anomaly	n.	an oddity, inconsistency; a deviation from the norm
antipathy	n.	a natural dislike or repugnance
apposite	adj.	suitable; apt; relevant
arcane	adj.	obscure; secret; mysterious
archetype	n.	the first model from which others are copied; prototype
arduous	adj.	laborious, difficult; strenuous
arid	adj.	extremely dry, parched; barren, unimaginative
articulate	adj.	clear, distinct; expressed with clarity; skillful with words
	v.	to utter clearly and distinctly
ascetic	1.–n.	one who leads a simple life of self-denial
	2.–adj.	rigorously abstinent

(continued)

The most frequently tested words on the GRE

Word	Part of Speech	Meaning
aseptic	*adj.*	germ free
aspersion	*n.*	slanderous statement; a damaging or derogatory criticism
assiduous	*adj.*	carefully attentive; industrious
assuage	*v.*	to relieve; ease; make less severe
astringent	*1–n.*	a substance that contracts bodily tissues
	2–adj.	causing contraction; tightening; stern, austere
atrophy	*v.*	to waste away, as from lack of use; to wither
attenuate	*v.*	to make thin or slender; to weaken or dilute
autocracy	*n.*	an absolute monarchy; government where one person holds power
autocrat	*n.*	an absolute ruler
baleful	*adj.*	harmful, malign, detrimental
banal	*adj.*	trite; without freshness or originality
beneficent	*adj.*	conferring benefits; kindly; doing good
bilateral	*adj.*	pertaining to or affecting both sides or two sides; having two sides
bombast	*n.*	pompous speech; pretentious words
burgeon	*v.*	to grow or develop quickly
cacophony	*n.*	a harsh, inharmonious collection of sounds; dissonance
cant	*n.*	insincere or hypocritical statements of high ideals; the jargon of a particular group or occupation
caprice	*n.*	a sudden, unpredictable, or whimsical change
catharsis	*n.*	a purging or relieving of the body or soul
chicanery	*n.*	trickery or deception
churlishness	*n.*	crude or surly behavior; behavior of a peasant
circumlocution	*n.*	a roundabout or indirect way of speaking; not to the point

The most frequently tested words on the GRE		
Word	Part of Speech	Meaning
cloture	n.	a parliamentary procedure to end debate and begin to vote
cloying	adj.	too sugary; too sentimental or flattering
coda	n.	in music, a concluding passage
codify	v.	to organize laws or rules into a systematic collection (code)
cogent	adj.	to the point; clear; convincing in its clarity and presentation
cogitate	v.	to think hard; ponder, meditate
cognitive	adj.	possessing the power to think or meditate; meditative; capable of perception
cognizant	adj.	aware of; perceptive
coherent	adj.	sticking together; connected; logical; consistent
cohesion	n.	the act or state of sticking together
comeliness	n.	beauty; attractiveness in appearance or behavior
commodious	adj.	spacious and convenient; roomy
complaisance	n.	the quality of being agreeable or eager to please
compliant	adj.	complying; obeying; yielding
connotative	adj.	containing associated meanings in addition to the primary one
constrain	v.	to force, compel; to restrain
contentious	adj.	quarrelsome
contiguous	adj.	touching; or adjoining and close, but may not be touching
contravene	v.	to act contrary to; to oppose or contradict
conundrum	n.	a puzzle or riddle
converge	v.	to move toward one point (opposite: diverge)

(continued)

The most frequently tested words on the GRE

Word	Part of Speech	Meaning
coterie	n.	a clique; a group who meet frequently, usually socially
crass	adj.	stupid, unrefined; gross; materialistic
debacle	n.	disaster; collapse; a rout
debilitate	v.	to enfeeble; to wear out
decorous	adj.	suitable; proper; seemly
deleterious	adj.	harmful; hurtful; noxious
denigrate	v.	to defame, to blacken or sully; to belittle
deprecate	v.	to express disapproval of; to protest against
deride	v.	to laugh at with contempt; to mock
derision	n.	the act of mocking; ridicule, mockery
desiccate	v.	to dry up
diatribe	n.	a bitter or abusive speech
dichotomy	n.	a division into two parts
diffident	adj.	timid; lacking self-confidence
diffuse	adj.	spread out; verbose (wordy); not focused
discourse	v.	to converse; to communicate in orderly fashion
discrete	adj.	separate; individually distinct; composed of distinct parts
disingenuous	adj.	not frank or candid; deceivingly simple (opposite: ingenuous)
disinterested	adj.	neutral; unbiased (alternate meaning: uninterested)
disparate	adj.	unequal, dissimilar; different
disputatious	adj.	argumentative; inclined to disputes
dissemble	v.	to pretend; to feign; to conceal by pretense
dissonance	n.	musical discord; a mingling of inharmonious sounds; lack of harmony
dissonant	adj.	not in harmony; in disagreement

The most frequently tested words on the GRE

Word	Part of Speech	Meaning
ebullience	n.	an overflowing of high spirits; effervescence
ellipsis	n.	omission of words that would make the meaning clear
elucidate	v.	to make clear; to explain
emollient	adj.	softening or soothing to the skin; having power to soften or relax living tissues
encomium	n.	high praise
endemic	adj.	native to a particular area or people
enervate	v.	to weaken; to deprive of nerve or strength
engender	v.	to bring about; beget; to bring forth
ephemeral	adj.	very short-lived; lasting only a short time
eulogy	n.	words of praise, especially for the dead
evanescent	adj.	vanishing quickly; dissipating like a vapor
exigent	adj.	requiring immediate action; urgent, pressing
extemporize	v.	to improvise; to make it up as you go along
extrapolate	v.	to estimate the value of something beyond the scale; to infer what is unknown from something known
facetious	adj.	not meant to be taken seriously; humorous
feign	v.	pretend
gainsay	v.	to speak against; to contradict; to deny
garrulous	adj.	extremely talkative or wordy
iconoclast	n.	one who smashes revered images; an attacker of cherished beliefs
impassive	adj.	showing no emotion
imperturbable	adj.	calm; not easily excited
impervious	adj.	impenetrable; not allowing anything to pass through; unaffected
implacable	adj.	unwilling to be pacified or appeased

(continued)

The most frequently tested words on the GRE

Word	Part of Speech	Meaning
impugn	v.	to attack with words; to question the truthfulness or integrity
inchoate	adj.	not yet fully formed; rudimentary
incisive	adj.	getting to the heart of things; to the point
incredulous	adj.	skeptical
indigenous	adj.	native to a region; inborn or innate
inept	adj.	incompetent; clumsy
inert	adj.	not reacting chemically; inactive
ingenuous	adj.	noble; honorable; candid; naive
inherent	adj.	part of the essential character; intrinsic
insipid	adj.	uninteresting, boring, flat, dull
intractable	adj.	stubborn, obstinate; not easily taught or disciplined
intransigent	adj.	uncompromising
intrepid	adj.	fearless, bold
irascible	adj.	prone to anger
laconic	adj.	sparing of words; terse, pithy, concise
loquacious	adj.	very talkative; garrulous
luminous	adj.	emitting light; shining; also enlightened or intelligent
macerate	v.	to soften by steeping in a liquid (including softening food by the action of a solvent)
maculate	1.–adj. 2.–v.	spotted, blotched; hence defiled, impure (opposite: immaculate) to stain, spot, defile
magnanimity	n.	a quality of nobleness of mind, disdaining meanness or revenge
malevolent	adj.	wishing evil (opposite: benevolent)
malign	1–v. 2.–adj.	to speak evil of having an evil disposition toward others (opposite: benign)

\multicolumn{3}{c}{**The most frequently tested words on the GRE**}
Word	Part of Speech	Meaning
malleable	*adj.*	easy to shape or bend
misanthrope	*n.*	a hater of mankind
obdurate	*adj.*	stubborn
obsequious	*adj.*	servilely attentive; fawning
obviate	*v.*	to make unnecessary
ossify	*v.*	to turn to bone; to harden
palpable	*adj.*	touchable; clear, obvious
panegyric	*n.*	high praise
paradigm	*n.*	model, prototype; pattern
paradox	*n.*	a tenet seemingly contradictory or false, but actually true
parsimonious	*adj.*	very frugal; unwilling to spend
pedantic	*adj.*	overly concerned with minute details, especially in teaching
penurious	*adj.*	stingy, miserly
perfunctory	*adj.*	done in a routine, mechanical way, without interest
petulant	*adj.*	peevish; cranky; rude
placate	*adj.*	to appease or pacify
plethora	*n.*	a superabundance
prevaricate	*v.*	to speak equivocally or evasively, i.e., to lie
pristine	*adj.*	primitive, pure, uncorrupted
propensity	*n.*	an inclination; a natural tendency toward; a liking for
putrefaction	*n.*	a smelly mass that is the decomposition of organic matter
putrefy	*v.*	to decompose; to rot
quiescence	*n.*	state of being at rest or without motion
rancor	*n.*	strong ill will; enmity
recalcitrant	*adj.*	stubbornly rebellious

(*continued*)

The most frequently tested words on the GRE		
Word	Part of Speech	Meaning
recondite	*adj.*	hard to understand; concealed; characterized by profound scholarship
redundant	*adj.*	superfluous; exceeding what is needed
sagacious	*adj.*	wise
salubrious	*adj.*	promoting good health
sinuous	*adj.*	full of curves; twisting and turning
specious	*adj.*	plausible, but deceptive; apparently, but not actually, true
spurious	*adj.*	not genuine, false; bogus
squalid	*adj.*	filthy; wretched (from squalor)
subjugate	*v.*	to dominate or enslave
sycophant	*n.*	a flatterer of important people
taciturn	*adj.*	inclined to silence; speaking little; dour, stern
tenuous	*adj.*	thin, slim, delicate; weak
tortuous	*adj.*	full of twists and turns; not straightforward; possibly deceitful
tractable	*adj.*	easily managed (opposite: intractable)
truculent	*adj.*	fierce, savage, cruel
ubiquitous	*adj.*	omnipresent; present everywhere
vacuous	*adj.*	dull, stupid; empty-headed
viscous	*adj.*	thick and sticky (said of fluids)
welter	*n.*	a confused mass; turmoil

Drill 1

DIRECTIONS: Write the word next to its definition.

ABERRANT	ABSTEMIOUS	CODA
COGENT	COMPLIANT	DISSONANCE
ENERVATE	OBVIATE	OSSIFY
PARADIGM		

1. _____ model; example; pattern
2. _____ sparing in eating or drinking
3. _____ obedient; easily managed
4. _____ change or harden into bone
5. _____ abnormal or deviant
6. _____ the concluding section of a musical or literary composition
7. _____ convincing
8. _____ make unnecessary; to get rid of
9. _____ discord; lack of musical agreement
10. _____ to weaken

Drill 2

DIRECTIONS: Write the word next to its definition.

ASSIDUOUS	ATTENUATE	BANAL
DESICCATE	DIFFIDENCE	EXTEMPORANEOUS
FACETIOUS	INTRANSIGENCE	LACONIC
PREVARICATE		

1. _____ to dry up
2. _____ humorous; jocular
3. _____ diligent

4. _____ trite; commonplace

5. _____ unprepared; off the cuff

6. _____ state of stubborn unwillingness to compromise

7. _____ to lie

8. _____ make thin; weaken

9. _____ shyness

10. _____ terse; using few words

Drill 3

DIRECTIONS: Write the word next to its definition.

ASSUAGE	CACOPHONY	DICHOTOMY
DIFFUSION	DISCRETE	EXTRAPOLATION
GAINSAY	INTRACTABLE	PRISTINE
QUIESCENT		

1. _____ primitive; unspoiled; having its original purity

2. _____ branching into two parts; division into two mutually exclusive groups

3. _____ wordiness; spreading in all directions like a gas

4. _____ projection; conjecture; from what is known to infer what is not known

5. _____ unruly; stubborn; obstinate; not docile

6. _____ ease; lessen (pain)

7. _____ separate and distinct

8. _____ at rest; dormant

9. _____ deny

10. _____ harsh noise

Drill 4

DIRECTIONS: Write the word next to its definition.

ASCETIC	BURGEON	DERISION
DISINTERESTED	DISPARATE	EPHEMERAL
EULOGY	GARRULITY	INGENUOUS
MALLEABLE		

1. _____ capable of being shaped or formed
2. _____ basically different; unrelated
3. _____ to grow quickly; to sprout
4. _____ talkativeness
5. _____ neutral; impartial
6. _____ ridicule
7. _____ short-lived; fleeting
8. _____ naive; young; unsophisticated
9. _____ austere; practicing self-denial
10. _____ praise; often for the dead

Drill 5

DIRECTIONS: Fill in the blanks in the sentences using the words from Vocabulary Drills 1 through 4.

1. The _____ national debt forced the president and Congress finally to take action before the debt grew so large that it overwhelmed us.

2. The school assembly was filled with discord. The fire alarm rang; one band played "Dixie" while another played "The Battle Hymn of the Republic." Dozens of children screamed at each other in several languages while teachers shouted at them to be quiet. It was a moment of pure _____ at P.S. 90.

3. The dispute between the next-door neighbors became so bitter that others on the block urged them to take their disagreement to a _____ arbiter, a third party with no axe to grind, who might help them solve their problem.

4. She was an extremely _____ person. One moment she was going to be a nuclear scientist, the next a fashion model. Even going to lunch was a challenge: she'd change her mind about restaurants a dozen times before finally settling on one.

5. His _____ seemed endless. He just talked a blue streak.

6. In the hot, dry desert air, the cut flowers eventually became completely _____. Their fragile beauty was perfectly preserved.

7. She was a Gemini, and there was a real _____ between the two sides of her personality. One side was fun loving and sweet tempered; the other was very hard working and somewhat tense.

8. Jack tried to estimate the height of the house by making a(n) _____ from the height of the garage, which he knew was 15 feet high.

9. He was very _____ in preparing the report. He worked nights and weekends for weeks, checking and double-checking everything.

10. He had a very _____ manner. He constantly kidded around, and it was hard to get him to be serious.

11. At the banquet she was suddenly called upon to make a(n) _____ speech. She was so surprised by the request that all she could say was, "Thanks for everything."

12. The child was so _____ that the teacher could do nothing with him. He was very stubborn and would not cooperate in any way.

13. Her _____ was so great that she never went to parties because she was afraid to meet new people.

14. Steven had a tendency to _____. Even though his father was a shoe salesman, Steve told his classmates stories about his royal ancestry and his weekends spent at luxurious country estates.

15. Looking at the littered beach and garbage-filled water, Joe longed for the _____ beach before the settlers arrived to spoil it.

Prefixes

Prefixes	Meaning	Examples
ab –, a –, abs –	away, without, from	absent – away, not present apathy – without interest abstain – keep from doing, refrain
ad –	to, toward	adjacent – next to address – to direct toward
ante –	before	antecedent – going before in time anterior – occurring before
anti –	against	antidote – remedy to act against an evil antibiotic – substance that fights against bacteria
be –	over, thoroughly	bemoan – to mourn over belabor – to exert much labor upon
bi –	two	bisect – to divide biennial – happening every two years
cata –, cat –, cath –	down, against, back, according to	catacombs – underground passageways catalog – descriptive list catheter – tubular medical device
circum –	around	circumscribe – to draw a circle around circumspect – watchful on all sides
com –	with	combine – to join together communication – to have dealings with
contra –	against	contrary – opposed contrast – to stand in opposition
de –	down, from	decline – to bend downward decontrol – to release from government control
di –	two	dichotomy – cutting in two diarchy – system of government with two authorities

(continued)

Prefixes

Prefixes	Meaning	Examples
dis –, di–	apart, away	discern – to distinguish as separate dismiss – to send away digress – to turn aside
epi –, ep –, eph –	upon, among	epidemic – happening among many people epicycle – circle whose center moves round in the circumference of a greater circle epaulet – decoration worn to ornament or protect the shoulder ephedra – any of a large genus of desert shrubs
ex –, e –	from, out	exceed – go beyond the limit emit – to send forth
extra –	outside, beyond	extraordinary – beyond or out of the common method extrasensory – beyond the senses
hyper –	beyond, over	hyperactive – over the normal activity level hypercritic – one who is critical beyond measure
hypo –	beneath, lower	hypodermic – pertaining to parts beneath the skin hypocrisy – to be under a pretense of goodness
in –, il –, im –, ir –	in, on, into	instill – to put in slowly illation – action of bringing in impose – to lay on irrupt – to break in
in –, il –, im –, ir –	not	inactive – not active illogical – not logical imperfect – not perfect irreversible – not reversible

Prefixes

Prefixes	Meaning	Examples
inter –	among, between	intercom – to exchange conversations between people interlude – performance given between parts in a play intra – within intravenous – within a vein intramural – within the walls, as of a town or university
meta –	beyond, over, along with	metamorphosis – to change over in form or nature metatarsus – part of foot beyond the flat of the foot
mis –	badly, wrongly	misconstrue – to interpret wrongly misappropriate – to use wrongly
mono –	one	monogamy – to be married to one person at a time monotone – a single, unvaried tone
multi –	many	multiple – of many parts multitude – a great number
non –	no, not	nonsense – lack of sense nonentity – not existing
ob –	against	obscene – offensive to modesty obstruct – to hinder the passage of
para –, par –	beside	parallel – continuously at equal distance apart parentheses – sentence or phrase inserted within a passage
per –	through	persevere – to maintain an effort permeate – to pass through

(continued)

Prefixes

Prefixes	Meaning	Examples
poly –	many	**polygon** – a plane figure with many sides or angles **polytheism** – belief in the existence of many gods
post –	after	**posterior** – coming after **postpone** – to put off until a future time
pre –	before	**premature** – ready before the proper time **premonition** – a previous warning
pro –	in favor of, forward	**prolific** – bringing forth offspring **project** – throw or cast forward
re –	back, against	**reimburse** – to pay back **retract** – to draw back
semi –	half	**semicircle** – half a circle **semiannual** – half-yearly
sub –	under	**subdue** – to bring under one's power **submarine** – to travel under the surface of the sea
super –	above	**supersonic** – above the speed of sound **superior** – higher in place or position
tele –, tel –	across	**telecast** – to transmit across a distance **telepathy** – communication between mind and mind at a distance
trans –	across	**transpose** – to change the position of two things **transmit** – to send from one person to another

Prefixes		
Prefixes	Meaning	Examples
ultra –	beyond	ultraviolet – beyond the limit of visibility ultramarine – beyond the sea
un –	not	undeclared – not declared unbelievable – not believable
uni –	one	unity – state of oneness unison – sounding together
with –	away, against	withhold – to hold back withdraw – to take away

Drill: Prefixes

DIRECTIONS: Provide a definition for each prefix.

1. pro– _____
2. com– _____
3. epi– _____
4. ob– _____
5. ad– _____

DIRECTIONS: Identify the prefix in each word.

6. efface _____
7. hypothetical _____
8. permeate _____
9. contrast _____
10. inevitable _____

Roots		
Root	Meaning	Examples
act, ag	do, act, drive	activate – to make active agile – having quick motion
alt	high	altitude – height alto – highest male singing voice
alter, altr	other, change	alternative – choice between two things altruism – living for the good of others
am, ami	love, friend	amiable – worthy of affection amity – friendship
anim	mind, spirit	animated – spirited animosity – violent hatred
annu, enni	year	annual – every year centennial – every hundred years
aqua	water	aquarium – tank for water animals and plants aquamarine – semiprecious stone of sea-green color
arch	first, ruler	archenemy – chief enemy archetype – original pattern from which things are copied
aud, audit	hear	audible – capable of being heard audience – assembly of hearers audition – the power or act of hearing
auto	self	automatic – self-acting autobiography – a history of a person's life written or told by that person
bell	war	belligerent – a party taking part in a war bellicose – war-like
ben, bene	good	benign – kindly disposition beneficial – advantageous

Roots

Root	Meaning	Examples
bio	life	biotic – relating to life biology – the science of life
brev	short	abbreviate – make shorter brevity – shortness
cad, cas	fall	cadence – fall in voice casualty – loss caused by death
cap, capit	head	captain – the head or chief decapitate – to cut off the head
cede, ceed, cess	to go, to yield	recede – to move or fall back proceed – to move onward recessive – tending to go back
cent	hundred	century – hundred years centipede – insect with a hundred legs
chron	time	chronology – science dealing with historical dates chronicle – register of events in order of time
cide, cis	to kill, to cut	homicide – the act of killing incision – a cut
claim, clam	to shout	acclaim – to receive with applause proclamation – to announce publicly
cogn	to know	recognize – to know again cognition – awareness
corp	body	incorporate – to combine into one body corpse – dead body
cred	to trust, to believe	incredible – unbelievable credulous – too prone to believe

(continued)

Roots		
Root	**Meaning**	**Examples**
cur, curr, curs	to run	current – flowing body of air or water excursion – short trip
dem	people	democracy – government formed for the people epidemic – affecting all people
dic, dict	to say	dictate – to read aloud for another to transcribe verdict – decision of a jury
doc, doct	to teach	docile – easily instructed indoctrinate – to instruct
domin	to rule	dominate – to rule dominion – territory of rule
duc, duct	to lead	conduct – act of guiding induce – to overcome by persuasion
eu	well, good	eulogy – speech or writing in praise euphony – pleasantness or smoothness of sound
fac, fact, fect, fic	to do, to make	facilitate – to make easier factory – location of production confect – to put together fiction – something invented or imagined
fer	to bear, to carry	transfer – to move from one place to another refer – to direct to
fin	end, limit	infinity – unlimited finite – limited in quantity
flex, flect	to bend	flexible – easily bent reflect – to throw back

Roots

Root	Meaning	Examples
fort	luck	**fortunate** – lucky **fortuitous** – happening by chance
fort	strong	**fortify** – strengthen **fortress** – stronghold
frag, fract	break	**fragile** – easily broken **fracture** – break
fug	flee	**fugitive** – fleeing **refugee** – one who flees to a place of safety
gen	class, race	**engender** – to breed **generic** – of a general nature in regard to all members
grad, gress	to go, to step	**regress** – to go back **graduate** – to divide into regular steps
graph	writing	**telegraph** – message sent by telegraph **autograph** – person's own handwriting or signature
ject	to throw	**projectile** – capable of being thrown **reject** – to throw away
leg	law	**legitimate** – lawful **legal** – defined by law
leg, lig, lect	to choose, gather, read	**illegible** – incapable of being read **ligature** – something that binds **election** – the act of choosing
liber	free	**liberal** – favoring freedom of ideals **liberty** – freedom from restraint

(continued)

Roots		
Root	Meaning	Examples
log	study, speech	archaeology – study of human antiquities prologue – address spoken before a performance
luc, lum	light	translucent – slightly transparent illuminate – to light up
magn	large, great	magnify – to make larger magnificent – great
mal, male	bad, wrong	malfunction – to operate incorrectly malevolent – evil
mar	sea	marine – pertaining to the sea submarine – below the surface of the sea
mater, matr	mother	maternal – motherly matriarch – government exercised by a mother
mit, miss	to send	transmit – to send from one person or place to another mission – the act of sending
morph	shape	metamorphosis – a changing in shape anthropomorphic – having a human shape
mut	change	mutable – subject to change mutate – to change or alter
nat	born	innate – inborn native – a person born in a particular place
neg	deny	negative – expressing denial renege – to deny
nom	name	nominate – to put forward a name nomenclature – process of naming

Roots		
Root	Meaning	Examples
nov	new	**novel** – new **renovate** – to make as good as new
omni	all	**omnipotent** – all powerful **omnipresent** – all present
oper	to work	**operate** – to work on something **cooperate** – to work with others
pass, path	to feel	**passionate** – moved by strong emotion **pathetic** – affecting the tender emotions
pater, patr	father	**paternal** – fatherly **patriarch** – government exercised by a father
ped, pod	foot	**pedestrian** – one who travels on foot **podiatrist** – foot doctor
pel, puls	to drive, to push	**impel** – to drive forward **compulsion** – irresistible force
phil	love	**philharmonic** – loving harmony or music **philanthropist** – one who loves and seeks to do good for others
port	carry	**export** – to carry out of the country **portable** – able to be carried
psych	mind	**psychology** – study of the mind **psychiatrist** – specialist in mental disorders
quer, ques, quir, quis	to ask	**querist** – one who inquires **question** – that which is asked **inquire** – to ask about **inquisitive** – inclined to ask questions

(continued)

Roots

Root	Meaning	Examples
rid, ris	to laugh	ridiculous – laughable derision – mockery
rupt	to break	interrupt – to break in upon erupt – to break through
sci	to know	science – systematic knowledge of physical or natural phenomena conscious – having inward knowledge
scrib, script	to write	transcribe – to write over again script – text of words
sent, sens	to feel, to think	sentimental – to feel great emotion sensitive – easily affected by changes
sequ, secut	to follow	sequence – connected series consecutive – following one another in unbroken order
solv, solu, solut	to loosen	dissolve – to break up absolute – without restraint
spect	to look at	spectator – one who watches inspect – to look at closely
spir	to breathe	inspire – to breathe in respiration – process of breathing
string, strict	to bind	stringent – binding strongly restrict – to restrain within bounds
stru, struct	to build	strut – a structural piece designed to resist pressure construct – to build
tang, ting, tact, tig	to touch	tangent – touching, but not intersecting contact – touching contiguous – to touch along a boundary
ten, tent, tain	to hold	tenure – holding of office contain – to hold
term	to end	terminate – to end terminal – having an end

\multicolumn{3}{c	}{Roots}
Root	Meaning	Examples
terr	earth	**terrain** – tract of land **terrestrial** – existing on earth
therm	heat	**thermal** – pertaining to heat **thermometer** – instrument for measuring temperature
tort, tors	to twist	**contortionist** – one who twists violently **torsion** – act of turning or twisting
tract	to pull, to draw	**attract** – to draw toward **distract** – to draw away
vac	empty	**vacant** – empty **evacuate** – to empty out
ven, vent	to come	**intervene** – to come between **prevent** – to stop from coming
ver	true	**verify** – to prove to be true **veracious** – truthful
verb	word	**verbose** – use of excess words **verbatim** – word for word
vid, vis	to see	**video** – picture phase of television **vision** – act of seeing external objects
vinc, vict, vang	to conquer	**invincible** – unconquerable **victory** – defeat of enemy **vanguard** – troops moving at the head of an army
vit, viv	life	**vital** – necessary to life **vivacious** – lively
voc	to call	**vocation** – a summons to a course of action **vocal** – uttered by voice
vol	to wish, to will	**involuntary** – outside the control of will **volition** – the act of willing or choosing

Suffixes		
Suffixes	Meaning	Examples
–able, –ble	capable of	**believable** – capable of being believed **legible** – capable of being read
–acious, –icious, –ous	full of	**vivacious** – full of life **delicious** – full of pleasurable smell or taste **wondrous** – full of wonder
–ant, –ent	full of	**expectant** – full of expectation **eloquent** – full of eloquence
–ary	connected with	**disciplinary** – relating to a field of study **honorary** – for the sake of honor
–ate	to make	**ventilate** – to make public **consecrate** – to dedicate
–fy	to make	**magnify** – to make larger **testify** – to make witness
–ile	pertaining to, capable of	**docile** – capable of being managed easily **infantile** – pertaining to infancy
–ism	belief, condition	**Mormonism** – belief in the teachings of the Book of Mormon **idiotism** – utterly foolish conduct
–ist	one who	**artist** – one who creates art **pianist** – one who plays the piano
–ose	full of	**verbose** – full of words **grandiose** – striking, imposing
–osis	condition	**neurosis** – nervous condition **psychosis** – psychological condition
–tude	state	**magnitude** – state of greatness **multitude** – state of quantity

Drill: Roots

DIRECTIONS: Provide a definition for each root.

1. cede _____
2. fact _____
3. path _____
4. ject _____
5. ver _____

DIRECTIONS: Identify the root in each word.

6. acclaim _____
7. verbatim _____
8. benefactor _____
9. relegate _____
10. tension _____

Drill: Suffixes

DIRECTIONS: Provide a definition for each suffix.

1. –ant, –ent _____
2. –tude _____
3. –ile _____
4. –fy _____
5. –ary _____

DIRECTIONS: Identify the suffix in each word.

6. audacious _____
7. expedient _____
8. gullible _____
9. grandiose _____
10. antagonism _____

ANSWER KEY

Drill: 1

1. paradigm
2. abstemious
3. compliant
4. ossify
5. aberrant
6. coda
7. cogent
8. obviate
9. dissonance
10. enervate

Drill: 2

1. desiccate
2. facetious
3. assiduous
4. banal
5. extemporaneous
6. intransigence
7. prevaricate
8. attenuate
9. diffidence
10. laconic

Drill: 3

1. pristine
2. dichotomy
3. diffusion
4. extrapolation
5. intractable
6. assuage
7. discrete
8. quiescent
9. gainsay
10. cacophony

Drill: 4

1. malleable
2. disparate
3. burgeon
4. garrulity
5. disinterested
6. derision
7. ephemeral
8. ingenuous
9. ascetic
10. eulogy

Drill: 5

1. burgeoning
2. cacophony
3. disinterested
4. ephemeral
5. garrulity
6. desiccated
7. dichotomy
8. extrapolation
9. assiduous
10. facetious
11. extemporaneous
12. intractable
13. diffidence
14. prevaricate
15. pristine

Drill: Prefixes

1. forward
2. with
3. upon, among
4. against
5. to, toward
6. e-
7. hypo-
8. per-
9. contra-
10. in-

Drill: Roots

1. to go, to yield
2. to do, to make
3. to feel
4. to throw
5. true
6. claim
7. verb
8. ben(e)
9. leg
10. ten

Drill: Suffixes

1. full of
2. state
3. pertaining to, capable of
4. to make
5. connected with
6. -acious
7. -ent
8. -ible
9. -ose
10. -ism

Appendix D
Drills and Practice Questions

MATH WARM-UP DRILL

The following 25 questions are not in the current GRE format, but they cover the same level of math found in the revised GRE. Use these as a warm-up for the 25 GRE-format questions that follow.

> DIRECTIONS: Each of the following given sets of quantities is placed into either Quantity A or B. Compare the two quantities to decide whether

Ⓐ the quantity in Quantity A is greater;
Ⓑ the quantity in Quantity B is greater;
Ⓒ the two quantities are equal;
Ⓓ the relationship cannot be determined from the information given.

        Quantity A   **Quantity B**

1. $x > 0, y > 0$

    $x^2 + y^2$ $(x + y)^2$

2. The average (arithmetic mean) of 40, 20, 30, 24, 27, and 15.

    $\bar{x}$ 26

3. $4w = 6x = 12y$

    w y

4.

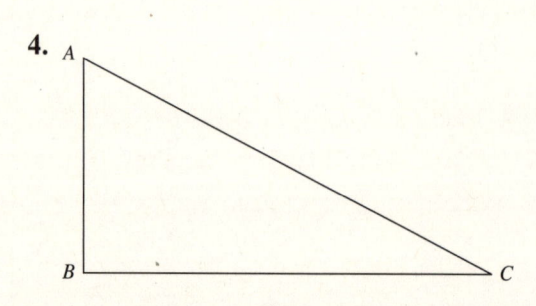

    $AB = 8, BC = 15, AC = 17$

    $\angle ABC$ 90°

Ⓐ the quantity in Quantity A is greater;
Ⓑ the quantity in Quantity B is greater;
Ⓒ the two quantities are equal;
Ⓓ the relationship cannot be determined from the information given.

Quantity A **Quantity B**

5.

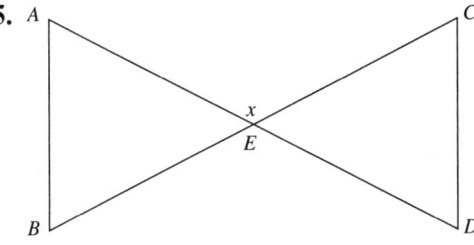

$2(\angle x)$ $\angle A + \angle B + \angle C + \angle D$

6.

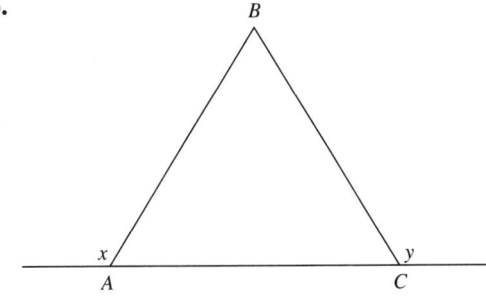

x y

  $BA = BC$

7. $m > n > 1$

w^n w^m

8. Given $2a = b$

Area of a square, side $= a$ Area of an isosceles right triangle with leg $= b$

For the following questions, select the best answer choice to the given question.

9. What part of three-fourths is one-tenth?

   Ⓐ $\frac{1}{8}$

   Ⓑ $\frac{15}{2}$

   Ⓒ $\frac{2}{15}$

   Ⓓ $\frac{3}{40}$

   Ⓔ None of these

10. Peter has five rulers of 30 cm each and three of 20 cm each. What is the average length of Peter's rulers?

    Ⓐ 25
    Ⓑ 27
    Ⓒ 23
    Ⓓ 26.25
    Ⓔ 27.25

11. Two pounds of pears and one pound of peaches cost $1.40. Three pounds of pears and two pounds of peaches cost $2.40. How much is the combined cost of one pound of pears and one pound of peaches?

    Ⓐ $2.00
    Ⓑ $1.50
    Ⓒ $1.60
    Ⓓ $.80
    Ⓔ $1.00

12. One number is 2 more than 3 times another. Their sum is 22. Find the numbers.

    Ⓐ 8, 14
    Ⓑ 2, 20
    Ⓒ 5, 17
    Ⓓ 4, 18
    Ⓔ 10, 12

13. The length of a rectangle is 6L and the width is 4W. What is the perimeter?

   (A) 12L + 8W
   (B) $12L^2 + 8W^2$
   (C) 6L + 4W
   (D) 20LW
   (E) 24LW

14. If the length of a rectangle is increased by 30% and the width is decreased by 20%, then the area is increased by

   (A) 10%.
   (B) 5%.
   (C) 4%.
   (D) 20%.
   (E) 25%.

DIRECTIONS: Each of the following given sets of quantities is placed into either Quantity A or B. Compare the two quantities to decide whether

(A) the quantity in Quantity A is greater;
(B) the quantity in Quantity B is greater;
(C) the two quantities are equal;
(D) the relationship cannot be determined from the information given.

Quantity A   **Quantity B**

15. Number of minutes in 2½ hours   Number of hours in 6¼ days

16. $w : x = y : z$
    $x \neq 0, z \neq 0$

    $wz - xy$ 0

17. $\dfrac{2}{3} - \dfrac{1}{2}$ $\dfrac{4}{5} - \dfrac{2}{3}$

412 | Appendix D

Ⓐ	the quantity in Quantity A is greater;
Ⓑ	the quantity in Quantity B is greater;
Ⓒ	the two quantities are equal;
Ⓓ	the relationship cannot be determined from the information given.

	Quantity A	**Quantity B**
18.	$x + y = 6$ $3x - y = 4$ $x - y$	0
19.	$(1 - \sqrt{2})(1 - \sqrt{2})$	$(1 - \sqrt{2})(1 + \sqrt{2})$
20.	Distance between $A(3, 4)$ and $B(-1, 1)$	Distance between $C(4, -2)$ and $D(-2, -2)$

21.

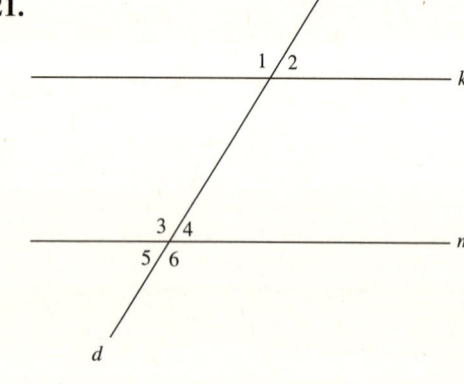

$k \parallel m$
$\angle 2 = 60°$

$\angle 5$ $60°$

22.

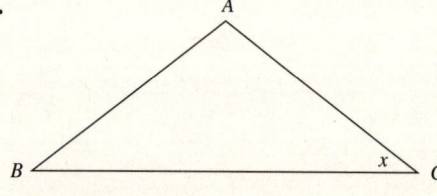

$\angle A = 100°$
$\angle B = 48°$

Side AB Side BC

23.	Product of the roots of $x^2 + 3x - 4 = 0$	Product of the roots of $x^2 + 4x + 4 = 0$
24.	$\dfrac{a+2}{a+1} = \dfrac{a-4}{a-3}$	
	Value of a	1
25.	The sum of all angles of a polygon whose sides are all equal	The sum of all angles of a square

ANSWER EXPLANATIONS

1. B

To compare the expression $x^2 + y^2$ in Quantity A with $(x + y)^2$, one should first assume that these expressions are equal. Then

$$x^2 + y^2 = (x + y)^2 \text{ implies } x^2 + y^2 = x^2 + 2xy + y^2. \qquad (1)$$

If x and y are both positive, their squares are also positive. So, a one-to-one comparison of the expression in Quantity B with the expression in Quantity A indicates that Quantity B is larger because it has an extra term, $2xy$, which is positive. Hence, response (B) is correct.

Response (C) is not possible. To see this, add $-x^2$ and $-y^2$, respectively, on both sides of (1). So, one obtains

$$x^2 + y^2 - x^2 = x^2 + 2xy + y^2 - x^2$$
$$y^2 = 2xy + y^2$$
$$y^2 - y^2 = 2xy + y^2 - y^2$$
$$0 = 2xy$$

Note that $2xy = 0$ means that either $x = 0$, $y = 0$, or $x = y = 0$. So, the assertion of equality between the two statements leads to a contradiction because the original assumption is that both x and y are positive.

2. C

The average (arithmetic mean), $\bar{x}$, of a set of numbers is defined as the sum of all the numbers in the set divided by the number of numbers, n. That is,

$$\bar{x} = \frac{\text{sum of all numbers}}{n}$$

In this problem, calculating the average, $\bar{x}$, of the given numbers, we get

$$\bar{x} = \frac{40 + 20 + 30 + 24 + 27 + 15}{6}$$
$$= \frac{156}{6} = 26$$

So the two quantities in Quantities A and B are equal.

3. D

To determine the outcome consider the following:

If $4w = 6x = 12y$, then $\dfrac{4w}{4} = \dfrac{12y}{4}$ or $w = 3y$. Thus, in general for positive numbers the value of w is always three times as large as the value of y. So response (A) would be correct. But, if one substitutes 0 for w, then w and y have the same value 0. So, the quantities are equal and response (C) is correct. Finally, if the values of w and y are both negative, then response (B) is correct. (For example, if $w = -12$, then $y = -4$ which is larger than w.) Thus, there is not enough information given to make a comparison.

4. C

To understand this problem, first assume that $\triangle ABC$ is a right triangle. With this assumption the Pythagorean theorem applies as follows:

$$(AC)^2 = (AB)^2 + (BC)^2.$$

Because the length of the sides of the triangle are given ($AC = 17$, $AB = 8$, $BC = 15$), substitute in the formula and observe whether the result is an equality.

$$(17)^2 = (8)^2 + (15)^2$$
$$289 = 64 + 225$$
$$289 = 289$$

Because the result is an equality, the assumption that the triangle is a right triangle is correct. So, the angle opposite the longest side ($\angle ABC$) must be a right angle. The quantities in the two columns are equal.

5. C

To explain this answer one needs to first know that the exterior angle of a triangle equals the sum of the measure of both remote interior angles of the triangle. The exterior angle of $\triangle CDE$ is $\angle x$ and the remote interior angles are C and D. So, the sum of angles C and D equals $\angle x$. Similarly, the exterior angle of $\triangle ABE$ is angle x and the remote interior angles are A and B. So, the sum of angles A and B equals $\angle x$. Hence, by substitution, one gets that the quantities in the two columns are equal as follows:

$$\angle x + \angle x = (\angle A + \angle B) + (\angle C + \angle D) \text{ or}$$
$$2(\angle x) = \angle A + \angle B + \angle C + \angle D$$

6. C

Because *BA* equals *BC*, $\triangle ABC$ is isosceles. Thus, according to a well-known theorem, the angles *BAC* and *BCA* are equal. Because angles *x* and *y* are supplementary angles to *BAC* and *BCA*, respectively, it is clear that

$$\angle x + \angle BAC = 180° \text{ and } \angle y + \angle BCA = 180°.$$

But, because $\angle BAC = \angle BCA$ one can conclude that $\angle x = \angle y$. So, the quantities in the columns are equal.

7. D

Because nothing is given about the value of *w*, the value could be negative or positive. If the *w* is negative, the value of w^n and w^m can be negative or positive values. If *w* equals 0 or 1, Quantity A and B will be equal. If *w* is greater than 1, then Quantity B will be greater than Quantity A.

8. B

The area of the square = a^2

The area of the right triangle in terms of $a = \dfrac{(2a)^2}{2} = \dfrac{4a^2}{2} = 2a^2$

Therefore, Quantity B is greater than Quantity A.

9. C

First, observe that three-fourths is $\dfrac{3}{4}$ and one-tenth is $\dfrac{1}{10}$. Let *x* be the unknown part that must be found. Then, one can write from the statement of the problem that the *x* part of three-fourths is given by

$$\dfrac{3}{4}x$$

The equation for the problem is given by $\dfrac{3}{4}x = \dfrac{1}{10}$. Multiplying both sides of the equation by the reciprocal of $\dfrac{3}{4}$, one obtains the following:

$$\left(\dfrac{4}{3}\right)\dfrac{3}{4}x = \left(\dfrac{4}{3}\right)\dfrac{1}{10} \text{ or } x = \dfrac{4}{30} \text{ or } x = \dfrac{2}{15}$$

which is choice (C).

Response (D) is obtained by incorrectly finding the product of $\dfrac{3}{4}$ and $\dfrac{1}{10}$ to be the unknown part. Response (B) is obtained by dividing $\dfrac{3}{4}$ by $\dfrac{1}{10}$.

10. D

$$\text{Average} = \frac{5 \times 30 + 3 \times 20}{8}$$

$$\text{Average} = \frac{150 + 60}{8} = \frac{210}{8} = 26.25$$

11. E

Let X = cost of one pound of pears
Let Y = cost of one pound of peaches

$$2X + Y = 1.4 \quad (1)$$
$$3X + 2Y = 2.4 \quad (2)$$

$$4X + 2Y = 2.8 \quad \text{(3) Multiply equation (1) by 2}$$
$$\underline{3X + 2Y = 2.4} \quad \text{(4) Subtract (2) from (3)}$$
$$X = .4 \quad \text{Substitute } X = .4 \text{ in (1)}$$
$$Y = .6$$

Therefore, $X + Y = 1.00$

12. C

Based on the information given in the first sentence of the problem, one needs to first represent the unknown numbers. So let x be a number. Then, the other number is given by $3x + 2$, which is two more than 3 times the first number. So the two numbers are x and $3x + 2$.

Next, form an equation by adding the two numbers and setting the sum equal to 22 and then solve the equation for the two numbers.

$$x + 3x + 2 = 22$$
$$4x + 2 = 22$$
$$4x = 20$$
$$x = 5, \text{ one of the numbers.}$$

The other number is given by

$$3x + 2 = 3(5) + 2 = 15 + 2 = 17, \text{ the other number.}$$

Hence, answer choice (C) is correct. The other answer choices fail to satisfy the equation $x + 3x + 2 = 22$.

13. A

In order to find the perimeter of the rectangle, it is important first to understand the definition—that is, perimeter equals the sum of the dimension of the rectangle. Hence, for the given rectangle,

Perimeter = $6L + 4W + 6L + 4W$ (Add like terms)
Perimeter = $12L + 8W$

Answer choice (E), $24LW$, is incorrect because it represents the area of the rectangle, which is the product of the length and width. Answer choice (C), $6L + 4W$, is incorrect because it represents only one-half of the perimeter of the rectangle. Answer choice (D), $20LW$, is incorrect because this response is obtained by simply adding the coefficients of L and W, which is an incorrect application of algebra. Finally, answer choice (B), $12L^2 + 8W^2$, is incorrect because it is obtained by using the definition of the perimeter of a rectangle incorrectly as follows: perimeter = $2L(6L) + 2W(4W)$.

14. C

Let x be the length of the rectangle. Then, a 30% increase in the length of the rectangle is given by $x + .3x$. Let y be the width of the rectangle. Then, a 20% decrease in the width of the rectangle is given by $y - .2y$. The original area is given by $A = xy$ and the new area is given by:

$$A = (x + .3x)(y - .2y)$$
$$= xy - .2xy + .3xy - 0.06xy$$
$$= xy + 0.04xy$$
$$= 1.04xy$$

So, the new area is 104% of the original area, which is a 104% − 100% = 4% increase, which is answer choice (C). The other answer choices are found by either using the perimeter formula or incorrectly finding the increase and decrease in the length and width, respectively.

15. C

Quantity A $2\frac{1}{2}$ hours = $\dfrac{60 \text{ minutes}}{1 \text{ hour}} \times \dfrac{5}{2}$ hours = 150 minutes.

Quantity B $6\frac{1}{4}$ days = $\dfrac{24 \text{ hours}}{1 \text{ day}} \times \dfrac{25}{4}$ days = 150 hours.

16. C

Note that $w : x = \dfrac{w}{x}$ and $y : z = \dfrac{y}{z}$. Thus, $\dfrac{w}{x} = \dfrac{y}{z}$. Adding the opposite of $\dfrac{y}{z}$ to both sides of the equation, we get

$$\dfrac{w}{x} + \left(-\dfrac{y}{z}\right) = \dfrac{y}{z} + \left(-\dfrac{y}{z}\right)$$

$$\dfrac{w}{x} - \dfrac{y}{z} = 0$$

Multiplying through by xz, the LCD, we have

$$(xz)\left(\dfrac{w}{x}\right) - (xz)\left(\dfrac{y}{z}\right) = (xz)(0)$$

$$wz - xy = 0$$

Hence, the quantities in both columns are equal.

17. A

Quantity A $\quad \dfrac{2}{3} - \dfrac{1}{2} = \dfrac{4}{6} - \dfrac{3}{6} = \dfrac{1}{6}$

Quantity B $\quad \dfrac{4}{5} - \dfrac{2}{3} = \dfrac{12}{15} - \dfrac{10}{15} = \dfrac{2}{15}$

Find a common denominator and compare the fractions.

Quantity A $= \dfrac{5}{30}$ $\quad$ Quantity B $= \dfrac{4}{30}$.

Therefore, Quantity A is greater than Quantity B.

18. B

The given equations form a system that can be easily solved by the elimination method. By elimination one simply adds the two equations together in order to easily eliminate the y variable and solve for the x variable as follows:

$$x + y = 6$$
$$\underline{3x - y = 4}$$
$$4x = 10 \quad \text{(sum of the equations)}$$

$$\dfrac{4x}{4} = \dfrac{10}{4} \quad \text{or} \quad x = \dfrac{10}{4} = \dfrac{5}{2}$$

The next step is to substitute the value of x in $x + y = 6$ and solve for the variable y. The result is

$$\frac{5}{2} + y = 6$$

$$\frac{5}{2} + y + \left(-\frac{5}{2}\right) = 6 + \left(-\frac{5}{2}\right)$$

$$y + 0 = \frac{12}{2} + \left(-\frac{5}{2}\right)$$

$$y = \frac{7}{2}$$

Finally, note that $x - y = \frac{5}{2} - \frac{7}{2} = -1$. Hence, the quantity in Quantity B is greater than the quantity in Quantity A.

19. **A**

In Quantity A expand the indicated product by using the foil method. Thus, the product of

$$(1 - \sqrt{2})(1 - \sqrt{2}) = 1 - \sqrt{2} - \sqrt{2} + (\sqrt{2})(\sqrt{2})$$
$$= 1 - 2\sqrt{2} + \sqrt{4}$$
$$= 1 - 2\sqrt{2} + 2$$
$$= 3 - 2\sqrt{2}$$

which is positive.

Similarly, in Quantity B one expands the indicated product to get

$$(1 - \sqrt{2})(1 + \sqrt{2}) = 1 - \sqrt{2} + \sqrt{2} - (\sqrt{2})(\sqrt{2})$$
$$= 1 - \sqrt{4}$$
$$= 1 - 2$$
$$= -1$$

Thus, the quantity in Quantity A is larger.

20. B

To determine the comparison one needs to know the formula for finding the distance between two points in the plane. The distance between $A(3, 4)$ and $B(-1, 1)$ is found by using the following formula, where the subscript 1 refers to coordinates in point A and subscript 2 refers to coordinates in point B.

$$\sqrt{(x_2 - x_1)^2 + (y_2 - y_1)^2} = \sqrt{(-1 - 3)^2 + (1 - 4)^2}$$
$$= \sqrt{16 + 9}$$
$$= \sqrt{25} = 5$$

The distance between $C(4, -2)$ and $D(-2, -2)$ is found using the same formula, as follows, where the subscript 1 refers to coordinates in point C and subscript 2 refers to coordinates in point D.

$$\sqrt{(-2 - 4)^2 + (-2 - (-2))^2} = \sqrt{(-6)^2 + (0)^2}$$
$$= \sqrt{36} = 6$$

Hence, the distance from C to D is greater than the distance from A to B.

21. C

By definition $\angle 4$ and $\angle 5$ are vertical angles and by a theorem vertical angles are equal. Because line segments k and m are parallel, by a theorem the corresponding angles are equal. What are the corresponding angles? They are $\angle 1$, $\angle 3$, and $\angle 5$ on the left side of the diagonal d and $\angle 2$, $\angle 4$, and $\angle 6$ on the right side of the diagonal. It is given that $\angle 2 = 60°$. Because $\angle 4 = \angle 2$, then $\angle 4$ equals $60°$. Finally, because $\angle 4$ and $\angle 5$ are equal vertical angles, then $\angle 5$ equals $60°$. So the quantities in both columns are equal.

22. B

Recall that $\triangle ABC$, as well as any triangle, contains $180°$. Thus, the measure of $\angle x$ must be the smallest because $\angle A$ is $100°$ and $\angle B$ is $48°$. That is,

$$100 + 48 + x = 180°$$
$$148 + x = 180$$
$$148 + x - 148 = 180 - 148$$
$$x = 32°$$

Now because $\angle A$ (100°) is the largest in $\triangle ABC$, then it is a well-known theorem that the side (BC) that is opposite this angle is the largest side. Thus, it follows that side BC in Quantity B is greater than side AB in Quantity A.

23. B

Factor each equation.

Quantity A
$$x^2 + 3x - 4 = (x - 1)(x + 4)$$
$$x = 1, -4$$
$$\text{Product} = -4$$

Quantity B
$$x^2 + 4x + 4 = (x + 2)^2$$
$$x = -2, -2$$
$$\text{Product} = 4$$

Therefore, Quantity B is greater than Quantity A.

24. C

$$\frac{a+2}{a+1} = \frac{a-4}{a-3}$$
$$(a+2)(a-3) = (a-4)(a+1)$$
$$a^2 - a - 6 = a^2 - 3a - 4$$
$$a^2 - a - a^2 + 3a = -4 + 6$$
$$2a = 2$$
$$a = 1$$

Therefore, the two quantities are equal.

25. D

Observe that in order to attempt to compare the two statements there is a need to analyze each. The statement in Quantity B indicates that a representation of the sum of the angles of a square must be made. Because each of the four angles of a square is a right angle, one can write the sum of the angles as follows:

$$4(90°) = 360°.$$

On the other hand, the statement in Quantity A indicates that a representation of the sum of all the angles of a polygon whose sides are equal must be made. The sum of all the angles of any polygon with equal sides will increase with the increasing number of sides of the polygon. For example, the sum of the angles of a triangle is 180° and the sum of the angles of a pentagon is 540°. Thus, it is not possible to compare the results from the two columns.

GRE MATH PRACTICE SET

Now that you have completed your warm-up, try these 25 GRE-format math questions.

Define $x \square y \Delta z$ as $x - y^2 \div z$

	Quantity A	**Quantity B**
1.	$3 \square 2 \Delta 5$	$4 \square 3 \Delta 6$

- (A) Quantity A is greater.
- (B) Quantity B is greater.
- (C) The two quantities are equal.
- (D) The relationship cannot be determined from the information given.

2.

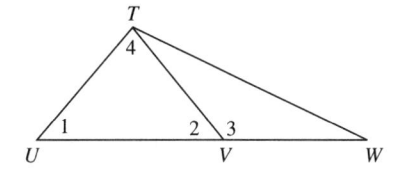

$m\angle 1 = m\angle 2$, $m\angle 4 < 90°$, and points U, V, and W are collinear

Quantity A	**Quantity B**
135°	$m\angle 3$

- (A) Quantity A is greater.
- (B) Quantity B is greater.
- (C) The two quantities are equal.
- (D) The relationship cannot be determined from the information given.

3. $|a|<|b|<|c|$

Quantity A	**Quantity B**
$a + b - c$	$a - b + c$

- (A) Quantity A is greater.
- (B) Quantity B is greater.
- (C) The two quantities are equal.
- (D) The relationship cannot be determined from the information given.

4. Car A travels a distance of 3 miles in 5 minutes. Car B travels at a speed of 30 miles per hour for 2 minutes, then 40 miles per hour for 3 minutes.

Quantity A	**Quantity B**
The average rate in miles per hour for car A	The average rate in miles per hour for car B

- (A) Quantity A is greater.
- (B) Quantity B is greater.
- (C) The two quantities are equal.
- (D) The relationship cannot be determined from the information given.

5. m is an odd integer between 10 and 20
n is a member of $\{30, 60, 90, 120\}$

Quantity A	**Quantity B**
The number of prime factors of m	The number of prime factors of n

- (A) Quantity A is greater.
- (B) Quantity B is greater.
- (C) The two quantities are equal.
- (D) The relationship cannot be determined from the information given.

6. List R consists of 15 numbers arranged in ascending order, for which the sixth number is 30, the seventh number is 33, and the eighth number is 35. List S consists of 15 numbers whose total is 500.

Quantity A	**Quantity B**
The median of list R	The mean of list S

- (A) Quantity A is greater.
- (B) Quantity B is greater.
- (C) The two quantities are equal.
- (D) The relationship cannot be determined from the information given.

7.

Quantity A	**Quantity B**
The positive root of $2x^2 + 5x - 3 = 0$	The positive root of $x^2 + 6x - 1 = 0$

- (A) Quantity A is greater.
- (B) Quantity B is greater.
- (C) The two quantities are equal.
- (D) The relationship cannot be determined from the information given.

8. In the xy-plane, the slope of $6x + by = c$ is 2 and the x-intercept is (1, 0).

   Quantity A   **Quantity B**
   $\dfrac{c}{b}$ $\dfrac{b}{c}$

   Ⓐ Quantity A is greater.
   Ⓑ Quantity B is greater.
   Ⓒ The two quantities are equal.
   Ⓓ The relationship cannot be determined from the information given.

9. Given a circle with center O, $m\angle AOB = 40°$, where $\angle AOB$ is a central angle. Also, $m\angle ADC = 10°$, where $\angle ADC$ is an inscribed angle.

   Quantity A   **Quantity B**
   $m\overarc{AB}$ $m\overarc{BC}$

   Ⓐ Quantity A is greater.
   Ⓑ Quantity B is greater.
   Ⓒ The two quantities are equal.
   Ⓓ The relationship cannot be determined from the information given.

10. The total weight of 12 people in a room is 1,680 pounds. After two people leave the room, the mean weight of the remaining people is 10% less than the mean weight of the original 12 people. What is the total weight in pounds, of the people left in the room?

    Ⓐ 1,512
    Ⓑ 1,428
    Ⓒ 1,344
    Ⓓ 1,260
    Ⓔ 1,176

11. Which of the following are equivalent to $\dfrac{(x^4)^6(x^9)}{\sqrt[3]{x^8}}$? Indicate all correct answers.

    [A] $\dfrac{x^{31}}{\sqrt[3]{x^2}}$

    [B] x^{31}

    [C] $\dfrac{x^{19}}{\sqrt[3]{x^2}}$

D $\dfrac{\left(x^3\right)^{11}}{\sqrt[3]{x^8}}$

E $\dfrac{\left(x^3\right)^{11}}{\sqrt[3]{x^2}}$

F $\dfrac{x^{14}}{\sqrt[3]{x^2}}$

12. In a normal distribution of 800 data, the mean is 60 and the standard deviation is 5. Which of the following is the best approximation of the total number of data whose value is between 55 and 65 or greater than 70?

   A) 384
   B) 400
   C) 528
   D) 544
   E) 560

13. For a certain medical insurance plan, the co-payment for any service is dependent upon the actual cost. If the cost of service is under $1,000, the co-payment is $25. If the cost of service is greater than $1,000 but less than $10,000, the co-payment is $50. For each additional $100 above $10,000 for the cost of service, the co-payment increases by $5. Last year, Jennifer had four visits to doctors' offices. The respective actual costs for these visits were $800, $2,000, $10,500, and $15,000. What was the total of Jennifer's co-payments for these visits?

   $ ☐

For questions 14–17, use the following information.

The Math Heaven store sells four major products related to mathematics, namely puzzle books, toys, games, and T-shirts (with imprinted math formulas). The total number of these items in stock is 1,800. Below are two graphs that identify important features about this store.

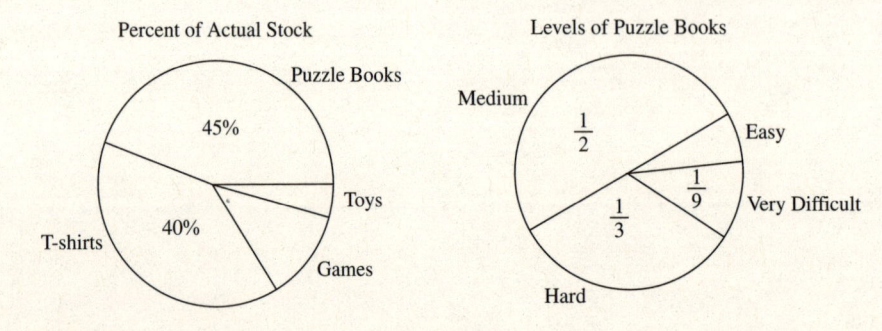

Percent of Actual Stock: Puzzle Books 45%, T-shirts 40%, Toys, Games

Levels of Puzzle Books: Medium $\tfrac{1}{2}$, Easy, Very Difficult $\tfrac{1}{9}$, Hard $\tfrac{1}{3}$

14. If the number of games is five times the number of toys, how many games are in stock?

   ☐ games

15. The mean price of a toy is $16 and the mean price of a T-shirt is $9. If the store can sell 40% of its stock of toys and 60% of its stock of T-shirts, what would be the total sales? (Disregard any sales tax.)

   Ⓐ $3,750
   Ⓑ $4,176
   Ⓒ $5,472
   Ⓓ $6,380
   Ⓔ $7,074

16. The company expects to sell all its puzzle books this year because they are extremely popular. Puzzle books rated as "Easy" sell for $3 each and those rated as "Medium" sell for $5 each. The puzzle books rated as "Very Difficult" sell for twice the price as those rated as "Hard." If the total sales of all puzzle books is $5,580, what is the cost of each puzzle book that is rated as "Very Difficult"?

   Ⓐ $14.40
   Ⓑ $14.80
   Ⓒ $15.20
   Ⓓ $15.80
   Ⓔ $16.40

17. The president of Math Heaven is planning to reduce the number of toys in stock by 40%, but to increase the total stock by at least 10%. Which one(s) of the following will meet that requirement? Indicate *all* correct answers.

   A Increase the number of puzzle books rated as "Hard" by 50%
   B Increase the number of T-shirts by 30%
   C Increase the number of games by 72%
   D Double the number of puzzle books rated as "Very Difficult"
   E Increase the number of puzzle books rated as "Medium" by $\frac{3}{5}$

18. Seven people are to be seated in a row. Amy and Ted are two of the seven people. Ted will not sit on either end seat and Amy does not want to sit next to Ted. In how many different ways can these seven people be seated?

Ⓐ 2,400
Ⓑ 3,600
Ⓒ 5,040
Ⓓ 31,250
Ⓔ 62,500

19. If $f(x) = 3x^2 - 1$, which of the following is the expression for $f(f(x))$?

Ⓐ $9x^4 - 6x^2$
Ⓑ $9x^4 - 6x^2 + 2$
Ⓒ $27x^4 - 18x^2$
Ⓓ $27x^4 - 18x^2 - 1$
Ⓔ $27x^4 - 18x^2 + 2$

20. Look at the figure below.

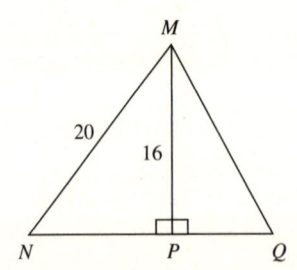

If $NQ = 18$, what is the length of $\overline{MQ}$? Round off your answer to the nearest tenth.

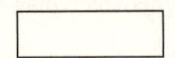

21. Four apples and seven pears cost $11.80, whereas seven apples and four pears cost $10.75. What is the cost of three apples and three pears?

Ⓐ $4.80
Ⓑ $5.30
Ⓒ $5.75
Ⓓ $6.15
Ⓔ $6.70

22. A box contains 12 green disks, and a number of white disks. The probability of selecting a green disk is 0.4. After three more white disks are then placed into the box, Jason randomly selects two disks, one at a time with no replacement. What is the probability that both selected disks are green?

- (A) $\dfrac{4}{7}$
- (B) $\dfrac{16}{49}$
- (C) $\dfrac{16}{121}$
- (D) $\dfrac{1}{8}$
- (E) $\dfrac{4}{49}$

23. In a group of 70 students, 8 have studied both the French and German languages. Fifteen of the students have studied neither language. The number of students who have studied German is $2\dfrac{1}{2}$ times the number who have studied French. How many of these students have not studied French?

- (A) 37
- (B) 45
- (C) 52
- (D) 55
- (E) 62

24. A sequence of numbers is defined as follows: $a_1 = 4$, $a_2 = 7$, and $a_n = a_{n-1} + 2a_{n-2}$ for $n > 2$. What is the sum of the first five terms of this sequence?

- (A) 146
- (B) 138
- (C) 130
- (D) 122
- (E) 114

25. Which of the following functions has *both* a domain of all real numbers greater than -6, and a value of zero whenever x equals -1 or 2?

(A) $f(x) = \dfrac{\sqrt{x+6}}{x^2 + x - 2}$

(B) $f(x) = \dfrac{3x^2 + 3x - 6}{\sqrt{\dfrac{1}{2}x + 12}}$

(C) $f(x) = \dfrac{2x^2 - 2x - 4}{\sqrt{\dfrac{1}{2}x + 3}}$

(D) $f(x) = \dfrac{2x^3 - 2x^2 - 4x}{\sqrt{6 - x}}$

(E) $f(x) = \dfrac{\sqrt{4 - \dfrac{2}{3}x}}{x^3 - 3x - 2}$

ANSWER EXPLANATIONS

1. B

$3 \square 2 \Delta 5 = 3 - 2^2 \div 5 = 3 - 0.8 = 2.2$ and
$4 \square 3 \Delta 6 = 4 - 3^2 \div 6 = 4 - 1.5 = 2.5$

2. A

The sum of the measures of angles 1, 2, and 4 is 180°. Because $m\angle 4 < 90°$, we know that $m\angle 1 + m\angle 2 > 90°$. This implies $m\angle 1 > \frac{90°}{2} = 45°$ and $m\angle 2 > \frac{90°}{2} = 45°$. But $m\angle 2 + m\angle 3 = 180°$. Thus, we conclude that $m\angle 3 < 180° - 45° = 135°$.

3. D

As numerical examples, suppose that $a = 3$, $b = 4$, and $c = 5$. Then $a + b - c = 2$ and $a - b + c = 4$. This would imply that Quantity B is larger. But if $a = 3$, $b = 4$, and $c = -5$, then $a + b - c = 12$ and $a - b + c = -6$. This would imply that Quantity A is larger. Therefore, the relationship between $a + b - c$ and $a - b + c$ cannot be determined.

4. C

Let x represent the average rate in miles per hour for car A. Then $\frac{x}{60} = \frac{3}{5}$. Cross-multiply to get $5x = 180$, so $x = 36$.

For car B, the distance it travels at 30 miles per hour for 2 minutes is $(30)(\frac{2}{60}) = 1$ mile. When car B travels at 40 miles per hour for 3 minutes, its distance is $(40)(\frac{3}{60}) = 2$ miles. Average speed equals total distance divided by total time. Thus, for car B, its average speed is 3 miles divided by 5 minutes, which is equivalent to $(3)(\frac{60}{5}) = 36$ miles per hour.

5. B

If $m = 11, 13, 17$, or 19, the number of prime factors for m is 1. If $m = 15$, the corresponding number of prime factors is 2 (namely 3 and 5). Each of the numbers 30, 60, 90, and 120 has 3 prime factors (namely 2, 3, and 5). Thus, the number of prime factors for n is 3.

6. A

The median of list R is the $\frac{15+1}{2}$ = 8th number, which is 35. The mean of list S is $\frac{500}{15} = 33.\overline{3}$.

7. A

$2x^2 + 5x - 3 = 0$ can be written as $(2x - 1)(x + 3) = 0$, so its positive root is $\frac{1}{2}$. In order to find the roots of $x^2 + 6x - 1 = 0$, we use the Quadratic formula. Then $x = \frac{-6 \pm \sqrt{6^2 - (4)(1)(-1)}}{2} = \frac{-6 \pm \sqrt{40}}{2}$. Thus, its positive root is $\frac{-6 + \sqrt{40}}{2} \approx 0.16$, which is less than $\frac{1}{2}$.

8. B

Rewrite $6x + by = c$ as $y = -\frac{6}{b}x + \frac{c}{b}$, where $-\frac{6}{b}$ represents the slope. Then $-\frac{6}{b} = 2$, which means $b = -3$. Now we have $6x - 3y = c$. Substituting (1, 0) leads to $(6)(1) - (3)(0) = c$, which means $c = 6$. Finally, $\frac{c}{b} = -2$, which is less than $\frac{b}{c} = -\frac{1}{2}$.

9. D

Because $\angle AOB$ is a central angle, $m\overarc{AB} = m\angle AOB = 40°$. Because $\angle ADC$ is an inscribed angle, $m\overarc{AC} = (2)(m\angle ADC) = 20°$. We can conclude that $m\overarc{AB} > m\overarc{AC}$, but we cannot determine the relationship between $m\overset{\frown}{AB}$ and $m\overset{\frown}{BC}$. Here are two scenarios, one of which shows $m\overset{\frown}{AB} > m\overset{\frown}{BC}$ and the other shows $m\overset{\frown}{AB} < m\overset{\frown}{BC}$.

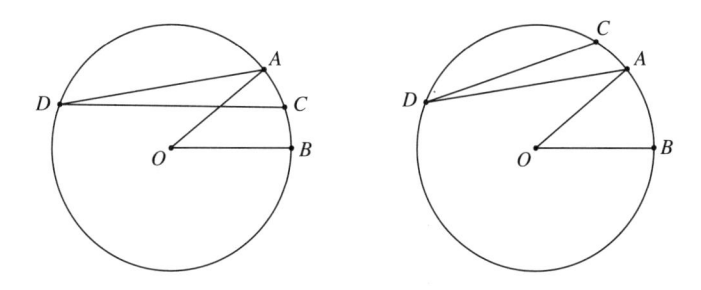

10. D

The mean weight of the original 12 people is $\frac{1,680}{12} = 140$ pounds. After two people leave the room, the mean weight becomes $(140) - (0.10)(140) = 126$ pounds. Thus, the total weight of the 10 remaining people is $(10)(126) = 1,260$ pounds.

11. A, D

$$\frac{(x^4)^6(x^9)}{\sqrt[3]{x^8}} = \frac{(x^{24})(x^9)}{\sqrt[3]{(x^6)(x^2)}} = \frac{x^{33}}{(x^2)(\sqrt[3]{x^2})} = \frac{x^{31}}{\sqrt[3]{x^2}}.$$ This is the exact form

of answer choice A. Note that for answer choice D,

$$\frac{(x^3)^{11}}{\sqrt[3]{x^8}} = \frac{x^{33}}{\sqrt[3]{(x^6)(x^2)}} = \frac{x^{33}}{(x^2)(\sqrt[3]{x^2})} = \frac{x^{31}}{\sqrt[3]{x^2}}.$$

12. E

Convert each of 55, 65, and 70 to standard scores. 55 changes to $\frac{55-60}{5} = -1$, 65 changes to $\frac{65-60}{5} = 1$, and 70 changes to $\frac{70-60}{5} = 2$. The percent of data that lies between the standard scores of -1 and 1 is $34\% + 34\% = 68\%$. The percent of data that lies above the standard score of 2 is 2%. Then the required number of data that lie either between the standard scores of -1 and 1 or above the standard score of 2 is $(70\%)(800) = 560$.

13. 450

For the visit in which the cost was $800, Jennifer paid $25. For the visit in which the cost was $2,000, she paid $50. When her visit cost $10,500, her co-payment would be calculated as follows: $10,500 - $10,000 = $500 and $\dfrac{\$500}{\$100} = 5$. So, her co-payment for that visit would be $50 + (5)($5) = $75. Similarly, when her visit cost $15,000, we first calculate $\dfrac{\$15,000 - \$10,000}{\$100} = 50$. So her corresponding co-payment would be $50 + (50)($5) = $300. Finally, her grand total in co-payments was $25 + $50 + $75 + $300 = $450.

14. 225

100% - 45% - 40% = 15% of the stock is allocated to games and toys. Then (0.15)(1,800) = 270 games and toys. Let x = number of toys and $5x$ = number of games. So, $x + 5x = 6x = 270$, which means that $x = 45$. Thus, the number of games is (5)(45) = 225.

15. B

The store has (0.025)(1,800) = 45 toys and will sell (0.40)(45) = 18 of them. So, the sales from toys will be (18)($16) = $288. The store also has (0.40)(1,800) = 720 T-shirts and will sell (0.60)(720) = 432 of them. The sales from the T-shirts will be (432)($9) = $3,888. Thus, the total sales will be $288 + $3,888 = $4,176.

16. C

The number of puzzle books is (0.45)(1,800) = 810. The number of "Medium" books is $(\dfrac{1}{2})(810) = 405$; the number of "Hard" books is $(\dfrac{1}{3})(810) = 270$; the number of "Very Difficult" books is $(\dfrac{1}{9})(810) = 90$; the number of "Easy" books is 810 - 405 - 270 - 90 = 45. The sales from all books rated as "Easy" and "Medium" is (45)($3) + (405)($5) = $2,160. Let x = cost of each "Hard" book and $2x$ = cost of each "Very Difficult" book. Then $270x + (90)(2x) + \$2,160 = \$5,580$. This equation simplifies to $450x = \$3,420$, so $x = \$7.60$. Thus, the cost of each "Very Difficult" book is (2)($7.60) = $15.20.

17. B, E

We have established that the number of toys in stock is 45 (from #14). A decrease of 40% will mean that $(0.40)(45) = 18$ toys will be removed, which will leave 1,782 items in stock. An increase of at least 10% in original stock means that there must be at least $(1,800)(1.10) = 1,980$ items in stock. Then the store must supply an additional $1,980 - 1,782 = 198$ items. Answer choice B is correct because there are currently $(0.40)(1,800) = 720$ T-shirts. An increase of 30% means that $(720)(0.30) = 216$ more T-shirts will be in stock. Answer choice E is correct because we have already established (from #16) that there are 405 puzzle books rated as "Medium." An increase by $\frac{3}{5}$ means that $(405)(\frac{3}{5}) = 243$ more such puzzle books will be in stock. Answer choice A is wrong because there will only be an increase of $(270)(0.50) = 135$ puzzle books rated as "Hard." Answer choice C is wrong because there will only be an increase of $(225)(0.72) = 162$ games. Answer choice D is wrong because there will only be an increase of 90 puzzle books rated as "Very Difficult."

18. A

Excluding the two end seats, we have five ways in which Ted may be seated. After Ted is seated, there will be two seats on either side of him. Because Amy does not want to sit next to Ted, there are only four available seats for her. The remaining 5 people can be seated in $5! = 120$ ways. Thus, the total number of ways to seat all seven people is $(5)(4)(120) = 2,400$.

19. E

$$f(f(x)) = f(3x^2 - 1) = 3(3x^2 - 1)^2 - 1 = 3(9x^4 - 6x^2 + 1) - 1$$
$$= 27x^4 - 18x^2 + 2.$$

20. 17.1

Using the Pythagorean theorem in $\triangle MNP$, $NP = \sqrt{20^2 - 16^2} = \sqrt{144} = 12$. This means that $PQ = 18 - 12 = 6$. Now use the Pythagorean theorem in $\triangle MPQ$. Thus, $MQ = \sqrt{6^2 + 16^2} = \sqrt{292} \approx 17.1$.

21. D

Let x = cost of one apple and y = cost of one pear. Then $4x + 7y = \$11.80$ and $7x + 4y = \$10.75$. Add these equations to get $11x + 11y = \$22.55$. This means that $x + y = \$2.05$. Thus, $3x + 3y = (3)(\$2.05) = \$6.15$.

22. D

Let x represent the total number of disks in the box. Then $\dfrac{12}{x} = 0.4$, which can be written as $12 = 0.4x$. So, $x = 30$, which means that there are 18 white disks in the box. After three more white disks are added, there are 12 green disks and 21 white disks, for a total of 33 disks. Thus, the probability of selecting two green disks, one at a time, with no replacement is $\left(\dfrac{12}{33}\right) \times \left(\dfrac{11}{32}\right)$, which reduces to $\dfrac{1}{8}$.

23. C

$70 - 15 = 55$ students who are studying at least one of French and German. Let x represent the number of students who are studying only French and let y represent the number of students who are studying only German. Then we can write $x + 8 + y = 55$, which simplifies to $x + y = 47$. The number of students studying German, which is represented by $y + 8$, is $2\dfrac{1}{2}$ times the number of students studying French, which is represented by $x + 8$. So $y + 8 = 2.5(x + 8)$, which becomes $y + 8 = 2.5x + 20$, and so simplifies to $2.5x - y = -12$. Now add the equations $x + y = 47$ and $2.5x - y = -12$ to get $3.5x = 35$. This means that $x = 10$, which leads to $y = 37$. Thus, the required number of students who are not studying French is $37 + 15 = 52$.

Here is a completed Venn diagram.

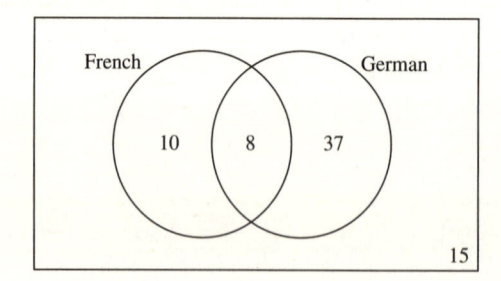

24. E

$a_3 = 7 + (2)(4) = 15$, $a_4 = 15 + (2)(7) = 29$, and $a_5 = 29 + (2)(15) = 59$. Thus, the sum of the first five terms is $4 + 7 + 15 + 29 + 59 = 114$.

25. C

When a function consists of a numerator and denominator, the domain is all real numbers except for those values for which the denominator is either zero or undefined. The value of the function is zero if its numerator is zero. For answer choice C, $\sqrt{\frac{1}{2}x + 3}$ is defined and not equal to zero if $\frac{1}{2}x + 3 > 0$.

This inequality is equivalent to $\frac{1}{2}x > -3$, which implies that $x > -6$.

The numerator can be factored as $2(x^2 - x - 2) = 2(x + 1)(x - 2)$. This expression equals zero if $x = -1$ or if $x = 2$. Answer choice A is wrong because the domain is all real numbers except -2 and 1; it has a value of zero if $x = -6$. Answer choice B is wrong because the domain is all numbers greater than -24; it has a value of zero whenever $x = -2$ or 1. Answer choice D is wrong because the domain is all real numbers less than 6; it has a value of zero whenever $x = 0, -1$, or 2. For answer choice E, the denominator can be factored as $(x + 1)^2 (x - 2)$. So, this answer choice is wrong because the domain is all real numbers except -1 or 2; in addition, it has a value of zero if $x = 6$.

VERBAL WARM-UP DRILL

The following 25 questions are not in the current GRE format, but they cover the same level of verbal skills as found in the revised GRE. Use these as a warm-up for the 25 GRE-format questions that follow.

1. The frightened mother _____ her young daughter for darting in front of the car.

    (A) implored
    (B) extorted
    (C) exhorted
    (D) admonished
    (E) abolished

2. The family left the country to _____ to Utopia and escape _____ because of religious beliefs.

    (A) emigrate ... prosecution
    (B) peregrinate ... extortion
    (C) immigrate ... persecution
    (D) wander ... arraignment
    (E) roam ... censure

3. She responded so quickly with a _____ that it was evident the remark had been _____ until the proper time to use it.

    (A) repartee ... dormant
    (B) wit ... latent
    (C) satire ... hibernating
    (D) humor ... camouflaged
    (E) sortie ... disguised

4. After reading the letter, she _____ that the manager was attempting to _____ a contract with her.

    (A) implied ... abrogate
    (B) inferred ... negotiate
    (C) imposed ... nullify
    (D) surmised ... breech
    (E) included ... annihilate

5. The defense attorney was satisfied with the acquittal, but the prosecutor believed the judge's decision was _____ .

- (A) ambiguous
- (B) astute
- (C) arduous
- (D) auspicious
- (E) arbitrary

6. Perhaps the most famous speech in all of Shakespeare's plays is Hamlet's _____.

- (A) colloquy
- (B) palindrome
- (C) soliloquy
- (D) quandary
- (E) obloquy

7. During the Middle Ages, many people were inspired to lead more religious lives by the _____ of St. Francis of Assisi.

- (A) abnegation
- (B) turpitude
- (C) calumny
- (D) vacillation
- (E) dichotomy

> DIRECTIONS: Each passage is followed by questions based on its content. After reading a passage, choose the best answer to each question. Answer all questions based on what is stated or implied in that passage.

Established firmly in popular culture is the notion that each of the two hemispheres of the brain has specialized functions. The left hemisphere, insist proponents of this theory, controls language and logic; the right hemisphere, espousers contend, is the more creative and intuitive half. Many proponents try to classify a person as "right-brained" or "left-brained," suggesting that the two hemispheres do not work together in the same person, and thus can be considered independent. Because of the supposed independent functions of the two hemispheres and because of their difference in specializations, an activity might engage one part of the brain while the other part is not used at all, they believe. "Right-brained" individuals are the creative, intuitive persons (artists, for instance) of society; "left-brained" persons are the verbal, language-oriented, logical individuals of civilization.

Opponents of the split-brain theory dispute the premise that the hemispheres operate independently simply because of specialized functions; they state that the very fact that the two hemispheres differ in purpose indicates that they must integrate activities and therefore result in processes that are different from and even greater than the processes of either hemisphere. These split-brain theory opponents base their arguments on the fact that when surgery is performed to disconnect the two sides, each can still function well (but not perfectly). They also argue that when a person writes an original story, the left hemisphere works to produce a logical work, but the right hemisphere helps with creativity. The third argument is based on the fact that if a patient has right hemisphere damage, major logical disorders are manifested; in fact, more logical disorders appear than if the left hemisphere suffers damage. The opponents to split-brain theory state that it is impossible to educate one side of the brain without educating the other. They state that there is no evidence that one can be purely right-brained or left-brained.

Educators, then, who seek to modify the curriculum and methods to accommodate the split-brain theory must justify their demands. The burden of proof rests with these innovators who seek to restructure education as it currently exists.

8. To the assertion that the split-brain theory is accurate, the author would probably respond with which of the following?

   (A) Unqualified disagreement
   (B) Unquestioning approval
   (C) Complete indifference
   (D) Strong disparagement
   (E) Implied uncertainty

9. Which of the following titles best describes the content of the passage?

   (A) A Reassertion of the Validity of the Split-Brain Theory
   (B) A Renunciation of the Split-Brain Theory
   (C) Split Opinions on the Split-Brain Theory
   (D) Modifying the Curriculum to Accommodate the Split-Brain Theory
   (E) A New Theory: The Split-Brain Theory

10. The author uses the term "integrate activities" to mean all of the following EXCEPT

    (A) share synaptic connections.
    (B) work together.
    (C) coordinate functions.
    (D) break down tasks into left- and right-brain segments.
    (E) pass information from one hemisphere to the other.

11. According to the information given in the passage, which of the following statements is (are) true?
    I. The left hemisphere of the brain controls language and logic.
    II. The two hemispheres of the brain control different functions.
    III. Evidence exists that suggests that some logical functions are controlled by the right hemisphere.

    (A) I only
    (B) II only
    (C) I and II only
    (D) III only
    (E) II and III only

12. The most compelling argument that the opponents of the split-brain theory present for their beliefs, according to the author, is which of the following?

    (A) When surgery is performed to disconnect the two sides of the brain, both sides continue to operate well—but not perfectly.
    (B) When a patient has right hemisphere damage, no logical disorders are manifested.
    (C) Because of the independent functions of the two hemispheres, an activity might engage one hemisphere of the brain and not another.
    (D) The hemispheres operate independently because of specialized functions.
    (E) It is impossible to educate one side of the brain without educating the other.

13. According to the passage, the most significant distinction between proponents and opponents of the split-brain theory is which of the following?

    (A) Their beliefs about teaching methods and the curriculum
    (B) Proponents state that the two hemispheres differ in purpose, and therefore must integrate activities.
    (C) Opponents state that the hemispheres differ in function, and therefore cannot integrate activities.
    (D) Their beliefs about the functions of the hemispheres of the brain
    (E) Their beliefs that the brain is divided into hemispheres

14. Which of the following statements is most compatible with the principles of the split-brain theory?

    (A) The fact that the two hemispheres differ in purpose indicates that they must integrate activities.
    (B) "Right-brained" individuals are the creative, intuitive persons of society; "left-brained" persons are the verbal, language-oriented, logical individuals of civilization.
    (C) It is impossible to educate one side of the brain without educating the other.
    (D) More logical disorders appear if the right hemisphere is damaged than if the left hemisphere is damaged.
    (E) When surgery is performed to disconnect the two sides of the brain, each can function well.

15. To an assertion that education curriculum and methods should be altered to accommodate proponents of the split-brain theory, the author would most likely respond with which of the following?

    (A) This is a definite need in our schools today.
    (B) Educators have already made these important modifications.
    (C) Justification for these alterations must be provided by proponents of the split-brain theory.
    (D) It is impossible to educate one side of the brain without educating the other.
    (E) Such alterations might be necessary because "right-brained" persons are the verbal, language-oriented, logical individuals.

Being born female and black were two handicaps Gwendolyn Brooks states that she faced from her birth, in 1917, in Kansas. Brooks was determined to succeed. Despite the lack of encouragement she received from her teachers and others, she was determined to write, and found the first publisher for one of her poems when she was 11.

In 1945 she marketed and sold her first book; national recognition ensued. She applied for and received grants and fellowships from such organizations as the American Academy of Arts and Letters and the Guggenheim Foundation. Later she received the Pulitzer Prize for Poetry; she was the first black woman to receive such an honor.

Brooks was an integrationist in the 1940s and an advocate of black consciousness in the 1960s. Her writing styles show that she is not bound by rules; her works are not devoid of the truth, even about sensitive subjects like the black experience, life in the ghetto, and city life.

Brooks's reaction to fame is atypical. She continues to work—and work hard. She writes, travels, and helps many who are interested in writing. Especially important to her is increasing her knowledge of her black heritage and encouraging other people to do the same. She encourages dedication to the art to would-be writers.

16. Which of the following phrases best describes the passage?

    (A) A discussion of the importance of Gwendolyn Brooks's writings
    (B) An essay on the achievements of Gwendolyn Brooks
    (C) An essay on Gwendolyn Brooks as a black female role model
    (D) A biographical sketch on Gwendolyn Brooks
    (E) A discussion of the handicaps faced by black women writers

17. The passage implies that Brooks received less credit than she deserved primarily because of which of the following?

    (A) She tried to publish too early in her career.
    (B) She was aided by funds received through grants.
    (C) She was a frequent victim of both racial and gender discrimination.
    (D) Her work was too complex to be of widespread interest to others.
    (E) She had no interest in the accolades of her colleagues.

18. According to the passage, Gwendolyn Brooks

    (A) marketed her first book when she was 11 years old.
    (B) achieved national recognition when she received the Pulitzer Prize.
    (C) advocated black consciousness in the 1940s.
    (D) received little encouragement from her teachers.
    (E) avoided "black" topics in her writing.

DIRECTIONS: Each of the given sentences has blank spaces that indicate omitted words. Choose the best combination of words that fit into the meaning and structure within the context of the sentence.

---

19. The unmitigated truth is that the author of the essays was _____ in his writing; their publication _____ the teacher's chances for a promotion.

    (A) abusive ... enhanced
    (B) laconic ... obliterated
    (C) obtuse ... obviated
    (D) profound ... diminished
    (E) prolific ... necessitated

20. The sales associate tried to _____ trade by distributing business cards.

    (A) elicit
    (B) solicit
    (C) illicit
    (D) elliptic
    (E) conciliate

21. Many doctors now believe that a pregnant woman's _____ for odd foods supplements some lack in her regular diet.

    (A) quirk
    (B) profusion
    (C) pittance
    (D) penchant
    (E) stipend

22. The chairman complained that the committee was wasting too much time on _____ issues, instead of concentrating on the _____ one.

    (A) peripheral ... essential
    (B) scurrilous ... tedious
    (C) trenchant ... superfluous
    (D) superficial ... whimsical
    (E) munificent ... desultory

23. The acquisition of exact knowledge is apt to be _____, but it is essential to every kind of excellence.

    (A) wearisome
    (B) equable
    (C) erratic
    (D) amorphous
    (E) eccentric

24. The biophysicist's lecture on molecular dynamics was too _____ for many of the students in the audience.

- Ⓐ erudite
- Ⓑ eclectic
- Ⓒ abstruse
- Ⓓ inchoate
- Ⓔ amorphous

25. All her attempts to _____ the situation not only failed, but actually seemed to exacerbate the problem.

- Ⓐ excoriate
- Ⓑ disseminate
- Ⓒ ameliorate
- Ⓓ exculpate
- Ⓔ objurgate

ANSWER EXPLANATIONS

1. D

IMPLORED (A) is a verb meaning begged; it does not fit well into the content of the sentence and is not the right answer. EXTORTED means having drawn something (like money) from someone by force; (B) is not the correct answer. EXHORTED means urged by words of good advice or cautioned; because urging is not the issue here, (C) is incorrect. ADMONISHED seems to fit best because it means warned, reproved, cautioned against specific faults. (D) is the correct answer. ABOLISHED (E) means destroyed or to have put an end to something; this word is too strong for the sentence.

2. C

EMIGRATE is usually accompanied by the preposition *from;* this word does not fit. Neither is it likely that there would be a PROSECUTION (a legal suit against) simply because of beliefs, not actions. (A) is not the best answer. PEREGRINATE means to travel, but EXTORTION (drawing something from someone by force) does not fit logically in the sentence. (B) is incorrect. One IMMIGRATES to another place; PERSECUTION (torment, abuse) might be typical for one's beliefs. These are logical choices; (C) is correct. Because WANDER implies no set destination; this choice does not fit well. Coupled with the word ARRAIGNMENT (the act of bringing before a court), (D) is clearly not a suitable choice. ROAM implies no set destination, this choice does not fit well. CENSURE indicates blame or criticism, but is not acceptable coupled with ROAM. Choice (E) is incorrect.

3. A

A REPARTEE is a clever, witty retort; DORMANT suggests inactivity of that which is present. A person who bides her time before giving a statement would hold that retort or REPARTEE DORMANT. (A) is the best answer. WIT suggests the power to evoke laughter by remarks showing quick perception; it is not usually preceded by the article *a*. Only one statement is suggested by the sentence. LATENT stresses concealment. (B) is not the best answer. SATIRE is wit used for the purpose of exposing vice. HIBERNATING is the passing of winter in a lethargic state. These two words of choice (C) are not the best choices for the sentence. HUMOR is an ability to see the absurd and the comical in life's situations; it suggests a series of incidents rather than just one retort. CAMOUFLAGED implies that which is disguised. The sentence suggests not a disguising of the witty statement but rather a concealment of it until the proper moment. (D) is not the best answer. A SORTIE is a mission or an attack. It does not fit the sentence at all. DISGUISED could fit the sentence, but not when paired with SORTIE. (E) is not the best answer.

4. B

IMPLIED is a transitive verb; it must have an object. There is no direct object here so IMPLIED does not fit well. ABROGATE is to annul, to abolish. Because IMPLIED does not fit well, (A) should not be selected. INFERRED is an intransitive verb in this sentence; it means to draw conclusions from data given. It fits well in this sentence. NEGOTIATE (procure) fits well in this sentence also. (B) is the correct answer. IMPOSED is to pass off or to obtrude. The word does not fit the meaning of the sentence well at all. NULLIFY (to make or render of no value) fits the sentence but not when coupled with IMPOSED. (C) is not the best choice. SURMISED is to imagine or to guess on slight charges. BREECH is to cover with breeches; a person who selected (D) probably confused BREECH with BREACH (to cancel). INCLUDED means contained; a person who chose (E) probably read the word as concluded, rather than INCLUDED. ANNIHILATE means to make void.

5. E

The prosecutor was not satisfied with the judge's decision. That means that the correct adjective must be negative, to express this dissatisfaction. AMBIGUOUS (vague), ASTUTE (shrewd), ARDUOUS (laborious, difficult), and AUSPICIOUS (favorable) do not carry a negative connotation. Choices (A), (B), (C), and (D) are all inappropriate adjectives to complete the sentence. Only ARBITRARY (based on one's preference, not on reason) is the logical adjective to complete the sentence. (E) is the correct choice.

6. C

The missing word must be some form of speech, so PALINDROME (B), a sentence that reads the same forward and backward, and QUANDARY (D), a state of doubt or perplexity, cannot be correct. COLLOQUY (A) is a dialogue, requiring two or more speakers; the sentence refers only to

Hamlet, implying that there are no other speakers in the speech referred to. (A) is not the correct choice. SOLILOQUY (C) means a monologue that usually presents the character's inner reflections to the audience and is treated as if unheard by the other actors. Because the sentence refers to a speech and to only a single character, (C) is the correct answer. OBLOQUY (E) means to speak abusively or offensively. It is not an appropriate choice.

7. A

People were inspired by the ABNEGATION, or self-denial, of St. Francis. (A) is the correct choice. TURPITUDE, which means depravity, is the opposite of the word sought. (B) is not an appropriate choice. CALUMNY (C) refers to false charges or misrepresentation; it is not the correct choice. VACILLATION (D) means indecision; it is not an appropriate word to complete the sentence. DICHOTOMY (E) means a division into two, often contradictory, groups.

8. E

There is no evidence that the author disagrees so vehemently with the split-brain theory as to respond with UNQUALIFIED DISAGREEMENT. (A) is not the best answer. UNQUESTIONING APPROVAL is not the attitude of the author; rather she seems willing to listen to both sides, though she seems more inclined to disagree with the theory. (B) is not the best answer. The very fact that the author wrote the articles negates the idea that COMPLETE INDIFFERENCE is the best answer; (C) is not the best choice. Although the author seems to disagree with the split-brain theory, STRONG DISPARAGEMENT is not the best answer; (D) should not be chosen. IMPLIED UNCERTAINTY seems to be the best of the choices. (E) is the best answer.

9. C

(A) is incorrect because the split-brain theory is not reasserted by the author in the article. Because the split-brain theory is not renunciated by the author, (B) is not the correct choice. (C) is the best answer because it implies what the article does—present both sides of the theory. Because modifying the curriculum is only one part of the article, (D) is incorrect. Because the split-brain theory is not new, (E) is inaccurate.

10. C

The author is saying that, according to the opponents of the split-brain theory, both hemispheres work on tasks that proponents try to label "left-" or "right-brained," and that the cooperation between hemispheres yields a better result than if only one hemisphere had functioned. In this context, to "integrate activities" means to "coordinate functions" to produce the better result. This meaning includes working together (B), separating the task into functions for each hemisphere (D), and sharing needed information between hemispheres (E). There is no reference in the passage to synapses or synaptic connections, so (A) is an inappropriate choice.

11. E

The passage states that proponents of the split-brain theory insist that "[t]he left hemisphere … controls language and logic." However, opponents of the theory do not think this is correct, so Statement I is false. Both proponents and opponents of the theory agree that the different hemispheres control different functions; that is not a point of contention. Therefore, Statement II is true. The passage states that the third argument presented by opponents of the split-brain theory is the fact that patients who sustain damage to the right hemisphere often show major logical disorders. This suggests that the right hemisphere controls at least some logical functions; therefore, Statement III is true. Choice (E), II and III only, is correct.

12. A

(A) is the correct answer. (B) is not the correct answer because damage to the right (as well as the left) side of the brain may result in logical disorders. (C) is not the right answer because it has not been proven to the satisfaction of everyone that one hemisphere may be engaged to the exclusion of the other. The article suggests that the two sides work cooperatively. (D) is therefore incorrect. The writer suggests that education involves both (not just one) sides of the brain. (E) is incorrect.

13. D

Proponents and opponents do disagree about methods and curriculum but that is not a fundamental difference; (A) is incorrect. (B) is false; proponents do agree that the purposes of the hemispheres do differ but that the integration of activities is not urged, or even thought possible, by many. Opponents do not always state that the two hemispheres differ significantly in function nor do they always believe that integration of the activities is impossible; (C) is incorrect. The beliefs about the functions of the two hemispheres of the brain are the fundamental differences between proponents and opponents of the split-brain theory; (D) is the correct answer. Both groups agree that the brain is divided into hemispheres; this is not the DISTINCTION between the two groups. (E) is not the correct answer.

14. B

(B) is the correct answer, as it is a statement used by proponents of the split-brain theory. (A), (C), (D), and (E) are all incorrect, as these are statements made by opponents of the split-brain theory.

15. C

The author would disagree with (A). (B) is certainly incorrect; the modifications have neither already been made nor are they on the agenda of most educators. (C) is the correct answer. (D) is incorrect; the author's open-minded point of view is not illustrated by this statement. The reader should immediately see (E) as erroneous because it reverses the hemisphere associated by proponents of the theory with language and logic.

16. D

The passage does include a discussion of the importance of Brooks's writing (A), mentioning the awards she's won and her use of black topics; a list of her achievements (B); a discussion of her importance as a role model (C), referring to her helping young writers and encouraging blacks to learn about their heritage; and does discuss the handicaps of being black and female (E). All of these phrases, however, are too specific to describe the passage well, because the passage encompasses all of these themes. The best phrase to describe the passage is (D), a biographical sketch on Gwendolyn Brooks.

17. C

Brooks was a published writer by age 11; (A) is incorrect. Grants did not lessen, but heightened, her prestige. (B) is incorrect. (C) is the correct answer. After her first book was sold, she received nationwide recognition; (D) is wrong. Brooks takes an interest in others; (E) is incorrect.

18. D

All of the statements are false except (D). It was Brooks's first poem that was published when she was 11; her first book was not marketed until 1945. Choice (A) is false. Brooks received national recognition after her first book was published, before she won the Pulitzer Prize; choice (B) is false. Brooks was an integrationist in the 1940s and advocated black consciousness in the 1960s; choice (C) is false. Brooks did write about the black experience; so choice (E) is false. Brooks did receive little encouragement from her teachers (D), and succeeded despite this lack (line 3).

19. C

(A) is incorrect; ABUSIVE means treating badly or harshly. The term does not fit the sentence very well; ABUSIVE writing probably would not ENHANCE one's chance for a promotion. (B) is not an appropriate choice. Because LACONIC means brief and to the point, this type of writing does not seem grounds to OBLITERATE (wipe out) a teacher's chances for promotion. (C) is the correct answer. OBTUSE means blunt, stupid, not sharp. (For instance, an obtuse angle is not sharp, like an acute angle; it is larger than a right angle.) Such writing might OBVIATE (eliminate) one's chances of a promotion. (D) is incorrect; because PROFOUND means not superficial and clearly marked by intellectual depth, it does not stand to reason that such writing would DIMINISH (or make less) one's chances for a promotion. The best answer is not (E). The publication of PROLIFIC (many) writings alone does not make necessary (NECESSITATE) the promotion of a teacher.

20. B

(A) is not the best choice. ELICIT means to draw out in a skillful way something that is being hidden or held back. Giving business cards is not unique. The best answer is (B). SOLICIT means to ask earnestly, to try to get. Because ILLICIT (C) means illegal, it is an incorrect choice. ELLIPTIC (D) means shaped like an ellipse (with ovals at both ends) and is an inappropriate choice. CONCILIATE (E) is to win over, to soothe. The word is an inappropriate choice.

21. D

A QUIRK is a peculiar behavior trait; a pregnant woman's desire for odd foods is a temporary condition, not a behavior trait; (A) is incorrect. Choice (B), PROFUSION (abundance), is inappropriate. A PITTANCE is a small amount of money; (C) is not the correct choice. A STIPEND is a monetary payment; therefore, (E) is also incorrect. (D) is the appropriate choice; a PENCHANT is a desire or craving.

22. A

Of the choices, (A) makes the most sense. A chairman would be likely to complain that time was being wasted on PERIPHERAL (auxiliary or side) issues, instead of on the ESSENTIAL (central or main) one. SCURRILOUS means coarse or indecent language; TEDIOUS means boring. (B) is not an appropriate choice. TRENCHANT, meaning distinct or clear-cut, and SUPERFLUOUS, meaning unnecessary, would be appropriate choices if their order was reversed, but as it is, (C) is incorrect. SUPERFICIAL, or surface, is an appropriate adjective for the first blank, but WHIMSICAL (fanciful) is not appropriate for the second; (D) is not the correct answer. MUNIFICENT (lavish) and DESULTORY (without order) are not logical adjectives for this sentence. Choice (E) is incorrect.

23. A

AMORPHOUS (D), ECCENTRIC (E), and ERRATIC (C) are all synonyms meaning inconsistent, sporadic. EQUABLE (B) suggests a uniform methodical occurrence. WEARISOME (A) is the correct choice, indicated by the key words "exact," "and," "but," and "essential."

24. C

ABSTRUSE (C), meaning difficult to comprehend, is the most appropriate choice. A lecture on molecular dynamics would be inherently ERUDITE, or learned; (A) is not the correct choice. The lecture focused on a single topic, so it was not ECLECTIC (varied, diverse). (B) is not the correct answer. INCHOATE (unformed) and AMORPHOUS (having no determined form) are unrelated to the sentence topic, so (D) and (E) are incorrect answers.

25. C

The clues to this sentence are "not only failed" and "exacerbate." These words imply that the correct choice must be the antonym of EXACERBATE (to worsen). EXCORIATE (to abrade), DISSEMINATE (to spread), EXCULPATE (to clear from fault), and OBJURGATE (to chide vehemently) are all inappropriate choices. AMELIORATE (to improve, to make better) is the necessary antonym; the correct answer is (C).

GRE VERBAL PRACTICE SET

> For each of questions 1 to 4, select one answer choice unless otherwise instructed.

> Questions 1 to 3 are based on the following reading passage.

The leader of a search-and-rescue operation must sometimes consider whether it would be more efficient to organize a careful, methodical search, or to simply scatter whatever people are available to begin searching immediately and perhaps, even frantically. The latter "messy" approach can be especially appropriate when mere seconds count, as in the abduction of a person, or when someone is missing in water near a beach or shore.

> For the following questions, consider each of the choices separately.

1. Which of the following can be inferred from the passage regarding efficiency?

- [A] "Messy" systems can often accomplish goals effectively.
- [B] "Messiness" is often taken as a sign of weakness.
- [C] Improvisation can lead to effective results.

2. Select the sentence in the passage in which the author introduces a specific example of a haphazard approach to a desired result.

3. In the context in which it appears, "messy" most nearly means

- (A) dirty.
- (B) grimy.
- (C) haphazardly.
- (D) slovenly.
- (E) caustic.

Health education needs to be instituted into preschool child development programs across the United States. Unless we can begin proper health habits in our country at an early age, **we cannot hope to see the health of adults and senior citizens improving in the future.** Investing in preschool health education can benefit society as a whole and may result in a financial savings for taxpayers who now support the sick and disabled.

4. In the passage above, the two portions in **boldface** play which of the following roles?

   Ⓐ The first is a claim made to support a certain position; the second refutes the position.
   Ⓑ The first is a judgment made by an explanation; the second is the explanation.
   Ⓒ The first sums up the position; the second provides grounds for that position.
   Ⓓ The first expresses an objection; the second reinforces that objection.
   Ⓔ The first and second contradict each other.

> For questions 5 to 8, select one entry for each blank from the corresponding column of choices. Fill in the blanks in a way that best completes the text.

5. Despite its promotion into the serious canon of literature, travel writing has remained like opera: (i) _____ of an imperialist past and inherently (ii) _____.

Blank (i)	Blank (ii)
Ⓐ idiosyncratic	Ⓓ transcendent
Ⓑ redolent	Ⓔ marginalized
Ⓒ cautious	Ⓕ bourgeois

6. Both cacti and other succulents require a minimum of care, provided that they have the required amount of sunlight and that their condition of hardiness is _____.

   Ⓐ ignored
   Ⓑ imitated
   Ⓒ marginalized
   Ⓓ respected
   Ⓔ relevant

7. In contemplation there is a greater psychic action than in the most attentive self-observation; this is also known by the wrinkled brow of (i) _____, in contrast with the restful features of (ii) _____.

Blank (i)	Blank (ii)
Ⓐ contemplation	Ⓓ suppression
Ⓑ consequence	Ⓔ attention
Ⓒ perception	Ⓕ self-observation

8. The novel is a particularly deep-thinking entry in a tradition of using the _____ resources of science fiction to address how language shapes culture and society.

- Ⓐ speculative
- Ⓑ dogmatic
- Ⓒ cautious
- Ⓓ alienated
- Ⓔ reactive

Questions 9 and 10 are based on the following passage.

Painting should have for its object the expression of ideas, and as such "it is invaluable, being by itself nothing." In art an idea may be expressed in ways that differ, principally according to the two modes, the subjective and the objective. To state the matter more explicitly, a painter may use the object he delineates chiefly for expressing his own thought, instead of revealing the idea inherent in the object itself. On the contrary, another painter strives to bring out the spirit of the object he portrays, rather than to express ideas of his own that may arise in association with the object. In general, Western painters belong to the latter class, while those of Japan to the former; the one laying stress on objective, and the other on subjective ideas. This distinction discloses the fundamental differences between Eastern and Western painting, which causes wide dissimilarities in conception and execution.

9. In the passage, the author is primarily concerned with

- Ⓐ summarizing the findings of a research project.
- Ⓑ analyzing a method of expression.
- Ⓒ evaluating a point of view.
- Ⓓ arguing a point of view.
- Ⓔ determining boundaries.

10. According to the passage, Western painters

- Ⓐ create art both subjectively and objectively.
- Ⓑ do not express the spirit of the object in their painting.
- Ⓒ are primarily concerned with objective ideas.

For questions 11 to 13, select one entry for each blank from the corresponding column of choices. Fill all blanks in the way that best completes the text.

11. Although there is a healthy and growing environmental (i) _____ in the United States, there are many who prefer to remain (ii) _____.

Blank (i)	Blank (ii)
Ⓐ movement	Ⓓ aware
Ⓑ crisis	Ⓔ satisfied
Ⓒ victory	Ⓕ unenlightened

12. Her weekly program on NPR is the most _____ means of educating the public about the congressional hearings on educational reforms.

   Ⓐ proficient
   Ⓑ effusive
   Ⓒ effectual
   Ⓓ capable
   Ⓔ competent

13. When the financial managers realized the corporation was losing money, they hired outside consultants to _____ the billing process and determine the causes of loss.

   Ⓐ predetermine
   Ⓑ scrutinize
   Ⓒ fabricate
   Ⓓ disavow
   Ⓔ distinguish

14. For competitive cyclists, many of whom achieve maximum aerobic efficiency by adopting a highly varied conditioning program, continually altering the speed, length, and frequency of their cycling routines, _____ often pays off.

   Ⓐ intervention
   Ⓑ elimination
   Ⓒ inconsistency
   Ⓓ authorization
   Ⓔ inflation

> Questions 15 to 16 are based on the following passage.

Stalagmites grow upward from the floor of a cave generally as a result of water dripping from overhanging stalactites. A column forms when a stalactite and a stalagmite grow until they join. A "curtain" begins to form on an inclined ceiling when the drops of water trickle along a slope. Gradually a thin sheet of calcite grows from the ceiling and hangs in decorative folds like a curtain. Sheets of calcite that are deposited on the walls or floor by flowing water are called flowstone.

15. The primary purpose of the passage is which of the following?

    (A) To analyze a situation
    (B) To define a phenomena
    (C) To propose a solution to a problem
    (D) To describe a specific place
    (E) To argue a position

16. According to the passage, stalagmites are formed when water

    (A) drips from underground caves.
    (B) drips from overhanging stalactites.
    (C) seeps through the ceiling of the cave.
    (D) trickles through cracks in the cave walls.
    (E) seeps through cracks in the cave floor.

> For questions 17 to 20, select one entry for each blank from the corresponding column of choices. Fill all blanks in the way that best completes the text.

17. A _____ decision was made so that both partners reaped equal benefits from the same amount of work.

    (A) defensible
    (B) bilateral
    (C) benign
    (D) sectarian
    (E) deferential

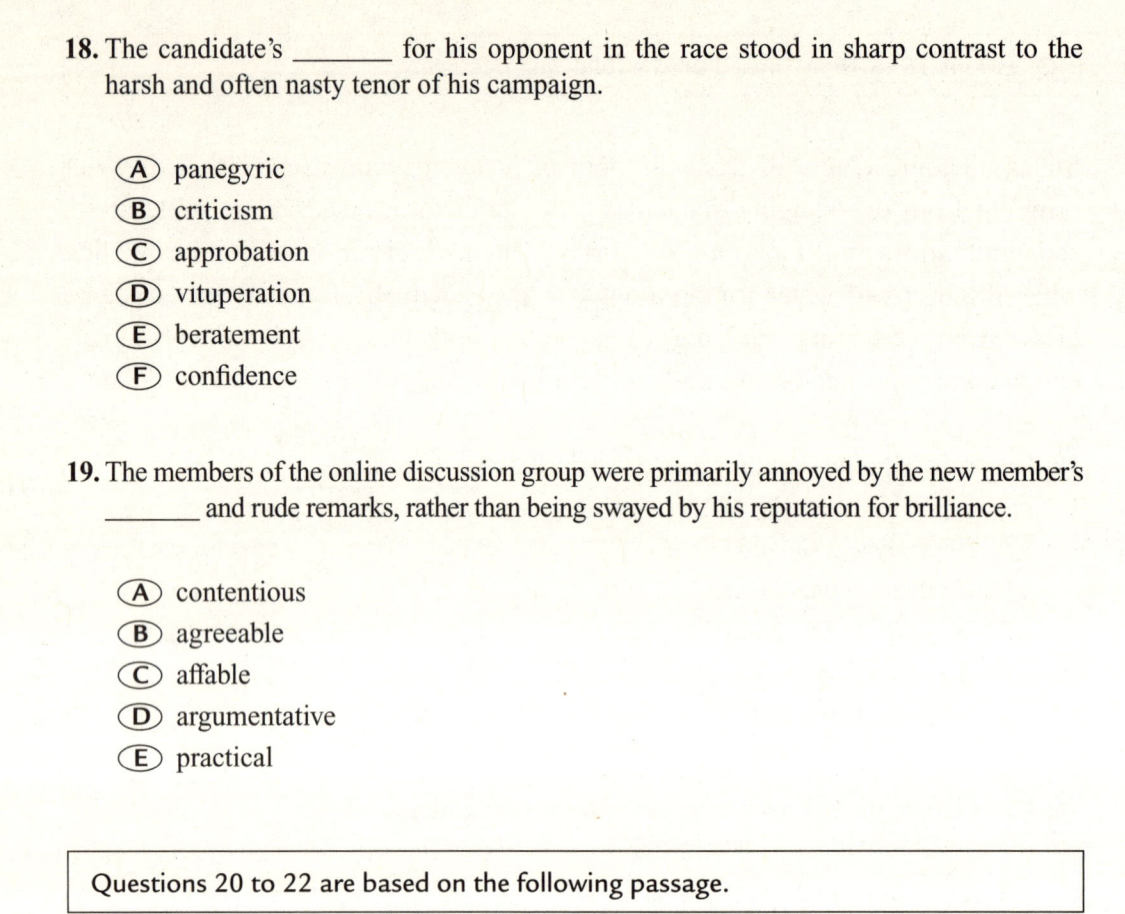

18. The candidate's _____ for his opponent in the race stood in sharp contrast to the harsh and often nasty tenor of his campaign.

   (A) panegyric
   (B) criticism
   (C) approbation
   (D) vituperation
   (E) beratement
   (F) confidence

19. The members of the online discussion group were primarily annoyed by the new member's _____ and rude remarks, rather than being swayed by his reputation for brilliance.

   (A) contentious
   (B) agreeable
   (C) affable
   (D) argumentative
   (E) practical

Questions 20 to 22 are based on the following passage.

American dancer, choreographer, and director Agnes de Mille was born into a theatrical family. Her father was a playwright and a director; her uncle was Cecil B. De Mille, the director and producer of movies. As a young child in California, de Mille was captivated by the allure of the dance and professed a desire to become a ballerina. However, her family did not encourage her ambition and made her all too aware that she lacked the "ideal" ballerina's long, sinuous limbs and compact torso. Crestfallen, she gave up dancing and studied English, graduating with honors from the University of California in Los Angeles.

When de Mille returned to New York in the late 1920s, she was drawn again to the dance. She began her career as a performer and then became a choreographer as well, creating and staging works for European and American ballet companies. These early dances were largely in the classical tradition of European ballet, but in 1942, de Mille broke new ground with *Rodeo*. This blithe look at courtship in the American West was a ballet, but it also included square dancing and tap. Its success led de Mille directly to Broadway. In 1943, de Mille composed and staged the dances for the Rodgers and Hammerstein musical *Oklahoma*. The show was a triumph and it put her in the vanguard of the American musical theater. *Oklahoma* was the first musical to make dance a part of the dramatic action. De Mille's choreography, which included ballet and modern dance forms, revolutionized the function of dance in the musical theater.

> For the following question, consider each of the choices separately and select all that apply.

20. The author of the passage suggests that de Mille's family fell short in which of the following respects?

    (A) It did not appear to recognize an opportunity to encourage de Mille's desire to become a ballerina.
    (B) The family seemed to reject all forms of creative expression.
    (C) It focused on de Mille's apparent lack of talent.

21. In the context in which it appears, "vanguard" most nearly means

    (A) forefront.
    (B) conductor.
    (C) center.
    (D) messenger.
    (E) stragglers.

22. Select the sentence in the passage in which the author solidifies his admiration for Agnes de Mille.

> For questions 23 to 25, select one entry for each blank from the corresponding column of choices. Fill all blanks in the way that best completes the text.

23. A heightened sense of (i) _____ has induced the government to adopt a more (ii) _____ policy toward illegal aliens.

Blank (i)	Blank (ii)
(A) elation	(D) indulgent
(B) compassion	(E) dormant
(C) incisiveness	(F) inflexible

24. Combining data, the scientists have been able to determine whether current climate changes have resulted from natural phenomena or have been induced by human _____.

- (A) interference
- (B) idiosyncrasies
- (C) creativity
- (D) fundamentals
- (E) benefits

25. The figures in the surrealistic painting had the _____ appearance of characters in a nightmare.

- (A) savory
- (B) complacent
- (C) zealous
- (D) somnolent
- (E) grotesque

ANSWER EXPLANATIONS

1. A and C

The passage suggests through examples that in some situations, the more efficient solution may be, in fact, one that some may believe to be "messy" and inefficient.

2.

Sentence 2, beginning with "The latter 'messy' approach ..."

3. C

The first sentence sets up the seemingly contradictory solution to what would normally call for a "careful methodical search." The concept of "messy" in this context most nearly means "in a haphazard manner."

4. C

The author presents his position to an issue in the first sentence and in the second, provides the grounds for his position. Because the highlighted portions represent the main content of the third sentence, the task in this question is to find the answer choice whose two parts fit those sentences' roles. Answer choice C fits the requirement.

5. B and F

The sentence is clearly conveying a contrast because "despite" is used to indicate something positive and something negative about travel writing. The clue to the negative aspect is in the latter part of the sentence in the word "imperialist."

6. D

The first part of the sentence attributes the care of cacti as one of very little attention and care, provided that care is given with the respect that the succulents require.

7. A and F

It is possible to analyze the sentence by starting with either blank. The first part of the sentence states that there is more "action" when contemplating than when engaged in self-observation.

8. A

The only choice that fits the meaning of this sentence is choice A, "speculative."

9. B

The passage analyzes the distinctions between Western and Japanese painting as contrasting methods of expression.

10. B and C

The author believes that Western painters, in contrast to Japanese painters who use the object for expressing their own thoughts, are primarily concerned with the object itself.

11. A and F

The point of the sentence is to emphasize contradictory aspects of how many people view environmental concerns.

12. C

The clue in this sentence is "means of educating the public." *Effectual* means having the power to produce the exact effect.

13. B

It is necessary to determine an additional function of a consultant to correctly fill in the blank. None of the other choices make sense when added to the sentence.

14. C

The word that fills in the blank must fit with the idea that in order for cyclists to achieve aerobic efficiency, their training program should vary.

15. B

The passage describes the phenomena of stalagmites.

16. B

The passage states that "stalagmites grow upward from the floor of the cave as a result of water dripping from overhanging stalactites."

17. B

The blank must be filled with a word that describes a decision that is beneficial to "both (or two)" partners, equally. *Bilateral* means "affecting both sides or two sides."

18. A and C

The sentence sets up a contrasting concept. The word in the blank must contrast with "harsh" and "nasty." Both panegyric and approbation are the best choices.

19. A and D

In the sentence the words "annoyed" and "rude" imply that the new member brings some negativity to the group. The two words that express negativity are choices A and D.

20. A

Choice C is an attractive distracter; however, the passage does not suggest that her family believed her to be without talent; only that she did not possess a ballerina's "ideal" form.

21. A

To be in the "vanguard" is to be in the forefront or on the cutting edge.

22.

The last sentence ("De Mille's choreography, which included ballet and modern dance forms, revolutionized the function of dance in the musical theater.") is the best choice. It is in this sentence that the author expresses an opinion.

23. B and D

The sentence sets up two parallel concepts. The word in the first blank should be roughly synonymous with the second.

24. A

The sentence sets up two contrasting concepts: "natural" or "induced." The word in the blank must contrast with "natural." Thus the correct answer is "interference."

25. E

Because a nightmare is a "bad dream or experience," the word in the blank should be roughly synonymous with something considered "aberrant" or "monstrous." Only choice E fits that description.

Appendix E
A Quick Reference Guide to Graduate School

WHO GOES TO GRADUATE SCHOOL?

Whether you are interested in scholarship, professional development, or personal enrichment, the decision to pursue graduate school requires a commitment to the application process as well as to your intended field of study. Here, we will provide you with a guide to graduate school, how to pick a program, and how to make the most of your opportunity to study at the graduate level.

According to the U.S. Census Bureau, about 7% of the American population goes on to earn a master's degree, and only about 3% of the population earns a doctorate or professional degree. Who are the people you are likely to meet and work with as you pursue advanced education? Who tends to go to graduate school?

Compared to 1995–1996, your graduate student classmates today are almost as likely to be over 40 as they are to be under 25, more likely to be international students, and much more likely to be female than male. In addition, about half of your classmates are married and/or have children, have come from families that have attained higher education, and they are more likely to be from diverse backgrounds than at any time in the past. Take a look at some of the changes in the chart below.

How do you fit into the changing nature of the graduate student body? Your personal circumstances will dictate how you can embark upon your road to advanced education.

Percentage Distribution of Master's Degree Students, by Selected Student Characteristics: 1995–1996, 1999–2000, 2003–2004, and 2007–2008

Student Characteristics	1995-96	1999-2000	2003-04	2007-08
Total	100.0	100.0	100.0	100.0
Age				
Younger than 25	16.6	15.6	18.5	19.7
25–29	33.4	34.0	32.3	30.8
30–34	17.9	17.6	16.5	16.6
35–39	10.9	11.2	11.0	12.2
40 or older	21.2	21.6	21.7	20.7

Percentage Distribution of Master's Degree Students, by Selected Student Characteristics: 1995–1996, 1999–2000, 2003–2004, and 2007–2008

Student Characteristics	1995–96	1999–2000	2003–04	2007–08
Sex				
Male	43.7	40.8	40.2	38.7
Female	56.3	59.2	59.8	61.3
Race/ethnicity (1)				
White	76.2	70.6	67.8	66.1
Black	7.5	10.0	10.5	12.9
Hispanic	4.9	6.9	8.3	8.5
Asian/Pacific Islander	9.6	9.7	10.3	10.3
American Indian	0.5	0.4	0.6!	0.3
Other or two or more races	1.2	2.4	2.5	1.9
Marital/dependent status (2)				
Unmarried, no dependents	49.9	44.5	45.9	48.0
Married with no dependents	18.2	18.6	18.4	16.4
Unmarried with dependents	10.5	10.0	9.8	10.5
Married with dependents	21.4	26.9	25.9	25.0
Citizenship				
U.S. citizen	93.6	88.0	88.1	88.7
Resident alien	2.6	3.0	4.3	3.4
Foreign/international student	3.7	9.0	7.6	7.9

(continued)

Percentage Distribution of Master's Degree Students, by Selected Student Characteristics: 1995–1996, 1999–2000, 2003–2004, and 2007–2008

Student Characteristics	1995–96	1999–2000	2003–04	2007–08
Highest education attained by either parent *(3)*				
High school diploma or less	33.0	32.3	27.9	24.5
Some postsecondary education	14.4	16.3	18.2	22.1
Bachelor's degree	23.4	23.1	25.7	23.9
Graduate or first-professional degree	29.2	28.3	28.2	29.5
Interpret data with caution (estimates are unstable).				

(1) Black includes African American, Hispanic includes Latino, American Indian includes Alaska Native, Asian/Pacific Islander includes Native Hawaiian, and Other includes respondents having origins in a race not listed. Questions concerning race/ethnicity changed over time. In 1995–96, respondents of more than one racial background were asked to choose one category, whereas in subsequent studies respondents could choose to identify themselves as multiracial.

(2) Divorced, separated, and widowed students are included in the unmarried categories.

(3) Some respondents did not know their parents' highest education level and are not included in the estimates for this table. These respondents represented 5.5% of the population in 1999–2000, 0.9% in 2003–04, and 0.7% in 2007–08. Graduate and first-professional students in NPSAS:96 were not given the option to indicate whether they knew their parents' highest level of education.

Note: Estimates include master's degree students enrolled in Title IV eligible postsecondary institutions in the 50 states, the District of Columbia, and Puerto Rico. Detail may not sum to totals because of rounding.

Source: U.S. Department of Education, National Center for Education Statistics, 1995–96, 1999–2000, 2003–04, and 2007–08 National Postsecondary Student Aid Study (NPSAS:96, NPSAS:2000, NPSAS:04, and NPSAS:08).

STRATEGIES FOR YOU

Recent College Graduate

More than 70% of students who pursue professional degrees do so within 2 years of receiving their bachelor's degree. Recent college graduates have the advantage of a fresh memory of the study environment, including doing the assigned readings, writing, and note taking in class. You can readily transfer these skills to your graduate work, but one major difference between undergraduate and graduate education is the level of independence your instructors expect from you. Graduate faculty tend to be more understanding than undergraduate faculty when it comes to commitments that conflict with your coursework, but they also expect you to communicate with them before your commitments interfere with assignment deadlines. Your graduate faculty will treat you not as subordinates or "kids," but as colleagues.

Mid-Career Changer

The other 30% of professional degree students are those who have been out of school for 3 years or longer, and as the preceding table shows, about half of all graduate students are aged 30 or over. If you are between jobs, you may be able to use this time to strengthen your qualifications in your field, or explore an entirely different profession. Alternatively, if you plan to work while you go to school, see the discussion on tuition reimbursement in the later Financial Aid section.

Students who have been out of the school environment have the advantage of an experienced perspective and practice in the field. If you have not been in a classroom in a number of years, you may be surprised to find yourself falling into old study habits as soon as you take your seat in a classroom or get your first syllabus. It's a good idea to schedule a consistent block of time every day in which to study and read, and to try to minimize distractions during that time.

Students with Special Needs

Graduate schools and universities are required to accommodate students who need physical access to campus buildings and facilities. However, not all universities offer accommodation if you have a learning disability or require academic support. Unfortunately, your preferred graduate program may not offer services for students with special academic needs. After you narrow your search for a program as described in this appendix, you should investigate the extent to which the program can accommodate your needs and adjust your plans accordingly.

THE IMPACT OF GRADUATE EDUCATION

As a prospective graduate student, you need to consider how graduate study will impact your day-to-day life. Aside from financing, your main question is likely to be one of how much time you can devote to your progress, and how far you intend to go. Will you attend full time or part time? If you decide to attend full time, you may need to calculate how long you can afford to be out of the workplace in order to make the commitment to finish the program on time.

Beyond the Bachelor's Degree

Master's programs usually take 1 to 2 years of full-time study beyond the bachelor's degree; law school takes 3 years and medical school takes 4 years beyond the bachelor's degree. At the Ph.D. level, most science and engineering programs generally take 6 to 7 years and humanities programs take about 10 years on top of your bachelor's degree. If you choose to attend part time, you may need to think about how you will find time to study along with balancing your full-time job, as well as tend to any child-care needs or your share of the household work.

Although the vast majority (over 80%) of graduate students are taking a full-time course load of 12 credits or more, over 60% continue to work either full or part time while they study.

Bachelor's and Advanced Degrees Combined

When you include the time spent getting a bachelor's degree, you will have invested on average anywhere from 6 to 15 years in your professional studies.

Average Number of Years for Completing Bachelor's and Advanced Degrees, Combined				
	Master's Degree	Professional Degree	Doctorate Degree
TOTAL	7.1	6.0	9.8
Field of Training			
Business	7.1	6.7	B
Computers	6.0	6.0	10.1
Liberal arts	6.8	0.0	12.9
Social science	6.2	5.5	9.0
Natural science	6.5	5.1	7.1
Education	8.5	11.1	14.4
Other	6.8	6.4	9.7

Derived measure is not shown when base is less than 100,000.

Note: This table was updated November 2010 from original table posted January 2008. Weights used in this table are those contained in the SIPP core files released July 2010. Coding of education has been changed as described in the document "Re-Calculation of Educational Attainment in the 2004 Panel of SIPP" located at: *www.census.gov/sipp/notes.html*.

Source: U.S. Census Bureau, Survey of Income and Program Participation, 2004.

Is this investment of time and resources worth the sacrifice? Aside from the scholarly achievement, statistics show that if you have an advanced degree you are likely to experience both higher rates of employment and higher income levels throughout your working life, as illustrated below:

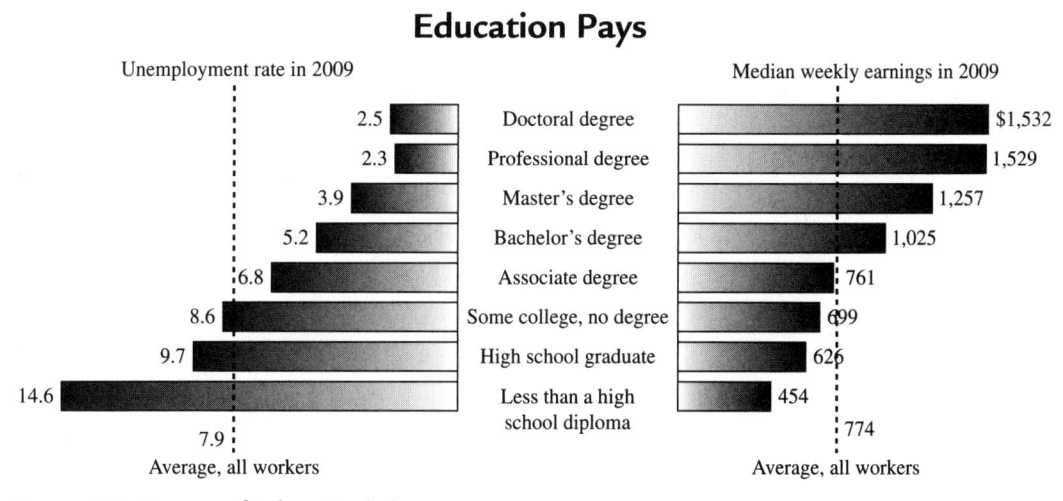

Education Pays

Unemployment rate in 2009		Median weekly earnings in 2009
2.5	Doctoral degree	$1,532
2.3	Professional degree	1,529
3.9	Master's degree	1,257
5.2	Bachelor's degree	1,025
6.8	Associate degree	761
8.6	Some college, no degree	699
9.7	High school graduate	626
14.6	Less than a high school diploma	454
7.9 Average, all workers		774 Average, all workers

Source: U.S. Bureau of Labor Statistics

In addition, the Bureau of Labor Statistics shows that the unemployment rate among individuals with master's degrees is nearly 4% lower than the national average, and the unemployment rate for those with professional and doctorate degrees is more than 5% less than the national average.

HOW TO PICK A GRADUATE SCHOOL

Your Intended Career and Your Field of Study

Your first step should be to try to pin down your professional goals. About 75% of students who pursue a Ph.D. intend to do research and/or teach, so your own strategies for success will vary according to what you want to do.

Begin with a consideration of your undergraduate major as well as your work experience so far. Do you want to advance in your current field or are you looking for a change? Graduate admissions officers will base the decision to admit you on how well you will fit into the program, and if you are changing fields that means they need to consider if your change makes sense for their admissions decision.

Location

Think about the school's location and size. Ask yourself whether you are in a position to relocate, and whether you prefer a big city or a small town. Among the factors you might want to consider are cost of living, access to transportation and recreation, diversity, crime statistics, and the quality of the schools if you have school-age children. Determining these choices before you apply may help determine whether you'll need to relocate in order to secure your future after you graduate.

EVALUATING THE PROGRAM

You should plan to have a final list of at least five schools to send applications to. To narrow your choices, you can use:

- Faculty recommendations
- Program rankings
- Online searches
- Campus visits

You need to ask questions, do some searching on your own, and spend some time visiting as many of your prospects as you can. One of the best resources for your evaluation is your undergraduate college; invest some time in a visit to campus if you can or at least in a phone call to your college's career placement office. If you aren't able to visit in person, a phone call is preferable to an e-mail. Not only is a personal contact faster, you run the risk that your e-mail may not get a response, end up in a spam folder, or perhaps not get through. Once you contact the placement office, the career advisors can help you get an idea of which programs might be best for you, no matter how recently you've graduated.

Faculty Recommendations

In addition to your college placement office, your former professors are also very valuable resources for information. Contact former professors and schedule an appointment to meet with them; college professors take pride in students who go on to graduate work, and they can tell you which programs and professors have the best reputation in the field.

Program Rankings

Another way to begin comparing programs is to check the magazines and catalogs that rank institutions, such as *U.S. News and World Report* (*http://grad-schools.usnews.rankingsandreviews.com/best-graduate-schools*). Although these rankings can be valuable, they should really serve to help you begin your search, rather than to help you evaluate and pick a program. This is because rankings can vary in methodology from each other, as well as from year to year, within the same catalog. These rankings often organize their information by region, so they can give you some good ideas as you consider the location of your intended program. Remember, however, that rankings are useful to provide preliminary guidance, and it's best to form your opinion from people in the field as well as from the people you meet during the admissions process.

Online Search

Once you have begun to organize a list of graduate programs to research, you can begin searching online. Search each website and click through the information available, including the graduate program details, faculty information, the admissions deadlines and requirements, facilities, and location. Also search for the school's reputation by looking for information about what kinds of activities alumni are now doing or what fields they are in. Do the answers fit in with what you are looking for? If so, they can help you finalize your list of programs.

Campus Visit

After you've searched and gathered as much information as you can on each school, the next step is to contact the admissions office to ask for written information from each of your choices. This will let you get a feel for the culture of the admissions office, and by extension a hint about the culture of the school's student services. Pay attention if you are looking for certain attributes: precision, promptness, courtesy, and an ability to put you at ease will tell you if this is a school in which you want to spend at least two years.

You won't be able to learn everything you need to know just by searching online and asking about the program. You need to visit as many of your prospective choices as you can. Most admissions offices accommodate walk-in inquiries, or you can make an appointment to discuss your questions with the admissions counselor. Also, consider your personal needs when you visit your prospective campus. Some universities offer on-campus housing for students and their families and some may offer day care, so be sure to inquire about these services.

You may want to get details on how long the program might take, and if you can speak to faculty directly. If you do get the chance to speak to faculty members, you could ask them for any recommendations about the program, or perhaps something about their publication or research.

NON-MATRIC ENROLLMENT—A WAY TO SAMPLE THE EXPERIENCE

A non-matriculating student is one who is taking one or two courses at a time, without enrolling in the program. Whether you plan to attend full or part time, this can be a good option for you to get a sense of how much coursework you can handle while getting to know the professors and the campus. If you can, try to take a course with the chair of the department or the professor you might wish to work with as an advisor. Finally, a good performance as a non-matric student in the program will give you a very nice credential in your application package.

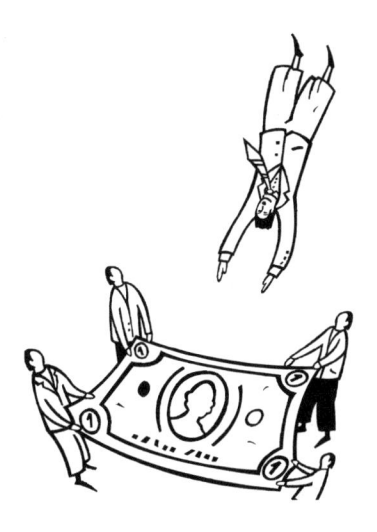

FINANCIAL AID OPTIONS

The cost of attending graduate school can be overwhelming and is usually one of the factors that makes students hesitate about undertaking an advanced degree. However, there are a variety of resources available, including:

- Scholarships
- Grants
- Tuition reimbursement

- Fellowships
- Assistantships
- Loans

You can often get financial help for your books and living expenses as well as tuition if you are able to use more than one source of aid.

Scholarships

Scholarships are sources of funding that do not have to be repaid, unlike student loans. Scholarships are financial awards usually offered by organizations, foundations, or individuals, and the money must be used specifically for tuition. Some scholarships are dependent on your grade point average.

Grants

Grants can also be awarded by organizations and foundations and, like scholarships, do not have to be repaid. Grants are usually awarded by federal and/or state governments, and often they can be used to cover your living expenses as well as tuition.

Tuition Reimbursement

Depending on your field of study and your employer, you may have the opportunity to get reimbursed for your graduate school tuition if you keep your job while you attend school. Some larger corporations go so far as to offer tuition reimbursement to children of employees, so check with the human resources department or your supervisor.

Fellowships

Research fellowships are grants that support research work as well as your tuition and living expenses. You can find out what's available on your campus by contacting your department chair, or the financial aid office, and you can also ask your professors about scholarly associations in your discipline.

There are some prestigious fellowship programs available from the federal government, such as the National Science Foundation and the Department of Defense. There are also discipline-specific programs at your university that pay for you to conduct research. Also, scholarly associations such as the Modern Language Association or the American Physical Society, for example, often have information on scholarships and fellowships.

Graduate Assistantships

Graduate assistantships are on-campus jobs, usually teaching, research, advising, or working with undergraduate students in some way. These jobs are unique to each academic department, and sometimes the financial aid office or the graduate admissions office will have a central listing of the jobs. Competition for these jobs is usually tough, and you should be prepared with your resume and networking skills to keep your name at the top of each department's list. Assistantships usually pay full tuition for a certain number of credits per semester and provide a monthly stipend or wage. Most colleges require you to be admitted to their program of study before you can apply for a graduate assistantship. Take advantage of any contacts you make with professors about available openings.

Student Loans

Most graduate students take out loans to fund their studies. The main loan program available to graduate students is the federal student loan program. In order to receive federal student loans, you must fall into one of these categories:

1. A U.S. citizen or national;

2. A U.S. permanent resident;

3. Citizens of the Freely Associated States: the Federated States of Micronesia and the Republics of Palau and the Marshall Islands;

4. Other eligible noncitizens. This is a complicated category and you should check with your school's financial aid office to see if you fall into this category. The category of "Other eligible noncitizens" include refugees, victims of human trafficking, persons granted asylum in the United States, conditional entrants, persons paroled into the United States for at least one year, and Cuban-Haitian entrants. If you are an eligible noncitizen, you must usually provide some evidence (such as having filed a valid permanent resident application) from the Department of Homeland Security that you intend to become a citizen or permanent resident in the United States.

(*Source:* Information for Financial Aid Professionals; Student Aid on the Web)

In addition to citizenship/visa status, you must be registered for at least half time in a degree program (more than 5 credits) If you are male student between the ages of 18 and 25, you must have registered with the Selective Service.

You cannot qualify for a federal student loan if you have defaulted on a prior federal student loan, or if you owe a refund on a federal grant.

Federal Stafford Loan

The federal Stafford loan program is the most common source of funding for advanced study. The Stafford loan can cover tuition and fees as well as provide aid for other expenses, such as books, living expenses, and travel. You can qualify for a subsidized loan at no interest, based on your financial need, or an unsubsidized loan, which does come with interest. You don't need to prove financial need for an unsubsidized loan, and your university's financial aid office can help you determine how much to borrow.

Direct PLUS Loans for Graduate and Professional Degree Students

If the maximum you can borrow on the Stafford loan doesn't cover all of your expenses, you can also apply for a Direct PLUS loan to help cover your costs. Direct PLUS loans have a fixed interest rate of 7.9%, and you need to be able to qualify with a satisfactory credit history.

Free Application for Federal Student Aid (FAFSA)

You must fill out the Free Application for Federal Student Aid (FAFSA) to begin the process of obtaining any federal, state, or institutional financial aid, and you must complete a FAFSA for each academic year that you are enrolled in your program. The FAFSA is available online and students are encouraged to use the online process at *www.fafsa.ed.gov* rather than the paper application process. You will need to use a federal PIN in order to sign your application, and you can apply for your PIN online at *www.pin.ed.gov*.

You can find a comprehensive list of frequently asked questions about how to fill out the FAFSA on the website at *http://studentaid.ed.gov/PORTALSWebApp/students/english/faqs.jsp*, including how to check on the status of your application and how to ask questions about your loan amount.

Private Loans and International Student Financing Options

Many universities work with private lenders to help you if you do not meet the eligibility requirements for the federal Stafford loan, or if the amount awarded through the federal Stafford loan is insufficient to cover your costs, or if you are an international student. Contact the financial aid office of your intended programs and ask them about these options, as well as fellowships and assistantships.

The federal student loan program is not available to international students, including anyone who falls under the following categories:

1. Family unity status—individuals who have been granted relief from deportation under the Family Unity program.

2. Temporary residents—individuals who are allowed to live and work in the United States under the Legalization or Special Agricultural Worker program.

3. Persons with non-immigrant visas—individuals who have work visas, as well as students, visitors, and foreign government officials.

(*Source:* Information for Financial Aid Professionals; Student Aid on the Web)

Repaying Your Loan

Your federal student loans will become due 6 months from your last day of attendance at school, whether or not you graduate from your program. Although the standard repayment term on the federal Stafford loan is 10 years, you can work out longer repayment terms with lower monthly payments through your school's financial aid office.

Finally, program graduates who work in certain public service jobs, such as teaching, nursing, and medical doctors, qualify for loan forgiveness programs, so ask your financial aid office about the eligibility requirements for loan forgiveness.

HOW TO APPLY

The application process itself is lengthy. Including preparing for and taking your standardized tests, you should plan to invest 2 years from the selection of your schools to the start of your first class. You should send out enough applications so that you have options when the acceptance letters come in. Just as with the undergraduate admissions process, you should apply not only to your ideal graduate programs but also to at least one "safe" school, one you are sure you can get into.

Many master's programs have application deadlines from January to March, and Ph.D. programs usually have application deadlines for December or January. Most programs will be accepting applications about 1 year in advance of the start of classes. Programs that offer rolling admissions accept applications all year, but you run the risk of getting shut out of your intended semester if the class has filled up. Programs that maintain application deadlines are usually inflexible about those deadlines, so it's best to plan at least 2 years ahead to evaluate and pick your programs, as well as to gather all of the documentation and materials that will go into your application.

A complete application package for most graduate schools requires an entrance exam, official undergraduate transcripts, professional recommendations, an essay, and often a personal interview. The admissions office or committee is looking for students who are not only capable of doing the academic work, but those who are committed to the field and demonstrate an ability to complete the degree. Your transcripts and test scores tell the story of your command of the subject matter; and your recommendations, the essay, and the interview tell the story of how you approach your obligations, manage your time, and if you will make it through to become a good colleague in the discipline. So, how can you show the admissions committee that you have what it takes? It depends largely on the discipline, but there are a few special guidelines to keep in mind depending on your intended field.

Business Programs

Admissions committees at business programs are evaluating your work experience, skills, and future career plans in addition to your academics. You can leave a positive impression in the interview, and be prepared to explain gaps in your resume just as you would in a job interview. The best difference between the two is that you are coming to school to improve your skills and credentials and the committee tends to listen supportively.

Education, Psychology, Public Affairs, Communications

You should go into programs like these with some experience working with people, whether in your work experience, extra-curricular activities, as a volunteer, or in any capacity. You can enhance your appeal as a candidate if you can demonstrate that you value and enjoy interacting with the population you'll be training to serve. Also, be sure you know which certification tests, such as the NCATE or Praxis, are required by your state for certification in your field. Take them as soon as you can.

Engineering and Science

Your knowledge of research in the field can boost your chances here; try to find and become familiar with the faculty research that matches your research interests, and explain in your application essay how your interests fit into those of the department. Also, your recommendations from professors and employers carry a lot of weight with these admissions committees. Science and engineering faculty often sit on admissions committees, so you should do your best to contact them and make a connection before you apply to the program.

Humanities, Social Sciences, Fine Arts

Advanced degrees in the humanities, social sciences, and fine arts require a commitment to scholarship and research in the field, and can lead to university teaching jobs. Management positions in college administration and museum administration also require advanced degrees. Be prepared to demonstrate your command of the subject; your GPA in the discipline will have a lot of weight. If your undergraduate GPA is not a strong point, you can compensate by doing very well on the GRE and by doing well in a non-matric course before you apply.

MAKING THE MOST OF THE GRE

Your GRE scores are valid for 5 years. On the revised general test, both the math and verbal sections will now be scored in ranges between 130 and 170 in one-point increments. The writing section remains graded on a scale of 0 to 6. You can take the GRE more than once, but you should not take the actual GRE just for practice because all of your scores will be sent to your intended schools, although the admissions committee will often just consider your highest combination of scores.

Admissions committees tend to use GRE scores as a way to thin their volume of applications. Applicants with low scores are placed at the bottom of the list. The committee can then take applicants with high scores and move on to evaluate the other parts of the applications. Doing well on the GRE allows you to remain in the stack of applications that will be considered, whereas low GRE scores give the admissions committee a reason to pick someone else for the program over you.

Most competitive graduate programs will be looking for scores above the 50th percentile, and highly selective programs will probably screen at the 90th percentile. There may be programs that weigh the GRE more heavily than others, and programs will differ with respect to which sections of the test they pay attention to in obvious ways. If you're applying to a program in literature or communications, your verbal score will be paramount and your math score will count for relatively little. On the other hand, if you are applying for math, engineering, or any of the hard sciences, your analytical and math scores will carry more weight than your verbal score.

TRANSCRIPTS

Your official transcripts are never sent to you, the student. They travel only between schools, and you can and should contact the admissions office to confirm that your transcript has arrived. Undergraduate colleges may or may not charge a fee to send your official transcripts, and some colleges send a certain number out for you at no charge (up to five, for example) before they charge a fee.

If you have attended more than one undergraduate program, check with your graduate school to see if they want official transcripts from each institution. Some programs will, whereas others will only need the official transcript from the school where you earned your bachelor's degree.

LETTERS OF RECOMMENDATION

Your letters of recommendation offer the admissions committee a look at the professional and/or academic impression you have made on people in the field. It may be intimidating to reach out and contact people to ask a favor, but college professors are familiar with this process. Don't be shy; just be polite.

Admissions committees expect you to get recommendations from people who like you, so whom you can get to recommend you can be as impressive as what is written about you. Get as many recommendations from faculty in the discipline as you can. Also, you should approach professors who actually know you and can write about your abilities and strengths. Something specific will reflect better than something generic, such as that you were a student and you did well.

You can approach employers in addition to professors for your letters of recommendation, especially for certain degrees such as business and public affairs. If you do request letters from employers, you will need them to emphasize how well you handled your job responsibilities and how your work experience prepared you for the transition to the graduate program.

Your letter writers will need about 2 months of lead time. Make a note to yourself on when to double-check that the letters have gone out. Offer the people you ask all of the assistance they might need to write knowledgeably about your candidacy. When you call or e-mail for your recommendation, go ahead and send a copy of your resume and let your recommenders read your personal statement. If you are asking a professor and you've been out of school for a while, include in your request what courses you took with him or her and when, and take some time to discuss your current academic and professional goals and what you've been doing since graduation.

THE PERSONAL STATEMENT ESSAY

Whether your schools are asking for a general statement or asking you to respond to specific prompts, the way you craft your essay will give the admissions committee a lot of information about you. Your essay will indicate not only your goals, but how you approach the task of writing and how you articulate your ideas. Some questions to consider before you write:

- When did you become interested in this discipline? What keeps you interested and why are you suited to this type of study?

- What are your career goals?

- What details of your personal history have influenced your choices? Be careful here; you don't want to discuss anything that is intimate or too controversial. Focus on what obstacles you have overcome and what in your life has made you who you are, not biographical "tell-all" details.

- What skills have you developed in your work experience?

- What makes you a strong candidate for the program?

Brainstorm and Organize Your Ideas

Brainstorm your answers; just jot down and note anything that comes to mind to get started on the writing process. Then organize your notes into three sections: the first part of the essay should explain what it is about your field that most appeals to you. The second section should explain what in your experience and background demonstrates that you have the abilities and skills that will help you succeed in your goals, and your final section should discuss your long-term goals and what you will bring to the program.

Draft, Revise, and Rewrite

Write well, and be sure your grammar and usage are correct. Pay attention to basic rules such as subject-verb agreement, pronoun agreement, and keeping in the same tense when it's appropriate. In addition, avoid using clichés (for example, "I give 110%" or "I am a people person") and be meticulous about avoiding common spelling mistakes, such as confusing "to," "two," and "too." The essay is your first opportunity to show the admissions committee that you have the ability to write at the academic level.

Plan to spend time on perfecting your essay, and keep in mind that you may not be able to use the same essay for all your applications. Also, like most students, you may have to write and re-write until you are satisfied with your essay; don't let yourself procrastinate concerning this essential process.

THE INTERVIEW

Your program application may or may not require an interview, but if it does the admissions interview provides you with an opportunity to cement your candidacy. Also, the admissions interviewers are attempting to determine how you will fit in as a person whom the faculty will have to work with—possibly as a colleague—over the next few years.

Discussing Yourself

You will most likely be asked why you want to pursue a graduate degree. This is your opportunity to show that you belong at the graduate level, while giving the interviewers a chance to evaluate your personality. Give some thought to your research interests and why they interest you. You can be prepared to talk about what you've achieved, relative to the program, that gives you the most pride. Also, you should be able to describe what's unique or novel about your accomplishments. Focus on your strengths and your willingness to learn.

The questions about the work will be specific to each institution, but you should be able to discuss the field articulately and give the impression that you understand the commitment that advanced study entails, and that you have the discipline and intelligence to succeed. Be polite, but show confidence and ask questions of your own when you get the opportunity. Try to learn the department members' names, their faces from the website, and one basic thing about each of their research/teaching areas to help you formulate questions or show your interest.

What to Wear

As with a job interview, your clothing choices can send a message, so it's a good idea to try to find out how formal the interview will be. You can ask your undergraduate career services office, or the professors you approached for your recommendation, for ideas on what to wear. If you have no way of finding out how to dress beforehand, as a rule it's usually best to dress for the position you want. Most universities will have pictures of the faculty up on their website, so you can take some cues from how formally they are dressed to represent the university.

AN APPLICATION TIMELINE

The timeline for the application is the culmination of all of the work you've done so far to search out potential programs and make your final choices. Now, it's just a matter of gathering your materials and making sense of them for each school.

First, make a checklist for each school that you apply to. Keep track of each item and make copies for yourself. Your deadlines will vary for each element of the application as well as for each school. It's a good idea to plot out your own version and try to anticipate what you'll do in case things get lost or are not received when you expect them. This sample timeline is for a planned start date of September; so add 3 months if you plan to begin in January.

One year before classes begin; July and August:

- *Prepare for the GRE*

- *Prepare for the TOEFL, if applicable*

    Plan for your test dates and take practice tests to get an idea of your strengths and weaknesses. Create a schedule for studying if you need better command of the material and for becoming familiar with the tests. Take the tests early, so that you can retake them if you need to.

- *International student planning*

    If you are an international student, contact the U.S. embassy for visa wait times, and begin to collect your visa materials.

September:

- *Take a non-matric course (if applicable)*

    Register in September if you plan to take any graduate courses as a non-matriculated student. There are usually no academic entrance requirements for non-matric courses, except proof that you have an undergraduate degree.

- *Statement of purpose*

    Begin work on your essay or statement of purpose and take advantage of your undergraduate college's career counseling office, or the writing center, or ask a faculty member to review it with you. You won't need to have it finalized until December, so make sure it's an honest reflection of what you hope to achieve at the graduate level.

October:

- *GRE subject test*

    Take the GRE subject test, and retake it in November if you need to.

- *Letters of recommendation*

    Ask faculty or employers for letters of recommendation. Give them the school's form, the deadline for submission, and sample letters if they need them. The letters of recommendation will require the most follow-up; keep track of their due dates and give your letter writers a polite reminder if the deadline is approaching.

November:

- *Financial Aid*

    Research your sources and become familiar with the documentation each application requires. Apply for any fellowships and scholarships, but the FAFSA for loans will not be due until January. If you are an international student, gather your materials for your student visa as well.

- *Official transcripts*

    Contact the registrar at your college and arrange for your official transcript to be sent to each of your programs.

- *Make contacts*

    Go ahead and make contact with a professor or two in your discipline at your prospective schools. Just call or e-mail, introducing yourself as a student who is applying next fall, and ask if they mind if you call or come by during office hours or whenever it might be convenient. Be yourself, and be prepared for the conversation with a few specific questions about the field or the research.

December:

- *Final check*

    Confirm the due dates for the applications of each school, as well as the application fees. Confirm that your letters of recommendation have come in. Follow up on your test scores and arrange to retake them if you need to.

    Write the final draft of your statement of purpose and be sure to proofread as well as spell check. Spell check alone will not catch an error if you have spelled the mistake correctly, such as mistaking "form" for "from," for example.

The year classes begin—January:

- *Send everything in*

    Submit your application forms, fees, essays, and statements of purpose for each of your programs. Keep a copy of each for yourself.

    The school should send you an acknowledgement when it receives your application. Keep a record of these and contact the admissions office to confirm that your application has been received before the deadline if you do not get an acknowledgement.

    Gather your income tax information from the previous year and fill out your Federal Student Aid (FAFSA) application.

February and March:

- *The interview*

    Review your essays and statements of purpose and begin to prepare for your admissions interviews.

April:

- *Decision time*

    Congratulations on your acceptances! Inform the program that you choose to attend and give notice to the programs that you decline.

    Send thank-you notes to the people who wrote your letters of recommendation.

    If it should happen that you are not admitted to your first choice of program, you may want to contact any professors you know and ask them if they might point out how you might successfully reapply the following year.

- *International students*

    Begin the process for applying for your student visa, as described in the next section. If you plan to bring any members of your family with you, you will need to show the U.S. embassy documentation that proves your relationship to your spouse and children, such as marriage and birth certificates. You are encouraged to apply with your family at the same time that you apply for your own visa.

INTERNATIONAL STUDENTS

As an international student, you will need to satisfy additional requirements, along with submitting the documentation for the application process as described in the timeline. You will most likely need a category F visa for attending a university, and you need to be sure that the schools you are applying to are certified by the Student and Exchange Visitor Program.

The Student and Exchange Visitor Program (SEVP) is designed to help the Department of Homeland Security (DHS) and Department of State better monitor school and exchange programs and F, M, and J category visitors. Exchange visitor and student information is maintained in the Student and Exchange Visitor

Information System (SEVIS). SEVIS is an Internet-based system that maintains accurate and current information on non-immigrant students (F and M visa), exchange visitors (J visa), and their dependents (F-2, M-2, and J-2). SEVIS enables schools and program sponsors to transmit mandatory information and event notifications, via the Internet, to the DHS and Department of State (DOS) throughout a student or exchange visitor's stay in the United States. (*Source:* U.S. Department of State)

The U.S. Bureau of Consular Affairs, *http://travel.state.gov/visa/temp/ types/types_1268.html*, is a very good resource for student visa information. There, you can find rules and regulations, as well as definitions and links to financial aid resources.

Among the extra materials international students must submit are:

- documentation to support a U.S. student visa;

- college or university transcripts evaluated and translated by accepted agencies; and

- proof of proficiency in the English language.

In addition, international students must be enrolled full time, which means you must be taking at least nine credits. Most American graduate schools require you, the student, to become familiar with U.S. immigration regulations.

How to Qualify for U.S. Student Visa

If you need a student visa, you must have documentation required by the United States Citizenship and Immigration Services (USCIS). To be able to qualify for a student visa, you need to:

- Have a residence abroad, with no immediate intention of abandoning that residence;

- Intend to depart from the United States upon completion of the course of study; and

- Possess sufficient funds to pursue the proposed course of study.

(*Source:* Bureau of Consular Affairs, U.S. Department of State)

The Application Process for a U.S. Student Visa

Visas are processed by the U.S. embassy or consulate located in your country of origin. You should contact the embassy to find out about how long the wait time is for visa processing, so you can incorporate it in your graduate school application timeline. To apply for a student visa, you will need:

1. *Form I-20A-B, Certificate of Eligibility for Nonimmigrant (F-1) Student Status—for Academic and Language Students.* You will need to submit a SEVIS-generated form, I-20, which is provided to you by your school. You and your school official must sign the I-20 form.

   This is usually the most complicated requirement for most international students. Many American universities will work with you to review your documents and determine if they are sufficient to issue the Certificate of Eligibility I-20 form. The documentation necessary for an I-20 includes the following:

   - Request for Certificate of Eligibility (I-20) form.

   - Declaration and Certification of Finances, with proof of your ability to pay for the cost of your education. Your funding can come from a variety of sources, such as private funds, university funds, or a sponsoring company/agency/government fund. If you will be supported by private funds, you need to provide current bank statements, or a declaration of financial support from the person or agency that will be supporting you during your studies.

   - International students who currently live in the United States must also fill out a Visa Sponsorship Transfer Form indicating the SEVIS release date.

   Your I-20 must come from a school that is approved to participate in SEVIS by the Department of Homeland Security (DHS), so look for this approval when you are deciding on schools to apply to. Your I-20 then goes to DHS, and the school is responsible for entering your information for the I-20 student visa form into SEVIS.

   Your I-20 is then recorded electronically through the SEVIS system, so that the U.S. embassy or consulate can process your student visa application.

2. *Online Nonimmigrant Visa Electronic Application, Form DS-160.* The DS-160 form is sent electronically to the Department of State website. Consular officers use the information entered on the DS-160 to process the visa application and, combined with a personal interview, determine an applicant's eligibility for a non-immigrant visa.

3. *A passport* valid for travel to the United States and with a validity date at least 6 months beyond the applicant's intended period of stay in the United States (unless *country-specific agreements* provide exemptions). If more than one person is included in the passport, each person desiring a visa must complete an application.

4. *One (1) 2x2 photograph.*

5. *A receipt for payment* of the visa application fee (called an MRV fee).

6. *The receipt* for the SEVIS I-901 fee.

7. *Transcripts and diplomas* from your previous schools.

8. *Scores from standardized tests* required by the educational institution, such as the TOEFL, and GRE.

9. *Financial evidence* that shows you or your parents who are sponsoring you have sufficient funds to cover your tuition and living expenses during the period of your intended study. For example, if you or your sponsor is a salaried employee, bring income tax documents and original bank books and/or statements. If you or your sponsor owns a business, bring business registration, licenses, and tax documents, as well as original bank books and/or statements.

(*Source:* Bureau of Consular Affairs, U.S. Department of State)

Evaluation of Academic Credentials

American graduate schools require an evaluation of your undergraduate work to determine that you have earned the equivalent of an American bachelor's degree. Most schools accept one of the following transcript evaluation services:

- World Education Services, *www.wes.org*

- Center for Applied Research, Evaluation, and Education, Inc., *www.iescaree.com*

- Evaluation Services, Inc., *www.evaluationservice.net*
- Global Credential Evaluators, Inc., *www.gceus.com*
- Educational Credential Evaluators, *www.ece.org*

English Proficiency

The most common requirement for American graduate schools is the Test of English as a Foreign Language (TOEFL). The TOEFL is made up of four sections, each designed to demonstrate your command of speaking, writing, listening, and reading in English at the university level. EducationUSA, a service of the U.S. Department of State, at *www.educationusa.info/pages/students/app-grad-exams.php*, is a good source of information about the TOEFL, including how to register and what to expect on the test. The most current and widespread format of the exam is the Internet-Based TOEFL (iBT); however, in several countries where iBT is not yet available, the Paper-Based TOEFL (PBT) is still offered. You must pre-register for whichever form of testing you choose, even the Internet-based option; it is not possible to go to the testing center and hope to find space available that same day.

The Internet-Based TOEFL administration generally lasts up to 4 hours and includes four sections:

- **Reading:** Measures the ability to understand short lectures similar to the academic texts used in schools and universities in North America.

- **Listening:** Measures the ability to understand North American English as it is spoken in an academic setting.

- **Speaking:** Measures the ability to speak English in an academic context.

- **Writing:** Measures the ability to write in English on the assigned theme. This section is equivalent to the previously administered Test of Written English (TWE).

Some of the assigned tasks in the iBT will measure your capacity to combine several of the measured skills. For example, you may be asked to read, listen, and speak your answer to a question.

The Computer-Based TOEFL (CBT) measures English language proficiency in listening, structure, reading, and writing.

The Paper-Based TOEFL (PBT) measures listening comprehension, structure and written expression, and reading comprehension.

(*Source*: EducationUSA)

YOU'RE IN!

Now that you've achieved your goal and have been admitted to the program, some of the pressure is off but a new set of pressures begins. It's natural to be a bit nervous about the new challenges you face, but most professors will confirm that you would not have been admitted if they had no confidence in your abilities.

Keys to Success

In the first semester, just watch and learn and start looking for research interests if you have not yet developed any. Don't hesitate to approach your professors for help. Your professors will most likely assume that, if you are not asking any questions, you don't need any help. Make a point of introducing yourself to the department's administrator or secretary, and be polite and courteous to him or her. These professional staff members often have years of experience at the university, and usually possess a wealth of information on many of the questions you may have about moving through the program.

The Coursework

Most successful graduate students create a schedule and stick to it. Your success will depend in great measure on your ability to handle your time. Do the readings for your courses and get in the habit of taking notes on the material. You'll find you have to discuss the readings in your seminar courses, and in your labs the professors will assume that you have done the reading and will conduct class accordingly. Participate in the discussions. Identify the main themes of your reading assignments and prepare to contribute on those, rather than side, issues.

Try to be friendly with your cohorts. You'll probably find that they are as enthusiastic—and probably as anxious—as you. Comparing notes and understanding what you have in common with them can help you adapt more quickly to the graduate school environment. If you are required to collaborate with your classmates and produce a paper or conduct some research as part of a group, never be the one who fails to do their fair share. Offer help to your classmates when they need it and accept help when you can. Advanced scholarship depends a great deal on collegiality, and being a good colleague will always let you stand out in a positive way.

The Qualifying Exam

Some programs will require a comprehensive exam before you can move on to the thesis or dissertation. Those that do seldom offer guidance on how to study and prepare, but your good relationships with your peers can help you. Forming a study group to review the main themes of each course and sharing class notes can help to get ready for your exam.

The Thesis and Dissertation

When the time comes to pick a thesis or dissertation advisor, you should take the professor's personality into account when considering whom to approach. By the time you are ready for such extended work, you'll know what style of advising will work best for you. Do you prefer to work at your own pace? Do you perform better with firm deadlines? Are you comfortable tackling portions of the thesis on your own, or would you need the advisor to be accessible? You will discover your style during your coursework. Being observant, communicating with your professors about their advising methods, and talking with your fellow students will help you make the right choice.

Time Management

The ability to manage your time is crucial to completing your dissertation. Work hard, be efficient, take time off, but beware of the pitfalls of procrastination. It's easy to turn away from the dissertation after you have moved beyond the routine of taking classes. You'll have to find a balance that works for you, but remember that it's easy to let your studies consume all of your time. If you spend all of your time on your work, and in the company of your graduate school peers, you could unintentionally alienate your family and friends and put yourself under additional strain. If you are holding down a job in addition to your courses, it's definitely to your benefit to try to relax on occasion, even if you have to schedule the time. The most successful graduate students treat the program like a job—keep a set schedule, work late when the need arises, and keep your social life to the best of your ability.

YOU'RE READY TO GO

Entering graduate school means entering a profession, albeit as a student. As such, graduate faculty will expect a great deal of initiative from you; what you get out of your experience will depend on what you put in. Many programs offer you an opportunity to teach and to work in the profession, and most programs also require you to contribute to the accumulated knowledge of the field. However you plan your course, you'll have everything you need to accomplish your goals at this important stage of your academic and professional career. Good luck on your journey.

REFERENCES*

Bureau of Consular Affairs, U.S. Department of State
http://travel.state.gov/visa/temp/types/types_1268.html

EducationUSA
www.educationusa.info/pages/students/app-grad-exams.php

*As of this printing all web address are accurate, but they are subject to change. See *rea.com/gre* for updates.

Information for Financial Aid Professionals; Student Aid on the Web
http://ifap.ed.gov/sfahandbooks/attachments/0809FSAHbkVol1Ch2.pdf

Overseas Association for College Admissions Counseling
www.oacac.com/links.htm

Students.gov
www.students.gov/STUGOVWebApp/Public?topicID=82&operation=topic

United States Bureau of Labor Statistics Occupational Outlook Handbook
http://www.bls.gov/oco/

United States Bureau of Labor Statistics Occupational Outlook Handbook Chart—Education Pays: More Education Leads to Higher Earnings, Lower Unemployment
http://www.bls.gov/opub/ooq/2010/summer/oochart.pdf

United States Census Bureau; Data on Educational Attainment
http://www.census.gov/hhes/socdemo/education/data/sipp/index.html

United States Citizenship and Immigration Services
http://www.uscis.gov/portal/site/uscis

United States Department of Education, NCES 2011-219—Profile of Graduate and First-Professional Students: Trends from Selected Years, 1995–96 to 2007–08
http://nces.ed.gov/surveys/npsas/graduate.asp

INDEX

Numbers

3:4:5 triangle, 92, 94
5:12:13 triangle, 92
30:60:90 triangle, 92
45:45:90 triangle, 91–92

A

Aberrant, 377
Absolute value, 355
Abstemious, 377
Acerbic, 377
Acute angles, 71–72, 355
Addition, 76–78
Alacrity, 377
Algebra
   and the Cartesian plane, 96–97
   common alert signals for, 368–370
   examples of, 95–99
   and factoring, FOILing, 99–106
   formulas, rules for, 361–362, 363–364
   origins of, 95
   and slope, 97–99
Allude, 377
Allusion, 377
Altruism, 377
Amalgam, 377
Amalgamate, 377
Ameliorate, 377
Anachronism, 377
Analytical writing section, of GRE, 2, 6, 171–172
   See also Essays
Angle bisector of a triangle, 355
Angles, 71–72
Anomaly, 377
Antipathy, 377
Apothem, 355
Application timeline, 486–489
Apposite, 377
Arc, 74, 77

Arcane, 377
Archetype, 377
Arduous, 377
Arid, 377
Arithmetic, 366–368
Articulate, 377
Ascetic, 377
Aseptic, 378
Aspersion, 378
Assiduous, 378
Assuage, 378
Astringent, 378
Atrophy, 378
Attenuate, 378
Autocracy, 378
Autocrat, 378
Average (mean), 107, 109

B

Baleful, 378
Banal, 378
Bases, 77–79
Beneficent, 378
Bilateral, 378
Binomial, 355
Biochemistry, Cell, and Molecular Biology Subject Test, 8–9
Biology Subject Test, 9
Bombast, 378
Box plot, 355
Box-and-whisker plots, 109
Burgeon, 378
Business programs, 481
Business school students, 2, 10

C

Cacophony, 378
Cant, 378
Caprice, 378
Cartesian plane, 96–97, 106

Catharsis, 378
Central angle, 355
Chemistry Subject Test, 9
Chicanery, 378
Chord, 72, 355
Churlishness, 378
Circles
  equations for, 72–74, 77, 80–81, 83–88, 90
  illustrated, 354
Circle-volume, 81
Circumference
  defined, 355
  equations for, 72–74, 77, 83, 86–88
Circumlocution, 378
Cloture, 379
Cloying, 379
Coda, 379
Codify, 379
Cogent, 379
Cogitate, 379
Cognitive, 379
Cognizant, 379
Coherent, 379
Cohesion, 379
Combination items, 111–112
Comeliness, 379
Commodious, 379
Common pitfalls
  for algebra, 368–370
  for arithmetic, 366–368
  for data analysis, 370–371
  for geometry, 370
Communications programs, 481
Complaisance, 379
Complement of a set, 355
Complementary angles, 355
Compliant, 379
Composite number, 355
Computer Science Subject Test, 9
Computer vs. paper testing, 3–4
Computer-based TOEFL (CBT), 493–494
Concentric circles, 355
Cone, 354, 355
Congruence, 71
Congruent, 355

Congruent figures, 355
Connotative, 379
Consecutive integers, 355
Constant, 355
Constrain, 379
Contentious, 379
Contiguous, 379
Contravene, 379
Conundrum, 379
Conventional wisdom (CW), 50
Converge, 379
Coordinate geometry, 96–97
Correct items per section percentage, xvi
Coterie, 380
Crass, 380
Credentials, academic, 492
Cube, 356
Cube function, 81–82, 90, 354
Cylinder, 354, 356

D

Data analysis items
  and algebra, 106
  common alert signals for, 370–371
  defined, 68
  examples of, 69–70
  formulas, rules for, 364–365
  guided practice for, 141–143
  independent practice explanations for, 145–146
  independent practice for, 144
  strategies for, 138–140
Debacle, 380
Debilitate, 380
Decimals, 112
Decorous, 380
Degrees, in a circle, 74
Deleterious, 380
Denigrate, 380
Denominator, 356
Deprecate, 380
Deride, 380
Derision, 380
Descartes, 96
Desiccate, 380
Details, of item, 54

Diagnostic test score, xv, xvi
Diameter, 72, 356
Diatribe, 380
Dichotomy, 380
Diffident, 380
Diffuse, 380
Direct PLUS loans, 478
Discourse, 380
Discrete, 380
Disingenuous, 380
Disinterested, 380
Disparate, 380
Disputatious, 380
Dissemble, 380
Dissertation, thesis, 495
Dissonance, 380
Dissonant, 380
Distractors, 26
Distribution, 99–100
Domain, of function, 106, 356
Drills
    answer explanations for math, 414–422
    answer explanations for verbal section, 446–452
    answer keys for vocabulary, 404–405
    math, 408–413
    verbal, 438–445
    vocabulary, 385–403
    See also Practice sets

E

Ebullience, 381
Education programs, 481
Elapsed time, per test section, xvi
Element, 356
The Elements of Style, 148
Ellipsis, 381
Elucidate, 381
Emollient, 381
Empty set, 356
Encomium, 381
Endemic, 381
Enervate, 381
Engender, 381
Engineering programs, 481

English proficiency, 493
Ephemeral, 381
Equilateral triangle, 91, 356
Essays
    about, 2, 148
    guided practice for, 155–168
    method for, 149–155
    personal statement, 483–484
    samples of, 153–155, 166–168
Eulogy, 381
Evanescent, 381
Even number, 356
Exigent, 381
Exponents, 76–79
Extemporize, 381
Extrapolate, 381

F

Face, 356
Facetious, 381
Factoring, 99, 101–106
Factors of a number, 356
FAFSA (Free Application for Federal Student Aid), 478
Federal Stafford loan, 478
Feign, 381
Fellowships, 476–477
Fill-in, 4
Fine arts programs, 481
FOIL (first, outers + inners, lasts), 100, 102
Format, of GRE, 3
Formulas, rules
    for algebra, 361–362
    for data analysis, 364–365
    for geometry, 363–364
Fractions, 92–93, 112
Free Application for Federal Student Aid (FAFSA), 478
Function, 356

G

Gainsay, 381
Garrulous, 381
Geometric figures, 354
Geometry formulas, 71–72, 370

Graduate assistantships, 477
Graduate school
　application process for, 480–481
　application timeline for, 486–489
　choosing, 472
　comprehensive exam for, 495
　coursework for, 494–495
　evaluating programs, 473–474
　financial aid for, 475–479
　and GRE, 2
　and GRE scoring, 482
　for international students, 489–494
　and interviews, 485
　keys to success for, 494
　letters of recommendation for, 483
　non-matriculating enrollment, 475
　personal statement essays for, 483–484
　profile of students, 466–468
　references for, 496–497
　strategies for, 469–470
　thesis, dissertation for, 495
　time invested in, 470–472
　time management for, 495–496
　transcripts for, 482
Grants, 476
Greatest common factor, 356
Guided practice
　for RCs, 62–63, 65
　for SEs, 29–30
　for TCs, 41–43

H

Hexagon, 354, 356
Highlighters, 4
Histogram, 356
Horizontal axis, 356
Humanities programs, 481
Hypotenuse, 91

I

Iconoclast, 381
Impassive, 381
Imperturbable, 381
Impervious, 381
Implacable, 381
Impugn, 382

Inchoate, 382
Incisive, 382
Incredulous, 382
Independent practice
　for RCs, 63–65
　for SEs, 31–33, 35–38
　for TCs, 44–47, 48–52
Indigenous, 382
Inept, 382
Inert, 382
Inferences, of item, 55
Ingenuous, 382
Inherent, 382
Insipid, 382
Integer, 356
International student financing, 479
International students, 489–494
Internet-based TOEFL (iBT), 493
Interquartile range, 108
Intersection of sets, 356
Interviews, 485
Intractable, 382
Intransigent, 382
Intrepid, 382
Irascible, 382
Irrational number, 356
Isosceles trapezoid, 357
Isosceles triangle, 91–92, 134, 357
Item, as question, 4
Items, and RCs, 54–55

K

Kite, 354, 357

L

Laconic, 382
Least common multiple, 357
Letters of recommendation, 483
Line graph, 357
Lines, 71–72
Literature in English Subject Test, 9
Loans, 477–478, 479
Logic, rhetoric, 24
Long passage sets, 19–22
Loquacious, 382
Luminous, 382

Index 503

M

Macerate, 382
Maculate, 382
Magnanimity, 382
Main idea, of item, 54
Malevolent, 382
Malign, 382
Malleable, 383
Math section, of GRE
   about, 71–72
   answer explanations for, 431–437
   data analysis items, 68, 69–70
   definitions, conventions for, 70–71
   drills for, 408–413
   form and function, 68–70
   geometry formulas, 71–72
   practice set for, 423–430
   problem-solving items (PS), 68–69
   quantitative comparison (QC), 68
   quantitative comparison strategies
      for, 120–128
Mathematical symbols, 352–353
Mathematics Subject Test, 9
Mean (average), 107, 109, 119, 357
Measures of dispersion, 108
Measures of position, 107
Median, 107, 119
Median of a set of data, 357
Median of a trapezoid, 357
Median of a triangle, 357
Metacognition, focused, 12
Midline, 357
Midpoint, 357
Misanthrope, 383
Mode, 107, 119, 357
Monomial, 357
Multiple-choice items, 4
Multiple-response items, 4
Multiplication, 76–78

N

Natural number, 357
Non-matriculating enrollment, 475
Normal distribution, 119–120
Normal strategies
   for RCs, 55–65
   for SEs, 25–33
   for TCs, 38–47
Numerator, 357

O

Obdurate, 383
Obsequious, 383
Obtuse angles, 71–72, 357
Obviate, 383
Odd number, 357
Order of operations (PEMDAS), 95–96
Origin, 357
Ossify, 383
Outline, for essay, 151–152, 161
Outline, of book, vii–viii

P

Palpable, 383
Panegyric, 383
Paper vs. computer testing, 3–4
Paper-based TOEFL (PBT), 493–494
Paradigm, 383
Paradox, 383
Parallel lines, 357
Parallelogram, 88–89, 354, 357
Parsimonious, 383
Passages, and RCs, 53–54
Pedantic, 383
PEMDAS (order of operations), 95–96
Pentagon, 354, 358
Penurious, 383
Percentage, of correct items per section, xvi
Percentile rank, 6
Percentiles, 107–108
Percents, 112–115
Perfunctory, 383
Perimeter, 72–75, 77, 80–90
Permutations item, 111
Perpendicular lines, 358
Personal statement essay, 483–484
Petulant, 383
Physics Subject Test, 9–10
Pi symbol (π)
   and circles, 72–75
   defined, 358
   in formulas, 77, 80–82

Pie graph, 358
Placate, 383
Plethora, 383
Point of view, of item, 55
Points, 71
Polygon, 73–76, 80–90, 358
Polynomial, 358
Power Prep software, 170
Practice, guided
   for RCs, 62–63, 65
   for SEs, 29–30
   for TCs, 41–43
Practice, independent
   for RCs, 63–65
   for SEs, 31–33, 35–38
   for TCs, 44–47, 48–52
Practice sets
   answer explanations for math, 431–437
   answer explanations for verbal section, 461–464
   math, 423–430
   verbal, 453–460
   See also Drills
Prefixes, 389–393
Preparation, for GRE, xviii–xxi, 170–171
Prevaricate, 383
Prime number, 358
Prism, 86–90
Pristine, 383
Probabilities, 115–116, 119
Problem-solving items (PS)
   and form, function, 68–69
   guided practice for, 129–130, 136–138
   independent practice explanations for, 132–134
   independent practice for, 131–132
   reverse engineering for, 134–136
   strategies for, 128–129
Product, 358
Prompt, for essay, 150, 155–157
Propensity, 383
Proportion problems, 93, 358
Psychology programs, 481
Psychology Subject Test, 10
Public affairs programs, 481
Putrefaction, 383

Putrefy, 383
Pyramid, 354, 358
Pythagorean theorem, 91–92, 94

Q

Quadratic formulas, 102–104, 122f
Quadrilateral, 73–76, 80–90, 358
Quantitative comparison (QC), 68, 120–122
Quantitative section, of GRE
   about, 2
   independent practice explanations, 124–125
   independent practice for, 123
   reverse engineering for, 126–128
Quartiles, 107, 109, 358
Quiescence, 383
Quotient, 358

R

Radius, 72, 97, 134, 358
Rancor, 383
Range, 108
Range of a data set, 358
Range of a function, 358
Ratio, 358
Rational number, 358
Ratios, 92–93
Raw score, xvi
Reading comprehension sets (RCs)
   about, 52–53
   content review for, 53–55
   examples of, 18–19
   normal strategies for, 55–65
   and SEs, TCs, 22
Recalcitrant, 383
Reciprocal operations, 96, 99, 358
Recommendation, letters of, 483
Recondite, 384
Rectangle
   defined, 358
   equations for, 73–76, 80–84, 86–87, 89–90
   illustrated, 354
Rectangular prism, 354, 358
Redundant, 384
Reflection, 359
Registration, for GRE, 6–8

Regular polygon, 359
Reverse engineering
　for Problem Solving, 134–136
　for Quantitative Comparisons, 126–128
　for Sentence Equivalences, 33–38
　for Text Completions, 47–52
Rhetoric, logic, 24
Rhombus, 354, 359
Right angle, 359
Right circular cone, 359
Right isosceles triangle, 91–92
Right triangle, 91, 94
Root. *See* Square root
Roots, of words, 394–401, 403
Rotation, 359
Rules. *See* Formulas, rules

S

Sagacious, 384
Salubrious, 384
Scaled score, xvi
Scalene triangle, 359
Scatterplot, 359
Scholarships, 476
Science (S), 50
Science programs, 481
Scoring, of GRE
　about, 5–6
　in the application process, xvi
　elements of, xvi
　importance of, 482
Secant of a circle, 359
Section-level adaptivity, 5
Sector, 74, 83, 86–88
Sentence equivalence questions (SEs)
　examples of, 16–17
　normal strategies for, 25–33
　reverse engineering for, 33–38
　and TCs, 22–25
Sentence structure, 23
Similar figures, 359
Sinuous, 384
Sitzfleisch, 3
Skipping ability, in GRE test, 12
Slope, 97–99, 359
Social sciences programs, 481
Specious, 384

Sphere, 81, 90, 354, 359
Spurious, 384
Squalid, 384
Square (noun)
　defined, 359
　formulas for, 73–76, 80–81, 83, 86–87, 89–90
　illustrated, 354
Square (verb), 75–76
Square root, 79, 352
Stafford loan, 478
Standard deviation, 109–111, 119
Standard deviation of a data set, 359
Straight angle, 359
Structure, timing, of GRE, 2–5
Student and Exchange Visitor
　Information System (SEVIS), 490
Student and Exchange Visitor Program
　(SEVP), 489
Student loans, 477–478
Subject Test, GRE, 8–10
Subjugate, 384
Subscore by category, xvi
Suffixes, 402, 403
Supplementary angles, 359
Surface area, 79–80, 82–83, 85–88
SVO language, 23
Sycophant, 384
Symbols, mathematical, 352–353

T

Taciturn, 384
Tangent, 72
Tangent to a circle, 359
T-chart, for essay, 150–151, 157–161
Technology (T), 50
Tenuous, 384
Test anxiety, 12–13
Test of English as a Foreign Language
　(TOEFL), 493–494
Testlet, 4–5
Text completions (TCs)
　examples of, 17–18
　normal strategies for, 38–47
　reverse engineering for, 47–52
　and SEs, 22–25
Thesis, dissertation, 495

Third dimension, 80, 86
Time management, 495–496
TOEFL (Test of English as a Foreign Language), 493–494
Tone, of item, 55
Tortuous, 384
Tractable, 384
Transcripts, 482
Translation, 359
Transversal, 359
Trapezoid, 89, 360, 354
Triangles
    defined, 360
        isosceles, 91–92, 134, 357
        formulas for, 84–90
        illustrated, 354
        types of, 91–92
Truculent, 384
Tuition reimbursement, 476

U

Ubiquitous, 384
Union of sets, 360
Universal set, 360
U.S. student visa, 490–492

V

Vacuous, 384
Variable, 360
Variables, with equations, 104
Venn diagram, 116–118, 360
Verbal section, of GRE
    about, 2
        answer explanations for, 446–452, 461–464
        drills for, 438–445
        form and function, 16–22
        practice sets for, 453–460
Vertex of a polygon, 360
Vertical angles, 360
Vertical axis, 360
Visa, U.S. student, 490–492
Viscous, 384
Vocabulary, 24–25
Vocabulary enhancer
    about, 375
    drills for, 385–388, 393, 403
    frequent GRE words, 377–384
    prefixes, 389–393
    roots, 394–401, 403
    suffixes, 402, 403
    tips for, 374
    using, 375–376

W

Welter, 384
Whole number, 360

X

x-intercept, 360

Y

y-intercept, 360